YORK NOTES COMPANIONS

Medieval Literature

Carole Maddern

Longman
is an imprint of

 York Press

Harlow, England • London • New York • Boston • San Francisco • Toronto
Sydney • Tokyo • Singapore • Hong Kong • Seoul • Taipei • New Delhi
Cape Town • Madrid • Mexico City • Amsterdam • Munich • Paris • Milan

I would like to thank all my teachers, colleagues and students over the years. In particular, I am truly grateful to those who inspired within me a love of the medieval period, including Amanda Walls, James Simpson, Marie Collins, Pam King, Janet Bately, George Kane, Jane Roberts and Janet Cowen. I owe a debt also to George, Gladys, and Bryony Maddern for their invaluable support.
Carole Maddern

YORK PRESS
322 Old Brompton Road, London SW5 9JH

PEARSON EDUCATION LIMITED
Edinburgh Gate, Harlow CM20 2JE. United Kingdom
Tel: +44 (0)1279 623623   Fax: +44 (0)1279 431059
Website: www.pearsoned.co.uk

First edition published in Great Britain in 2010

© Librairie du Liban *Publishers* 2010

The right of Carole Maddern to be identified as author of this work has been asserted by her in accordance with the Copyright, Designs and Patents Act 1988.

ISBN: 978-1-4082-0475-7

British Library Cataloguing in Publication Data
A CIP catalogue record for this book can be obtained from the British Library

Library of Congress Cataloging-in-Publication Data
Maddern, Carole.
  Medieval literature / Carole Maddern.
    p. cm. -- (York notes companions)
  Includes bibliographical references and index.
  ISBN 978-1-4082-0475-7 (pbk. : alk. paper)
  1. English literature--Middle English, 1100-1500--History and criticism. I. Title.
  PR255.M25 2010
  820.9--dc22
  2010003270

10 9 8 7 6 5 4 3 2 1
14 13 12 11 10

Phototypeset by Chat Noir Design, France
Printed in Malaysia, CTP-KHL

Contents

Contents

Part One
Introduction

The period covered by this book is an extensive one. Whereas most discretely defined literary periods occupy the space of a hundred years or so, the medieval period covers over eight hundred years, from the first writings in English by the Anglo-Saxons in the eighth century to the sixteenth-century Renaissance. The death of the Tudor poet John Skelton in 1529 is often taken as a convenient, if somewhat arbitrary, cut-off point for medieval English literature. This book concentrates on the literature of the post-Conquest period (following the Norman Invasion of 1066). This entails a time-span of five centuries, during which enormous social, political and linguistic changes transformed life in Britain.

Part Two: 'A Cultural Overview', is designed to set the scene so as to help readers find their way through this wide-ranging period (alongside the Timelines in Part Five). The chapter provides an overview of key historical events, broadly dividing the period into three main sections. These divisions roughly correspond with changes in the ruling dynasties: the Normans, the Plantagenets and the Lancastrians. Using the framework of successive monarchies helps to shape the account of some of the major social and political developments. Among the topics discussed are the changing status of English, the development of the English language, the power of religion, and a series of crises which marks the later period, including the Great Plague of 1349 and the Peasants' Revolt of 1381. Each of these had an important impact on literature. At the beginning of the period, English coexisted alongside higher-status languages in common use; namely, Norman-French and Latin. It was only gradually that English reasserted itself as a literary medium, beginning with lyrical poetry in the late twelfth century and culminating in the extraordinary flowering of vernacular poetry and prose which marks the 'Ricardian'* era of the late fourteenth century.

The prominence and power of the Church is one of the most striking differences between medieval England and today. Just about every area of life was touched to some degree by religious precepts and practices. The church gained in wealth and prestige in the centuries after the Conquest, exploiting its international connections and asserting its jurisdiction over manners and morals as well as religious ritual. It promoted marriage as a sacrament, seeking to displace older, more casual forms of union, and supervised conduct through ecclesiastical courts. Meanwhile, pilgrimages and the worship of relics grew in popularity, generating an enormous revenue in addition to the income from substantial landholdings. This meant a ubiquitous presence of ecclesiastical figures, ranging from the parish priest to itinerant friars, pardoners (dispensing pardon)† and summoners (prosecuting malefactors). As time passed, the church became a target for widespread criticism and, increasingly, came under pressure to reform. A more questioning, challenging and less deferential attitude grew among certain groups, which eventually led to the radical reshaping of religion that would constitute the Reformation.

Clergy, the 'lerned', were distinguished from secular laity,¶ the 'lewed', primarily by their (Latin) literacy, essential for a religion founded upon the Latin Bible. This learned clerical elite occupied a special position in society, in a culture where the majority of people were functionally illiterate (unable to read or write) and books were expensive items laboriously produced by hand. Boundaries between Church and State became ever more blurred, as clerics attained high secular office

---

* This term designates the reign of Richard II (1377–99) but is also applied to the literature of the period.

† Religious pardon is the formal forgiveness and remission of part, or all, of the temporal penalty in purgatory earned for sins (embodied in papal indulgences).

¶ The laity is the body of religious worshippers, as distinguished from the clergy.

and formed the bureaucracy required by burgeoning processes of law and government. This led to writers such as Langland and Chaucer satirising careerists and corrupt self-seekers who merely used religion as a cloak for ambition. One linguistic outcome of the rise of lawyers and bureaucrats was the development of a new script, Chancery, and the spread of a more regularised spelling system, the Chancery Standard. Lay and female literacy, which was negligible at the beginning of the period, grew steadily so that by 1500 almost half of the population were able to read, if not to write. This contributed to a larger and more diverse audience for literary texts of many kinds, from religious tracts to scurrilous poems. Medieval literature is the product of a complex, sophisticated culture, whose vitality and inventive spirit is apparent in the sheer quantity and diversity of material which was produced.

The main body of this book comprises six chapters in Part Three which are organised systematically according to genre. The most important and influential medieval genres are considered in detail, with reference not just to English works but also to key writings in Latin, Anglo-Norman, French and Middle Scots. The multi-lingual culture of the Middle Ages is represented by the inclusion of works by Geoffrey of Monmouth, Marie de France, Chrétien de Troyes and Wace. Selected, representative examples of each genre are appraised in turn, beginning with the Breton lay, then moving through medieval lyrics, Arthurian romance, dream-vision, medieval drama and mystical writings. Examining texts within distinct generic groupings clarifies the essential nature of each genre, while conveying some sense of evolution over time, for each of these literary forms underwent significant development during the period. Each chapter is self-contained, in that it can be read in isolation. But, as the chapters advance, the interconnectedness of many texts will become apparent. Some texts feature in several different chapters, since they are composites of several genres. This allows for certain sections of the *Canterbury Tales*, for instance, to be highlighted and compared with similar and associated works by different authors, thus developing a fully representative picture of the literary culture. Some of the best-known works of the period assume new meaning when set against preceding and subsequent works. Chaucer is the most famous poet of the period but, like Shakespeare, does not exist in a vacuum. Several of his less frequently studied poems, such as *The Legend of Good Women* and *Troilus and Criseyde*, are discussed alongside works by some of his outstanding fellow-poets, such as the *Gawain*-poet and William Langland, and successors such as Robert Henryson and Thomas Hoccleve. In this way, the rich interplay of ideas and styles which medieval literature attests becomes more readily apparent. Major canonical works by named authors are discussed in relation to and alongside the many anonymous works of the period. The lyrics, for example, constitute a vast and underused corpus of literary material which illuminates any reading of the major writers. Throughout, the selections have been chosen so as to reveal a sense of dynamic interplay, displaying the creative processes of fashioning and refashioning at work.

The variety and vitality of medieval literature is clear from the wide range of texts and topics covered. Among the important literary phenomena treated are the invention and innovative deployment of notions of courtly love, chivalry, affective piety, satire and fantasy. One of the most significant features of medieval literature is its exploration of personal experience and personal expression – the beginnings of a new self-awareness and subjectivity. The earliest forms of autobiographical writing emerge in the writings associated with the mystical movement, along with a new mode of narrative which explores voice through distinctive narrative personae.

These trends are discussed with reference to a range of specific works, so that meaningful connections and comparisons can be made within and across genres. The critical discussion focuses on the essential themes of each text. The emphasis is on rendering medieval literature accessible, regardless of the superficial cultural and linguistic differences which appear to intervene between the Middle Ages and the present day. Once a few unfamiliar features such as archaic letter forms and variable spellings are accepted, the texts present attitudes and issues which are perhaps surprisingly familiar. The preoccupations and concerns of medieval writers are not unlike our own, as they grapple with issues of identity, purpose and meaning. Particular recurrent topics include personal and collective responsibility, relationships of all sorts with family, society and God and, above all, with the difficulties of communication. The discussion aims above all to be elucidating and informative, glossing vocabulary wherever necessary and clarifying key concepts, with footnote comments and endnotes supplying further information.

In each chapter, the survey of key works concludes with an extended commentary. This provides a close reading of a single work or section of a work, analysing its literary qualities, while commenting on some of the main formal, structural and linguistic effects. Detailed consideration is given to such features as lexis, rhyme, rhetorical tropes, stylistic nuance and imagery. A variety of critical theories are applied, at times contrastively, so that multiple interpretative possibilities are illustrated. These commentaries are designed to explore the range of meaning language can achieve, and to offer models for further textual analysis. Close reading is a necessary core skill for literary studies of any period, and these sample analyses offer a variety of techniques designed to interrogate and articulate meaning.

Part Four consists of four chapters, each adopting a particular theoretical perspective and applying it to a range of medieval texts. In 'The Emergent Individual', reader-response theory informs a reading of a variety of Chaucerian narrators, particularly regarding the invention of a female perspective and voice, in the characterisation of Criseyde and the Wife of Bath. Chaucer's imaginative exploration of female subjectivity is discussed with reference to *Troilus and Criseyde* and *The Legend of Good Women* as well as to *The Canterbury Tales*. Two personal testimonies, by William Thorpe and Thomas Hoccleve, provide first-hand accounts of trial and tribulation, each asserting an individual integrity in the face of persecution for non-conformity, although of very different types – one as a religious dissenter, the other as a madman. 'Gender and Power' takes account of several strands of feminism: in relation to examples of the saint's life, personification allegory, cycle drama and prose romance. In each case, the central question posed is, how far does gender determine agency and define parameters? The results show that gender boundaries are far from fixed, and that various genres are engaging with notions of contingency and partiality in ways which critique the prevailing anti-feminist rhetoric.

Bakhtin's notion of the carnivalesque is surveyed thoroughly in 'Fun and Games', with particular attention on aspects of bodily and linguistic dismemberment which find plentiful expression in medieval literature. A wide variety of genres is discussed, using texts which demonstrate lively humour and dangerously edgy playfulness. Robert Henryson's beast fables are predicated upon the value of diversion and entertainment. The unsettling effect of the dramatic juxtaposition of the sacred and the profane is apparent in plays from the York and Wakefield Cycles as well as in passus 5 of *Piers Plowman*. Finally, five of Chaucer's *Canterbury Tales* are considered as idiosyncratic versions of the fabliau genre. 'Society and Class' concerns cultural materialism as a method of enquiry into the constitution of society and class in the Middle Ages. The beast fable as an instrument of satire is considered as it is used to different ends by Henryson, Chaucer and Langland. The important concept of social estates is explored from a variety of perspectives, fictional and non-fictional, including sermons and satire. The intensifying conflict among elements of society, as old hierarchies were being fractured, is witnessed by several texts which reconfigure assumptions of Estates Satire, as well as letters attributed to the rebel leader, John Ball.

No single 'correct' reading is recommended; rather, the theories are employed lightly, drawing attention to certain features and offering some critical interpretation intended to stimulate the reader's own comparative and critical thinking. The theoretical analysis is designed as a starting point, one which aims to foreground the shifting and subjective nature of meaning by demonstrating how different texts can be read in a multiplicity of ways.

Part Five contains further reading suggestions, as an annotated list, so that supplementary study of particular topics of interest may be easily undertaken. The selections include recommended web resources, detailing some of the many excellent websites which specialise in resources relating to the medieval period. Also, the two Timelines present the major historical and literary events of the period in a condensed manner which permits easy reference to chronological developments and the situating of texts in relation to each other and to historical and cultural landmarks.

Carole Maddern

Part Two
A Cultural Overview

The Domesday Book of 1086 provides an evocative snapshot of the lives of ordinary people at the beginning of the period. It shows an agricultural society of small settlements, peasants farming scattered strips of land in and around villages, owing various services to the local lord. He in turn owed military service to his overlord and so on up to the king, the titular head of this system of loyalties known as feudalism (from Latin *feodum*, 'fief', a parcel of land, from OE *feoh* – cattle, property). In many respects, this hierarchical system has come almost to represent the Middle Ages as a time of strict social distinction according to rank: the rich man in his castle, the poor man at his gate. Medieval society was categorised as comprising three separate 'estates' or ranks; namely, peasantry (*laboratores* – those who labour), knighthood (*bellatores* – those who fight, headed by the king) and priesthood (*oratores* – those who pray). Such an image of an organically designed, stratified community lies at the heart of the 'Merrie England' mythology still current in the popular imagination. As with all such models, such theories of orderliness are overly simplistic and, in many respects, far removed from reality.* In fact, later medieval society was experiencing intense pressure and fragmentation, as economic and cultural changes took place. Established hierarchies and certainties

---

* Chaucer's 'General Prologue' to the *Canterbury Tales* provides a good example of the estates model being reconfigured.

crumbled slowly but surely over the period. Certain key events and personalities contributed to these developments but fundamental processes were at work, intellectually, socially and economically, that transformed English society.

The six centuries covered by this period can be usefully divided into three distinct parts. Initially, there was a period of integration and assimilation following the Norman Invasion of 1066, as Norman culture imposed itself upon the Anglo-Saxons. Under the Plantagenet dynasty, English power expanded into Europe, a cash economy developed, and there were substantial advances in science and learning. Finally, the tumultuous pre-Renaissance centuries fashioned many institutions and practices which are recognisably modern in nature, as well as shattering long-established beliefs and power structures.

The Norman Influence

The victory of William, Duke of Normandy, at Hastings in 1066 ended centuries of Anglo-Saxon rule and had a drastic impact on the organisation and composition of English society. The Conqueror's power rested essentially on a small band of knights owing him personal allegiance, governing the land from their strategically placed castles. Battle Abbey, built on the site of his victory, remains a solid reminder of William's methods of establishing power. He and his successors were energetic in demolishing Anglo-Saxon churches, establishing new, fortified towns, erecting scores of imposing castles and churches – literally stamping their presence on the landscape. Many of these Romanesque buildings survive and are formidable stone constructions designed to impress and to endure. Within ten years of the Conquest, at least a thousand castles were built, largely of the rapidly erected motte-and-bailey type. The English forces had been weakened by the losses at Hastings and sporadic rebellion was put down with brutal force. William's destructive reprisals on the north of England had a long-lasting impact on the region's economy. Anglo-Saxons in positions of influence were systematically removed from office, the last English earl being executed following a rebellion in 1075. Thereafter, power was conspicuously in Norman hands. William instituted a thorough survey of his kingdom, known from later centuries on as the *Domesday Book*, on account of its unavoidable, absolute authority, akin to that of God at the Last Judgement. The two mighty volumes of the nationwide survey, completed in a matter of months, testify to the efficiency of the new regime. Tellingly, William himself emerges in possession of twice as much land as the Wessex kings whom he displaced. At this time, land equated with power; in fact, the Old English word *rice* (Modern English 'rich') meant 'dominion' (cf. German *reich*). The Norman system of vassalage was a hierarchical one of mutual obligation between lord and subordinates. Feudalism essentially entailed a chain of allegiance, beginning with tenant farmers working small parcels of land held in grant from a local lord, who in turn owed military service to the king. Rigid quotas of labour and service, along with penalties and exactions comprised the matter of government, and led to new law courts and bureaucracy.

For women in particular, Norman culture meant a loss of status and liberty. Anglo-Saxon women had enjoyed considerable power.[1] An abbess such as Hilda, who convened a major church assembly, the synod of Whitby, in 664 held authority over a community of monks as well as nuns. Such double houses were abolished by the Norman Church. Secular women were deprived of their rights to own property independently of their husbands, to inherit or to act as executors, effectively becoming reduced in law to a subject status, *femme couverte* (lit. 'covered woman'). Not until the fourteenth century, when an urban environment favoured more liberty, were women able to assert some financial independence, acquiring *femme sole* (lit. 'lone woman') status.

The Status of English

The arrival of Norman-French had a major impact on English culture. The dialect of the invaders is known as 'Anglo-Norman' to distinguish it from continental French. It is significant that the Normans, 'men from the North', had easily yielded up their original Scandinavian language to assume that of their recently settled territory in the North of France (the Viking Rollo became the first Duke of Normandy in 911). Similarly, in England too, the Normans showed themselves linguistically adaptable. For a time, however, Anglo-Norman displaced the native vernacular as a medium for government, recordkeeping, law and literature. New words entering the language include many indicative of the new order: court, crime, government, tax, justice, religion, sermon, noble, royal, castle, army, battle, enemy and, indeed, literature. At the time of the Conquest, the English language was in a robust state, far more developed than comparable European vernaculars such as French and Italian that were just emerging from Vulgar Latin. For centuries, Old English had flourished as an expressive vehicle for a wide range of ideas and imaginative writings. Something of a written national standard had developed under the direction of Alfred the Great (849–99), with the Wessex dialect becoming generally accepted across the whole of England. The arrival of Norman-French led to the disintegration of this common form of language. It would be another five hundred years before such a shared form would reappear. Displaced as the language of the ruling elite, English became relegated to a primarily spoken function and fragmented into hundreds of different regional versions, so that by the fourteenth century, some dialects were mutually unintelligible. The effective ending of literary English for a century and a half had a major impact on the language. Yet it is easy to exaggerate the effect of Norman-French, as English before the Conquest had already been evolving into a looser form, one less dependent on inflexional endings and more prone to use prepositions. Anglo-Norman quickened the pace of linguistic change, so that when documents in the vernacular re-emerge in the early thirteenth century, the language is recognisably closer to modern English than the pre-Conquest vernacular.

Another of King Alfred's projects had been to institute national recordkeeping, in the form of monastic chronicles. Remarkably, some of these annals continued to be written in English until 1154. The earliest post-Conquest literary writings in English date from the early thirteenth century so, although there is a gap in the record, it is smaller than is commonly presumed. *The Anglo-Saxon Chronicle* records events in sequence, so the continuous nature of the entries offers a remarkable opportunity to witness the language in the process of evolution. New letters appear (such as w, k, j, th), old letters decline (æ, ð, insular g), endings weaken and syntax changes before our eyes. One late section of the *Peterborough Chronicle* shows many of these features in action:

> For ævric rice man his castles makede ... ond fylden þe land ful of castles. Hie swencten suyðe þe wrecce men of þe land mid castelweorces ... wile Stephne was king ... ævre it was werse and werse. Hie læiden gældes on the tunes ... ond clepeden it *tenserie*.
>
> [For every powerful man built his castles ... and they filled the land full of castles. They sorely burdened the wretched people of the country with forced labour on the castles. While Stephen was king ... things grew worse and worse. They imposed taxes on the villages ... and called it 'tenserie'.][2]

Literary texts in English, such as *The Owl and the Nightingale* and Laȝamon's *Brut*, begin to appear early in the thirteenth century. Clearly the language is evolving, and there are new French-derived forms, such as rhyming octosyllabic couplets, in place of the native alliterative line. The opening of the *Owl and the Nightingale* contains only one French word, however, attesting to the resilience of the vernacular:

> Ich was in one sumere dale;
> In one suþe diȝele hale
> Iherde ich holde grete tale
> An Hule and one Niȝtingale.
> þat plait was stif & starc & strong,
> Sum wile softe & lud among,
> An aiþer aȝen oþer sval
> & let þat vvole mod ut al;
> & eiþer seide of oþeres custe
> þat alre worste þat hi wuste.
> & hure & hure of oþeres songe
> Hi holde *plaiding* suþe stronge.

11

[I was in a sunny valley, in a very secluded place, when I heard a noisy exchange between an owl and a nightingale. The debate was hard and fierce and powerful, sometimes soft, sometimes loud. Each became swollen with rage against the other and expressed passionate objections to the other. Each spoke of the other's character, the worst that they knew, and voiced very powerful complaints, especially about their singing.][3]

Some scholars date this poem to the late twelfth century, others slightly later. Whatever its precise date of composition, it shows English continuing as a flourishing literary medium at a time when Anglo-Norman was dominant.

The Angevin Empire: Continental Expansion and Contraction

The firm foundation of the Norman dynasty soon crumbled. After William died in 1087 his realm was split into two, with one of his sons inheriting the throne of England, another the Duchy of Normandy. After a period of conflict, the third and youngest son, Henry, eventually acquired control of both but his death in 1135, without leaving a legitimate male heir, left a power vacuum which developed into violent civil war. There followed a period known as the 'Anarchy', so vividly depicted by the Peterborough Chronicler. Henry's daughter Mathilda and her faction fought to contest the throne claimed by Stephen of Blois. Empress and Countess by virtue of her successive marriages to the German Emperor and the Count of Anjou, Mathilda was evidently a forceful character, disparagingly referred to by the historian William of Malmesbury as *eadem virago*, 'that mannish woman'. Extensive continental possessions now featured in the equation as factions formed and stakes grew. Following Stephen's death in 1154 the Plantagenets, in the form of Mathilda's son, Henry, and his sons, Richard 'the Lionheart' and John, settled to rule what was now a vast territory extending across more than half of modern France. This

A Cultural Overview

Angevin* empire resulted from Henry's marriage to Eleanor of Aquitaine in 1152, which brought him vast territory in southern France two years before becoming king of England, still aged only twenty. Again, strategically appointed castles were the key to control, as many fine remains testify. Systematically, Henry greatly increased the number of royal castles while depriving many barons of their own seats of power. He also undertook the conquest of Wales and Ireland. Economically, the empire was thriving during the twelfth century, as many new markets opened up for French wine and English wool. New ports such as Grimsby and Boston were developed, along with new towns founded as business enterprises. Part of the progress involved clearing forests and fenlands, with land increasingly becoming a saleable commodity rather than a feudal holding. This sowed the seeds for what later developed into a proto-capitalist economy with towns and cities offering opportunities for newly prosperous 'middle' classes. However, the era of prosperity was punctuated by several calamities.

'Bad' King John is a figure familiar from Robin Hood stories, and primarily remembered for issuing Magna Carta. This 'great charter' stands as a monument to fledgling democratic concepts, acknowledging as it does a range of principles of liberty and constraints upon royal power. In fact, far from being a willing gesture towards democracy, the charter was forced upon John by rebellious barons after his heavy-handed rule had roused intense opposition. Particularly disastrous for John was military defeat at the hands of a resurgent French monarchy, resulting in the symbolically potent loss of Normandy in 1204. John's relations with the Church were also spectacularly dismal. In a dispute reminiscent of his father's quarrel with Thomas à Becket, John opposed the Archbishop of Canterbury, Stephen Langton, in open defiance of the pope. The resultant Papal Interdict between 1208 and 1214 meant that John was excommunicated, and that no church services were held, no masses or baptisms performed. God was seen by chroniclers to have withdrawn from the land. When John died in 1216, he left an embittered, fragmented elite embroiled in civil war, and a nine-year-old heir. Fortunately, the regent, William Marshal, was an exceptional man

* Angevin is an adjective relating to Anjou in southern France.

who maintained the kingdom successfully, resolving the widespread discord so that Henry III could accede to the throne, which he held for over fifty years. Although long, his reign was far from untroubled. Henry III spent lavishly, constructing impressive monuments such as Westminster Abbey, and being forced to resist a series of rebellions. As his ability to raise taxation grew weaker, he had to resort to convening parliament* more frequently, negotiating and establishing principles of accountability and restraint of royal prerogatives. In 1259, Henry III was militarily humiliated, forced to yield most of his continental territories to the French king. The pope, far from neutral, denounced England as being 'in a boiling whirlpool of universal disruption'. For the warrior elite who directed national policy, loss of the empire was a disaster but, more generally, relief from taxation to fund expensive wars on the continent resulted in increased wealth and a more effective focus of resources. The result was economic prosperity and a growth of community enterprise, with new trade guilds formed and expanding towns and villages.†

The Power of the Church

The power of Roman Catholicism had succeeded that of the Roman Empire by this time, as a unifying force for Europe. Latin continued to be the language of power, with the Church controlling access to the divine word, as the Bible was available only in St Jerome's fourth-century Vulgar Latin translation. Under the Normans, a system of church organisation in the image of secular feudalism had been fostered. Archbishops were at the pinnacle of power, bishops beneath them, controlling their individual dioceses, with lesser clergy and parish priests in charge of local parishes. At the top of the structure, in the position of ultimate ruler of Christendom, was the pope, Christ's vicar on earth. As stronger monarchies emerged however, rivalries intensified. From Thomas à Becket in the thirteenth century to Thomas More in the

---

* At this time, parliament was an occasionally convened debating chamber consisting of two Houses, the Commons and the Lords. Its primary purpose was to grant taxation to the king in time of war. The term 'parliament' was used from the mid-thirteenth century onwards.
† This civic prosperity helped to foster the development of the Mystery play cycles.

sixteenth, much of the history of the Middle Ages revolves around the competition for power between the secular and religious orders.

It used to be commonplace to regard the medieval period as one of ubiquitous piety, indeed to define it as the 'Age of Faith'. Fixed order and inscrutable divine purpose are the twin poles of authority in the period, justifying the power of rulers and social structures alike. Overarching theories of fixity and divine ordering are plentiful. The universe was perceived as an intricate machine, with each element fixed in position, operating in harmony according to the divine plan. Nine planets were known to exist, each in orbit around the earth, the centre of the cosmos.

This harmonious mechanism is described in *The Dream of Scipio*, 'In nine circles, or rather spheres, all things are connected. The outermost sphere, which contains all the rest, is the celestial, and is itself the supreme God, enclosing and holding together all the other spheres in itself.'[4] This image of divine order, conceiving of the universe as a superb piece of machinery, is prominent in one of the most influential works of the Middle Ages, Boethius's *The Consolation of Philosophy*. Chaucer translated this work (*Boece*) and frequently employs philosophical passages drawn from it in his writings. Theseus in 'The Knight's Tale' is a notable exponent of the theory of immutable order, describing 'the fayre cheyne of love' which binds all of creation, and the 'Firste Moevere', the controlling force of life on earth in an eternally fixed system.[5] Such a conservative theory could lend itself easily to social control but, in practice, was beset by challenges.

It is a fact that the power and prestige of the Church were prominent aspects of life in the Middle Ages. The Church's authority extended into many areas of everyday life, as it functioned as a major landholder, tax and tithe gatherer, as well as moral arbitrator (ecclesiastical courts punished moral and sexual offences, such as adultery and sexual intercourse outside marriage). But the medieval Catholic Church was not the unassailable monolith of popular imagination. The pan-European entity of Christendom gathered itself in a series of eight Crusades between 1096 and 1271, seeking to regain the Holy Land from the Muslim infidel. Far from achieving unifying glory, the episodes ended in spectacular defeat and ignominy. Major benefits in the longer term resulting from contact with Muslim society were advances in science and learning. Classical texts such as works by Aristotle and Ovid became available in the West for the first time, through Arabic sources. New, more easily manipulated numerals were adopted, modern 'Arabic' numerals as opposed to the unwieldy Roman system. There was something of an international renaissance during the twelfth and thirteenth centuries. Scholars such as Peter Abelard, Thomas Aquinas and Roger Bacon engaged with the new intellectual possibilities opening up, and contributed to subtle and sophisticated debates about the universe and man's place within it. The established Church had to contend with challenging new ideas, many deriving from suspect pagan and Islamic sources.

As the Roman Catholic Church had grown in power and wealth, concomitant corruption and malpractice duly led to widespread disapproval. There were recurrent efforts to reform and reconstitute religious life. In the twelfth century, several new religious orders were founded, which sought to recover and emulate the apostolic virtues of poverty, chastity and obedience. New monastic orders, devoted to a life of humble devotion, spread rapidly so that in 1215 the fourth Lateran Council* banned any further foundations. The monastic orders in England comprised mainly Augustinians (also known as Black or Benedictine monks and Augustinian canons) and Cistercians (Grey or White monks). The Augustinians were few in number but influential, forming small but stable priories at important centres such as Walsingham, and St Bartholomew's in London. The Cistercians established large communities in the North of England, founding abbeys such as Waverley in 1129, Rievaulx in 1131, and Fountains in 1135. They quickly grew wealthy from the wool trade, profiting from enormous flocks of sheep on monastic estates, but were falling into sharp economic decline by the late thirteenth century. The causes of the economic decline remain obscure but may well be related to warfare between the English and the Scots occurring in the Yorkshire region (e.g., the Battle of Byland, 1322).

---

* The Lateran Council is one of the five general councils of the Western Church held in the church of St John Lateran, in Rome.

At the same time, alternative models of pious service were being developed, extending into the secular community. There were four orders of friars, who roamed at large rather then being enclosed within a monastic community. Known as 'mendicants' (Latin *mendicare*, 'to beg'), these fraternal orders proliferated rapidly, much to the chagrin of the established church. There were Carmelites (White Friars), Dominicans (Black Friars), Augustinians (Austin Friars) and Franciscans (Friars Minor, or Minorites). Rivalry between the various church organisations lies behind an intense hostility, which is evident in a wave of anti-fraternal literature. Antagonism between the secular clergy* and friars is clear from early thirteenth-century disputes in Paris. The archbishop of Ireland, Richard Fitzralph, wrote and delivered sermons in the 1350s, in which he vociferously denounced friars for usurping clerical rights to preaching, confession and burial. He formally petitioned the Avignon pope to strip the friars of their privileges. The mendicant orders became a target for widespread literary satire, with perceived fraternal corruption continuing to be a rich source of satirical writings for Jean de Meun, Chaucer and others.†

Religious Tension and Crisis

It was not only the mendicant orders who were targets for criticism. As the papacy became increasingly a secular and political power, one of many competing Italian states, the very centre of Christian authority was itself a site for dispute. In 1309, under pressure from the French king, Pope Clement V left Rome to set up his base in Avignon, in Provence. The city was bought by Pope Clement VI in 1348. Only in 1377 did Pope Gregory XI return the seat of the papacy to Rome. This initiated a farcical period when rival claimants contested the papacy in arms. Successively, Clement VII and Benedict XIII occupied Avignon as 'anti-popes', until being expelled from the city in 1408. This time of the

* Secular clergy are clergy living in the community, not subject to a religious rule or enclosure.
† By the time of Chaucer, many different religious practices were widely conceived of as corrupt, so that satire extended to itinerant clerical figures such as the Pardoner and the Summoner (see Chaucer's *Canterbury Tales*).

Great Papal Schism between 1378 and 1417, when Benedict XIII died, split Christendom and contributed to an erosion of the sacrosanct status claimed by the papacy as an institution.

Religion may have been a prominent force in society, but universal piety would be a gross misassumption. Documentary evidence for scepticism, agnosticism or even atheism is slender but, occasionally, as in trials for heresy, less-than-orthodox opinions are recorded. While in Europe from an early period there were heretical sects such as the Cathars in France, religious radicalism in England appears rather late. By the fourteenth century, ideas of religious reform and radicalism emerge with the Wycliffites and Lollards (the latter term is of obscure origin, related to the Dutch word for 'mumbler'). Scepticism spread, filtering down into village life, as evident in the records of the Norwich heresy trials in 1428–31. One suspect, Hawissia Mone, spoke forthrightly against her parish priest and Christian practices such as confession, 'Confession shuld be maad oonly to God ... no prest hath poar to remitte synne ... no man is bounde to do no penaunce whiche onyy prest enjoyneth hym to do.'[6] This independent and authority-resistant outlook cannot have been unique. Throughout most of the period, literacy and education were the preserve of the Church: dissent lacks record. It may be fair to presume a widespread if basic, nominal Christianity but, beyond the devout who left their tracts and poetry, the piety of the masses is a matter for conjecture. Time and again writers deplore the woeful ignorance of people, possessing a meagre grasp of what their faith actually entailed. Going to church to confess one's sins was only required annually. Birth, marriage and death were also occasions for church attendance. Saints' days and religious festivals were more of a regular experience for most people, effectively reducing the peasants' working week to an average of just three days.

Towards the end of the period, the concept of a unified Christendom was visibly crumbling, with a proliferation of dissenting tracts, satirical writings and unorthodox theological works. Ecclesiastical control over the dissemination of learning was proving impossible to maintain. There were radical new proposals for vernacular bibles to render the Word of God accessible to all. The Wycliffites produced two English translations of the Bible, and even went so far as to demand the disendowment of the Church. Reforming the Church to a state of apostolic poverty was not a notion confined to radical dissenters, but was shared by even relatively moderate reformers such as Langland.[7] Religion was becoming a more individual, personal experience, increasingly laicised, from the fourteenth-century mystics to the dawn of the Reformation, when the Church of England finally split from Rome. Martin Luther encapsulated the spirit of reform, when he declared (1513), 'There has been a fiction by which the pope, bishops, priests and monks are called the "spiritual" estate ... This is an artful lie and hypocritical invention ... all Christians are truly of the spiritual estate.'[8] Radical sectarianism only came to the surface in England much later, in the seventeenth century, when state censorship was relaxed, allowing the unorthodox to publish their views. Numerous splinter groups suddenly asserted themselves, with convictions and principles as varied as those of the communistic Levellers, sexually liberated Ranters, and pacifist Quakers.

The Fourteenth and Fifteenth Centuries: Crisis and Change

By 1300, the population was growing steadily and society was diversifying, with significant shifts in status. The manorial system under which the vast majority of the population lived as agricultural labourers gradually weakened its dependence on unfree tenants in favour of more flexible arrangements, with cash rents and leaseholding increasingly displacing formal serfdom. The nobility was losing its *raison d'être*, its military function being supplanted to some extent by newly prominent and decisive roles for footsoldiers and archers, as demonstrated at the battle of Crécy. Protective armour could not keep pace with technological advances in weaponry, as the fighting knight grew ever more anachronistic. Warfare was evolving from being a chivalric performance by mounted cavalry to a more pragmatic and democratic massed engagement, with more hired, mercenary forces. Froissart's glamorising description of knighthood provides an idealised portrait of chivalry:

All these warlike men set out in full array and took the field, and the whole country began to tremble before them ... the French and English behave chivalrously and have always done so.⁹

This contrasts strongly with other more realistic accounts of warfare as destructive:

Stone steeples full stiff in the street ligges,	[lie]
Chambers with chimnees and many chef inns,	
Paised and pelled down plastered walles; [demolished and struck]	
The pine of the pople was pitee for to here!	
...	
Towers he turnes, and tourmentes the pople,	
Wrought widowes full wlonk wrotherayle singen,	[bright]
Oft were and weep and wringen their handes;	[curse]
And all he wastes with war there he away rides.¹⁰	

Royalty and aristocracy were experiencing what would prove to be a gradual but definite descent into pageantry and ceremonial. This is evident in the development of tournaments and jousts as entertainment, and the creation of knightly castes such as Edward III's Order of the Garter (1348) and Richard II's Order of the White Hart (1390). Knighthood was increasingly less of an honour and more of an imposition, the unrewarding expense of which many sought to avoid. New Knights of the Shire were created, to serve as parliamentary spokesmen and enforce the king's laws in their home counties. Over time, this new governing class of minor landed gentry displaced the aristocracy as the effective centre of power, through the institution of the House of Commons.

New employment opportunities contributed to a greater variety of social status. Educational provision expanded, as the growing universities of Oxford and Cambridge (later Scottish universities too) produced candidates equipped for careers in government and law, well beyond the earlier medieval ecclesiastical sphere. A burgeoning middle class of merchants and artisans was emerging, who actively sponsored trade fairs, crafts guilds and religious fraternities, along with self-government in the form of town councils. During the fourteenth century, religious festivals such as the feast of Corpus Christi evolved into occasions for exuberant civic ceremonial. The great cycles of religious drama express bourgeois confidence, promoting and demonstrating the power of the urban elite. This expanding class included merchants, profiting from thriving exports of wool and cloth, skilled artisans producing exquisite Decorated Style architectural wonders such as Gloucester Cathedral, and also lawyers, scholars and a myriad of other emerging professions. In the countryside, a new landlord class was developing, benefiting from more intensively farmed and efficiently managed estates, through the means of managing intermediaries such as reeves, stewards and franklins. At the same time, an emerging capitalist economy was transforming life in the expanding cities, frequently connected with trading ports. Although small by modern standards, prospering towns across Britain were growing to accommodate many thousands of people. York and Norwich are estimated to have contained around 10,000 and 12,000 people respectively. The City of London dwarfed all others, containing as it did about 12 per cent of the entire population, some 60–70,000 citizens.

National confidence stood high towards the middle of the fourteenth century. Edward III was at the height of his successful rule, having enjoyed a string of military victories over the Scots and the French, most spectacularly at Sluys, Crécy and Calais. But the bubble was soon to burst. The protracted Hundred Years' War (1337–1453), during which a succession of English kings asserted their claim to the French throne, was an expensive business. Edward was extravagantly in debt to Italian bankers, desperately extracting taxation at unprecedented and unsustainable levels, and even pawned his crown to the archbishop of Trier. So desperate was Edward to maintain the expensive war against France that he tried to set up an Estate of Merchants, the class upon whom he depended for finance. Underlying these developments was a disruption of traditional social strata, along with a progressive decline in importance of the warrior elite. Shored up by proto-capitalists and the wealth generated by trade with Europe, the English monarchy's assertiveness and prestige were fragile. Ironically, the very source of economic prosperity, the extensive trading of commodities across Europe and the East, was about to deliver a deadly cargo: the devastating new import known to history as the 'Black Death'.

The Great Plague

What became known much later as the Black Death was referred to by contemporaries as the 'pestilence'. A virulent infection originating in China first reached Europe in January 1348 on a ship docked in Genoa. Within months, the disease, probably carried by fleas on black rats, had spread to afflict most of Western Europe. Plague had been unknown in the West since AD 750. This fresh outbreak proved catastrophic in its severity. A lyrical account survives from a Welsh poet which captures the awful horror of the physical symptoms:

> We see death coming into our midst like black smoke, a plague which cuts off the young, a rootless phantom which has no mercy for fair countenance. Woe is me of the shilling in the armpit: it is seething, terrible … a head that gives pain and causes a loud cry, a burden carried under the arms, a painful angry knob, a white lump.[11]

The terrifying impact of sudden, widespread death is audible in the hushed tones of Chaucer's serving boy in 'The Pardoner's Tale':

Ther cam a privee theef men clepeth Deeth   [secret]
That in this contree al the peple sleeth.[12]   [is killing]

It has been calculated that between a third and a half of the population of England (and Europe) died, approximately one and a half million people in England. The clergy seem to have suffered disproportionately, their greatly reduced numbers perhaps contributing to the re-emergence of English as the dominant national language during the latter part of the century. Many accounts survive, offering glimpses of the horror and trauma of the devastation. One English chronicler described the severe impact on Bristol, 'There died suddenly overwhelmed by death, almost the whole strength of the town, for few were sick more than three days, or two days, or even half a day'.[13]

The epidemic raged for two and a half years, devastating the country. Immediate responses must have included much hysteria, panic and violent reaction, one visible example of which is the phenomenon of the flagellants. Sizeable groups of people chastised their bodies in mass self-floggings, in order to atone for the sins which were believed to have provoked the divine retribution. The plague's long-term effect is incalculable. The traumatic effect has been compared to that of the First World War. Even after the first wave subsided, subsequent outbreaks occurred every dozen years or so, with particular force in 1361–2 and 1368. For the next three hundred years, until the Great Fire of London in 1666, plague was a recurrent affliction. Disastrous harvests, especially that of 1369, contributed further to a collapse of the economic and social order. It is no coincidence that the later medieval period is marked by a cult of death. A rampant morbidity is evident in art, literature and architecture, with deep anxiety fuelling the explosion of endowments of chantry chapels to pray in perpetuity for the souls of the wealthy dead.

The economic effects varied, but widespread hardship is attested. There was a period of rapid inflation, as prices rose while income from rents and taxation fell. Many tenant farmers deserted their manors to seek higher wages elsewhere. The labour shortage and economic volatility shattered relations between landlords and their tenants, so much so that the government tried to impose harsh measures restricting peasant mobility. In 1349, the Ordinance of Labourers was issued, aiming to freeze wages and prices, and to bind men to their lords. The 1351 Statute of Labourers and 1352 Statute of Treasons went further, attempting to define a range of rebellious behaviour as 'treason', punishable by death. As ever, at this time, the theory and the reality of enforcing the law were divergent. Little definite unrest among the peasants is recorded, but there are several known cases of attacks on the clergy and landlords, such as the Chester uprising in 1353.

While historians disagree about the precise effects of the plague, it is safe to presume that it shattered old habits of faith and deference. Existing tensions were exacerbated and certain tendencies given heightened impetus, such as the shift towards a more loosely structured society.

A World Turned Upside Down

Events such as the plague intensified processes at work in society which were creating critical tensions. As we have seen, feudal practices of sworn allegiance as sacramental bonds of mutual service were being weakened during the period. Shorter-term, flexible contracts and indentures based on cash payments were replacing the older system. K. B. McFarlane coined the phrase 'bastard feudalism' for this new arrangement.[14] As social relations became more voluntary and contingent affairs, intense reactions were provoked. There were widespread denunciations of personal liveries, hired retainers and inappropriate clothing. A series of Sumptuary Laws sought to regulate clothing according to rank, specifying which orders were entitled to wear rich fabrics and furs, carefully delineating social status. The reissuing of such laws demonstrates their inefficacy, while also revealing unassuaged anxieties. Social tensions are evident in 'The Wakefield Second Shepherds' Play', where a shepherd complains:

We are so hamyd,	[hamstrung]
For-taxed and ramyd,	[over-taxed and oppressed]
We are mayde hand tamyd	[submissive]
With thys gentlery men.	[gentry]
...	
There shall com a swane as prowde as a po,	[peacock]
He must borrow my wane, my ploghe also,	[cart]
... I were better be hangyd	
Then oones say hym nay.[15]	[once]

The same deep unease at social mobility, although from the different end of the social scale, is evident in Chaucer's *Lak of Stedfastness*:

Somtyme the world was so stedfast and stable
That mannes word was obligacioun,
And now it is so fals and deceivable
That word and deed, as in conclusioun,
Ben nothing lyk, for turned up-so-doun   [are]
Is al this world for mede and wilfulnesse   [payment/bribery]
That al the world is lost for lak of stedfastnesse.[16]

The notion of the social order in disarray becomes a leitmotif in the literature of the period. On all fronts, tensions are evident, as greater social mobility contributed to a climate of radical change; old certainties, established authorities, centres of power, came under attack. Even sacred institutions such as monarchy were subject to radical reconstitution. Royal power increasingly required parliamentary cooperation, as the 1388 'Merciless' Parliament's impeachment and execution of the king's favourites demonstrated. The deposition and murder of a king twice in the fourteenth century is a grim sign of the times.* The following century witnessed increasing fragmentation of society, with civil war no longer a matter of spasmodic baronial conflicts but developing into extensive regional anarchy during the Wars of the Roses (1455–85).†

The Peasants' Revolt

In the summer of 1381 there were a number of uprisings in Essex and Kent, labelled by later historians as the 'Peasants' Revolt'. The name is misleading, as peasants comprised a minority of the rebels, combining with artisans, independent farmers and minor landowners to protest against perceived injustices. Often seen as an inevitable consequence of the mid-century disaster of the plague, the revolt stands out as a symbol of the breakdown of the old social order. One of the main catalysts was an ill-conceived series of poll taxes, imposed on every adult. Resistance

---

* Edward II (d. 1327) and Richard II (d. 1399).
† This war was a protracted contest for the English throne between the rival Houses of York and Lancaster.

was widespread, one collector being told that the villagers of Fobbing in Essex 'would have nothing to do with him nor give him a penny'. Under the leadership of Wat Tyler, disaffected groups from Kent and Essex assembled in London. They were addressed at Blackheath by John Ball, a radical preacher they had released from prison in Canterbury. He preached a sermon on the text:

When Adam delved and Eve span,
Who was then the gentleman?

For several days, riots ensued, during which Flemish immigrants were targeted and killed, while the Priory of St John in Clerkenwell and John of Gaunt's Savoy Palace were destroyed. Taking over the Tower of London, the rebels beheaded the Archbishop of Canterbury, Simon Sudbury, and the Chancellor, Sir Robert Hales. The young king, Richard II, met them at Mile End where he agreed to their demands, including the abolition of serfdom and punishment of 'traitors'. There were simultaneous outbreaks of violence in Bury St Edmunds and St Albans, revealing the townspeople's resentment of landowners' exactions and a lack of corporate independence. The rebellion soon collapsed, after Wat Tyler was killed by the Mayor of London. Richard swiftly revoked his concessions and carried out harsh reprisals, but underlying resentments remained. Villeinage* was practically in decline, as the high price of labour and the low price of grain were making traditional landholding practices uneconomic. Agrarian tensions persisted, erupting periodically, as with the rebellion led by Jack Cade in 1450 and the Cornish revolt in 1497. Cade and his Kentish followers followed the earlier rebels by marching to London, killing various aristocrats and a sheriff, and freeing prisoners from Southwark jail, as depicted in Shakespeare's *Henry VI Part Two*. By the end of the medieval period, traditional serfdom had virtually disappeared, crumbling away as an anachronistic system without value. Land was given over more and more to sheep rather than arable farming. Many

---

* Villeinage is a system by which an unfree peasantry owes allegiance and services to a lord.

tenant farmers progressed from renting to owning their land, and began to acquire the status of minor gentry. Meanwhile, landless poor flocked to the growing towns. The dynamics of social mobility in play would continue for several centuries to come, leading up to the Industrial Revolution.

The Status of English and English Literature

Growing nationalism in the course of protracted war against France helped to foster an interest in a separate language to define England. Gradually, political factors also influenced the decline of French in favour of English at all levels of society. From the early fourteenth century onwards, plenty of texts articulate a new linguistic self-consciousness. The *Cursor Mundi* poet (*c.* 1300) declares that he is translating for the 'commun' people:

> For the love of Inglis lede   [English people]
> Inglis lede of Ingland.[17]

William of Nassyngton (*c.* 1325) describes a widely varying facility in French and Latin, enthusiastically proposing English as a common tongue:

> Both lered and lewed, olde and ȝonge,
> Alle vunderstonden English tonge.

Ralph Higden (*c.* 1320) admits the superior social status accorded to French speakers, 'Gentil men children beeþ i-tauȝt to speke Frensche ... and vplondisshe [country-dwelling] men wil likne hym self to gentil men, and fondeþ [exert themselves] wiþ greet besynesse for to speke Frensche, for to be more i-tolde of'. But, fifty years later, in 1385, John Trevisa, translating Higden's *Polychronicon*, remarks on the changes which have taken place since Higden wrote, 'Now ... in al the gramerscoles of Engelond children leueþ [leave] Frensch, and construeþ [analyse grammar] and lurneþ [learn] an [in] Englysch ... Also gentil

27

men habbaþ now moche yleft [stopped] for to teche here [their] children Frensch'.[18] The fact that he remarks upon it shows that learning English rather than French was evidently still a novelty.

By the time of Chaucer, English had gained prestige while provincial French was a target for ridicule, in the person of the pretentious Prioress, with her 'Frenssh … After the scole of Stratford atte Bowe'.[19] It was 1362 that marked a turning point in the history of the English language when, for the first time, parliament was opened with a speech in English, and proceeded to pass a statute by which all laws were henceforth to be in English. From its position as the dominant, high-status language, at the heart of the Church, Latin had been displaced by the vernacular, remaining only as a scholarly *lingua franca*. English literature enjoyed a Golden Age during the reign of Richard II, with exceptional poets such as Chaucer, Langland and the *Gawain*-poet, as well as many less well-known authors, producing outstanding works.

Functional literacy grew, so that by 1500 about half the population were able to read if not to write. Collections of private letters survive, such as the family correspondence of the Paston family in Norfolk. These demonstrate a lively, colloquial prose style developing:

> I let yowe pleynly undyrstond that my fader wyll nomore money parte wythall in that behalfe but an hundred pound and fifty marke, which is ryght far fro the acomplyshment of yowr desire. Wherefor, yf that ye cowed be content with that good and my por persone, I wold be the meryest mayden on grounde.[20]

With the invention of moveable type in Germany, the production and dissemination of texts was transformed. Instead of laborious hand copying of manuscripts, new printing presses could produce large quantities of identical texts quickly and cheaply, using paper rather than expensive parchment. In 1476, William Caxton set up the first English printing press at Westminster. His editions fed the appetites of a greatly expanded reading public. For the first time, authorship became important, something to be stated boldly on the cover and title pages. In the earlier medieval period, anonymity was the norm, identification of the author being rare and tending to be oblique, frequently acrostic. William Langland's sly insinuation of his name, 'My name is Will … I have lived in lande longe', is in the same spirit of self-effacement as the Anglo-Saxon poet Cynewulf, who encrypted his name in runes. By the fourteenth century, a new class of semi-professional writers such as Chaucer and Gower felt confident enough to declare their name and to claim credit for their creativity.

The later Middle Ages led up to and helped to create the English Renaissance. Far from being a primitive prologue, the medieval period nurtured to fruition many ideas, and laid much of the foundations upon which the sixteenth century built, such as robust scholarly thinking, engagement with the Classical past and extended lay piety. Humanism grew out of Aristotelian studies from much earlier, based on principles of systematic enquiry and experiential methodology. Continuity was as important as innovation.

Notes

1   For an excellent study of the impact of the Norman Conquest on women, see Christine Fell, *Women in Anglo-Saxon England* (London: British Museum Publications, 1984).

2   Extracts with a facing-page Modern English translation can be found in Elaine Treharne (ed.), *Old and Middle English c. 890-c. 1400: An Anthology* (Oxford: Blackwell, 2004), pp. 254–9.

3   Eric Gerald Stanley (ed.), *The Owl and the Nightingale* (Manchester: Manchester University Press, 1960; repr. 1982).

4   This account forms part of Book 6 of Cicero's *De Re Publica* (*c*. 270 BC). It was very popular in the Middle Ages. See Michael Grant (trans.), *Cicero: On the Good Life* (Harmondsworth: Penguin, 1971), pp. 337–55.

5   'The Knight's Tale', pp. 65–6, ll. 2987–3074, in *The Riverside Chaucer*, ed. Larry D. Benson (Oxford: Oxford University Press, 1989).

6   Cited by David Aers in *Faith, Ethics and Church: Writing in England, 1360–1409* (Cambridge: Brewer, 2000), p. 47.

7   James Simpson, *Piers Plowman: An Introduction to the B-Text* (London: Longman, 1990), pp. 179, 227–8.

8   Martin Luther, 'Appeal to the German Nobility', cited in Peggy Knapp, *Chaucer and the Social Contest* (London: Routledge, 1990), p. 45.
9   *Froissart: Chronicles*, trans. Geoffrey Brereton (Harmondsworth: Penguin, 1978), p. 176.
10 *The Alliterative Morte Darthur*, in *King Arthur's Death*, ed. Larry D. Benson (Exeter: University of Exeter Press, 1986), pp. 3040–3, 3153–6.
11 Cited in Philip Ziegler, *The Black Death* (Harmondsworth: Penguin, 1998), p. 197.
12 'The Pardoner's Tale', p. 199, ll. 675–6, in *Riverside Chaucer*.
13 Ziegler, *The Black Death*, p. 138.
14 K. B. McFarlane, 'Bastard Feudalism', *Bulletin of the Institute of Historical Research* 20, pp. 161–80. Rpt. in K. B. McFarlane, *England in the Fifteenth Century: Collected Essays* (London: Hambledon, 1981), pp. 23–43.
15 'The Second Shepherds' Play' (Play 14), ll. 16–19, 37–8, 44–5 in *English Mystery Plays*, ed. Peter Happé (Harmondsworth: Penguin, 1975).
16 *Riverside Chaucer*, p. 654, ll. 1–7.
17 Extracts from *Cursor Mundi* can be found in Elaine Treharne (ed.), *Old and Middle English c. 890-c. 1400: An Anthology* (Oxford: Blackwell, 2004), pp. 417–21.
18 Extracts can be found in Derek Pearsall (ed.), *Chaucer to Spenser: An Anthology* (Oxford: Blackwell, 1999), pp. 230–1.
19 'General Prologue', p. 25, l. 125, in *Riverside Chaucer*.
20 Cited in Alexandra Barrett (ed.), *Women's Writing in Middle English* (Harlow: Longman, 1992), pp. 254, 227–32.

Part Three
Texts, Writers and Contexts

Fantasy and Fairy: The Breton Lay

The Breton lay is an early and influential genre. Sometimes regarded as a transitional genre between lyric and romance, it is a kind of short romance often featuring love and the 'fairy' and usually claiming descent from 'lays' sung by Bretons. Poems designating themselves 'Breton lays' appear in England from the twelfth century onwards. Essentially short narrative poems sung to a harp accompaniment, no Breton originals survive. If there were a lay tradition in Brittany, it was short-lived and has left no trace other than the poems purporting to be translations of Breton works. The claim for Breton sources may be grounded in reality or may be a fictive device, akin to Geoffrey of Monmouth's 'very ancient book' – a fraudulent ancestry for authenticating purposes.

The poems that survive form a fairly coherent body of work with distinct features in common: a self-consciously simple style; recognisable character 'types'; recurrent plot elements; folklore motifs; highly formulaic expression. Above all, these poems are particularly concerned with magic and the supernatural, and occupy a realm charged with exotic and symbolic connotations. About thirty such poems survive from the medieval period, mainly in French. They cover a wide variety of moods and themes, ranging from tragedy to comedy. One of the main ways in which these works invite modern critical attention is in their preoccupation with psychological and fantasy worlds, exploiting the power of suggestive symbolism. Their brevity and obliqueness often contribute to their enigmatic quality. Like fairy stories in general, they can be as challenging as they are charming. They offer rich materials in the modern critical climate where scholars debate and interrogate the nature and function of signs, symbols and meaning.

'Little Britain'

Central to the Breton lay is material derived from folktales, transmitted orally as part of an ancient storytelling tradition. The literary lay provides a valuable window into the transposition and reconstruction processes at work as oral tales were recorded in written form. The story types and plot elements tend to be drawn from a common stock with widely recurring patterns classified by anthropologists, such as the Calumniated Wife, the Man tried by Fate, and Exile and Return. The Breton origin attributed to many of the lays suggests the transmission of Celtic tales via Brittany, a north-westerly region of France colonised by Celts fleeing the Anglo-Saxon invaders from the sixth century onwards. The proximity of a Celtic kingdom geographically and culturally close to England is reflected in the terms applied to the region – 'Britoun', 'Bretoun' and 'Lytyll Bretayne', which are not to be confused with the British Isles. One remnant of the Celtic regions' shared cultural heritage survives today; namely, the Five Nations rugby union tournament contested by England, Wales, Ireland, Scotland and France (now called the Six Nations, including Italy). Medieval romance in general and the Breton lay in particular are suffused with Celtic material. In *Sir Gawain and the Green Knight,* for example, Celtic analogues exist for the figure of the Green Knight, and for the Temptation and Beheading trials, while Sir Gawain appears to have originated as a Celtic sun god. The 'faraway' world that frequently provides the setting for the Breton lay is at once historically and culturally grounded in reality, and a timeless fantasy realm of psychological displacement.

The Transmission of Stories

The Breton lays are key texts inasmuch as they demonstrate the nature of medieval storytelling processes at work. They are products of cultural assimilation, showing how stories were diffused and refashioned over several centuries, and meeting the demands of a variety of audiences from the courtly elite to the lower bourgeoisie. They also provide valuable insight into the transition from a primarily oral to a literate culture, as revealed by Michael Clanchy's seminal work, *From Memory to Written Record*.[1] The texts to be discussed in this chapter exist along a continuum, but one which is not marked by any straightforward lineal development; rather, there is notable crossover and coexistence. This complexity of transmission is typical of the medieval period.

Pre-12th cent.		Breton lays	
		Songs	
		Oral performance	
		↓	
12th cent.		Marie de France,	
		Lais, incl. *Lanval*	
		Octosyllabic couplets	
		← Courtly environment →	
Early 14th cent.	*Orfeo, Sir Degaré,*		*Sir Landevale*
	Lay le Freine		Octosyllabic couplets
	Tail-rhyme stanzas		Popular
	Popular (contained in		
	the mid-14th cent.		↓
	Auchinleck manuscript)		
Mid-14th cent.	↓		*Emaré*, Thomas
			Chestre, *Sir Launfal*
			Tail-rhyme stanzas
			Popular (contained in
			mid-15th cent. Cotton
			Caligula A ii manuscript)
Late 14th cent.	Chaucer, *Franklin's Tale*		
	Five-stress couplets		
	Courtly		

Marie de France

In the second half of the twelfth century, probably at the court of Henry II (reigned 1155–89), a poet known as Marie de France produced a dozen short poems called 'lais'.[2] She wrote in Anglo-Norman using the refined octosyllabic form then in favour for courtly literature in England as well as continental France, where Chrétien de Troyes was writing the first chivalric romances. The form has some similarities with native Old English verse in that it has lines of four stresses, although the rhyme and regularity of meter are very different from Old English poetry, which was structured around alliterative patterns. There is a distinct musicality to the form, resonant of oral tradition, whereby rhyme and regular metre function as aids to memorising by the performer. The attribution of the *Lais* to 'Marie de France' dates from the sixteenth century. Within the *Lais* themselves, there is only one reference to the author as 'Marie', in the tale of *Guigemar*, and the authenticity of this is doubtful. The only other contemporary reference comes from the poet Denis Piramus (*c.* 1180) who mentions a certain 'Dame Marie' who is a writer of verse lays and very popular with ladies. The popularity of Marie's work is attested by the fact that thirteen manuscripts of the *Lais* survive.* Her identity remains a mystery, although several candidates have been proposed – among whom the most favoured is an abbess of Shaftesbury, a putative illegitimate daughter of Geoffrey of Anjou and thereby Henry II's half-sister. Marie's writing, however, is self-conscious enough to convey a vivid impression of the author as a learned and assured woman. She prefaces her collection of lays with a Prologue in which she confidently announces her literary skill:

> Anyone who has received from God the gift of knowledge and true eloquence has a duty not to remain silent: rather should one be happy to reveal such talents. (p. 41)

---

* The other major work attributed to Marie de France, the *Moral Fables*, survives in twenty-three manuscripts.

This is remarkably assertive for the time, when even male writers traditionally deployed the 'modesty' topos, expressing humility. The poet situates herself within a literary tradition of 'the ancients' and 'men of learning', associating her work with lofty moral purposes of helping people who wish 'to guard against vice'. The *Lais* are clearly conceived of as serious and worthy of attention, not as frivolous entertainment. Marie presents herself by implication as one seeking 'to study intently and undertake a demanding task'. Her first inclination to translate 'some good story' from Latin is superseded by a more 'worthwhile' project:

> I thought of lays which I had heard ... composed, by those who first began them and put them into circulation, to perpetuate the memory of adventures they had heard. ... I set myself to assemble lays, to compose and to relate them in rhyme. (p. 41)

Clearly the lines between oral transmission and literary composition and translation are being blurred here. Marie is using folktale materials but writing for an aristocratic public – the Norman ruling class. Her work is marked by courtly vocabulary and concerns; her writing style is poised and sophisticated, employing clear, simple, yet elegant expressions. Her artistry is controlled, finely contained within the brevity of the lay (individual tales vary in length between 118 and 1184 lines, with an average length of 477 lines). She can be compared in some respects to another superb miniaturist although one working in a very different medium – the novelist Jane Austen. Like Austen, Marie has a distinct preference for writing about women from a woman's point of view. The tales tend to be domestic and family-oriented, treating of marriage and love affairs. Marie's heroines are markedly forceful and resourceful. Old, jealous husbands receive short shrift, there is plentiful sympathy for lovers, and the narrator even explicitly approves one adulterous liaison, 'I never saw so fair a couple'. Marie's lovers display admirable endurance, asserting their individual need for self-fulfilment. Most of the *Lais* present marvellous adventures, usually containing a central emblem or magical token such as a ring or sword. The natural world figures prominently, often as a place of enchantment or supernatural agency: key symbolic elements include the nightingale (*Laustic*), the hazel tree and honeysuckle (*Chevrefeuil*), a hawk-lover (*Milun*) and a swan messenger (*Yonec*). One of her *Lais* is, unusually, focused on a male protagonist, Sir Lanval, and offers an intriguing view of a fantasy, combining female heroism, male wish-fulfilment and insightful psychological development.

Marie de France's *Lanval*

At just 646 lines, this poem[3] is a typical miniature gem. It retains many features of orality with the narrator being a firm if occasional presence, addressing the audience early on, interjecting a speculative comment about the hero, 'Alas, what will he do?' (p. 77), and concluding with a teasing disavowal, 'No one has heard any more about him, nor can I relate any more' (p. 81). The opening of the poem declares a typically confident narratorial control:

> L'aventure d'un autre lai,
> Cum ele avient, vus cunterai,
> Fait fu d'un mut gentil vassal;
> En bretans l'apelent Lanval.

> [The story of another lay, just as it happened, I shall relate to you.
> It was made about a very noble young man whose name in
> Breton is Lanval.]

Lanval is a young knight at the court of King Arthur. He suffers neglect and impoverishment until one day he meets a mysterious lover who enriches him and pledges her love on condition that he keep their affair secret. Numerous elements deriving from Celtic tales of the supernatural are obvious: the river, acting as a boundary between worlds; the trembling horse, intuiting magic; the hero being 'taken' as he sleeps. Lanval is goaded into declaring his mistress's supreme beauty when Gwenever tries to seduce him, thereby breaking his promise of secrecy. The rejected Gwenever accuses him of homosexuality, 'I have been told often enough that you have no desire for women. You have well-trained young men and enjoy yourself with them' (p. 76). Such surprising sexual explicitness is another feature of Marie's work. Several of her *Lais* treat topics such as pre-marital sex, adultery and illegitimate children with an ease perhaps borne of familiarity with the cosmopolitan court. On trial for treason, Lanval is saved at the eleventh hour when his mistress appears and triumphantly vindicates him. The two of them depart for Avalon. The story exists in many versions, some of which conclude happily with union, while others end in separation and loss. The narrative structure of Marie's lay presents events as a diptych, contrasting the sexual advances of the fairy mistress with those of the wicked queen. The climax is managed in a leisurely way with a prolonged, suspenseful trial followed by Lanval's surprising rescue. The suspense is intensified by the protracted dénouement in three stages, culminating in the long-anticipated reappearance of the fairy lover. The sparse style employs few conventional similes: the mistress's neck is said to be whiter than snow on a branch, her hair brighter than a golden thread; the luxurious bedding is observed to be extraordinarily costly, 'the coverlets cost as much as a castle' (p. 74). There are rare touches of precise detail, 'In the same year, I believe, after St. John's day' (p. 76), combining with incidents of a recognisably feudal nature, such as Arthur summoning his barons and granting bail 'on surety of all that you hold from me, lands and fiefs, each man separately' (p. 78).

This 'very noble young man' (p. 73) at the centre of the tale is far from a typical chivalric hero. Lanval performs no noble deeds; in fact, he is a remarkably passive and marginalised figure. Lanval's fate and fortune depend entirely on his chance encounter with a magical lover, whose dramatic rescue at the end provides the climax of the tale. This reconfigures the traditional power relations of romance. Marie carefully avoids explaining the nature of the mistress's magic power and never explicitly designates her as a fairy, unlike later versions and analogues. The Fairy Mistress motif, related to that of the Wooing Woman, which is common in Anglo-Norman romance, provides a site of female empowerment as well as male gratification. Such fairy mistresses have been described by Judith Weiss as, 'a special case: exotic outsiders, free from social and moral restraints'.[4] Given the prominent and resourceful roles of Marie's heroines throughout the *Lais*, the mistress's conclusive power is less exceptional. Read from a psycho-analytical perspective, Lanval's dependency and painful progress can be seen to represent stages in a narcissistic fantasy. His sexual and egoic gratification must necessarily be kept secret to preserve his fragile sense of self. Rejecting threatening or neglectful parents (Arthur and Gwenever) enables him to move beyond his infantile state, but only into a projected realm of fantasy (Avalon). The two women work as binary opposites – the one nurturing, seductive, protective, the other vindictive, sexually un-alluring, threatening. The story can be seen to be exploring an Oedipal complex, dramatising the processes of maturation and sublimated desire. Lanval in this reading is a child passing into adolescence. Gwenever is depicted unfavourably (through the lens of Lanval's hostile gaze) as a dangerous, despised mother figure replaced by a more nurturing alternative.

Lays in Middle English

Marie's *Lais* were copied in manuscripts for at least two hundred years. Of the dozen or so Middle English lays which survive, three are based directly on Marie's tales – *Lay le Freine*,[5] *Sir Landevale* and Thomas Chester's *Sir Launfal*.[6] The lay enjoyed a considerable popularity in England, although it disappeared early on in France. Most of the Middle English translations are directed at a non-courtly audience, as evident in their style and orientation. However, the concept of 'popular' literature has been hotly debated in recent years. There are those who argue for a widely diverse audience composed of menials and artisans, with access to minstrel performances in the lord's manor hall or the town square. Others, such as Stephen Knight, consider popular romances as literary productions, euphemising chivalric life for the consumption of the aspiring lower gentry/bourgeois classes.[7] Middle English Breton lays are generally regarded as inferior to the French originals, judged on purely aesthetic grounds. Literature designed for a more general public than that of the court or elite is necessarily different but not necessarily less important. 'Popular' remains a term of abuse in some quarters, but applied to the Middle English lays it enables fresh responses to texts which have been traditionally held in disdain.

Sir Landevale is an anonymous couplet version of Marie's tale written in a homely vernacular idiom. Stylistically it can be crude and most unromantic in its expression:

> 'Landavale,' she seid, 'myn hert swete,
> For thy loue now I swete.' (ll. 113–14)

But the poem's strength lies in its accessibility and its robust turn of phrase as it represents the material. The couplets strive to reproduce in English effects which are easier to achieve in French. The later version by Thomas Chester, who takes care to name himself as author, 'Thomas Chestre made this tale' (l. 1039), is written in the tail-rhyme form associated with popular romance. This alternates rhyming couplets with a tail line or *cauda*, whose rhyme chimes throughout the stanza:

> Launfal turnede himself & low,   [laughed]
> Therof he hadde scorn ynow,   [plenty]
> And seyde to hys knyghtes tweyne:
> 'Now may ye se – swych ys seruice
> Vnther a lord of lytyll pryse! –   [worth]
> How he may therof be fayn' (ll. 115–20)   [glad]

This tends to result in a great deal of extraneous, redundant matter with semantically empty tags and stilted rhymes. It is the very form satirised by Chaucer in 'Sir Thopas', which drives the Host to interrupt, 'Thy drasty ryming is nat worth a toord!'[8] The manuscript context in which *Sir Launfal* is preserved, namely a household miscellany from the fifteenth century, suggests its appeal to an educated bourgeois family. This diversifying of the audience for the Breton lay affects the storytelling technique, so that the Middle English Breton lay generally tends to divest symbols of their mystery and rationalise the marvellous, regularly explaining and concretising. Chester's *Launfal* expands the narrative to well over a thousand lines in order to accommodate more and greater events with new characters, including magical sidekicks and a greedy town mayor. The hero's role is reconfigured to satisfy expectations, so that he wins a tournament, performs knightly deeds and defeats a giant. The narrator heightens the pathos, depicting Launfal in distress, begging and weeping. The new sensibility removes the reference to homosexuality and expresses intense moral hostility towards the promiscuous Gwenever, who is vilified from the outset and punished at the end by being blinded by the fairy mistress, Tryamour. Clearly, the lay provided material for a wider public to enjoy, transforming Marie's refined elegance into something far more action-packed and dramatic. Rather than measure the later versions against their original source text, it may be better to accord them a different kind of success, in that they met new criteria for engaging an audience. In this light, we can now consider another tail-rhyme Breton lay which is found in the same manuscript as *Sir Launfal* and illustrates the flexibility of the genre.

The Lay of *Emaré*

The lay of *Emaré*[9] is similar in length to *Sir Launfal*, at 1035 lines. Stylistically, too, it resembles Chester's work, employing a restricted vocabulary and simple diction. Its formulaic qualities are pronounced. Examples of the formulaic phrasing occur in descriptions of female beauty, 'worthy under wede', 'goodly under gore', 'comely under kelle'; 'fayr and fre', 'fayr and semely', 'fayr and bryght'. The elements of oral-formulaic poetry need not be disparaged or condemned as ineptitude. The insistent repetition with variation found in *Emaré* develops a structural as well as descriptive function, as the narrative relates a sequence of double exile, double rescue and double reunion. Cyclic patterning forms part of the divine order, inscribing shape upon apparently chance events.

The lay's religious focus is clear from the opening prayer. The tale exploits the directness of a minstrel narrative persona, delivering an orally transmitted tale, 'As y here singe in songe' (l. 24), although later referring to a written text, 'In romans as we rede' (l. 216). Its generic identity is delayed until the end (ll. 1030–2), just before its final prayer:

> Thys ys on of Brytayne layes,
> That was vsed by olde dayes:
> Mon callys 'Playnþ E-garye'.   [complaint/lament]

Having an eponymous heroine marks this lay as unusual. The female at the centre of the story seems to exist as a saint-like object of admiration. Emaré (OF *esmeré*, 'refined, purified') is an emperor's daughter who, following the gift of a wonderful robe, becomes the object of her father's incestuous desire. She even resists papal support for the union, constituting a fixed point of moral certitude:

> Nay, syr! God of Heuen hit for-bede   [forbid]
> þat euer do so we shulde! (ll. 251–2)

Emaré is then set adrift by her father, landing in pagan 'Galys' (possibly Wales, Galicia, or Galloway) where she calls herself Egaré (OF 'lost, displaced'). Her rescuer, Sir Kador, brings her to court where the king falls in love with her and converts to Christianity:

> þe cloth vpon her shone so bryȝth ...   [brightly]
> She semed non erdly þyng.   [earthly]
> (ll. 394, 396)

While her husband is called abroad, she gives birth but, due to the machinations of her mother-in-law, is accused of delivering a monster, 'A fowl, feltred [matted-haired] fend' (l. 540) and tried for adultery (the common folklore motif of the Accused Queen). She is set adrift with her son and lands in Rome where, after many years, her father and husband arrive to perform penance and she orchestrates a thorough reconciliation. The storyline falls into the 'family romance' category, covering several generations and positing an ideal nuclear family. Fantasy elements of a Cinderella-type exist alongside a didactic *exemplum*. The lay is designed for Christian teaching, depicting Emaré as a Job-like figure who endures hardship with unwavering faith which is ultimately rewarded. She is paradoxically a passive heroine who is an active agent of divine will. Her main function is as an instrument of redemption and salvation. There are distinct Marian* overtones to her presentation, especially as she is set adrift for the second time:

> The lady that was meke and mylde
> In her arme she bar her chylde. (ll. 640–1)

This lay represents another development of the Breton source material, being reconfigured as a semi-hagiography. It appropriates conventions of the genre for its own ends, exploiting the exile-and-reunion structure for religious purposes. Framed as a conversion myth, the lay deals with religious identity, the conversion of the heathen and the redemption of both emperor and pope. Clearly, the story appealed to later writers including Chaucer and Gower, who both retold it.[10]

The lay contains elements typical of the genre, notably the symbolic rudderless boat and the magical cloth from which her robe is made.[11] The mysterious potency of the robe as a symbol resides in its imprecise status. A gift from the King of Sicily, it is embroidered with scenes of lovers: Ydone and Amadas; Tristram and Isolde; Floris and Blanchflour; the Emir's daughter and the son of the Sultan of Babylon. The emperor's bedazzled reaction to it is typical of its impact:

> Sertes, þys ys a fairy   [magical enchantment]
> Or ellys a vanyte!   [illusion]
> (ll. 104–5)

The eight stanzas dedicated to describing this fabulous cloth are hugely disproportionate in such a short poem, yet mark it as a significant

* The word Marian means of, or pertaining to, the Virgin Mary.

object. The power associated with it varies, as it enchants and seduces but is at times associated with devilry. Whenever the robe is mentioned, desire or an emotional response is prompted. It may represent all sorts of things by implication, such as love, beauty, goodness and sexuality, but its value is never specified. It perplexes by its double nature as something at once casual and causal. Ad Putter considers the robe's imprecise agency to be its essential function, acting as a connecting thread which signifies the marvellous, a memorable hook, appropriately practical in the context of oral reception.[12] The magical robe's suppressed potency allows pagan magic to be subsumed by Christian miracle.

'The Franklin's Tale'

'The Franklin's Tale'[13] is famous for seeming to provide a 'solution' to the 'Marriage Debate' within the *Canterbury Tales*, proposing mutuality in place of dominance and submission, championed by 'The Wife of Bath's Tale' and 'The Clerk's Tale' respectively. As a late version of a Breton lay, it offers a fascinating example of how such stories generated new meanings and could be reshaped according to the individual writer's will. Chaucer adopts a form associated with a noble history, raising the audience's expectations of exotic fare from the distant, pre-Christian past:

> Thise olde gentil Britouns in hir dayes   [noble]
> Of diverse aventures maden layes,
> Rymeyed in hir firste Briton tonge;   [language]
> Whiche layes with hir instrumentz they songe,
> Or elles redden hem for hir plesaunce,
> And oon of hem have I in remembraunce   [one]
> Which I shal seyn with good wyl as I kan. (ll. 709–15)

The narrative voice here is specifically assigned to the middle-aged Franklin, self-consciously disclaiming any rhetorical skill or learning, 'I am a burel [uneducated, simple] man' (l. 716). The eloquence with which he goes on to relate his Tale belies his claim for simplicity. Like Chaucer, the Franklin ('freeholder') occupies a marginal status, not of noble birth but associating with and approaching gentle rank. By presenting itself as a lay, the story draws on the established attributes of the genre. The prologue is very close to those of *Sir Orfeo* and *Lay le Freine* in the Auchinleck manuscript, which it is believed that Chaucer may have seen or even owned.[14] As a sophisticated court poet, Chaucer develops the lay into a multi-layered and complex form posing challenging questions about identity and ideals. While retaining many 'popular' elements and typical features, Chaucer nevertheless creates something quite new.[15]

The story is concerned with love and magic but neither is in its traditional guise. At the outset, the Tale proposes an ideal arrangement of equality between the newly married couple, Dorigen and Arveragus (both Celtic names). Their policy is based on the principle that 'freendes everych oother moot obeye' (l. 762), yet with some social compromise necessary, 'Save that the name of soveraynhtee, / That wolde he have for shame of his degree' (ll. 751–2). This accord is tested by the events of the subsequent narrative, which, like the majority of lays, focuses on a woman's experience. As in so many of his works, Chaucer explores the nature of female strength in adversity, suffusing the lexis of the tale with terms such as 'pacience', 'suffre' and 'suffrance'. Dorigen is left distraught by her husband's absence abroad, tormented by thoughts of his possible shipwreck on the dangerous rocks along the coast of Brittany. Further tested by the unwelcome courting of the love-sick squire Aurelius, she seeks to assuage both causes of sorrow at once by declaring to Aurelius that she will accept his love provided that he remove the rocks. This Rash Promise is couched in confused notions of honour and obligation:

> Ne shal I nevere been untrewe wyf ...
> Taak this for final answere ...
> But after that in pley thus seyde she ...
> Yet wolde I graunte yow to been youre love,
> Syn I yow se so pitously complayne ...   [since]
> ... Have heer my trouthe. (ll. 984, 987, 988, 990–1, 998)

Aurelius engages a magician to create the illusion of the rocks' removal, to Dorigen's shock and distress. She considers suicide in a long, formal complaint and, upon Arveragus's return, confesses everything to him. He is troubled but insists that she keep her word. En route to fulfil her promise, Dorigen meets Aurelius, who is so moved by her grief and by Arveragus's noble behaviour that he renounces his claim. The magician is moved in turn to renounce payment and all ends happily. But the underlying issues are not so easily resolved. Every aspect of the Tale presents conflicting interpretative possibilities. The symbolic elements of the garden and the rocks connote multiple meanings. As a location for wooing, the garden is a traditional setting for romance, associated with love and sexuality from the time of the biblical Song of Songs, while echoes of the garden of Eden introduce hints of a Fall. The rocks are Chaucer's own addition to the story, a far more multivalent symbol than that of his principal source – Boccaccio's *Filocolo* (IV.4) where the condition is that the squire make a garden bloom in January. The rocks can be seen to represent hostile natural forces or, as Dorigen interprets them, unaccountable evil:

> That semen rather a foul confusion
> Of werk than any fair creacion. (ll. 869–70)

She has been criticised for objecting to their presence as if refuting the divine order, doubting God's 'purveiaunce' (l. 865). Readings of the rocks see them as representing divine wrath, inscrutability, the unconscious, ignorance or chance. They are clearly invested with forceful presence even as their import remains enigmatic. As the site of illusion and fraudulent magic, they can be seen to implicate a host of targets, including female credulity, the sham of courtly love and implacable masculine power.

The multiplying of interpretative possibilities is a feature of Chaucer's reworking of old stories. Here the lay form is invested with philosophical and moral significance far removed from the world of minstrel entertainment. Inviting more complex responses to characters and their predicaments renders meaning increasingly elusive. For example, the

45

status of the 'ideal' marriage is a contentious issue. Aurelius has been read as embodying a new masculinity, which regards personal integrity more highly than public performance; as the knight-hero, his unorthodox role here is to privilege words over deeds. Others see his celebrated acquiescence to Dorigen's sexual liaison as another form of male domination. Her role too is complicated. For some she is a new type of heroine, demonstrating admirable virtues of autonomy, while others deride her as feeble and victimised.[16] The central value at issue in the Tale is the concept of 'trouthe', centred on Dorigen's honour. The intense self-consciousness inscribed in Chaucer's rationalising, modernising version creates problems of interpretation which simply do not occur in earlier types of the Breton lay. In her long and operatic complaint (ll. 1355–456), Dorigen recalls the rape and suicide of twenty-two women treated in the notoriously misogynistic *Epistola Adversus Jovinianum.** Rather than revealing her less-than-heroic nature as she fails to emulate these role models, this text surely scrutinises and rejects such Classical ideals of self-sacrificing women. Whoever is finally deemed to be the 'moost fre', it is certainly not Dorigen. Her predicament, trapped amidst male rivalry, according to Elaine Tuttle-Hansen, 'exposes the illusory nature of the empowerment that courtly fictions seem to cede her'.[17] Questions of gender and genre coincide in numerous ways in a story riven with speculation as to meaning and power. Gentility itself may be illusory where appearances can be so deceptive, where authority is relative and where no one emerges honourably.

Among the many tensions within the Tale, the sudden resolution and happy ending are problematic, given the disturbing dilemmas presented. The final rhetorical question or *demande* invites the audience to judge who was the most 'fre' (noble, generous, unrestrained) as if it were an easy matter. This exploits the popularity at the time of inviting an audience debate. But questioning the nature of truth and gentleness, couched in terms of social rank ('a cherlyssh wrecchednesse / Agayns franchise [noble generosity] and alle gentillesse', ll. 1523–4), is a bold

---

* St Jerome's 'Letter Against Jovinianus' was a famous attack on marriage. This text also informs much of 'The Wife of Bath's Prologue' and 'The Merchant's Prologue', supplying plentiful material which represents women in derogatory ways.

manoeuvre at a time when social mobility was an unsettling notion.[18] Elsewhere, tellingly bourgeois practicalities impinge on the romance, such as the repayment of debt and the need to earn a living. The only real magic is the transformation of potential shame to honour on the part of several characters.

In Chaucer's hands the simplicity of the Breton lay is subtly transformed. Traditional motifs are redeployed in a typically Chaucerian way, so as to become teasing and ironic. This illustrates the lay's durability and flexibility, as a form able to expand and resonate with new meaning, to develop possibilities and to remain live and productive as a vehicle over several centuries.

Extended Commentary: *Sir Orfeo*

Sir Orfeo[19] is an anonymous early lay (*c.* 1330) of approximately 600 lines. Its octosyllabic couplets provide an insistent beat and speedy rhythm appropriate for a musically oriented piece. In its Epilogue the poem identifies itself as a 'lay of gode liking' (l. 599) made by 'Harpours in Bretaine' (l. 597), concluding:

> That lay 'Orfeo' is y-hote:
> God is the lay, swete is the note. (ll. 601–2)

The narrator immediately establishes his presence as a performer, addressing the listening audience, 'Herkneth, lordinges' (l. 23), and announcing his extensive knowledge of the lay genre:

> Sum ben of wer and sum of wo,
> And sum of joie and mirthe also,
> Sum of trecherie and sum of gile,
> And sum old aventours that fel while, [happened once]
> Sum of bourdes and ribaudy, [fun and games]
> And mani ther beth of fairy. (ll. 5–10)[20]

As the story proceeds, this narrative voice occasionally expresses sympathy and appreciation for the skill and vulnerable 'patron-dependent' status of its harper hero, developing a fairly coherent narrative persona.

Sir Orfeo is essentially a medievalised retelling of the classical myth of Orpheus, known to the Middle Ages through Ovid's *Metamorphoses*. In the original myth, Orpheus pursues his wife Eurydice to Hades after she dies from a serpent bite but loses her forever when he glances back at her, contrary to Pluto's injunction. The grief-stricken Orpheus ends up wandering in the wilderness with only his harp and wild animals as company until he is torn to pieces by a group of female Bacchantes.* The lay transforms the myth in many ways. In this version, Orfeo is an English king ruling in Winchester (previously known as 'Thrace'). Such reassigning of geography is found in other lays; for example, in *Lay Le Freyne*, whose location in Brittany is changed to the west of England. The identification of Orfeo's parents as King Pluto and Queen Juno, once regarded as gods (ll. 43–4), may be either a joke or innocent misapprehension.

The lay relates how Orfeo's wife, Herodis, falls asleep at noon in an orchard and in a dream is taken by the fairy king, who vows to return to claim her the following day. Despite all Orfeo's efforts, she is magically abducted and he leaves his kingdom in the care of his steward while he wanders for ten years in the wilderness. Tracking his wife to the fairy kingdom, Orfeo wins her back by his musical skill and returns to Winchester. Here, the second plotline unfolds, as the disguised Orfeo tests his steward – first by requesting alms, which are promptly granted, then by playing his harp at a feast, claiming to have found it beside a dead man. The steward's grief convinces Orfeo of his faithfulness and he reveals his true identity. He nominates the loyal steward as his heir, and the poem ends with the restoration of the king and queen. As in 'The Franklin's Tale', the various threads of the story cohere around the key moral concept of 'trouthe', as Herodis, Orfeo, the fairy king and the steward each in turn honour their word.

---

* An oblique allusion to this may lie behind the pretended death Orfeo reports on his return, 'With lyones a man totorn smale' (l. 538).

In the earliest account of fairies in English, symbolic Celtic elements abound: the May setting, the orchard, the 'ympe-tre' (l. 70), 'undrentide' (l. 65) – that is, noon, the traditional time of fairy abduction/encounter when the barrier between worlds is thin. In various Celtic analogues, such as the Irish tale of the *Wooing of Etain*, kings retrieve abducted wives; as in Irish *aithed* stories, Herodis is taken not killed. The poem presents a Celtic Otherworld quite different in nature from the Classical underworld.

Literary Qualities

Among the many features of the poem which are justly celebrated are the economy of the double narrative (the Abducted Damsel and Faithful Steward motifs), which is simply but effectively structured, and its use of contrast, juxtaposition and suspense. Close in style to oral-formulaic poetry, *Sir Orfeo* is marked by the simplicity of its diction, its plain register – with few, conventional similes (as bright as the sun, as withered as a tree) – and a fondness for minstrel tags and alliterating doublets:

The fairest levedi, *for the nones,*	[lady]
That might gon on *bodi and bones.*	[live]
(ll. 53–4)	

The simple style can achieve fine effects, as in Orfeo's simple yet moving declaration witnessing his wife's violent distress:

'Allas!' quath he, 'forlorn icham,	[I am]
Whider wiltow go, and to wham?	[will you]
Whider thou gost, ichil with thee,	[I will (go)]
And whider y go, thou shalt with me.'	[must]
(ll. 127–30)	

This is rhetorically impressive with its poised chiasmus but also poignant, as the declarations of will and intention (wil, shalt) are hollow assertions inscribing helpless grief even as they seek to assuage it. Juxtaposed with this outburst, Herodis's very plain, insistently negative reply serves to heighten the tension:

'Nay, nay, Sir, that nought nis!
Ichil thee telle al hou it is.' (ll.131–2)

Two of the most celebrated passages in the poem are the vividly descriptive accounts of the fairy kingdom and Orfeo's reunion with his wife. The 'fair cuntray' (l. 351) of 'the king o fairy' (l. 283) is hidden deep within the mountains and is approached by Orfeo in several stages. He marvels at the beauty and richness of the king's castle with its hundred towers, buttresses of red gold and halls made of precious stones. The luxury and sensuousness of the scene are so tantalising that it seems like paradise. The seductive vision is followed by a contrastingly chilling and grim description of the vast crowds of suffering people enclosed within the fortress. The castle is revealed suddenly as a nightmarish underworld, and the narrator catalogues the horrors, with stark simplicity:

Sum stode withouten hade,	[head]
And sum non armes nade...	[had not]
Som astrangled as thai ete,	
And sum were in water adreynt,	[drowned]
And sum with fire al forschreynt.	[shrivelled]
(ll. 391–2, 396–8)	

Orfeo's reunion with Herodis at the mid-way point in the poem (ll. 303–30) is a narrative tour de force, masterfully controlling the sequence of detail to intensify suspense:

And on a day he seighe him biside	[saw]
Sexti levedis on hors ride,	
Gentil and iolif as brid on ris,	[branch]
Nought a man amonges hem ther nis.	

And ich a faucun on hond bere,
And riden on haukin bi o rivere. (ll. 303–8)

Careful manipulation of detail maintains the audience's interest and prevents monotony as bursts of narrative action are regularly interspersed with description and direct speech. The deceptively casual phrase, 'And on a day' (l. 303) introduces a typical 'chance' encounter which marks the end of his ten-year exile. This vision of sixty mysterious, beautiful hunting ladies follows directly after a sequence recounting his general experiences: frequent glimpses of the fairy king hunting, 'Oft in hot underntides [morning/noon]' (l. 282), followed by sights of a thousand knights ready to fight, then groups of knights and their ladies dancing. Throughout, verbs of seeing dominate, 'He might se him bisides' (l. 281), 'And other while he might him se' (l. 289), 'And otherwile he seighe other thing' (l. 297). This lexical cluster informs the casual phrase, 'And on a day he seighe him biside' so as to cue expectation that this is more of the same – a passing interlude merely delineating the passing of time and lulling us into a false sense of familiarity. As another in a sequence of chance encounters, this meeting with the ladies strikes no jarring note and does not overly excite; they are presumed to be fairies too. The previous episodes led nowhere and proved to be passing events of no real significance, so there is no reason to assume that this encounter will be different; yet, on some level, primed by the key words, we are expecting it to be significant. The continuous nature of the dead ends cannot go on forever and we anticipate something climactic occurring. The unsuspecting audience may find itself misled once the importance of the event is clear, or an alert audience may be gratified – rewarded for their patience and attention.

In this way, the ostensibly simple language creates complex arenas of meaning. When the fairy ladies appear, they are immediately signified as aristocratic, engaged in falconry. The list of prey birds they hunt provides a factual, precise background for Orfeo's emotional reaction, attracted as he is by his former aristocratic pastime. His laughter seems to mark the beginning of his recovery. The oaths ('Parfay', 'God') remind us of the Christian context, helping to offset any unease about the potentially otherwordly company. Yet the all-female company bodes ill, as does their easy predation and their unnatural domination of nature:

> The foules of the water ariseth,
> The faucons hem wele deviseth,
> Ich faucoun his pray slough.   [killed]
> (ll. 311–13)

Narrative delay, with three verbs of seeing across three lines, sustains suspense before the revelation and naming:

> To a levedi he was y-come,
> Biheld, and hath wele undernome,   [understood]
> And seth bi al thing that it is-   [sees]
> His owhen Quen, Dam Heurodis. (ll. 319–22)

Herodis's silent tears even as she is under the enchantment seem to be the first sign of the spell loosening. Juxtaposed, Orfeo's emotional response is magnificently elaborated in an extended lament:

> Now me is wo! [...]
> Allas! to long last my lif,
> When y no dar nought with mi wiif,
> No hye to me, o word speke. (ll. 331, 335–7)

The key rhyme (my life / my wife) neatly encapsulates his agony. Here he expresses the intense love he feels for his wife in a passionate outburst in reaction to the pain of being so close to her and her pain. The longed-for reunion proves cruelly thwarted, raised hopes are dashed. The release of long pent-up feelings is conveyed in heightened language – the anaphoric 'Allas!' chiming through the passage. The formal lament announces its theme, 'wo' in the first line, and develops it through a series of rhetorical questions and cumulative negatives ('nil', 'no might', 'no dar', 'no hye', 'nil'). Orfeo contemplates suicide in a speech every bit as elaborate and heightened as Dorigen's. The recovery of composure hinges on the oath 'Parfay' (l. 339) as he resolves to recover Herodis, 'tide wat bitide' (l. 339). From misery he moves to determination, 'i-chil' (l. 341), and grim resolve, 'Of liif ne deth me no reche' (l. 342). The climactic negatives paradoxically carry a positive force of renewed purpose.

Allegorical Interpretation

As the hero of a romantic lay, Orfeo fulfils his role as lover and rescuer. The narrative of trial and ordeal clearly celebrates the redemptive power of love. Both Orfeo and Herodis (unlike the silent, objectified Eurydice of the Classical tale) speak expressively of their love. But on the level of allegorical meaning, the story is far from simple. Classical mythology was a new and suspect source of literary inspiration, acceptable primarily as primitive fictions veiling perennial moral truths. From a Christian perspective, Orfeo is an emblem of worldly pride, the archetypal king brought low by Fortune's wheel. His period of exile in the wilderness serves a moral purpose, illustrating penitence. One of the most celebrated passages (ll. 235–60) follows the *ubi sunt** convention, enumerating the losses he suffers:

He that had y-had knightes of priis	[renown]
Bifor him kneland, and levedis,	[kneeling]
Now seth he nothing that him liketh,	
Bot wilde wormes bi him striketh.	[snakes]
(ll. 249–52)	

The balanced alternatives accumulate, contrasting past and present, very much in the spirit of the *contemptus mundi* [despising the world] tradition, disdaining the transience of earthly wealth and glory. The miraculous becomes functional and more rational as Orfeo's musical skill enchants animals and birds, not extending, as in the Classical version, to trees and stones. Along with other Classical tales, that of

---

* *Ubi sunt* is Latin, part of the phrase *Ubi sunt qui ante nos fuerunt?* (Where are those who were before us?). The term '*ubi sunt*' designates writings which express nostalgic recollection of the past.

Orpheus was appropriated by medieval Christian commentators as material for allegorical interpretation. The *Ovid Moralisé*, for example, analyses Ovidian stories from a moral perspective, which identifies Orpheus as symbolising eloquence, the power of music, wisdom and reason. At the heart of this interpretation is the influential version found in Boethius's *Consolation of Philosophy*.[21] Here, where Orpheus looks back and loses Eurydice forever, the story is seen as a philosophical allegory, representing the blessed man freed from worldly attachment:

Happy he whose unchecked mind
Could leave the chains of earth behind.

Sir Orfeo provides no explicit moral exegesis. The very openness of the story to multiple interpretation is remarkable. Some regard *Orfeo* as a political allegory, depicting a dereliction of kingly duties existing in tension alongside romantic obligations. Herodis here can represent sensuous distraction. Alternative political readings posit her as a feminised personification of the state without whom government cannot function. Where Penelope Doob sees Orfeo as Christ-like in his exile in the wilderness, typologically signifying Christ's descent into hell, others detect an affinity with the wild man of the woods from Celtic myth. Primal elements of seasonal change underlie the myth, resonances of which are retained by the Middle English lay. The narrative circularity relates to the cyclical nature of human experience, suggesting something archetypal in the emotional and physical decay depicted. Herodis's madness functions as a psychological allegory, treating the dissolution of self, and explores disturbing notions so often situated in female experience – the site of mysterious power and instability.[22]

Simple stories simply told? On the contrary, the Breton lays present a diverse range of subjects covering complex issues. The genre was clearly stimulating to poets across several centuries. Its powerful stories are charged with meaning, despite the deceptive characteristics of brevity and plain style. Even the most formulaic elements can be seen to offer possibilities for very varied deployment. Each refashioning develops a new intertextual response, creating new layers and reconfiguring for varying audiences a multivalent and surprisingly 'open' form.

Notes

1   Michael T. Clanchy, *From Memory to Written Record: England 1066–1272* (Glasgow: Fontana, 1983).

2   *The Lais of Marie de France*, (trans.) Glyn S. Burgess and Keith Busby (Harmondsworth: Penguin, 1986) provides a useful 'plain prose translation'. All quotations are taken from this edition.

3   *The Lais of Marie de France*, pp. 73–81.

4   Judith Weiss, 'The Wooing Woman in Anglo-Norman Romance', in Maldwyn Mills, Jennifer Fellowes and Carol M. Meale (eds), *Romance in Medieval England* (Cambridge: Brewer, 1991), p. 149; see also Judith Weiss, 'The Power and the Weakness of Women in Anglo-Norman Romance', in Carol M. Meale (ed.), *Women and Literature in Britain 1150–1500* (Cambridge: Cambridge University Press, 1993), pp. 7–23, (p. 15).

5   T. C. Rumble (ed.), *The Breton Lays in Middle English* (Detroit: Wayne State University, 1965).

6   A. J. Bliss (ed.), *Sir Launfal: Thomas Chestre*, 2nd edn (Oxford: Oxford University Press, 1966). This edition also contains *Sir Landevale*, pp. 105–28.

7   See the Introduction to *The Spirit of Medieval and Popular Romance*, eds Ad Putter and Jane Gilbert (Harlow: Longman, 2000).

8   'The Tale of Sir Thopas' in *The Riverside Chaucer*, ed. Larry D. Benson (Oxford: Oxford University Press, 1989), pp. 216, l. 930.

9   Maldwyn Mills (ed.), *Six Middle English Verse Romances* (London: Dent, 1973), pp. 46–74.

10   See Chaucer's 'Man of Law's Tale' and Gower's *Confessio Amantis*, II, ll. 587–1598 both develop the analogous story of 'Constance'.

11   For the range of symbolic meanings ascribed to rudderless boats, see V. A. Kolve, *Chaucer and the First Five Canterbury Tales* (London: Arnold, 1984), pp. 308, 319, 325.

12   Ad Putter, '*The Narrative Logic of* Emaré', in Ad Putter and Jane Gilbert (eds), *The Spirit of Medieval English Popular Romance* (Harlow: Longman, 2000), pp. 157–80 (pp. 174–7).

13   'The Franklin's Tale' in *Riverside Chaucer*, pp. 178–89.

14   See Laura Hibbard Loomis, 'The Auchinleck Manuscript and a possible London Bookshop of 1330–40', *Publications of the Modern Language Association* 57 (1942), pp. 595–626.

15   For discussion of Chaucer's relationship with the native traditions of romance, see Derek Pearsall, *The Canterbury Tales* (London: Routledge, 1993) and W. A. Davenport, *Chaucer and his English Contemporaries: Prologue and Tale in the Canterbury Tales* (New York: St Martin's, 1998).

16   Susan Crane, *Gender and Romance in Chaucer's Canterbury Tales* (Princeton, NJ: Princeton University Press, 1994), explores correlations between the Franklin's social status and Dorigen's gendered role in his tale, seeing both as overpowered by the genre's demands. By contrast, Jill Mann, 'The Surrender of Maistrye' in *Geoffrey Chaucer* (Brighton: Harvester, 1991) regards Arveragus's role as one of support for Dorigen rather than dominance, with each surrendering to the other in an image of successful mutuality. For a less magnanimous reading, see Elaine Tuttle-Hansen, *Chaucer and the Fictions of Gender* (Berkeley: University of California Press, 1992).

17   Tuttle-Hansen, *Chaucer and the Fictions of Gender*, p. 276.

18   'The Franklin's Tale' follows directly after 'The Squire's Tale', which is praised for its 'gentil' quality, and forms part of a thread appraising noble behaviour which runs throughout the *Canterbury Tales*; cf. 'The Wife of Bath's Tale', 'The Clerk's Tale', as well as one of Chaucer's short poems, *Gentillesse* (*Riverside Chaucer*, p. 654).

19   Anne Laskaya and Eve Salisbury (eds), *The Middle English Breton Lays*, Consortium for the Teaching of the Middle Ages (Kalamazoo, MI: Medieval Institute Publications, 1995). Quotations shall be from this edition. The shorter version of the poem can be found edited by Francis Berry in Boris Ford (ed.), *The Pelican Guide to English Literature: Volume One: The Age of Chaucer*, 9 vols (Harmondsworth: Penguin, 1954; rept 1980), pp. 269–86.

20   This prologue is found in one of the three manuscripts in which *Orfeo* is preserved, namely British Library Harley 3810. The earliest version in the Auchinleck manuscript (*c.* 1330–40) suffers from a lost leaf at this point. The Harley prologue is very close to that of Auchinleck's *Lay le Freyne* but it is impossible to determine which preceded which. All three versions are in A. J. Bliss's 2nd edn (Oxford: Oxford University Press, 1966). All quotations's are taken from Anne Laskaya and Eve Salisbury (eds), *The Middle English Breton Lays* (Kalamazoo, MI: Medieval Institute Publications, 1995).

21   V. E. Watts (trans.), *Boethius: The Consolation of Philosophy* (Harmondsworth: Penguin 1969), III.m.12.

22   For discussion of the common literary location of madness in female form, see Elaine Showalter, *The Female Malady: Women, Madness and English Culture 1830–1980* (New York: Pantheon, 1985); and for a psychoanalytical reading of *Orfeo*, see Derek Pearsall, 'Madness in *Sir Orfeo*', in Jennifer Fellows, Rosalind Field *et al.* (eds), *Romance Reading on the Book* (Cardiff: University of Wales Press, 1996), pp. 51–63.

Short and (Bitter) Sweet: Medieval Lyrics

The lyric is one of the most common and yet diverse forms in medieval literature, and had a lasting influence on many other genres. It is a feature of Chaucer's work that, at points of heightened emotion and dramatic tension, he inserts short lyrical pieces into his narrative poems. His dream-vision poem, *The Parliament of Fowls*, ends pointedly with a sung roundel, while the lovesick hero of *Troilus and Criseyde* is given plaintive songs to sing at key moments, expressing his anguish and pain.[1] One of these is a version of a Petrarchan sonnet adapted into rime royal.*[2] As he tries to express the intensity of his inner conflict, the lover wrestles with oxymoronic paradoxes:

> Allas, what is this wondre maladie?   [strange disease]
> For hote of cold, for cold of hote, I dye.[3]

Such self-conscious exploration of emotion draws upon a vibrant contemporary tradition. Chaucer himself wrote at least nineteen short poems which survive, along with many more attributed to him but of less certain authorship. These attest to Chaucer's fondness for lyric poetry, in particular, the 'courtly' forms, such as the French-derived *ballade* and complaint, as well as popular religious forms, such as hymns

---

* The rime royal stanza is a demanding form comprising seven lines, rhyming *ababbcc*, which is credited to Chaucer's invention.

to Mary and meditative reflections. Chaucer's contemporaries and imitators, such as Lydgate and Dunbar, followed his lead, developing the lyric genre. The fifteenth century saw the flowering of the form with increasingly elaborate conceits and florid language, culminating in the so-called 'aureate' or golden style. The works of these well-known poets, however, represents but a small sample of the surviving lyric corpus, the vast majority of which is anonymous.

This anonymity is one of the contributory causes which have tended to relegate lyric poetry from the late medieval period into something of a specialist sideline rather than a mainstream concern. Until fairly recently, the many hundreds of short poems which survive have languished in relative obscurity, even though they represent a substantial corpus which relates fundamentally to the major works of the period. Many of the effects regarded as most innovative are less strange when read in the context of lyric poetry. For example, William Langland's depiction of Jesus as a knight entering a tournament is justly celebrated as an imaginative treatment of the crucifixion:

> Barefoot on an asse bak bootles cam prikye,   [riding]
> Withouten spores other spere; spakliche he loked,   [lively]
> As is the kynde of a knight that commeth to be dubbed.
> ...
> This Jesus of his gentries wol juste in Piers armes   [joust]
> In his helm and in his haubergeon – *humana natura*.[4] [mailcoat]

The creative imagination at work here is not operating in a vacuum. As with so many key motifs, the image is also present in lyrics. One lyric addresses Christ as a knight-lover, 'My fender of my fose [enemies], sa fonden [proven] in the felde'; others presents Christ in the guise of knight-hero, 'take myn armes pryvely', 'Restles I ride ... Mi palefrey is of tre [wood].'[5] Familiarity with the lyric corpus helps with recognition of the conventional nature of such imagery and appreciation of the intertextuality so often at work.

Various factors have contributed to the relative neglect of the lyrics. The state of their preservation and practical difficulties in naming and grouping the lyrics are among the primary obstacles to their being more widely studied. The poems labelled 'lyrics' by modern scholars are found scattered among disparate manuscripts, often in single copies and frequently scribbled unceremoniously onto flyleaves and book bindings.* They usually lack titles and provenance, as well as an identifiable author. None of this permits ready access or coherent treatment. Nevertheless, the material is not entirely intractable. Several sizeable collections of lyrics survive, copied into commonplace books along with all sorts of other literary and extra-literary material. These are traditionally referred to collectively by the name of the manuscript in which they survive (e.g. the Harley lyrics, the Findern lyrics and so on)[6] and individually, as is the case with untitled poetry in general, by their first lines or dominant phrases (e.g. *Maiden in the mor lay, Sumer is icomen in*).

The lyrics suffer on the one hand from their disparate and dispersed condition and, on the other, from their enormous quantity. The sheer number surviving presents editors with difficulties when it comes to the selection and organisation of lyrics into anthologies. In 1939, Carleton Brown published 192 religious lyrics, which represented a tenth of the number available to him by his own estimation. A comparable edition of non-religious lyrics by R. H. R. Robbins in 1952 contains 210 items chosen from around three hundred extant.[7] Grappling with such numbers is challenging for critics and students alike. There is also the question of variable quality to be taken into account. It has to be admitted that not all lyrics are equally accomplished or noteworthy, so criteria of aesthetic judgement also create hurdles for the poems to surmount in order to become more accessible. Despite all these handicaps, medieval lyrics have experienced renewed interest in recent years, so that their range and significance can be more readily appreciated.[8]

---

* There are twenty-four copies surviving of a prayer to Jesus written by Richard Caister, a vicar of Norwich who died in 1420, but this is a rare case of multiple copies of a lyric surviving.

Musicality

The term 'lyric' derives from the same Greek word which gives us 'lyre'. It is not a term used by medieval writers, who described their works variously as songs, ditties, lays and so on. The association of the word 'lyric' with short compositions set to music began in the Renaissance and continues today with pop songs and musical theatre. There is reason to suppose that the medieval texts commonly grouped under this umbrella term, diverse as they are, originated as pieces to be sung, intoned or rhythmically read to musical accompaniment. This essential musical element is obvious where the texts have survived along with their musical notation, as is the case with some two hundred pieces. Where the music has not been preserved however, the lyrics frequently show clear signs of their musical orientation. Many have a distinct chorus or refrain, while most employ a clear rhythm and group lines into regular units, or verses. It helps to retain this aspect of musical design when reading medieval lyrics, as much of the intended effect depends on vocal performance – the auditory experience of tone and rhythm. Medieval lyrics, even more than poetry *per se*, need to be read aloud with sensitivity to the sound and rhythm of the language in order to do justice to their design.

One subset of medieval lyrics expressly designed to be accompanied by music is the *carole*. The form seems to have originated as a round dance with the burden* sung by circling dancers while the verses were sung by a soloist. As an expression of popular culture, early versions of such songs were rarely written down. One rare exception seems to be *Maiden in the mor lay*, referred to above, which is specifically mentioned in a fourteenth-century sermon as 'A certain song, namely a karole'. Over four hundred medieval *caroles* survive, mainly from the fifteenth century, by which time it has developed into a distinctly literary form. These tend to conform rigidly to a set structure, typically rhyming *aaab* with a *bb* burden. About a quarter of the *caroles* which

* The burden is a repeated element which occurs not just at regular intervals throughout the song, as a refrain, but also at the beginning of the song.

survive have their original music preserved, primarily of a sophisticated, polyphonic type.

Origins and Development of Vernacular Lyrics

This brings us to the vexed question of how far medieval English lyrics owe their origin to traditional popular festivities, and how far they are a purely literary phenomenon. From the twelfth century onwards, continental Europe enjoyed a lively culture of wandering minstrelsy. The influence of the troubadours and trouvères* is a matter of debate, complicated by the historical accidents of the Norman Conquest and resultant Anglo-Norman culture. Since so few examples of English lyric poetry survive before the fourteenth century, scholars can only speculate about origins. Many critics support a theory by which English lyrics began as imitations and translations of Latin models, while others argue for a more popular native tradition. It is true that many lyrics have Latin originals. One medieval Latin song tune has even survived down to the present day, albeit with completely different words, as *Good King Wenceslas*. The role played by the Latin liturgy† in inspiring and informing English lyrics is the subject of another critical debate. Quotations from the liturgy are regularly employed, such as the refrain *Timor mortis conturbat me* [fear of death disturbs me], taken from the Office for the Dead,¶ which occurs in several different poems. The inclusion of such material need not necessarily imply derivation from the liturgy, so much as casual incorporation of its familiar material.

Vernacular poetry – poetry written not in Latin but in the emerging national languages of Europe – is frequently disapproved of in sermons from the Anglo-Saxon period onwards, yet the evidence suggests that such denunciations had little effect. The disproportionate number of religious to secular lyrics which survive surely attests to some

---

* Troubadours and trouvères are poet-composers, often itinerant, writing in Southern and Northern France respectively.
† The liturgy is a prescribed form of public worship consisting of set readings and songs.
¶ The Office for the Dead is the divine service accompanying a funeral.

ecclesiastical control, unsurprising in an age where literacy was the preserve of a clerical elite. Since most manuscripts were copied by monks, the secular material would have had less chance of being preserved. Yet, despite deep-rooted ecclesiastical disapproval of vernacular poetry, several new religious movements of the late medieval period gave a keen impetus to its creation and distribution. The new form of Affective Piety* inspired by Bernard of Clairvaux and his followers in the twelfth century contributed to a climate favourable to vernacular lyrics (see 'Acting Up: Medieval Drama'). In particular, two orders of mendicant (begging) friars founded in the twelfth century, namely the Franciscans and the Dominicans, were particularly influential since they travelled widely preaching to the laity. Friars' sermons developed narrative techniques of using *exempla* and embedded lyrics as effective ways of engaging the imagination of the faithful and disposing them to repentance and contrition. Three important collections of medieval English lyrics come directly from such sources. William Herebert (d. 1333), an Oxford scholar, copied out a collection of twenty-three English poems, including some possibly of his own composition. In 1372, the Franciscan friar John of Grimestone gathered together a compendium of appropriate lyrical material for use in sermons, organised into alphabetical sequence according to topics. As well as many Latin poems, his collection contains 239 English poems. Another valuable anthology from the late fifteenth century, comprising 163 lyrics, mainly *caroles*, is attributed to a Canterbury friar named James Ryman. Such deployment of English lyrics both exploited and encouraged the popularity of the genre. By gathering and disseminating English lyrics, Franciscan friars were adhering to the edict of the founder of their order, St Francis, who declared that his followers should be God's minstrels, *joculatores dei*.

The very existence of such an extensive body of poetry in English at this time is a remarkable fact. During the thirteenth and fourteenth centuries when these lyrics began to be composed, English was one among several languages in use and was considered an inferior medium

---

* Affective Piety is a form of late medieval religious devotion that focuses on an intense emotional response, particularly to the suffering of Jesus.

for literary expression. French and Latin were generally preferred, being of an appropriately dignified and elevated status. The early fourteenth-century Harley Manuscript is entirely representative in containing a mixture of Latin, French and English texts. By the end of the fourteenth century, Chaucer's friend and fellow poet John Gower was still producing major works in all three languages. The multi-lingual culture of the period is testified to by a group of lyrics known as 'macaronic' (mixing several languages). These demonstrate linguistic versatility, shifting easily between the three languages then in use:

> A celuy que pluys eyme en mounde
> Of alle tho that I have founde
> Carissima.

> [To the one whom I love most in the world, of all those that I have met, the dearest.]

Only towards the end of the fourteenth century does English begin to displace Latin and French, a change often attributed to the influence of Chaucer and some of his contemporaries whose works helped establish English as a literary medium.

Towards Defining the Genre

With few named authors, little precise chronology and rare provenance, the body of medieval lyrics resists easy classification. Given the variety of material surviving, it is not surprising that generic traits are difficult to define. Among the most basic features shared by the many hundreds of surviving poems grouped beneath the umbrella term 'lyric' are: brevity, plain diction (at least in the earlier period) and uniform stanzas. These could be regarded as essential, defining characteristics were it not the case that each of these features is subject to considerable qualification and exception. Lyrics range in length from two lines to several hundred lines; the later period is marked by the more elevated

Latinate diction of the aureate style; and individual poems experiment and play with form.

Very few elements are consistent enough to form anything approaching a norm. Alliteration is a common stylistic feature, whereas unrhymed lines are very rare indeed, usually indicating a corrupted text. One can detect developments over time. For instance, there is a shift from the earlier lyrics which tend to focus primarily on the human qualities of Jesus and Mary to later poems' depiction of both in a more majestic guise as king and queen of heaven. Similarly, there is an early emphasis on visual elements, with frequent invitations, both explicit and implicit, to 'look', 'see' and 'behold'; this changes later to a preference for more abstract and elaborate conceits, with a greater appeal to the intellect than to the visual imagination. But, generally, variety is the norm. Simple rhyming couplets at one end of the spectrum are offset at the other by elaborate rime royal stanzas; plain, colloquial diction can be set against some extremely ornate, verbose pieces. Stephen Hawes's *A Pair of Wings* is a late fifteenth-century example of particularly complex pictorial design – the words on the page set out to form the very image it describes.[9]

Despite the conspicuous variety of form and style, several key qualities can be asserted as characteristic at certain times. Douglas Gray offers a succinct assessment of early religious lyrics, 'Simplicity and unaffectedness are the characteristic features of the style'.[10] Rosemary Woolf supports this view in her praise of the lyrics' 'direct and dignified intimacy'.[11] It is true that medieval lyrics generally employ a simple vocabulary, with plain diction and syntax. The homely language is part of the appeal and accessibility. A fine example of how extreme simplicity can coexist with wit and imagination is *Adam lay i-bounden*.[12]

Adam lay i-bounden

The poem opens with a grim statement of extreme punishment (four thousand years being a traditional time period for Adam's imprisonment in Hell):

Adam lay ibowndyn, boundyn in a bond,
Fowre thowsand wynter thowt he not to long. (ll. 1–2)

This immediately sets up some challenging ideas by its straightforward attitude to grievous torment. The light tone continues with the mischievously minimising attitude, 'al was for an appil' (l. 3). This *reductio ad adsurdum** construes the central event of Creation history, the Fall of man, as a minor matter of stealing an apple. The speaker seems to distance himself from the weighty doctrinal concerns by referring to 'clerks' and their books rather disparagingly. Yet the unfolding logic reveals a complex design. Behind the compelling contrasts lies a theological paradox, the doctrine of the Fortunate Fall (*felix culpa*),† which derives from the *Exultet* (Lat. 'rejoice') hymn sung as part of the Easter Saturday liturgy. Within just eight lines, the divine plan is rapidly unfolded as the narrator guides the reader from long ago ('Adam') to the contemporary 'clerks' through to an inclusive 'we'. The poem exploits the challenge to human logic by which original sin is revealed as an occasion for joy. The movement from sin to redemption hinges upon a mid-way transition effected by strong repetition, with balanced phrases reassuring the reader of overarching pattern and symmetry:

Ne hadde the appil take ben, the appil taken ben,
Ne hadde never our Lady a ben hevene qwen. (ll. 5–6)

The poem is at once complex and homely, presenting the ineffable in ordinary terms so that the oddness is perceived as right by the final shared song of celebration.

---

* *Reductio ad adsurdum* (Lat. 'reduction to the absurd') is a form of logical disputation, arguing for extreme propositions, supported by irrefutable logic, however contradictory or paradoxical the conclusions.
† The notion of the Fortunate Fall celebrates original sin as the cause of Jesus's incarnation, with Eve (Eva) replaced by Mary (Ave), neatly fulfilling the divine plan for the redemption of mankind through Christ's sacrifice.

Classification of Lyric Types

Several attempts have been made to group the lyrics according to their stylistic aspects. Professor George Kane distinguished four types: *Plain*, with simple syntax and no special poetic diction; *Early Decorated*, with poetic diction and tending to be elaborate or artificial; *Polished*, enriched with romance vocabulary and increasingly sophisticated; and *Aureate*, very ornate, with excessive rhetorical colouring.[13] An alternative system of organising the lyrics groups them according to their dominant modes: *lyrical*, where feeling, emotion or reflection is usually mediated through an 'I' persona; *narrative*, which focuses on action, with a narrator or persona mediating; and *dramatic*, where the action is unmediated.

The Dramatic Mode

The link with drama is particularly notable, as many of the most accomplished lyrics develop features from the thriving vernacular drama. Two examples will serve to illustrate the imaginative deployment of dramatic elements. The lyric *Suddenly Afraid* opens with a burden which economically sets the scene:

> Sodeynly afraide,
> Half waking, half slepyng,
> And gretly dismayed –
> A woman sat wepyng.[14]

The abrupt, mysterious opening is almost worthy of the later master of metaphysical wit, John Donne. There is a disarming immediate directness as the speaker delivers a first-hand account of his experiences. The poem unfolds as personal recollection, re-enacting an encounter in which extensive reported speech contributes to a vivid intimacy. The narrator's confused state of awareness colours the poem, as he remains strangely unable to identify the woman even after her son is named in line 7, '"Jesu!" so she sobbid.' The reader is necessarily superior to the mediating narrator in understanding and feeling. This type of dramatic irony is typical of the dream-vision genre (see 'Dream and Vision: A Space Odyssey') as a means by which to engage the reader's response. The narrator's progress from hard-heartedness (l. 12) to tears (l. 18), coupled with the insistent end-of-stanza injunction, 'Who cannot wepe, com lerne at me', work to implicate the reader as active participant. The appeal is immediate and emotional, particularly as Mary describes her son's torment, 'So betyn, so wowndid, entreted so Jewly' (l. 22). Much of the poem consists of speech, contributing to the effect of personal presence and engagement in the scene. As an invitation to devotion, the lyric prompts a personal involvement by focusing on the human aspects of the crucifixion, thus involving aspects of human experience with which the audience can readily identify: a mother's grief, a son, death. The poem skilfully combines elements from several different traditions. It is primarily a *planctus* – a lament designed to evoke pity and devotion – but it is framed by motifs and situations deriving from secular poetry, opening as a *chanson d'aventure* (a chance encounter with a lady) and closing as a lay (evoking a supernatural realm of vanishing fairies). Above all, its semi-dramatic style contributes to the mood of felt awe and pain which creates an effectively fresh treatment of the subject matter.

This element is even more pronounced in *Farewell This World*, which begins with a powerful declaration:[15]

> Farewell this world! I take my leve for ever,
> I am arrested to apere afore Goddes face.

This shows a familiar mix of the simple and the complex. The speaker's tone is strikingly matter of fact even though the predicament is again surprising and abruptly declared. What is noticeable here is the casting of the poem as a monologue – in effect a soliloquy addressed to the reader. The personal situation is starkly related to the general human condition:

My hert, alas, is broken for that sorow;
Som be this day that shall not be tomorrow! (ll. 5–6)

The speaker's personality is lightly sketched in as the poem progresses. He reflects upon his life with a penchant for proverbial wisdom ('Experience teacheth me', l. 26), a certain wry humour ('Speke soft, ye folks, for I am laid aslepe', l. 15) and a playfully cryptic final enjoinder ('I say no more, but beware of an horne!', l. 21). Essentially it is a poem on the theme of mortality, a subject of pressing contemporary concern as evidenced by the vast numbers of literary and pictorial representations of death and dying. The standard fare of *memento mori** is given a peculiarly vivid twist, primarily through the use of personification allegory.[16] This begins with the depiction of Death arresting the speaker, a traditional image used by Hamlet, 'This fell sergeant Death / Is strict in his arrest' (V.ii.328–9). Another imaginative touch is presenting Death as winning a game of chess:

'Till sotil deth knocked at my gate   [subtle]
And unavised he said to me "Checkmate!"'   [without warning]
(ll. 11–12)

Much of the poem comprises gnomic utterance, along with conventional denunciation of the world as 'feckil ... false and ... unstable' (l. 21). So conventional is the final stanza that it occurs separately in other manuscripts and, as remarked upon by Wordsworth, was used as an epitaph on many fifteenth-century graves:

Farewell, my frendes! The tide abideth no man:
I moste departe hens, and so shall ye. (ll. 29–30)

But there are also novel aspects, such as the gothic touches of grim humour, as the speaker addresses us from the grave. References to

---

* *Memento mori* (lit. 'Remember that you have to die') denotes a prevalent attitude of the medieval period focused on awareness of mortality as a prompt to maintaining spiritual purity.

worms feeding on a corpse (l. 14) are commonplace, but rarely is a first-hand account given. This essential feature of treating ideas about mortality through the voice of an individual is what marks the poem as an inventive piece, heavily influenced by the drama.

Conventions of Religious Lyrics

As these examples show, the distinction between religious and secular lyrics is often far from absolute. Both of these religious lyrics incorporate elements of secular material to produce lively results. One of the primary phenomena associated with the lyrics is this exploitation of convention. The existence of recurrent topics, themes and styles allows for the classification of lyrics according to various types and sub-types. Religious poetry in particular operates from a common base in scripture and theology, so it is not surprising that imagery and ideas recur widely. Repetition, similarity, derivativeness: these are not attributes held in high regard today. In the medieval period, however, such qualities were the norm and creativity lay in the deployment of existing material rather than in invention or originality in the modern sense. One may compare Shakespeare's reliance on pre-existing stories. It is true that the lyrics share many features, particularly of style and diction, but this is not to be seen automatically as a defect. Rather, it needs to be borne in mind that the prevailing expectation of poetry was of a shared, communal experience – literature as a social event. Our post-Romantic notions of poetry as a private experience are anachronistic when applied to medieval lyrics.

There are a large number of sub-types which can be distinguished. Among religious lyrics the main categories are: hymns and prayers; narratives of biblical events; and meditational poems. Marian poetry (focused on the Virgin Mary) constitutes a sizeable proportion of surviving lyrics, with a range of sub-types covering her experiences of birth (lullabies and nativity poems), bereavement (the five sorrows of the Virgin), ascension to heaven and intercessory function on behalf of humanity. An extensive system of correspondences and typological resonance developed in lyrics expressing devotion to Mary. Chaucer's *ABC* is a prime example of the plethora of epithets which became the stock material of hymns of praise to the Virgin. Time and again poets speak of Mary as queen of heaven, rose without thorns, star of the sea, lily among thorns and so on. So highly formulated is the range of imagery that Davies, in his collection of lyrics, can include an appendix listing dozens of terms for the Virgin Mary alongside their relevant biblical and patristic sources. As the cult of Marian devotion grew, poets drew on courtly love to further extend the vocabulary of devotion. A particularly rich source for the vocabulary and imagery of love was the biblical *Song of Songs* with its sensuous depiction of passion. The lyric *In a tabernacle of a toure*, also called 'Song of Love' (*Canticus amoris*), demonstrates an imaginative blending of motifs.[17] Mary appears as 'crouned quene', lamenting the sinful state of mankind and longing to provide help:

> I byd, I byde in grete longyng,   [pray]
> I love, I loke when man woll crave,
> I pleyne for pyte of peynyng ...
> *Quia amore langueo.** (ll. 16–18, 24)

Among the most popular types of lyric associated with Jesus are poems contemplating the crucifixion, salvation and the last judgement. Primary sub-types include representations of Christ as suffering physical agony (Reproaches from the Cross), Christ as complaining lover or as heroic knight. Another large group of lyrics are penitential in design, urging contrition and reflecting upon mortality. Poems on the subject of life as a swift passing from dust to dust are particularly plentiful; one such lyric exists in forty-one different versions.[18]

These lyrics are poems to be used. Their practical purpose is often apparent, as they seek to elicit empathy, repentance or reform. Many function as aids to prayer and devotion. Repeated reading aloud of religious lyrics was even recommended as a way to access remission of

---

* 'I am suffering because of love'.

sin in one manuscript which specifies the benefits, 'Hosumever saith this praier in the worship of the passion shal have .c. [100] yere of pardon' and 'Whosumever saith this devotedly hathe granted be divers bisshopis saing at the last ende five pater nosters and five Aves .cccccc. [600] dayes of pardon.' This frankly calculating mentality is a feature of the proto-capitalistic culture of the late medieval period, yet strikes an oddly jarring note in the context of religious devotion.

Conventions of Secular Lyrics

Courtly love is the prime source of imagery and theme for secular lyrics. Popular forms derived from French sources include the *chanson d'aventure*, where a knight in low spirits encounters a woman, frequently in a spring setting, and the *pastourelle*, a related form where the couple engage in amorous conversation and the lady yields her favours – often quite suddenly – in the fourth stanza. This abrupt conclusion seems to have originated in a type of French and Provencal love poetry, known as the *envoi*, which usually employs apostrophe, encouraging a personal application (e.g., 'Take heed of me'). The *ballade* comprises three stanzas (with an optional fourth) and is marked by the use of concatenation – the last line of each stanza being repeated at the beginning of the next stanza. The *reverdie*, or spring song, originated as a dance in celebration of the new year. During the medieval period, April was the first month of the year, corresponding to the first month of Mary's pregnancy. The date of the Annunciation was calculated to be 25 March and was also regarded as New Year's Day.

Most secular love lyrics concern themselves with the refined form of courtly love, predicated upon devoted service to the beloved. This presents the experience of love as primarily painful but also ennobling and involves a whole set of conventions. The perspective is usually that of a male lover. Since most lyrics are anonymous, it is customary to presume male authorship. It is rare for such poems to be attributable to women but, in the case of over a dozen lyrics in the Findern manuscript, female authorship is reliably attested. *My Woeful Heart*[19] is one such poem, presenting what Sarah McNamer describes as 'authentic female experience'.[20] The speaker here sets out her pain in a progressive sequence, describing her long separation from her beloved and the loss of comfort she suffers:

> For lakke of syght nere am I sleyn,
> All joy myne hert hath in dissedeyn:
> Comfort fro me is go. (ll. 4–6)

The short lines condense emotion and lack a regular refrain, but are bound together by insistently chiming rhymes: so, go, do, wo, moo, to, so. Indeed, the poem is a formal tour de force, restricting its rhymes to just two sounds throughout. The result is an impression of emotional containment, beautifully balanced by the intensity of the feeling expressed. Liberally employed intensifiers add to the impression of pain, framed in poignant yet simple language:

> None butt he may me susteyn,
> He is my comfort in all payn,
> I love hym and no moo. (ll. 13–15)

The poem moves from anguish to resolve as if the speaker finds release from tension in the act of voicing her emotional distress. The language shifts from an insistent focus on grief (so, all, nothing, none but he) to confident assertions of enduring love (he is my comfort, I will be true, ever, certain, till death). The poem ends with a final flourish as the speaker commits herself wholeheartedly to loving:

> My hert shall I never fro hym refrayn,
> I gave hitt hym withowte constrayn,
> Ever to contenue so. (ll. 19–21)

Many secular lyrics are light hearted and playful. An altogether different female experience is attested in *Kyrie, so Kyrie*.[21] This opens with reminiscence, recalling a festive occasion:

As I went on Yol day in owre prosessyon
Knew I joly Jankyn be his mery ton: [tone]
Kyrieleyson.* (ll. 4–6)

The poem's main strategy is one of artful juxtaposition, as here, of the church service alongside flirtation. The religious setting provides an incongruous backdrop for some very impious activities. The story unfolds cryptically with past and present interspersed and snatches of Latin chant from the Christmas Day mass alternating with the speaker's memories. Jankyn's name dominates each stanza as the service proceeds and the flirtation intensifies. As the speaker reflects on the choirist Jankin's seductive singing, her artlessness creates a comic impression of her naivety, relying heavily on bathos; for instance, when she parenthetically recalls paying for his clothes (l. 14). Behind the extremely simple statements lie *double entendres* and underlying sexual excitement: 'Knew I joly Jankyn' (l. 5), 'it dos me good' (ll. 8, 11, 14). Other suggestive elements are the increased pace and delivery of Jankin's singing, the casual wink and touch as he passes:

Jankyn at the *Agnus* beryt the pax-brede;†
He twynkelid but sayd nowt and on myn fot he trede. (ll. 19–20)

The playful mood is suddenly undercut as the poem concludes with the revelation of the speaker's pregnancy and her plaintive prayer to Christ to shield her from shame, 'alas, I go with chylde!' (l. 24). But as the threads of the narrative coincide at the high point of the Mass, the final impression is comic as the mock-conception contrasts so strongly with the birth being commemorated in the service. This short lyric with its peculiar combination of charming simplicity and complex narrative procedures is an example of the lyric at its best.

---

* Kyrie eleison (Gk. 'Lord have mercy') is the opening of the Mass.
† Agnus (Dei) is the Lamb of God; pax-brede is a silver or gilt disc circulated for the faithful to kiss, emulating the riest's kiss of peace.

Extended Commentary: 'When the nyhtegale singes the wodes waxen grene'

At first glance 'When the nyhtegale singes the wodes waxen grene'[22] appears to be a typical love lyric with a male lover addressing his beloved and declaring his love for her. It is fairly simple in form, comprising five verses of four long lines each, rhyming *aaaa*. The regularity is disrupted only once, in the final line, where 'ylong' deviates from the established rhyme scheme. It is not a major discrepancy as the rhyme sound '-ounde' is quite close phonetically to '-ong'. Yet it marks a fitting final moment of a slightly unexpected kind. Overall, the poem is tightly woven, highly regular and constrained by its rhyme scheme. There is occasional use of internal rhyme for variety: lines 1 and 2 share a mid-line rhyme, 'springes'/'singes'; lines 5 and 7 have 'yer' and 'ner' mid-line; the final line has internal rhyme between 'song' and 'ylong'. This feature has led some editors to present the lyric as eight-line stanzas, but the rhyme-scheme is then seriously altered so as to appear highly irregular. Taking the long-line form as closer to the original, the poem displays constraint in its deliberate limitation as well as flexibility.

The lyric casts itself as a conventional appeal to a lady from a suffering lover, finally identifying itself explicitly as a lament, 'Y wole mone my song' (l. 20). Up until the relatively 'low' register endearment, 'lemmon' (l. 6), there is nothing which would not sit easily in a religious love lyric addressed to the Virgin Mary. Several aspects of the poem are reminiscent of lyrics addressed to Mary, such as the pose of respectful devotion, the request for 'ore' (grace, mercy) and the insinuated suggestiveness of the repeated word 'preye' (ll. 9, 13, 19). From line 6 onward, however, the secular nature of the lyric is clear. It is employing certain lexical items from the Marian repertoire, in a fashion typical of the period, as the discourse of Marian worship was opening up a new space and lexis for secular love poetry.

The poem deploys many conventional elements which establish the tone as 'romantic', raising the reader's expectation of standard fare. Most immediately, there is the springtime opening and the image of the nightingale, evoking associations of love. The second line, 'Lef and gras and blosme springes in Aueryl, y wene', could hardly pack in more seasonal conventions, yet the uncertainty implied by 'y wene' [I believe] may strike an odd note. There is already a tension between the confidently replicated details of standard springtime love and the first-person narrator's artless self-presentation as a less than typical lover. The tag, 'y wene', is awkward and strangely empty of meaning. It may be mechanically employed in order to fit the rhyme-scheme, but the hollow phrase could also be read in several ways as subtly reflective of the speaker: as a hint of his idiocy, naivety, sense of humour or even cynicism. The narrative persona of this poem in fact becomes harder and harder to respond to in a straightforward way.

Repetition is always a stylistic feature worth exploring, and here the terms emphasised in this way are revealing. 'Suete lemmon' [sweet beloved] chimes through the lyric in every stanza after the first, sometimes more than once. The recurrence of this phrase suggests the lover's intense fixation, but might also begin to grate and convey an excessive dependence on cliché. The word 'loue' is similarly ubiquitous and to similarly dual effect: it demonstrates a limited vocabulary, but may be none the less sincere.

It is possible to read the poem in two quite different ways. As it employs so many typical devices, there is plenty to fulfil traditional functions. The images of being wounded by love (l. 3) and of losing one's lifeblood in suffering (l. 4) are typical of love lyrics. The direct address to the beloved ('thin ore', 'the') which follows on from the opening scene-setting is a typical expression of amorous devotion. A modest request for even the slightest favour begins the central stanza, with protestations of the lover's dedication set alongside traditional imagery of the beloved as healer and bringer of joy ('blis', 'leche'). The lover's assertion of lifelong devotion seems impressive, 'Whil I live in world so wyde other nulle y seche' [will I not seek] (l. 10). The poem closes with praise of the unparalleled beloved, 'Ne wot y non so fayr' [I know no one so beautiful], with a final request for her to grant her love. This all attests to a conventional love poem, enlisting courtly love motifs, hyperbole and superlatives in order to express intense emotion.

However, a more cynical appraisal of the same material finds plenty to undercut the impression of sincerity. The love wound here is extraordinarily described: in place of the usual Cupidian arrow, this lover has been wounded by a spear, an altogether more substantial and alarming weapon. He uses a particularly intense verb which heightens the impression of overly determined pain, 'nyht ant day me blod hit drynkes' (l. 4). As the lover elaborates upon his devotion, many ambiguities emerge. His claim for longstanding ardour is less impressive on closer enquiry: is a year really too long? Can he really not go on? He is a rather feeble kind of lover then, in a tradition which embraces lifelong devotion to an ideal. This love certainly has no valid claim to have lasted 'yore' [long]. Extreme commitment it is not! The precise terms in which the lover formulates his appeals suggest unseemly haste: the limit of his desire moves quickly from the modest 'one speche' to a more physical desire, 'a suete cos of thy mouth'. When the lover proceeds to bring in a public perspective (l. 14), the mood of intimacy is shattered. Either this lover is singularly inept at expressing himself within the conventions or he is merely role-playing. The extreme diffidence of his thrice-evinced reserve ('Yef ... as y wene ... yef') can be construed as shyness or duplicity. In sharp contrast, a sudden tone of peremptory demand cuts through what is increasingly felt as a pretence, 'thou loke that hit be sene' (l. 15). It sounds suspiciously as if his patience is wearing thin.

Next the would-be suitor tries to align himself with the natural forces observed at the beginning of the poem, claiming to be 'turning green'. This is the traditional unhealthy pallor of the lovesick, but the small but highly significant modifier, 'al', plays a key part in exposing the image as a sham, another excessive claim. It could even be a crude joke ('every little bit of me is turning green'). At the very least, the intensifying adverb is somewhat self-pitying and over-precise.

The end of the poem is crucial in determining which of the alternative readings best suits the whole. The geographical sweep of line 17 sounds like an impressive asseveration until one realises that the range is actually quite small: 'from Lincoln to Lindsey' is hardly expansive, covering a modest region of the Midlands. As praise it is far from extravagant. The final request is equally underwhelming, if not jocular in intent, as he asks her to love him 'a stounde' [for a little while]. This can be interpreted as extreme humility, despair, or a frank avowal of all he really wants – a brief affair.

One way of responding to such poems – where the courtly love motifs are so abundant and yet handled in such a problematic way – is to see the whole thing as a pose, a game. This poem provides an intriguing sample of how skilfully poised a piece may be, between sincere and satirical. The deceptive simplicity of form and diction, the restricted codes and modes, allow for complex effects of multiplicity. Full 'explication' remains elusive.

As the variant readings for this lyric suggest, the finest lyrics provide richly nuanced material. The homogeneous nature of medieval lyrics can be exaggerated. In practice, much of the material is inventive and exploratory, as we have seen, even as it employs conventions. The best lyrics can be lively, personal, cryptic and ingenious as the poets delight in multiplicity of meaning, daring juxtaposition and creative combinations.

Notes

1   *The Parliament of Fowls*, in *The Riverside Chaucer*, ed. Larry D. Benson (Oxford: Oxford University Press, 1989), pp. 680–92.

2   *Troilus and Criseyde*, in *Riverside Chaucer*, I, pp. 478–9, ll. 400 ff., 'If no love is, O God, what fele I so?'.

3   *Troilus and Criseyde* in *Riverside Chaucer*, I, p. 479, ll. 419–20.

4   *The Vision of Piers Plowman: A Complete Edition of the B-Text*, ed. A. V. C. Schmidt (London: Everyman, 1984), passus 18, 11–13, 22–3.

5   Douglas Gray (ed.), *A Selection of Religious Lyrics*, Clarendon Medieval and Tudor Series (Oxford: Clarendon, 1975), Text 19, 21; Text 45, 7; Text 28, 11, 13.

6   'Harley' refers to British Library Manuscript Harley 2253, probably written in the West Midlands in the first quarter of the fourteenth century. The lyrics are contained in G. L. Brook (ed.), *The Harley Lyrics: The Medieval English Lyrics of MS. Harley 2253* (Manchester: Manchester University Press, 1948, repr. 1978). The 'Findern' manuscript, Cambridge University Library Manuscript, is a late fifteenth-century household book from South Derbyshire available in a facsimile edition by R. Beadle and A. E. B. Owen

(London: 1977). *Maiden in the mor lay* and *Sumer is icomen in* are two of the earliest extant lyrics in English.

7 Carleton Brown (ed.), *Religious Lyrics of the Fifteenth Century* (Oxford: Clarendon, 1939); R. H. R. Robbins (ed.), *Secular Lyrics of the Fourteenth and Fifteenth Centuries* (Oxford: Clarendon, 1952).

8 A representative sample of 187 lyrics from the thirteenth through to the sixteenth centuries can be found in R. T. Davies (ed.), *Medieval English Lyrics: A Critical Anthology* (London: Faber, 1963; repr. 1990). Forty-three lyrics from the late medieval period are included along with many from the early Renaissance in Derek Pearsall (ed.), *Chaucer to Spenser: An Anthology* (Oxford: Blackwell, 1999).

9 Davies (ed.), *Medieval English Lyrics*, item 152.

10 Douglas Gray (ed.), *A Selection of Religious Lyrics* (London: Oxford University Press, 1975), p. ix.

11 Rosemary Woolf, *The English Religious Lyric in the Middle Ages* (Oxford: Clarendon, 1968), p. 127.

12 Derek Pearsall (ed.), *Chaucer to Spenser: An Anthology* (Oxford: Blackwell, 1999), p. 387. Most of the poems discussed in some detail in this chapter can be found in this anthology of medieval literature.

13 Derek Pearsall memorably describes this as involving 'florid Latinate diction, with the Latin barely digested into English' (*John Lydgate*, London: Routledge and Kegan Paul, 1970, p. 262). A brief example from William Dunbar's *Hymn to Mary* will suffice to demonstrate the dense, polysyllabic flavour of the style: 'Hodiern, modern, sempitern/Angellical regine' (ll. 4–5); see Davies (ed.), *Medieval English Lyrics*, item 1.

14 Pearsall (ed.), *Chaucer to Spenser*, pp. 391–2.

15 Pearsall (ed.), *Chaucer to Spenser*, pp. 394–5.

16 Parallels are found throughout medieval drama, particularly in Morality Plays, e.g. the treatment of the World, the Flesh and the Devil in *The Castle of Perseverance* and the figure of Death in *Everyman*.

17 Pearsall (ed.), *Chaucer to Spenser*, pp. 391–3.

18 Item 87 in Davies (ed.), *Medieval English Lyrics*, 'Erthe oute of erthe', is one version of a lyric which graced many tombstones up until the eighteenth century.

19 Pearsall (ed.), *Chaucer to Spenser*, pp. 403–4.

20 Sarah McNamer, 'Female Authors, Provincial Settings: The Re-versing of Courtly Love in the Findern Manuscript', *Viator* 22 (1991), pp. 279–310 (p. 296).

21 Pearsall (ed.), *Chaucer to Spenser*, pp. 395–6.

22 Theodore Silverstein (ed.), *Medieval English Lyrics* (London: Arnold, 1971). All quotations shall be from this edition.

The Many Faces of Arthurian Romance

Arthurian romance is a sub-genre of romance similar in some respects to the Breton lay. Like the lay, it essentially occupies a courtly milieu and explores fantasy, magic and the supernatural. Unlike the lay, which is fairly easy to define according to formal characteristics and subject matter, Arthurian romance is a very elastic category. Whereas lays are typified by economy and simplicity, Arthurian romances are among the longest medieval works. They track the careers of Arthur and his knights, frequently structured around quests which explore chivalric ideals. No other concept held as much fascination for the period, as attested by the widespread and long-lasting literary phenomenon of Arthurian romance. From the twelfth century onwards, stories of Arthur's exemplary court accumulated to form what Jean Bodel (d. 1202) designated the 'Matter of Britain', alongside the 'Matter of France' (stories of Charlemagne) and the 'Matter of Rome' (stories of Classical heroes such as Alexander the Great). Centuries later in 1805, the miscellaneous romances not falling into these neat categories were labelled by the critic George Ellis as the 'Matter of England'. Arthurian romance was by far the most popular of all, accounting for more than a quarter of all surviving Middle English romances.

King Arthur and the Knights of the Round Table

Mention of King Arthur immediately conjures up images of knights and ladies, feasts and tournaments. The Arthurian story still holds widespread currency today thanks to innumerable treatments in many different media, from art to film, so that the names resonate with mystical and chivalric glamour: Uther Pendragon, Merlin, the Lady of the Lake, Excalibur, the Round Table, Camelot, Lancelot, Galahad, the Holy Grail and Avalon. Yet before the twelfth century they were virtually unknown. Arthur is a medieval creation. The familiar stories and figures which have cultural currency today rest on foundations from a specific moment in history when fact and fiction merged to produce a powerful legend.

The single most influential telling of Arthur's story in English was Sir Thomas Malory's *Morte Darthur*. Most subsequent versions, from Tennyson's sentimental *The Lady of Shalott* and *The Idylls of the King* (1859–1885), through the satire of Mark Twain's *A Connecticut Yankee at the Court of King Arthur* (1889) to the pastiche of *Monty Python and the Holy Grail* (1975) and its recent stage spin-off, *Spamalot*, have drawn on Malory as their source. The tragic love affair between Gwenever and Lancelot has been the subject of numerous films as varied as *Excalibur, Camelot* and *First Knight*. Malory's account may be the longest and best-known medieval English Arthurian romance, but it is relatively late and represents only one of many perspectives on the material. Other writers had developed the genre in highly individual ways: Chrétien de Troyes, Laʒamon and the poet of *Sir Gawain and the Green Knight* construct very different versions of the Arthurian world. In Chaucer's only Arthurian text, 'The Wife of Bath's Tale', the conventions of the genre are reconfigured to create a deeply subversive romance. This chapter will consider how and why Arthurian stories came to be such an appealing source of inspiration for writers, continuing to stimulate imaginative responses across many centuries.

King Arthur in History and Legend

Even today, Arthur's name is invoked by heritage sites scattered across Wales, Cornwall and Brittany, seeking to associate themselves with the legend. Tintagel Castle in Cornwall, for instance, claims to be 'King Arthur's legendary birthplace', while Avalon is associated with Glastonbury (reputedly the 'isle of glass' mentioned by Gerald of Wales) and Camelot with the iron-age hillfort at Cadbury. Even when Caxton first published Malory in 1485, he acknowledged in his preface the conflicting opinions about the historicity of Arthur, 'Dyvers men holde oppynyon that there was no suche Arthur and that all suche bookes as ben maad of hym ben but fayned and fables.'[1] Arthur exists at the interface between fact and fiction. His name is a warrior title (related to Celtic *artos*, meaning 'bear') and is more of a heroic epithet than a personal name, as is that of another legendary warrior, Beowulf ('bee-wolf', i.e. bear). When he first appears in literature, Arthur is an active heroic figure who rebels against foreign occupation, fights and conquers Rome, and achieves his apotheosis by being crowned emperor. He bears little resemblance to the elderly cuckold of later tales. The very lack of historical evidence for his existence allowed writers imaginative freedom.

It is important to note that the terms 'history' and 'story' were not separate concepts in the medieval period, when both served to translate the Latin *historia*. Medieval writings purporting to be history customarily occupy a fertile middle ground between fact and fiction. A few brief and imprecise references scattered across several texts form the slender basis for belief in a 'real-life' Arthur. The earliest record of a British chieftain opposing the invading Anglo-Saxons, named as Ambrosius Aurelianus, is in an account by Gildas (*c.* 545). Half a century later a Welsh chronicle, *Gododdin*, lists Arthur as a well-known hero. The chronicler known as 'Nennius' (*c.* 800) lists twelve battles fought by Arthur, while the *Annales Cambriae* (*c.* 960) mention the death of Arthur and Mordraut at Camlann. The Welsh *Mabinogion* (*c.* 1100) contains the earliest Arthurian story, *Culhwch and Olwen*.

The Invention of Arthur

It is in the twelfth century that Arthur emerges as a powerful figure with stories of his life being accorded widespread credence. The earliest full account of Arthur's reign is Geoffrey of Monmouth's *The History of the Kings of Britain*, written in Latin *c.* 1136.[2] This hugely influential account survives in hundreds of manuscripts and presents itself as resolutely factual. Geoffrey cites respectable historical sources such as the Venerable Bede and a putative 'very ancient book written in the British language' even while he inventively incorporates marvels from orally transmitted folklore. The dedication of the book to the king's illegitimate son, Robert of Gloucester, is clearly designed by Geoffrey to flatter a royal patron and ingratiate himself with the ruling dynasty. Geoffrey's history spans many centuries, but devotes a disproportionate amount of space, a fifth of its total length, to the reign of King Arthur. Passages such as the following illustrate how Geoffrey presents Arthur's time as a golden age:

> Indeed, by this time Britain had reached such a standard of sophistication that it excelled all other kingdoms in its general affluence, the richness of its decorations, and the courteous behaviour of its inhabitants. (p. 229)

As a mirror, a canvas upon which to project aspirations and self-image, Arthur served the Plantagenets well. The story of a great European ruler with expansionist ambitions provided a noble precedent helping to justify military conquest. An appealing parallel between the Britons overcome by Saxons and the English in turn conquered by Normans connects the Norman Conquest with divine providence. Arthur, although a native of the country conquered by their Norman ancestors, could be adopted by the Plantagenet dynasty as an illustrious predecessor. Using the same strategy as modern politicians, who try to associate with celebrities to improve their popularity, kings in medieval England effectively appropriated Arthur for propagandistic purposes, much as the emergent French monarchy was promoting Charlemagne as its glorious national figurehead.

Clear calculation can be seen to underpin the discovery in 1191 of the bodies of Arthur and Gwenever at Glastonbury Abbey, just as the monks were in need of a new income-generating attraction. A hundred years later in 1278, a solemn ritual of exhumation and reburial in the presence of King Edward and Queen Eleanor shows the reverence with which the Arthurian mythology was being deployed. The new marble tomb provided for the remains lasted until the dissolution of the monastery in 1539, as a sign displayed there today proudly relates. As a national icon and, in particular, an image of royalty, Arthur continued to appeal to British monarchs – from Edward III, who probably commissioned the Round Table hanging at Winchester and who founded the Order of the Garter in 1348, a pseudo-Arthurian brotherhood of knights, to the Welsh-born Henry Tudor naming his eldest son Arthur, and his successor, Henry VIII, who had the Winchester Table repainted to depict himself as Arthur. This appropriation of the Arthurian legend for political expediency accounts for his favour with the ruling orders but it is as a figure gripping the wider public imagination that Arthur is most notable.

Arthur as National Icon

Arthur became a literary hero as one of the Nine Worthies, alongside the historical Christian heroes Charlemagne and Godefroy of Bouillon.* Wace (*c.* 1155) and Laȝamon (*c.* 1200) were the first poets in Britain to take up Geoffrey's historical account of Arthur and turn it into vernacular poetry. The Plantagenets toyed with the idea of renaming London 'New Troy' to express their status as the inheritors of Rome. They traced the foundation of Britain back to the legendary Brutus, great-grandson of the Trojan Aeneas, supported by texts such as Wace's

---

* The tripartite system comprised these three Christian Worthies, along with three pagan Worthies (Hector, Alexander the Great and Julius Caesar), and three Jewish Worthies (Joshua, David and Judas Maccabeus).

Brut (History of the British). In this new poetic historiography, Arthur featured prominently as an icon of nationalism.

Laȝamon's Brut

The earliest English poem treating of Arthur was a translation of Wace's Anglo-Norman *Brut*³ by a priest based in Areley, near Worcester. This area was then geographically situated at the heart of national affairs, close to the disputed Welsh Marches. Laȝamon was perhaps witness to such important events as the burial of King John at Worcester Cathedral in 1216, or the pledging of allegiance by the Welsh leader Llywelyn in 1218. The date of Laȝamon's work is impossible to determine as, even though references in the text speak of King Henry married to Queen Eleanor, this could refer either to Henry II (d. 1189) or his grandson Henry III (acceded 1216). At 16,000 long lines, Laȝamon's poem dwarfs even Wace's poem. The elegant octosyllabic couplets of his source are completely refashioned into alliterative long lines with occasional rhyme, a highly idiosyncratic cultural blend. Two manuscripts survive (compared to twenty-six manuscripts of Wace): Cotton Caligula A ix and Cotton Otho C viii. Laȝamon's *Brut* has a distinctively odd lexis, employing very few French-derived words, preferring a self-consciously archaic vocabulary with many Old English words and Germanic compounds; this, coupled with the alliterative form favoured by Anglo-Saxon poets, suggests that Laȝamon may have had political intentions, presenting a defiantly English work. The later of the two manuscripts thoroughly revises the poem's vocabulary, eliminating many archaic words and introducing many more French terms, diminishing the poem's radical linguistic challenge.

Comparison of Laȝamon's account of Arthur with Wace's reveals a number of significant alterations. Wace had already expanded Geoffrey of Monmouth's text in a more courtly direction, with leisurely descriptions of elaborate ceremonial and etiquette at feasts and public occasions. He had invested the battle scenes with more epic grandeur by exploiting heroic formulae and diction. These features are heightened still further by Laȝamon, who favours insistently reiterated heroic epithets such as 'Arður, aðelist kingen'* (Arthur, noblest of kings) and extended similes frequently involving animal and hunting imagery for scenes of battle. Laȝamon also increases the amount of direct speech, rendering events more immediate and dramatic. Above all, he expands the romance elements and general appeal, 'even catering for women and young people' according to Rosamund Allen.[4] The marvellous is featured more plentifully and with less scepticism than in Wace, who regarded the stories about Arthur as 'Not all lies, not all truth, neither total folly, nor total wisdom' ('Ne tut mençunge, ne tut veir, / Tut folie ne tut saveir'). Laȝamon seems happy to include a good deal of folktale in his version, increasing the role of Merlin, being more attentive to prophesies and introducing several fairies and elves.

At this early stage in the story, many characters familiar from later versions are absent or unrecognisable: Arthur himself is primarily a warrior-king; there is no Lancelot; Gawain, the most prominent knight, at times voices sentimental praise of love and peace; Gwenever's adultery with Mordred is a matter of abduction and forced marriage, although beginning to develop greyer shades of complicity. Wace's most significant addition is the Round Table, a symbol of the monarchy's power over baronial factions. Laȝamon brings to his version a notable legalistic slant (possibly connected with his given name, 'Lawman') and intensely didactic attitude. His concept of Britain differs strikingly from Wace's, portraying a wider community rather than a centralised aristocratic rule. Laȝamon uses the word 'leode' to mean both the land and its inhabitants, perhaps indicating a personal concept of the nation.

It is the way in which each poet presents the death of Arthur that provides the clearest evidence of their differing temperaments and design. Laȝamon expands this scene, assigning a long speech to Arthur addressing his nominated successor, Cadwalader. This is deeply felt and emotional, culminating in Arthur's firm declaration that he will return. Wace narrates in a distanced, sceptical tone, 'If the chronicle is true', 'as they say and believe'. When reporting the Britons' belief in Arthur's

* Variations on this phrase occur, for example, at ll. 12,054, 12,240, 12,830, 12,840.

future return, Wace endorses as true only the doubtfulness foretold by Merlin, so that his statement 'Truly ... he did have himself carried to Avalon' serves to discount romantic notions of a return. Laȝamon has no such reservations. His Arthur is assuredly destined for magical reincarnation. Laȝamon introduces a ship full of women to carry Arthur away to Avalon, specifically to be healed by 'Argante there quene alven swithe sceorne' (l. 14,278) [Queen Argante, a very radiant elf]. This combines Celtic and Norse motifs which resonate with mystery and magic. For Laȝamon, Merlin's prophesy concerns the great grief attending Arthur's death rather than great doubt. Most tellingly of all, the poem's final line asserts that Merlin prophesied truly, 'That an Arthur sculde ȝete cum Anglen to fulste' (l. 14,297) [Of how an Arthur once again would come to aid the English].* Clearly Laȝamon is using the term 'English' in a loose sense to mean all the inhabitants of England rather than the Anglo-Saxons in particular. The revised Otho manuscript may be correcting what is seen as an error, or amending a dangerously democratic idea, by substituting the term 'Bruttes' [Celtic peoples, Britons] for 'English'.

Arthur in Romance

The literary treatment of Arthur coincided with the invention of 'Courtly Love', a term coined in the nineteenth century by Gaston Paris. A concept of *'fin' amors* (refined love) developed in the lyric poetry of the troubadours of Provence and the more northerly *trouvères*, which propagated a code of conduct in love in which it was deemed ennobling for a knight to serve and worship a beloved lady. Texts such as Andreas Capellanus's *De Amore* ('On Love', *c*. 1180) elaborated upon this 'Courtly Love' ethos in a playful and ironic way, constituting what the historian Georges Duby dubbed 'a man's game'.[5] Two female patrons in particular are associated with the cultivation of

---

* The odd reference to 'an' Arthur may possibly allude to the rival claimant to King John's throne, Prince Arthur of Brittany, who was killed in 1203.

this literary phenomenon: Marie de Champagne and her mother, Eleanor of Aquitaine. Under Marie's patronage, Chrétien de Troyes wrote the first French courtly romances (*c.* 1160–90), which constitute the birth of the genre, Arthurian Romance. In these tales, Arthur's role is reduced to that of an emblematic figurehead who is largely ineffectual apart from providing an emblem of respected central authority. Chrétien shapes the characteristically circular structure of Arthurian romance, which travels from court to quest and back to court. His stories focus on individual knights of the Round Table, following the wandering adventures of Erec, Cligès, Yvain, Perceval and Lancelot.

Lancelot, or the Knight of the Cart is the earliest text to feature Lancelot as the lover of Gwenever.[6] This extravagant tale sets out in detail the relative roles of knight and lady according to expected behaviour in the *fin' amors* tradition. Gwenever acts as a catalyst for chivalric enterprise by being abducted and requiring rescue, and fulfils the role of imperious *domna* [lady], requiring complete obedience from her devotee. Lancelot (remaining incognito until line 3660 of the poem) is inspired by his love for Gwenever to perform great acts of bravery and skill, but is also at times reduced to a besotted wretch forced to abase himself. The extremity of his servile state appears almost farcically exaggerated at times. Within the tale, Gawain regards Lancelot's behaviour, as he humiliates himself by riding in a lowly cart, as a 'grant folie' [great madness/folly]. It seems ludicrous that Lancelot's single second of hesitation before mounting the humble cart should be a grievous sin which causes the queen's furious rejection of him when he arrives to rescue her (p. 171). Lancelot's reverence for Gwenever almost amounts to idolatry, a quasi-religious devotion carried to excessive lengths, as when he falls enraptured, half-fainting, upon finding the queen's comb, to worship a few strands of her hair (p. 139). This unmanly display of emotion has been read by some as deliberately exposing him as excessive, an example of *demesure*, but by others as an idealised portrait of perfect love. The uncertain tone, shifting between comic, ironic and serious, adds to the tale's perplexity. Chrétien left the story to Godefroy de Leigny to complete, possibly suggesting his lack of interest in a story foisted upon him. The opening words create a sense of unwelcome imposition even as they claim subservience in what may be a playfully ironic mode:

> Since my lady of Champagne wishes me to begin a romance, I shall do so most willingly, like one who is entirely at her service ... the subject matter and meaning are furnished and given him by the countess, and he strives carefully to add nothing but his careful effort and attention. (p. 123)

Whether or not Chrétien is effectively disclaiming responsibility for an uncongenial task, his powerfully engaging Arthurian romances circulated widely and fostered an explosion of tales about Athur across Europe.

Sir Gawain and the Green Knight

Most medieval English romances are translations of French works. No such source is known for one of the most famous and sophisticated Arthurian romances in English, the anonymous *Sir Gawain and the Green Knight*[7] (*c.* 1380). *Sir Gawain and the Green Knight* is one of a dozen Middle English romances which have Gawain as their central figure. The poem tells of Gawain's partial success in fulfilling a beheading contest with the Green Knight, and his unwitting compromise of his ideals by being tempted to accept a love-token from his host's wife. Much about the poem is unique, not least its form, combining alliterative lines with rhyming couplets in a 'bob and wheel'. Part of the 'Alliterative Revival', it explicitly aligns itself with the native poetic tradition:

> With lel letters loken   [loyal/true]
> In londe so hatz ben longe.   [land]
> (ll. 35–6)

The alliterative style can achieve vividly felt passages, such as Gawain's severe suffering in freezing weather:

Ner slayn with þe slete he sleped in his yrnes   [irons, i.e. armour]
Mo nyt3ez þen innoghe, in naked rokkez   [rocks]
þeras claterande fro þe crest þe colde borne rennez   [river]
And henged he3e ouer his hede in hard iisseikkles. (ll. 729–31)

The poem survives in a single, unprepossessing manuscript, in a dialect identified with the North West Midlands.* Although in every way far from the court culture exemplified by Chaucer, *Sir Gawain and the Green Knight* is a sophisticated and imaginative achievement of the highest order. Pattern is everywhere: the opening line is echoed in its final line, completing 101 stanzas with a neat circularity;† there are parallel scenes between two courts – two New Year's celebrations, two scenes of a knight arming for battle, two beheading encounters; two symbolic objects are central to Gawain's challenge – the pentangle and the love lace; a complementary threefold patterning is also prominent with three days of hunting, three bedside temptations and three kisses.

Although the story begins as a typical challenge and quest, its real interests lie elsewhere. Deeds of daring are relegated to passing reference, a mere five lines dealing baldly with the heroic feats Gawain achieves on his journey:

Sumwhyle wyth wormes he werres, and with wolves als,
                                 [serpents]
Sumwhyle wyth wodwos that woned in the knarres,   [wild men
                                of the woods]
Both wyth bulle and beres, and bores otherqhyle,   [boars]
And etayns.   [giants]
(ll. 719–23)

The studied casualness of this description dismisses the usual fare of adventuring heroes in a perfunctory manner. The poem goes on to

---

* British Library Manuscript Cotton Nero A.x.

† The same close similarity between the opening and closing lines is found in *Pearl* and *Patience*, believed to have been written by the same poet.

develop a new concept of heroism, involving more subtle and internal trials of personal integrity. Gawain here embodies chastity and devotion to the Virgin Mary, hardly his usual guise. His knightly device is the mystical symbol of the Pentangle, 'a syngne ... In bytoknyng of trawthe' whose fivefold significance is elaborated as comprising five inter-dependent virtues: 'fraunchyse' (generosity), fellowship, cleanness (chastity), courtesy and piety (ll. 625–65). Gawain's flaw, as he accepts the lady's protective talisman and keeps it secret, may appear minor but it destroys the emblem of perfect 'truth'.

Gawain's moral virtue, like Galahad's, serves to critique secular chivalry. The poem exploits the romance genre, elevating piety over prowess.[8] Arthur here is 'childlike', presiding over a hedonistic court of immature and generally unheroic knights, loathe to face the challenger but fit to frolic with his decapitated head. Gawain is confronted by conflicting demands of moral virtue and courtesy. The roles played by women in the poem are as liability (Gwenever), as sexual temptress (Bercilak's lady) and arch villainess (Morgan le fay). Gawain, the exemplar of chivalry in other works, launches a furious tirade against women's perennial evil which would not be out of place in Jankin's 'Book of Wicked Wives' (ll. 2413–28). His anti-feminist rant may be a momentary aberration, juvenile pique, or comic release, depending on one's point of view. The ambivalence is typical of much of the poem. There is plenty of comic potential, especially during the scenes of attempted seduction, where Gawain cowers in bed as a lady enters his bedchamber:

A corner of the cortyn he caght up a lyttel,   [lifted]
And waytes warly thiderwarde quat hit be myght.   [looks warily]
Hit was the ladi. (ll. 1185–7)

Later, the lady tries to instruct Gawain in his expected role as a romance hero:

And of alle cheualry to chose, þe chif þing alosed	[praised]
Is þe lel layk of luf, þe letture of armes.	[loyal sport]
For to telle of þis teuelyng of þis trwe knyȝtez,	[deeds]
Hit is þe tytelet token and tyxt of her werkkez.	[title]

(ll. 1512–15)

Elsewhere, she insinuates that he is failing to live up to his name, 'Sir, yif ye be Wawen, wonder me þynkkes' (ll. 1481). This is part of an extraordinary self-reflexivity in the poem, situating its perspective in relation to textual traditions, established roles and generic expectation. During the exchanges between the two of them, courtly love becomes the site of a strategic contest as she asserts one version while he maintains another (hers involves sexual liaison, his mere gallantry). The delicate poise of their speeches assures that neither view emerges as definitive.

The poem perplexes until the end, where a bewildering variety of interpretations are supplied. Bercilak's lighthearted response to Gawain's 'failure' is complicated by his ambiguous identity. He has an awkward, dual role in the poem – as the enchanted giant adversary, the Green Knight, and also his later incarnation as Sir Bercilak, Gawain's jovial host. His dismissal of the trial as an elaborate jest lacks moral authority in view of his uncertain allegiance. When Gawain castigates himself for 'untrawthe' and decides to wear the green sash as a badge of shame, his opinion carries more weight:

This is the bende of my blame I bere on my nek,	[sign]
This is the lathe and the losse that I laught have	[injury]
Of couardise and covetyse that I haf caght thare.	[fell prey to]

(ll. 2506–8)

Set against this, however, is the completely contrasting response of Arthur and the rest of the court, who laugh loudly and adopt the same token as a sign of unity and honour:

That lordes and ladis that longed to the Table,
Uche burne of the brotherhede, a bauderyk schulde have. [each
(ll. 2515–16)   man]

This may defuse the stigma, or, alternatively, extend the culpability. The narrator remains resolutely silent on the matter, leaving such irreconcilable perspectives so that the meaning of the tale remains elusive – an 'endless knot' indeed.

Sir Thomas Malory's *Morte Darthur*

Malory's monumental Arthurian romance (*c.* 1469–70) is a relatively old-fashioned work, essentially nostalgic and elegiac in nature, lamenting the demise of a Golden Age.[9] Caxton's printed edition of 1485 which remained continuously in print until the seventeenth century was the standard text until the discovery of the Winchester manuscript in 1934.[10] In his preface, Caxton sets out clearly the nature of the work's edifying and entertaining appeal:

> To th'entente that noble men may see and lerne the noble acts of chyvalrye, the jentyl and virtuous dedes that somme knyghtes used in tho dayes ... Doo after the good and leve the evyl and it shal brynge you to good fame and renommee. And for to pass the tyme thys book shal be plesaunte to rede in.[11]

Malory's synthesis of Arthurian romance is an enormous accomplishment, filling seven hundred pages in Vinaver's edition, while greatly abridging and simplifying his sources. Several extremely prolix and interlacing narratives are skilfully condensed. Vinaver's algebraic analysis of the changes which Malory made to the thirteenth-century *Mort Artu* in the Fair Maid of Astolat sequence exemplifies Malory's technique.[12] The French text presents the episodes thus: a1 b1 a2 b2 x b2 y b2 z b2 m b2 n b2 p a3 a6 a4 b3 a5 (where the 'a' strand represents the tale of the Fair Maid, the 'b' strand the poisoned apple story, while other letters represent the sequence of several interspersed episodes). Compared to this, Malory's narrative structure, a1 a2 a3 a4 a5 a6 b1 b2 b3, is a model of linearity and clarity.

Plainness is at the core of Malory's work. By writing in prose, he is signalling the veracity of his story, aligning it with chronicle rather than romance. His style is emphatically formal and precise, as when he names each of the 110 knights present at the healing of Sir Urry. He favours specific geography (Windsor Forest) and broadly chronological treatment. The writing style is appropriately plain with few rhetorical ornaments, a rigorously limited lexis and occasional flourishes enlivening the regularly neutral tone. Formulaic epithets lend dignity, with Arthur always designated as 'noble' king, his 'full noble' knights endlessly associated with 'worship', and ladies always 'passing fair'. Perhaps the keynote to Malory's writing is his paratactic sentence structure (insistently additive, with few subordinate sentences), which tends to create a leisurely rhythm. The narrative is punctuated with over seventy references to his sources, the 'French Book', usually when Malory is at his most original and innovative, clearly marking his attempt to disguise or to authenticate his own innovations.

One such invention is the Oath of Knighthood sworn annually by the knights of Arthur's court, every article of which is breached at some time or other. The contingent, slippery nature of ideals and aspirations is a developing theme. Lancelot is Malory's prime interest, his supremacy acknowledged by Arthur even at the point of crisis, 'For sir Launcelot ys an hardy knyght, and all ye know that he ys the beste knyght amonge us all ... I know no knyght that ys able to macch hym' (p. 674). Malory's relative lack of interest in love is evident not just in the remarkable absence of intimate scenes between the central lovers, but also in the treatment of small-scale episodes, such as Pelleas's unrequited love for Ettarde in Book IV. Malory alters the mood of his sources completely, showing little sympathy for Pelleas's anguish and changing Pelleas into a pragmatist who readily renounces Ettarde in favour of a new mistress, Nineve. In Malory's French source, Pelleas remains devoted to Ettarde, even after finding her sleeping with Gawain, and wins her love in the end. Elsewhere, in the 'Knight of the

Cart' episode, Malory's unease with sexuality is readily apparent. Where the English source states frankly, 'to bede he gothe with the queen', following the French source ('se coucha avec la roine'), Malory is equivocal, 'whether they were abed other at other maner of disportis, me lyste nat thereof make no mencion, for love that tyme was nat as love ys nowadayes' (p. 676). When he elaborates his ideal of 'vertuouse love' it is strikingly devoid of passion:

> Nowadayes men can nat love sevennyght but they muste have all their desyres ... love nowadayes, sone hote, sone colde. Thys ys no stabylyté. But the olde love was nat so. For men and women coude love togydirs seven yerys, and no lycoures lustis was betwyxte them, and than was love truthe and faythefulnes. And so in lyke wyse was used such love in king Arthurs dayes. (p. 649)

The tragic tale of Elaine of Ascolat, who dies from inordinate ('out of mesure') and unrequited love for Lancelot, highlights the inequities of the Arthurian world. Her brother, Lavain, is free to join Lancelot while she is repudiated. Her last speech, 'Why sholde I leve such thoughtes? Am I nat an erthely woman?' (p. 639), poignantly asserts the naturalness of her love for Lancelot, although some detect irksome platitudes and self-pity where others respond to its simplicity and pathos. Above all, she represents innocence in sharp contrast with Gwenever, whose vindictiveness and quarrelsome nature are highlighted. The exchanges between her and Lancelot betray a brittle edge as she sends him away from court to avoid gossip:

> 'Sir, ye ar gretly to blame thus to holde you behynde my lorde. What woll youre enemyes and myne sey and deme?' ... 'Have ye no doute, madame ... I alow youre witte. Hit ys of late com syn ye were woxen so wise!' (p. 622)

The strained nature of their relationship is apparent throughout, even as Gwenever finally apologises for her treatment of him:

'Thys ys nat the firste tyme,' seyde sir Launcelot, 'that ye have ben displese with me causeles. But, madame, ever I muste suffir you, but to what sorow that I endure, ye take no forse.' (p. 642)

Male fellowship is Malory's main interest, in line with Arthur's pronouncement, 'Much more I am soryar for my good knyghtes losse than for the losse of my fayre quene; for quenys I myght have inow [plenty], but such a felyship of good knyghtes shall never be togydirs in no company' (p. 685). In this society, public persona is all. The interior life, so vital in French romances where lovers' internal monologues and thought processes are set out frequently at length, is irrelevant here. Readers of Malory simply do not know how his characters think or feel most of the time as he returns to a much earlier tradition where action is primary. Lancelot can assert his and Gwenever's innocence because, 'Within the logic of the knightly code, a liar is a man who cannot prove the truth of his words with his sword'.[13] The casuistry increases palpably in the final series of rescues and vindications of the queen, to the point where Lancelot is guilty as charged by Meliagant, facing death in combat, 'I rede you beware what ye do ... shulde ye be avysed to do batayle in a wronge quarell' (p. 659). Lancelot's assertion of Gwenever's innocence rests on a subterfuge as, although she did not sleep with any of the ten knights as charged, she did commit adultery with him. The strain of such moral compromise may underlie his tearful breakdown after the healing of Sir Urry but, typically, Malory offers no clarification, so that the tears might just as well stem from pure ecstasy as from contrition, 'And ever sir Launcelote wepte, as he had bene a chylde that had bene beatyn!' (p. 668).

It is in Book VI, the 'Quest for the Holy Grail', where religious piety clashes most blatantly with secular chivalry. Arthur's knights leave Camelot to pursue a spiritual quest, where familiar romance motifs are reconfigured, so that a damsel in distress, such as Heloise the Sorceress, is a female fiend in disguise and a knight cannot tell which is the 'right' side in a battle (cf. Melias' two paths; Lancelot's choosing wrongly to fight on the apparently weaker side). Percival and Galahad now represent the supreme heroic ideal – virginity. In this realm, power rests with wise hermits and priests, who interpret dreams and visions as spiritual revelation, and a knight's best weapons are prayer, confession, penance and signing with the cross against fiends. After the Grail Quest, a new piety permeates the narrative, as Amesbury and Glastonbury replace Camelot for the final sequence of events leading up to the climactic Crusade. The essence of the Grail material, its critique of secular knighthood, is, however, perversely toned down by Malory, who retains an undaunted admiration for Lancelot. Instead of being eclipsed in glory by his pious son, Malory's Lancelot emerges from the Grail Quest minimally humbled and is hailed for his relative success:

> Than, as the booke seyth, sir Launcelot began to resorte unto quene Gwenivere agayne and forgate the promyse and the perfeccion that he made in the queste; for, as the booke seyth, had nat sir Launcelot bene in his prevy thoughtes and in hys myndis so sette inwardly to the quene as he was in semyng outward to God, there had no knyght passed hym in the quest of the Sankgreall. (p. 612)

This sets the tone of the last two books, presaging disaster. The causes of the collapse of the Arthurian age involve a mixture of human failings and impersonal destiny. The numerous 'causes' inscribed in the text result in overdetermination. Arthur blames the troublemaking Agravain and Mordred (p. 685), his dream envisages an arbitrary Fortune (p. 711), Gawain blames himself (p. 709), a snake in the grass provokes the final battle (p. 712) and Gwenever judges herself and Lancelot responsible (p. 720). The most popular 'explanation' favoured by later writers and filmmakers, the sin of Arthur's incestuously begotten son, Mordred, remains unstated.

At the time when Malory was writing, the ideal of a brotherhood of loyal warriors had an urgent contemporary relevance. General lawlessness was prevalent during the civil war raging across the country, with bands of armed retainers and mercenaries terrorising people such as the Pastons in Norfolk. As a participant or criminal during the time of the Wars of the Roses, Malory ended his life in prison, by his own account. Occasionally a sense of personal grievance seems to break through the fictive frame as the narrator deplores the fickleness of the English, 'Lo ye all Englysshemen! ... Alas! Thys ys a greate defaughte of us Engysshemen, for there may no thynge us please no terme' (p. 708). Arthur's end is handled with skill and pathos. But the real climax of Malory's work is not the death of Arthur but that of Lancelot, the epitome of Malory's conception of knighthood as formulated in the famous eulogy delivered by Sir Ector:

> 'Thou were the curtest knyght that ever bare shelde ... the truest frende to thy lovar that ever bestrade hors ... the trewest lover, of a synful man, that ever loved woman ... the kyndest man that ever strake wyth swerde ... the godelyest persone that ever cam emonge prees of knyghts ... the mekest man and the jentyllest that ever ete in halle emonge ladyes ... the sternest knyght to thy mortal foo that ever put spere in the reeste.' (p. 725)

This celebrates a complex compounding of qualities, encompassing chivalrous, courtly and martial excellence. Yet the awkward expression and the clashing, contradictory attributes create a disharmony which exists in tension with the praise and intense grief.

Extended Commentary: Chaucer, 'The Wife of Bath's Tale'

Chaucer's only Arthurian romance is rather surprisingly assigned to the loud and crude Wife of Bath.[14] What is now 'The Shipman's Tale', a crude fabliau, was originally told by the Wife and would seem a genre better suited to her character. Critics debate how far the Wife's Tale functions as a vehicle for her to continue her pro-feminist agenda as an indulgent comic interlude and as wish-fulfilment.[15] Alison can be seen to project herself into her story as the powerful woman who gains dominance over her husband while regaining her youth and beauty.

Such mirroring is less persuasive when one considers the denigration of women which informs the plot, predicated upon generalisations about women's love of 'richesse ... riche array, lust abedde, / And oftetyme to be wydwe and wedde' (ll. 925–8). It is no surprise that the Wife, embodying all these traits, slips into first person pronouns at this point, speaking of 'oure hertes' and 'we', but it is surprising that such a vocal rebel against patriarchy should approve of such antifeminist views, 'He gooth ful ny [near] the soothe, I wol nat lye' (l. 931).

The Intersections of Gender and Genre

The Wife's Tale is set in a fairytale past, when 'Al was this land fulfild of faery' (l. 859).[16] Its grounding in romantic legend, 'In th'olde dayes of the Kyng Arthour, / Of which that Britons speken grete honour' (ll. 857–8), emphatically 'manye hundred yeres ago', may be a satirical manoeuvre. The Wife's casual observation of the displacement of fairies by predatory friars is a sharp attack on the fraternal orders. Although the story superficially resembles Arthurian romance, it is deeply subversive of generic expectation. By extension it may work satirically to unsettle not just audience expectation but also established social order, allegorical mindsets and glossing habits. In every respect, romance elements are confounded.

Chaucer's version of a widely known folktale about the disenchant-ment of a 'Loathly Lady' transforms the story in significant ways.* Personal names are largely erased, giving the tale a distanced, generalised quality. The catalyst for the knight's quest to find out 'What thyng it is that wommen moost desire' (l. 1007) is not an accidental killing of a knight but an altogether more directly relevant crime: the violent rape of a young girl.† This transforms the story into one of poetic justice as all expectations of gender are inverted. No chivalrous hero but 'a lusty bacheler', this knight's 'success' rests on submission to

---

* Two anonymous Arthurian romances, *The Marriage of Sir Gawain* and *The Wedding of Sir Gawain and Dame Ragnell*, are based on this folktale, as is Gower's 'Tale of Florent' in his *Confessio Amantis*.
† Cecily Champain's quitclaim in 1380, formally dropping charges of rape against Chaucer, may be an interesting side issue to consider.

female authority as he is forced to occupy a subject position. Constrained to sexual intercourse against his will, the unheroic knight is
mocked by the hag in a way which is reminiscent of Bercilak's mockery
of the Arthurian court in *Sir Gawain and the Green Knight*:

> 'Is this the lawe of kyng Arthures hous?
> Is every knyght of his so dangerous?'   [grudging]
> (ll. 1089–90)

The rape which sets the tale in motion is introduced with extreme casualness, 'on a day ... it happed that ... he saugh a mayde walking hym biforn'
(ll. 884–6), which makes the sudden violence all the more shocking:

> Of which mayde anon, maugree hir heed,   [against her will]
> By verray force, he rafte hire maydenhed.   [seized]
> (ll. 887–8)

Intensifying adverbs (anon, verray), the harsh tone and import of the
verb ('rafte') all combine with the unsubtle punning rhyme to convey a
brutal act of 'oppressioun'. Around this act of violence the Tale presents
a restorative process of educating the knight, which involves him being
forced to experience what the Wife's Prologue presented as a female
hardship, 'the wo that is in mariage' (l. 3). In this nightmare vision of
romance, a knight's sighs betoken despair over female domination:

> Wo was this knight, and sorwefully he siketh;   [sighs]
> But what! He may nat do al as hym liketh. (ll. 913–14)

Female Authority

Where unquestioned male 'authority' was the Wife's main bone of
contention in her Prologue, her Tale devotes a hundred lines (a quarter
of its total length) to the hag's pillow lecture, in which she instructs her
husband as to his erroneous judgement, dealing with each of his
objections to her:

'Thou art so loothly, and so oold also,
And therto comen of so lough a kynde.'   [lowborn origin]
(ll. 1100–1)

Tellingly, she rearranges the order of the topics for her own purposes, prioritising 'gentillesse' and dismissing any idea of inherited nobility as 'nat worth a hen' (l. 1112). Essentially she elaborates upon the proverb, 'Noble is as noble does', but delays making this explicit until line 1070, 'He is gentil that dooth gentil dedes'. Her speech is forceful as she declares that nobility is a gift to all from Christ not something bequeathed by 'oure elders for hire olde richesse' (l. 1118). References to Dante and Classical authors soften the radical implications of this and her disdain for possessions and property, 'temporel thyng, that man may hurte and mayme' (l. 1132). The most explicit social criticism comes towards the end of the section on nobility:

'For, God it woot, men may wel often fynde
A lordes sone do shame and vileyne.' (ll. 1150–1)

Insistent negatives dominate her extended discourse on social status:

[He who] nel hymselven do no gentil dedis   [is unwilling]
Ne folwen his gentil auncestre that deed is,   [dead]
He nys nat gentil, be he duc or erl,
For vileyns sinful dedes make a cherl. (ll. 1155–8)

Further emphasis is achieved by the limited lexis and repetition of key words in successive lines along with the noticeable awkwardness of the rhymes 'dedis', 'deed is'. Her subtext of radical topicality in the period of the Peasants' Revolt may be deflected by the naming of revered Classical authors – Valerius Maximus, Seneca and Boethius – in support of her philosophical pronouncements.

A short but pointed discussion of poverty (thirty lines long) is followed by a mere six lines on old age, comprising a few vague platitudes. The assured tone slips ('as I gesse') as her supportive authorities dwindle to an imprecise 'ye gentils of honour' (l. 1208). She strategically elides the topics of old age and ugliness, 'foul and old', chiming through this section. Her weak defence perversely endorses the knight's repulsion by praising old age and ugliness as guarantees of chastity. Overall, the lecture seems to diminish in force as it progresses. Her arguments are generally conservative as she urges the rich to behave nobly and the poor to be content with their lot. She appears to be a reformer rather than a rebel, much like the Wife, who seeks to invert gender power relations, not attain mutuality. Nevertheless, her discourse dominates the Tale and is fundamentally disruptive of patriarchal norms. A sermon delivered by a woman automatically opposes prevailing ideas about gender – it was considered inappropriate for a woman to speak of philosophy or to preach.* Allegorically, as in Chaucer's 'Tale of Melibee', this Tale shows Reason (embodied in a woman) winning over (male) brute force.

In the end, the story is resolved by a fantasy, 'happy ever after' conclusion as the knight gains a wife both beautiful and faithful, living with her 'in parfit joye' (l. 1258). The final accord mirrors the end of the Prologue, where the Wife and Jankyn kissed after their quarrel and established a happy union. Yet, the hag's ambivalent promise is less reassuring than it seems:

> I prey to God that I moote sterven wood,   [die insane]
> But I to yow be also good and trewe
> As evere was wyf, sin that the world was newe. (ll. 1242–4)

A critical eye might detect here an ominous, if oblique punning reference to original sin – a hollowness in her hyperbolic intention to be as virtuous as 'any woman ever' and an unpromising relativity ('as good as'). These hints are slight and easily missed, but the final shattering of the romance frame is brutally clear as the Wife prays for bad husbands to die:

---

* St Paul's doctrine forbad women to speak in church (I Corinthians 14:34) – a position enforced until recently when women were allowed to be ordained as priests, to the consternation of many traditionalists.

And olde and angry nigardes of dispence,   [misers in spending]
God sende hem verray pestilence! (ll. 1262–3)

The hag's prayer may be no less impious. It is worth noting that the 'verray pestilence' the Wife calls down upon miserly husbands was no empty metaphor then, but a terrible reality. This strikes a discordant note which destroys any reconciliatory mood at the climax of the Tale. We could hardly be further removed from the world of refined chivalry associated with the Arthurian romance. Chaucer's only Arthurian romance is constituted as a highly irregular, parodic piece which may suggest reservations towards the genre, or a sophisticated reshaping of it.

Notes

1   Caxton's preface is given as an appendix in Helen Cooper (ed.), *Sir Thomas Malory: Le Morte Darthur: The Winchester Manuscript* (Oxford: Oxford University Press, 1998), pp. 528–30 (p. 529).
2   Geoffrey of Monmouth, *Historia Regum Brittaniae*, trans. Lewis Thorpe, *The History of the Kings of Britain* (Harmondsworth: Penguin, 1966).
3   The standard two-volume edition contains both manuscripts as parallel texts, (eds) G. L. Brook and R. F. Leslie, Early English Text Society o.s. 250, 277 (London: Oxford University Press, 1963, 1978).
4   For a modern English translation of the Arthurian sections of both Laȝamon and Wace's *Bruts*, see Judith Weiss and Rosamund Allen (trans.), *The Life of King Arthur: Wace and Laȝamon* (London: Everyman, 1997), p. xxxix.
5   Georges Duby develops a searching analysis of 'Courtly Love' in *The Knight, The Lady, and the Priest: The Making of Modern Marriage in Medieval France*, trans. Barbara Bray (London: Penguin, 1983).
6   Chrétien de Troyes, *Lancelot, or the Knight of the Cart*, trans. William W. Kibler, in *The Romance of Arthur*, ed. James J. Wilhelm (New York: Garland, 1994), chapter 7, pp. 121–99.
7   A. C. Cawley and J. J. Anderson (eds), *Pearl, Cleanness, Patience, Sir Gawain and the Green Knight* (London: Dent, 1985).
8   Some religious, perhaps even allegorical significance, is likely in view of the

poem's manuscript context, alongside didactic Christian works, *Pearl*,
Patience, and *Cleanness*.

9   The division into eight books first proposed by Eugène Vinaver provides a
      convenient structure, although arguments for alternative divisions rage. All
      references to the text shall be to Vinaver's single-volume edition, *Malory:
      Works* (Oxford: Oxford University Press, 1971).

10   The structure of *Le Morte Darthur* was for a long time occluded by
      Caxton's rearrangement of the text into twenty-one books, subdivided into
      506 chapters, along with considerable revision, until the discovery of the
      Winchester manuscript revealed the original as constituting much larger
      units. Vinaver's edition presents the text as follows: Book I treats Arthur's
      rise to power, marriage and establishment of a knightly order; Book II his
      conquest of Rome; Book III relates the early adventures of Lancelot; Book
      IV concerns Gareth, Gawain's younger brother; Book V, the longest, is of
      Tristram, featuring Lancelot's enchanted fathering of a son on the Grail
      king's daughter; Book VI tells the Grail story, introducing a new concept of
      spiritual honour, which is achieved only by Galahad, Percival and Bors;
      Book VII includes the episode of the Fair Maid of Ascolat, part of a
      sequence of unfolding destructive events; Book VIII treats of Arthur's
      death, followed by that of the queen and Lancelot.

11   Cooper (ed.), *Le Morte Darthur*, p. 530.

12   Vinaver (ed.), *Malory: Works*, p. 767.

13   Terence McCarthy, *An Introduction to Malory* (Woodbridge: Brewer,
      1991), p. 98.

14   'The Wife of Bath's Tale' in *The Riverside Chaucer*, ed. Larry D. Benson
      (Oxford: Oxford University Press, 1989), pp. 105–21.

15   Jill Mann, *Chaucer* (Brighton: Harvester, 1991) regards the Tale as subtly
      elevating female status by demonstrating how surrender paradoxically
      empowers, while Mary Carruthers, 'The Wife of Bath and the Painting of
      Lions', *Publications of the Modern Language Association*, 94 (1979), pp.
      209–22, sees the tale as a comic self-indulgence by the Wife, whose 'streak
      of sentimentality' has already been glimpsed in her Prologue. Helen
      Cooper, *The Structure of the Canterbury Tales* (Athens, GA: University of
      Georgia Press, 1983), p. 126, regards this 'more than any other tale in the
      whole work [as] psychologically as well as rhetorically appropriate for its
      teller'.

16   Peter G. Biedler, *Chaucer's Wife of Bath's Prologue and Tale: An Annotated
      Bibliography 1900–1996* (Basingstoke: Macmillan, 1996) contains useful
      summaries of two contrasting interpretations of the opening section of the
      tale, pp. 171–88 and pp. 205–220.

Dream and Vision: A Space Odyssey

Dreams appear frequently in medieval literature, providing moments of powerfully focused meaning within longer narratives. They can offer access to the divine, usually presaging good or bad fortune (cf. Arthur's two dreams in Malory's *Morte Darthur* Book VIII – one an allegory of Fortune's wheel and the other a vision of Gawain prophesying on the eve of the final battle – and Cresseid's vision of the gods deciding her fate in Henryson's *Testament of Cresseid*). In many works, the dream forms the substantive basis for the poem, rather than incidentally crystallising a theme. This distinct genre, the dream vision, was immensely popular and was favoured by many medieval writers, including the finest 'Ricardian' poets – Chaucer, Langland and the *Gawain*-poet. Poems framed as dreams already formed a respected literary tradition. Boethius's *Consolation of Philosophy* and the thirteenth-century courtly love allegory the *Roman de la Rose* each inspired different types of dream vision concerned with philosophical, intellectual issues and with the emotional aspects of courtly love respectively (although, as ever, the two were not mutually exclusive). The late medieval mystical movement, which produced contemplative and devotional works exploring personal experiences of heightened ecstasy, also played a vital role in shaping and authorising dream vision.*

---

* For discussion of the late medieval mystical movement, see Part Three: 'Acting Up: Medieval Drama'.

Medieval dream vision flourished as a flexible vehicle for wide-ranging ideas, exploring boundaries between author and reader, fact and fiction, individual and community, and developing new concepts of character and identity. Dream vision may feature the journey of romance, adventure and quest, or the fantasy and symbolism of the lay, but it is distinctive in its form. Above all, dream vision provides a creative space in which the 'imagined' world of the dream can represent the creative imagination of the poet. This takes place via a dreamer who is by no means to be simply identified with his poetic persona, even though that figure often bears the same name. This 'I' persona is one of the genre's major contributions to literary technique, along with vivid realism. The dream framework is developed by poets to explore searching questions of meaning, identity and imagination in remarkable and innovative ways.

In surveying the genre of dream vision, four of the most important works of the later fourteenth century will be considered: two of Chaucer's four dream vision poems, which are among his earliest works, *The Book of the Duchess* and *The Parliament of Fowls*, the *Gawain*-poet's *Pearl*; and William Langland's *Piers Plowman*. Their themes are many and varied, ranging from courtly love and consolation to religious faith, salvation and political satire.

The Book of the Duchess is Chaucer's earliest major work (*c.* 1369–72). It is written in the French-inspired octosyllabic couplets associated with his earliest writings and treats the historical event of the death of John of Gaunt's wife, Blanche (on 12 September 1368 or 1369). *The Parliament of Fowls* seems to fall into Chaucer's period of Italian influence as it is written in rime-royal stanzas – an elaborate form popularised by Chaucer and known in England as the Chaucerian Stanza. The usual composition date proposed for the poem is May 1382, coinciding with the marriage of the fifteen-year-old Richard II to Anne of Bohemia, for which it would be a suitable celebratory piece.* The other two works considered here form part of the

---

* This, the earliest St Valentine's Day poem in English, is looking forward to the following 14 February 1383.

'Alliterative Revival' contemporary with Chaucer but associated with baronial courts rather than the royal court where Chaucer resided: *Pearl,* probably written by the same poet as *Sir Gawain and the Green Knight,* and *Piers Plowman* (*c.* 1367–85) by William Langland, a poet originally from the south-west Midlands who was living in London.

Form and Style

As is already evident, dream poetry encompasses a variety of forms: short rhyming couplets, elaborate Italianate stanzas and long lines of alliterative verse. It presents its themes using a range of techniques, including debate, dialogue, instruction, dramatic representation and reflection. Above all, in structure and style, dream poetry presents a dazzling array of shifting scenes and mixed modes (realistic, allegorical, tragic, comic, amatory and political). One of the most significant aspects of dream vision is that it liberates poets from narrative linearity and causality, enabling them to roam across space and time and to explore new ways of writing and imagining. The essentially fluid logic of the dream world finds lively poetic expression, perhaps most spectacularly in *Piers Plowman.* Here the poet creates a kaleidoscopic world of dazzling diversity encapsulating what T. S. Eliot called 'the logic of the imagination'.[1]

Piers Plowman uses a complex mix of allegorical styles:[2] *personification allegory,* where abstract concepts are represented as people (Hunger, Greed), concretising their nature, and aspects of a person are figured as external forces (Fear, Will, Memory); *dramatic allegory,* developing a topic through story/plot and character, investing concepts with a vivid, life-like presence and authenticating detail, approaching 'realism' – for example, Mede's marriage sequence; the four daughters of God; *iconographic allegory,* semi-pictorial presentation influenced by the visual arts, static tableaux, verbally painting and labelling diagrams, in a meticulously detailed way which can be dull – for example, the Tree of Jesse; and *non-visual allegory,* presenting ideas which are impossible to picture, often frustrating and perplexing; *exemplary allegory,* similar to the sermon technique, using short stories to illustrate and enliven didactic material, sometimes brief allusions, sometimes fledgling narratives within the main narrative.

The Status and Classification of Dreams in the Middle Ages

Across human history, dreams and visions have been accorded respect as experiences of privileged access to the higher realm of the divine. In Classical literature, the barrier between worlds, between life and death, earth and heaven, is often crossed by gods and epic heroes, with frequent apparitions, underworld journeys in search of enlightenment, and general consultation of oracles and the practice of divination. Belief in the potential power of dreams and visions to guide and to prophesy forms a major part of the Judeo-Christian tradition too, with many examples in both the Old and the New Testaments:

> By a dream in a vision by night, when deep sleep falleth upon men, and they are sleeping in their beds;
> Then he openeth the ears of men, and teaching instructeth them in what they are to learn. (Job 33:15–6)

Among the best-known Biblical precedents are the dreams of Joseph, Pharoah and Nebuchadnezzar, the whole Book of Ezekiel and, above all, the Book of Revelations by St John the Divine, the final book of the Bible which presents an apocalyptic vision of the end of the world.

Dream theory was widespread in the Middle Ages with various treatises cataloguing and clarifying the functions of dreams. The most influential work was Macrobius's commentary (*c.* AD400) on Cicero's *The Dream of Scipio* (*c.* 50BC). Macrobius's dream theory distinguished between five main types of experience: the three divinatory types are divinely inspired and revelatory – the *somnium* (enigmatic), the *visio* (prophetic) and the *oraculum* (an oracular authority foretells the future); two non-divinatory types are attributed to physiological causes

– the *insomnium* (nightmare) and the *visum* or *phantasma* (apparition). Chaucer frequently incorporates discussion of dreams, as in 'The Nun's Priest's Tale' where the chicken Pertelote voices a common-sense attitude to commonplace dreams, rejecting any supernatural significance:[3]

> Nothyng, God woot, but vanitee in sweven is.   [dream]
> Swevenes engendren of replecciouns.   [are caused by overeating]
> (ll. 2922–3)

The joke turns out to be that she is wrong, as Chantecleer's dream is a genuinely prophetic vision of impending danger. The dreamer in Chaucer's *The House of Fame* ponders the whole range of possible types while comically asserting his lack of comprehension:

> Why that is an avision
> And why this a revelacion,
> Why this a drem, why that a sweven [...]
> Why this a fantome, why these oracles. (ll. 7–9, 11)

The dismissive note is misleading in view of Chaucer's continuing interest in dreams, a clear reminder that the poetic persona is not to be equated with the poet.

Multiple Meaning: The Fourfold Method of Exegesis

Medieval people were encouraged to be experts in Exegesis, to be able to 'read' signs in the world around them, since Nature was a book wherein could be discerned God's providential design, according to authorities such as Alain de Lisle. From this perspective, meaning concealed in signs is an everyday experience and the medieval period developed a correspondingly allegorical outlook, which finds plentiful expression in its literature. Medieval scholars were trained to interpret scripture with an awareness of multiple layers of meaning; namely, the literal (historical), the allegorical (typological), the tropological (moral) and the anagogical (eschatological or theological). In practice, this means that 'Jerusalem' literally signifies the city in Judea, allegorically the Christian Church, tropologically the faithful soul and anagogically the 'New' Jerusalem, the future heavenly abode of Christians. We may well sympathise with the dim-witted dreamer in *Pearl*, a reader who struggles to grasp such multiple signifiers.[4] A well-known mnemonic by Nicholas of Lyra (*c.* 1270–1349) sets out a succinct account of the system:

> Littera gesta docet, quid credas allegoria,
> Moralis quod agas, quo tendas anagogia.

> [The literal sense teaches what happened, the allegorical what you believe, the moral what you should do, the anagogical where you are going.]

It is not that poets consciously sat down to write according to this method, but that at times the multivalence of their works responds to such an interpretative strategy. Allegory (Gk. 'speaking otherwise') is essentially about veiling, obliquity, encouraging the reader to interpret. The allegorical mode of expression at the heart of medieval literature can appear remarkably modern, as in *Piers Plowman*, which at times approaches a 'stream of consciousness' technique. Dream vision especially can present a challenge, structurally and conceptually, as its mode is symbolic and its allegory shifting and multiple.

Dreamers and Their Guides

The dream vision genre coheres around a number of key elements: the frame of the dream, the persona of the dreamer, the authoritative figure(s) met within the dream, the dream landscape and several common themes. The dreamer figure acts as a 'focaliser' – an inscribed observer who communicates the contents of his dream to the reader. He is often presented as naïve, even dim-witted, which creates a fruitful gap between narrator and reader even as we are being implicated or given a superior vantage point. The dreamer's exploratory experience is shared by the reader – a journey of interior searching and insight whose progress may be straightforward or convoluted. Primarily the dreamer serves as the connecting thread holding it all together, a narrator shaping what can be a bewildering sequence, operating at times as surrogate reader, guide, visionary, exegete or interpreter. Every dreamer needs a guide – an authoritative figure who acts as a further controlling presence (cf. Dante's Virgil, Boethius's Lady Philosophy). The guide leads and instructs the dreamer, entering into dialogue through answering questions so that the relationship between the two can develop aspects of dramatic interaction and tension.

Chaucer's dreamers share his name and certain characteristics, such as bookishness, but are constructed personas. They tend to be learned but dim-witted (although, taking account of Chaucer's irony, at times may possibly be less dense than they appear). His earliest dream vision, the *Book of the Duchess* is grounded in actuality and personal experience, as Chaucer knew Blanche, Duchess of Lancaster, the first wife of his patron John of Gaunt.* Chaucer probably wrote his *ABC* for her. In the poem, her name is given in English as White. The poem opens with an insomniac narrator reading in bed. He claims to be suffering from an unspecified, long-term malady (l. 37), which is usually presumed to be unrequited love. Yet the narrator appears to mostly comic effect in his self-obsession and self-pity, achieved primarily through his chatty style of speech, almost like a monologue, with its direct address ('ye') and anticipated audience responses ('men might axe me'). His clumsy rhymes, 'hom/ ... com/Hom' (ll. 77–9) and rambling, mock-heroic elaboration of his own reflections (ll. 230–70) contribute to the comedic mood. Priscilla Martin sums up the ludicrous impression of the poem nicely, describing the *Book of the Duchess* as 'a dream inspired by a book misunderstood, a view through windows painted with a poem, a conversation at cross purposes.'[5] The book in question is Ovid's

---

* John of Gaunt was one of the most powerful men in the country, king in all but name during Richard II's minority. His third marriage was to Chaucer's sister-in-law.

Metamorphoses, whose tale of Ceyx and Alcione is recounted at some length (155 lines) although conspicuously omitting the happy ending in which Ovid's lovers are reunited after death as seabirds.

The prolonged preliminaries end with a very abrupt falling asleep (l. 272ff.). In the dream, too, the narrative proceeds with great hesitancy and leisureliness before ending with comic suddenness. The guide is a deferred presence, as the dreamer briefly encounters a huntsman and then a young dog before finally reaching the Man in Black. This grieving figure provides the bulk of the narrative, relating his experiences of love and loss. The dreamer remains frustratingly hesitant, first approaching stealthily from behind, 'I stalked even unto hys back' (ll. 458), advancing with a ludicrously studied pace, 'I went and stood right at hys fet' (l. 502), 'y stood / before hym' (ll. 515–16). Before he is aware of the dreamer's presence, Black delivers a lyric complaint (ll. 475–86) which the dreamer calculates with comic vagueness as 'of rym ten vers or twelve' (l. 463). There is a marked contrast in demeanour and assertiveness between the dreamer and his aristocratic 'subject', evident even in their terms of address, respectively employing 'ye', 'you' and 'thee'. Their contrasting attitudes to love have been interpreted by Spearing as a staging of the common late medieval debate between Absolutists and Relativists – the one regarding phenomena as extraordinary and unique, the other promoting relativity.[6] Other critics, such as Strohm, regard the disparity as one of social class, distinguishing aristocracy from lesser gentry.[7] The climax is effected through an awkward final exchange, 'She ys ded!' 'Nay!' 'Yis, be my trouthe!' (ll. 1309–10). As the dreamer expresses 'trouthe', Black leaves to resume the hunt, 'al was doon' (l. 1311). The extremely laconic ending to such a prolonged presentation of Black's suffering feels quite odd and unsatisfactory. In place of the expected learning outcome, the poem concludes with its narrator none the wiser; his only comment on waking is that the dream was 'queynt' and worth putting into verse.

Similarly, in Chaucer's other early dream poem, the *Parliament of Fowls* the dreamer–narrator is presented as an extremely naïve and comedic figure who has only read about love's sufferings. He is learned in dream lore, referring to Cicero (l. 31), Macrobius (l. 111) and Alain de Lisle (l. 316), and scholarly, drawing on Boccaccio, the *Roman de la Rose* and Dante. Again, the catalyst for the dream is a Classical text, the *Dream of Scipio*, but this time the book produces the vision more directly as the first guide is Scipio Africanus*. In the manner of an oraculum, Africanus supplies the narrator with knowledge, 'I shal the shewe mater of to wryte' (l. 168). This dreamer is a poet manqué (an unsuccessful poet) who needs to be physically pushed through the double gates into the Temple of Venus, and then led by the hand (l. 154). It is the two goddesses, Venus and Nature, who instruct the dreamer – one revealing the destructive force of carnal and corrupt love before the other, God's 'vicaire' [deputy] (l. 379), presides over the generative, benign aspects of love.† Once again, the instruction and the vision of the bird parliament seem to have little effect on the narrator beyond supplying him with a good story to relate (inspiring the poem, *Parliament of Fowls*). The dreamer wakes suddenly and returns to his books, hoping for some future knowledge, 'som thing for to fare / The bet' (ll. 697–8). The conspicuous lack of meaning leaves the ending enigmatic, constituting, along with the unresolved avian debate, a kind of courtly game, a 'demande d'amour'.

The dreamer in *Pearl* is immediately less precisely drawn and more emotionally affecting than Chaucer's.[8] With no preliminary exposition or introduction of the narrative persona, the narrative begins in a curiously oblique way with an unnamed and insubstantial 'I' figure expressing his grief. The speaker appears to be a jeweller and a grieving lover, speaking of his 'luf-daungere' (l. 11), suffering caused by love, and describing his beloved in terms reminiscent of lyric poetry, 'So smal, so smothe her sydes' (l. 6). The mood is quickly established as elegiac, the dreamer's pearl buried in 'clot ... moul ... moldes dunne' (ll. 22–3, 30). The situation gradually emerges as a father grieving for his young daughter's death. The dream charts his struggle to accept this loss and his even more difficult progress towards understanding God's larger

---

* Roman general and statesman (235–183BC), a hero of the Second Punic War. In his *De Re Publica*, Cicero gives an account of Scipio Africanus appearing in a dream to his (adoptive) grandson, Scipio Aemilianus.

† The earlier 'Cytherea ... blissful lady swete' (l. 113) is the allegorical representation of the planet, not the goddess who appears later, embodying corrupt love and carnality.

purpose and the mysteries of the Christian faith. Surprisingly, the authority figure he encounters in his dream is his lost child, yet transformed into an ethereal presence. She addresses him coolly, remaining distant and authoritative in a way which confuses both the dreamer and the reader. Mysteriously transformed from two-year-old infant to bride, she addresses her father formally ('Sir') and rebukes him sternly for his excessive grief, calling him 'madde' (l. 290). This reversal of earthly roles, the child instructing the parent, offends and mystifies the materialistic and literally minded dreamer and the reader alike. The Pearl Maiden is quite unsympathetic according to human values, showing no pity, although her discourse and revelation of her heavenly life does ease his grief. Her 'inhuman' aspect, like the logic of some of the parables she relates, defies comprehension from the limited, earthbound perspective, pointing the way to a faith beyond understanding. The dreamer remains a father to the end, proud of his daughter, 'my lyttel quene' (l. 1147), trying to cross the river to join her, 'For luf-longyng in gret delyt' (l. 1152). He finally accords his vision the status of an elevated experience, a 'veray avysyoun' (l. 1184), whereas earlier it was more neutrally a 'sweven' (l. 62) and a 'drem' (l. 1170), but its effect is only partially consoling.

Everything about *Piers Plowman* is extraordinary. The poem is uniquely complex, presenting an elaborate, multiple dream-sequence of eight dreams with two inner dreams.[9] The poem begins with several romance motifs, 'In a somer seson' (l. 1), with the wandering dreamer, Will, experiencing 'a ferly, of Fairye' (l. 6) as he falls asleep beside a stream and has 'a merveillous swevene' (l. 11).[10] The alliterative long line is adept at suggesting the languid mood of drowsiness:

> And as I lay and lenede and loked on the waters,   [leaned over]
> I slombred into a slepyng, it swayed so murye.   [made so sweet
> (ll. 9–10)   a sound]

But the generic markers are misleading, for this is no romance or love vision but a startlingly original theological treatise with 'a serious claim to be the greatest English poem of the Middle Ages'.[11] Authority figures met by Will multiply exponentially, encompassing an array of allegorical figures who instruct and guide Will – primarily, Holy Church, Reason and Conscience. The eponymous Piers is an extraordinary composite figure who appears at irregular intervals in ever-changing guises – as ploughman, priest, pope, the incarnate Christ and the embodiment of the true Christian ethos. The kaleidoscopic series of adventures ranges across twenty passus (Lat. 'steps', here, the divisions of the poem) only to ends with an ongoing, unresolved quest as Conscience leaves to seek Piers. No dream vision ever concluded in such an unresolved fashion – in effect, denying closure, with the dream world continuing unobserved.

Dream Landscapes

The traditional setting of the love vision in French poetry is springtime or May, situated in a sensuous natural world or a garden of love, which blends the Classical *locus amoenus* (pleasant place) with the biblical *hortus conclusus* (enclosed garden) from the Song of Songs. The four dream visions under consideration in this chapter reconfigure this archetypal landscape to suit their own individual purposes. *The Book of the Duchess* defers entry into the dream landscape, beginning with the narrator's imaginative recounting of a story in a book, Alcione's dream of the House of Morpheus. The cave of the god of sleep is fittingly evoked as a place of strange and ominous power located in a 'derke valey':

> That stant betwixe roches tweye   [two mountains]
> That never yet grew corn ne gras ...
> Save ther were a few welles
> Came rennynge fro the clyves adoun,   [cliffs]
> That made a dedly slepynge soun. (ll. 156–7, 160–2)

This ominous setting, in a cave 'also derk / As helle-pit (ll. 170–1), conjures up grim associations before the mood is abruptly altered with a return to the bedroom. The frame and dream world then merge, blurring boundaries since the bedroom walls depict scenes in a forest. Birdsong signals transition, here initiating re-entry into the dream world (where in the *Parliament of Fowles*, it returns the dreamer to a waking state). The event is oddly realised as the dreamer moves from his bed onto horseback to follow the hunt depicted on his windows, 'up anoon / I ... Took my hors, and forth I wente / Out of my chamber' (ll. 356–8). Finally reaching the forest, he is led by a 'whelp' to a flowery meadow where the Man in Black sits beneath an oak tree. Here, Black's account of his suffering conjures up allegorical scenes of Fortune personified and love as a game of chess, in which Black loses his White queen. The *Parliament of Fowles* also proceeds in stages, from a recounted dream from a book to a hesitantly entered allegorical world in which he sees Cupid and various personifications:

> Tho was I war of Plesaunce anon-ryght,
> And of Aray, and Lust, and Curteysie.   [clothing]
> (ll. 218–19)

In the Temple of Venus, the dreamer sees languid Classical deities and painted depictions of tragic lovers (ll. 288–92) derived from Boccaccio's *Teseida*.[12]

From here the dreamer moves outside to an idyllic countryside where the goddess Nature is convening a gathering of birds seeking to choose a Valentine's Day mate. The impression is immediately lively and refreshing after the stultifying atmosphere of Venus's temple:

> And in a launde, upon a hill of floures,
> Was set this noble goddesse Nature,
> Of braunches were here halles and here boures. (ll. 302–5)

Pearl begins in a garden 'erbere' (l. 9) but soon shifts to a graveyard where the dreamer lost his pearl. The burial place is a flowery and aromatic meadow, 'þat spot of spysez mot nedez sprede' [must be overspread] (l. 25), with 'Gilofre [gillyflower], gyngure, and gromylyon, [gromwell] / And pyonys [peonies] powdered ay bytwene' (ll. 43–4). Set against this blossoming growth is the unusual time of year; the 'hyȝ seysoun' of August is one of imminent decay, like Keats's 'season of mists and mellow fruitfulness'.[13] Various biblical associations may be in play, with the imagery of seeds and harvests which dominates the opening of the poem, such as the destructive harvest metaphor in the Book of Revelation (14:15–16) and parables in the gospels of St Mathew (e.g. 13:4–8; 13:18–30) and St John (4:35–7; 15:1–6), which employ metaphors of crop-tending as suggestive images of gaining eternal life. The literal-minded dreamer is, as yet, oblivious to any such suggestions of possible salvation and resurrection. He falls asleep after a passionate expression of grief, 'I playned my perle' (l. 53), made drowsy by the heady scents of the flowers:

> Suche odour to my hernez schot [brains rushed]
> I slode vpon a slepyng-slaȝte [deep sleep]
> (ll. 58–9)

The intensifying verbs continue as the narrator's spirit 'sprang in space' (l. 61) on an 'aventure þer mervaylez meven' [a quest where marvels occur] (l. 64). He finds himself in a mysterious landscape, 'I ne wyste in þis worlde quere þat hit wace' (l. 65). The description is detailed and ornate, wonderfully visual with its crystal cliffs, blue woods, silver leaves, gravel path made of pearls – a place where his senses are acute and aware of the 'frech flauores of frytez' (l. 87) which nourish him like food. This strange otherworld contains brightly coloured birds producing music to compare with the 'sytole-stryng [citole] and gyternere [cithern]' (l. 91). Guided by a force he identifies as Fortune, he travels easily through this land until he reaches a river, whose bed is made of jewels with pebbles of emerald, sapphire and other precious stones. The river is the boundary between life and death, separating him from his daughter on the far bank. His vision ends when he is seized by a desire to cross the river and wakes.

116

The Dream of Consolation

The distancing effect of the dream frame can accommodate the painful personal emotion of bereavement. Some dream visions specifically explore the world of inner feeling, mental confusion, anguish and conflict in ways which foreshadow later developments of fictive characterisation. The dream vision necessarily constructs a narrative persona with an incipient self-awareness and psychology.

The dream proper in the *Book of the Duchess* begins only in line 445. Theory encounters experience when the dreamer meets Black and prompts a confession from him which eases his suffering, providing the original 'talking therapy', 'discure me youre woo, I wolde ... Amende hyt, yif I kan or may' (ll. 549–52). Under the dreamer's tutelage, Black laments his lost love (ll. 560–709), his speech constructed around a series of antitheses, 'my wele is woo, / My good ys harm' (ll. 603–4). Black's memories are staged via the metaphors of Fortune as falsehood personified (l. 618ff.) and himself as a beaten opponent in her game of chess. His suicidal desire is assuaged through textual exempla, enacting a cathartic process considering Classical and biblical figures who suffered similar grief – Socrates, Medea, Dido, Echo and Delilah. A further technique which diffuses Black's pain is the dreamer's manifestly obtuse questions, 'Good sir, telle me al hooly / In what wyse, how, why and wherfore' (ll. 746–7). The second stage of Black's therapeutic discourse is an encomium (ll. 758–1297) in which he revives happy memories of meeting and falling in love with White, recalling in detail her physical appearance and personality (ll. 841–1041). After finally naming her (l. 948), the Man in Black can voice his passion:

> For certes she was, that swete wif,
> My suffisaunce, my lust, my lyf,   [desire]
> Myn hap, myn hele, and al my blesse,   [health]
> My worldes welfare, and my goddesse,
> And I hooly hires and everydel. (ll. 1037–41)

The dreamer's conspicuously dull response of lukewarm assent provokes an intense reaction from Black, amassing examples from Classical mythology (Hercules, Hector, Alexander) to demonstrate White's exceptional nature. Black now realises that it is an honour 'To do hir worship and ... servise' (l. 1098) and is willing to proclaim his love in the face of the dreamer's continuing obtuseness, 'What los ... ? Nyl she not love thow?' (l. 1140). Black's love poetry enshrines the vocabulary and sentiment of courtly love with its lexis of service and grace and the ring as an emblem of love. Whether inadvertently or skilfully, the dreamer successfully leads Black to acceptance of the fact of White's death (l. 1309).

Pearl offers far less in the way of effective consolation. The main difference is that here the dreamer is the bereaved subject experiencing the dream vision. The situation is emphatically personal, directly voiced from the outset, 'I hardyly saye' (l. 3). The poem starts as an elegy in an allegorical mode, then moves on to encompass key theological doctrines through dramatised debate and spiritual revelation. The first stanza enigmatically introduces the lost love object, 'pryvy perle wythouten spotte' (l. 35), 'my own spotless pearl / Pearl', as both gem and beloved child, in terms which apply equally to both:

So rounde, so reken in uche araye,	[radiant]
So small, so smothe her sides were.	[slender]
(ll. 5–6)	

A widespread symbol of chastity and purity, the pearl is also literally valuable, 'to princes paye' (l. 1), pleasing or profitable to a prince. The metaphors create a complex mix of suggestion, which the rest of the poem develops in sophisticated ways.

Far from exploiting the potential pathos and empathy, the poem creates a challenging vision of the lost child, depicting her as a distant, otherworldly figure. The Pearl Maiden is effectively absent for half of the poem, entering at line 161, active between lines 241 and 976, and then receding before making one final appearance towards the end. While not offering comfort as we know it, she seeks to ease his suffering through instruction and revelation. The central part of the poem (sections 5–16) forms a debate in four stages. She relates the parable of the vineyard, elucidates the nature of grace and merit and the place of the innocent in heaven, explains Christ's suffering, her life with the Lamb, and presents the dreamer with a vision of the New Jerusalem. Along the way, she redefines terms such as 'deme', 'blysse' and courstesy, distinguishing between earthly and divine perspectives. The concatenation words,* which link each stanza via repetition, highlight key concepts such as 'more', plenty', what is 'just' and perfect. Although the dreamer breaks through the vision by trying to cross the river and remains saddened at the end, he seems to have moved from despair to a greater faith.

The Dream of Social and Political Commentary

The liberating possibilities of the dream vision enable poets to explore social commentary and reformist satire, perhaps most spectacularly in *Piers Plowman*, which is discussed in Part Four: 'Fun and Games'. A smaller-scale and more veiled social commentary appears in the *Parliament of Fowles*. The title itself suggests a parodic parliament, and Chaucer has altered his models by introducing greater social variety along with legal and procedural terms. Parliament (lit. 'talking place') was developing at the time from an occasional body comprising aristocracy, knights and bourgeoisie which primarily authorised taxation, to a regular debating-chamber seeking to influence policy, recently having gone so far as to indict and execute several of the king's favourites. The assembly of birds is an example of the popular beast fable genre which traditionally satirised human society.[14] Drawing on Alain de Lisle's *De Planctu Naturae* (The Complaint of Nature), where Nature's robes are covered in bird images, and Vincent of Beauvais's encyclopedia, *Speculum Naturale* (Mirror of Nature), Chaucer first summarises the many species of bird present then presents the

---

* Concatenation (Lat. 'bound in a chain') is a term for a system of verbal linking.

discussion between representatives of different classes: flesh-eating (corresponding to the aristocracy), seed-eating (the lesser nobility), worm-eating and water-fowl (the lower orders).[15] The mixed gathering of birds provides a lively debate in which contrasting voices feature, foreshadowing the *Canterbury Tales*'s interest in a diverse range of characters; there is a sharp divide between the noble eagles competing for the female formel*, who subscribe to notions of courtly love, and the lower-status birds, who mock and demystify such elaborate pretensions. To some extent, the opposition is complicated by differences between the eagles, the first voicing conventional devotion, 'my soverayn lady; merci ... grace ... my deere herte' (ll. 416, 421, 427). The second eagle betrays a less refined attitude, 'That shal nat be! I love hire bet than ye don, be seint John ... do me hangen by the hals!' (ll. 449–50), while the third speaks more hesitantly and briefly, 'at short wordes' (l. 481) and argues that long devotion is no more deserving than recent (a view perfectly in accord with the parable of the vineyard in *Pearl*). The poem poses the conundrum, 'which is the most worthy?' It is unclear whether the eagles' disappointment and the deferral of a decision is to be seen as an indictment of their attitudes or whether their refined aspirations are admirable, juxtaposed as they are with the less 'romantic', practical desires of the other birds to mate, which are fulfilled. The lower-status birds are sketched amusingly, using a colloquial idiom, 'Have don!' (l. 492), 'Com of!' (l. 494), ending in sheer animal noise, 'Kek kek! Kokkow! Quek quek!' (l. 499). The polyvocality is problematic. Incongruity and disparity remain unresolved. When Nature finally arbitrates, she unambiguously asserts the merit of the royal eagle:

> If I were Resoun, thanne wolde I
> Conseyle yow the royal tercel take [...]
> As for the gentilleste and most worthi. (ll. 632–3, 635)

However, she is not Reason, and she allows the formel a free choice:

* A formel is a female bird, especially the female of any of the species used in hawking.

120

That she hireself shal han eleccioun
Of whom hire lest; whoso be wroth or blythe,
Hym that she cheest, he shal hire han as swithe. (ll. 621–3)

However, the phrasing begs a good many questions about genuine choice and constraint. These become pronounced when the formel responds in terms which foreclose any notion of free will:

Soth it that I am evere under your yerde,   [authority]
As is everich other creature,
And mot be youres whil my lyf may dure. (ll. 640–2)

She makes an emotional plea for a year's respite, in tones approaching despair, 'Ye gete no more, although ye do me deye!' (l. 651). This unwillingness to choose a mate places her in the company of Emily in 'The Knight's Tale', the only other female figure in Chaucer who expresses such a disinclination. Although the debate is left unresolved, harmony appears restored in the musical finale of the roundel.

The Dream of Revelation and Apocalypse

The Book of Revelation supplies two very different scenarios exploited in dream vision texts – one of heavenly perfection fulfilled, the other of the attendant apocalyptic destruction. The B-text of *Piers Plowman* focuses on the latter in its climactic final passus with Antichrist and his followers, the friars, attacking the last bastion of Christendom, the Barn of Unity. After the devastation wrought by waves of plague and corruption, Conscience is driven to set out on pilgrimage to find the redemptive but elusive Piers. It is a grim ending refusing to supply a conclusive resolution. From Section 16 where the Maiden presents the dreamer with a vision of the Apocalyptic City of the New Jerusalem, *Pearl* uses the Book of Revelation following closely the biblical description:

As John the apostel hit syy with sight,
I syye þat city of gret renoun. (ll. 985–6)

The dreamer sees, 'This noble cite ... sodaynly ful ... Of such vergynes in the same gyse ... coronde wern alle of the same fasoun ... in perles and wedes qwyte' (ll. 1097–1102). From seeing his pearl as unique at the beginning of the poem, 'I sette hyr sengeley in synglure' (l. 8), he comes to appreciate her place in the massed ranks of the 144,000 brides of the lamb, the virgins betrothed to Christ. Seeing the Lamb's wound, 'ful wyde and weete' (l. 1135) bleeding profusely, the dreamer is moved to pity, 'Alas, thought I, who did þat spyt?' (l. 1138). His compassion marks a new stage in his development, enlightened by his experience even as his grief remains.

Journeys through space and time, imagining marvellous worlds and mythical encounters, constitute the 'space odyssey' of dream vision. The genre clearly appealed to poets as supplying opportunities for exploration and discovery. Dream vision poetry investigates all sorts of internal states, while finding new ways to convey meaning via symbols and allegory. As a realm where imagination can play freely, the liminal space of the dream allows literal and latent meanings to coexist. Dream vision probes the nature of meaning and authority, combining subtly subjective perspectives with cogent commentaries on contemporary issues.

Extended Commentary: Langland, *Piers Plowman*

Passus 18 forms the climax of the dream sequence, a moment of apotheosis for Will, enabling him to experience firsthand the events of the Crucifixion and Harrowing of Hell, which achieves mankind's redemption by reconciling the Old and New laws. The narrative exploits mixed modes, variously allegory, typology, sermon, vision, drama and narrative. Langland's language avoids the excessive rhetorical ornament favoured by many alliterative poets, while exploiting the possibilities of the alliterative long line. This proves a flexible medium for his idiosyncratic style, able to accommodate a range of expression from learned Latin citations and scholastic terminology to the most robust, colloquial and proverbial utterance.

The opening lines of passus 18 demonstrate Langland's style and technique. A few lines (1–3) sketchily present the dreamer, Will, in his typical lowly guise, 'wolleward and weetshoed' [shirtless and sockless], 'a recchelees renk' [man caring for nothing], 'lik a lorel' [a wastrel]. This humble figure experiences his sixth dream vision at the time of Lent as the waking world framing the dream dissolves into an Easter vision, which transports Will back in time to witness Jesus's crucifixion. Yet, unlike the Affective tradition, Langland's style is notably lacking in the visual detail which invites the reader imaginatively to be present. There is remarkable little to picture. The barest of details is given, merely naming personages in the dream, the 'gerles' [children] and 'olde folk' (ll. 7–8) who launch the vision with songs from the Easter liturgy to an organ accompaniment, merging seamlessly into 'the peple' (l. 9), to the figure of Faith who answers Will's questions, explaining the scene before him. The dream landscape is absent; there is no gradual approach but, instead, the most sudden of encounters presented in the most casual of ways as Will sees 'Oon sembable to the Samaritan, and somdeel to Piers the Plowman' (l. 10) [someone resembling the Samaritan, rather like Piers the ploughman]. This is exactly the kind of challenging allegory which defeats any attempt at visualising the figure, instead inviting intellectual consideration. The figure of the Samaritan, met in the previous dream, is associated with charity, selflessness and moral teaching, while Piers has been something of a shapeshifter, appearing irregularly throughout the poem. The immediate significance of the comparison is uncertain. Only when the dreamer asks whether Piers is present is the mysterious reference explained (ll. 22–3):

> This Jesus of his gentries wol juste in Piers armes,   [joust]
> In his helm and in his haubergeon – *humana natura*.   [mailcoat]

The peculiar nature of Piers, the tantalising and fractured presence weaving throughout the poem, is defined in this section as representative of humanity. The 'oon' (named as Jesus in line 19) is described on his entrance as a disguised knight riding into Jerusalem about to win his spurs (ll. 11–14), appropriately heralded by Faith, who announces the name of the combatant (l. 15). This metaphor presenting Jesus as knight is familiar from devotional poetry but Langland typically inverts the romance motifs so that this knight rides a humble ass and is conspicuously unarmed and without armour, 'Barefoot ... Withouten spores other spere'. This allegory is sustained throughout the passus – first presenting the crucifixion (ll. 11–36) and the Longinus episode (ll. 78–100) as jousting bouts in a tournament, later treating the Harrowing of Hell* – as a knightly quest (ll. 262–409). Langland masterfully combines the expected lexis and imagery with unexpected details and events which both enlist and frustrate assumptions, so that once again a keen attention is required to receive the cues and respond quickly to incongruent and innovative elements.

The crucifixion, the central event of Christianity, is in many ways the climactic moment of Will's journey, even though it occurs two passus before the end of the poem. Will experiences a privileged insight into the process of salvation, witnessing at firsthand not just the death of Jesus but also his triumphant assault on hell, freeing the damned and thus enacting the potential of release which applies to all Christians. In effect, a new image of heroism is formed whereby accepting death is a victory (cf. the much earlier Old English poem, *The Dream of the Rood*, depicting Christ as a Germanic warrior). The quiet pathos of the event is strikingly understated but powerful:

> Pitousliche and pale as a prison that deith,   [prisoner]
> The lord of lif and of light tho leide hise eighen todideres. [then]
> (ll. 58–9)

Momentarily the contemplative aspects are to the fore, inviting an emotional response to a sharply realised scene. Solid blocks of coherent

---

* The Harrowing of Hell is a Christian doctrine concerning the descent of Christ into Hell and his release of the good souls confined there.

narrative are juxtaposed with fragmented incidents and a range of disparate voices, disrupting any sense of neat progression. Voices are introduced suddenly, with direct speech from historical figures (Pilate) and typological ones (Faith=Abraham), pure abstractions (Death) exist side by side with the risen dead (l. 64), individual voices sound at intervals, from the 'pelour' (l. 40), to the 'cachepol' (l. 47), while an undifferentiated crowd is represented by snatches of reported comment, 'Some seide that he was Goddes sone, that so faire deyde ... And some seide he was a wicche' (ll. 68–9). The whole creates a mobile sound picture which is restless, unpredictable and fluid. The effect is unsettling and at times bewildering as at any moment a 'Goblin' may start speaking, appearing from nowhere; this element of surprise can as easily switch to patriarchs and prophets and many hundreds of angels!

Dividing the two scenes of Christ's triumph is the dramatised episode of the Four Daughters of God, a hugely expanded account of Psalm 85.* Langland's ear for voice is readily apparent as he invests the four women with distinctive personalities largely through their speech; clothing and gesture also play a part in contributing to the liveliness of their interactive debate. This scene epitomises dramatic allegory as a vivid, engaging technique. The four sisters embody the conflict between the Old and New Laws, their final reconciliation marking the climax of the passus, enacting the harmony made possible by Christ's sacrifice. Langland retains the symbolism while effectively humanising the abstract concepts, rendering the argument intelligible as a case of quarrelling siblings. Mercy first enters from the west followed by Righteousness (Justice) from the north, Truth from the east and finally Peace from the south. By suspending the main narrative, they provide both diversion and exposition as they argue about the justness of mankind's salvation. The dramatic mode expresses conflict and tension through speaking interaction. Mercy speaks courteously, with extended complex sentences filled with balance and easy authority, 'Have no merveille ... that was tynt thorugh tree, tree shal it wynne' (ll. 127, 140).

* The original psalm (cited in *Piers Plowman*, l. 424) consists of ten words, *Misericordia et veritas obviaverunt sibi; iusticia et pax osculate sunt* (mercy and truth are met together; justice and peace have kissed).

By contrast, Truth's manner of speaking is harsh and marked by negatives and cursory dismissal of Mercy's gentle narration, 'That thow tellest ... is but a tale of waltrot! [rubbish] ... Hold thy tonge, Mercy! ... I, Truthe, woot [know] the soothe' (ll. 142, 146, 147). Peace, clothed in 'pacience' (another of Langland's characteristically 'impossible' images!) runs in to join them, bearing a love-letter and speaking in a suitably innocent, even gushing, way, 'My wil is to wende ... and welcome hem alle ... Mercy shul [singe], / And I shal daunce therto – do thow so, suster!' (ll. 175, 178–9). Justice's 'personality' is even more clearly demarcated by her manner of speech, 'What, ravestow? [are you crazy?] ... or thow art right dronke!' (l. 187). Sin is final, in her grim opinion as she seeks to conclude the debate:

> Forthi, lat hem chewe as thei chosen, and chide we noght, sutres,
> For it is botelees bale, the byte that thei eten.   [incurable evil]
> (ll. 200–1)

The last word is not hers as Peace persists in hoping for a happier outcome. At this point, Book appears, personifying the Bible, and delivers a monologue (ll. 229–59). Langland's technique is complex here as he creates a personified abstraction who in turn deploys personification allegory. Far from sounding lofty and portentous, this prophesying figure is characterised by an enthusiastic energy enforced by run-on lines as he urges us to 'see' the amazing events of Christ's conception and death:

> 'I wol bere witnesse
> That tho this barn was ybore, ther blased a sterre   [when]
> That alle the wise of the world in o wit acordeden ... [one opinion]
> And lo! How the sonne gan louke hire light in hirselve   [conceal]
> When she seigh hym suffer ...
> Lo! Helle myghte nat holde, but opnede the roche.' (ll. 231–3,
> 245–6, 249).

The Harrowing of Hell sequence is also managed dramatically, marked by a predilection for direct speech (cf. the York 'Play of the Crucifixion'). A rabble of squabbling devils contrast with Christ's eloquence, 'I that am lord of lif, love is my drynke ... I that am kyng of kynges shal come' (l. 366). After a long legalistic exchange, addressing theological matters, the actual victory is literally achieved by the Word/word:

> 'Dukes of this dymme place, anoon undo thise Yates,   [immediately]
> That Crist may come in, the Kynges son of Hevene!'
> And with that breeth, helle brak. (ll. 320–2)

The effect of this vision on the dreamer is instant and energising as Will, woken by the Easter bells, rouses his family to go with him to church. In the final words of the passus, the everyday world returns with specificity, with Will addressing 'Kytte my wif and Calote my doghter' (l. 429). The return to waking reality is aligned with an appreciation of the universal access to salvation, symbolised by the cross, whose significance is now intensely clear to Will and available to all:

> For Goddes blissede body it bar for oure boote ...   [salvation]
> May no grisly goost glide there it shadweth! (ll. 432, 434)

This marks a climactic moment of revelation for Will but does not conclude the quest. Within a few lines of the poem, the restless spirit is soon once more engaged in dreaming.

Notes

1   Cited by D. S. Brewer (ed.), *The Parliament of Fowls* (Manchester: Manchester University Press, 1972; originally published London: Thomas Nelson and Sons, 1960), p. 17.

2   This classification is based on that of Elizabeth Salter and Derek Pearsall (eds), *Piers Plowman* (London: Arnold, 1967), pp. 9–19.

3   'The Nun's Priest's Tale' in *The Riverside Chaucer*, ed. Larry D. Benson (Oxford: Oxford University Press, 1989). All references to Chaucer's works

shall be to this edition unless otherwise stated.

4   Walter Hilton defines the four levels of exegesis in *The Scale of Perfection*, ed. E. Underhill (London: Watkins, 1923), II.43, p. 445: 'By the letter, that is lightest and most plain, is the bodily kind comforted; by morality of Holy Writ, the soul is informed of vices and virtues ... by mystihood it is illumined for to ... apply words of Holy Writ to Christ our head, and to Holy Kirk that is his mystical body. And the fourth, that is to heavenly, longeth only to the working of love, and for that is most like to heavenly feeling, therefore I call it heavenly.'

5   Priscilla Martin, *Chaucer's Women: Nuns, Wives and Amazons* (London: Macmillan, 1996), p. 28.

6   A. C. Spearing, *Medieval Dream Poetry* (Cambridge: Cambridge University Press, 1976), p. 72.

7   Paul Strohm, *Social Chaucer* (London: Harvard University Press, 1989), pp. 51–5.

8   A. C. Cawley and J. J. Anderson (eds), *Pearl, Cleanness, Patience, Sir Gawain and the Green Knight* (London: Dent, 1985).

9   There are three versions of *Piers Plowman*, thought to represent a series of revisions. They are designated as the 'A' 'B' and 'C' texts. A is the shortest, at 2,572 lines; B has 7,241 lines, with nine additional passus; C is a revision of B, with some additions, totalling 7,354 lines.

10   A. V. C. Schmidt (ed.), *The Vision of Piers Plowman: a Complete Edition of the B-Text* (London: Dent, 1984).

11   Schmidt (ed.), *Vision of Piers Plowman*, p. xii.

12   For a modern translation of the relevant section of Boccaccio's *Teseida*, see D. S. Brewer (ed.), *The Parliament of Fowls* (Manchester: Manchester University Press, 1972), Appendix IV.

13   John Keats, 'Ode to Autumn' (l. 1), in *Keats: Poetical Works*, ed. H. W. Garrod (Oxford: Oxford University Press, 1989).

14   For discussion of similar bird assemblies in medieval French poetry, see Helen Phillips and Nick Havely (eds), *Chaucer's Dream Poetry* (Harlow: Longman, 1997), p. 226.

15   Vincent names sixteen specific types of hawk (1.16.14). Bird lore traditionally ranked birds in a hierarchy, resembling social orders, the 'royal' eagle being the most noble, with other birds of prey such as the goshawk, falcon, sparrowhawk and merlin representing lesser aristocratic ranks (hunting with birds of prey and falconry being favourite pastimes of the aristocratic elite). In bestiaries and heraldry, different species were associated with human attributes; for example, the unclean and lustful owl who portended doom, the cowardly kite and so on.

Acting Up: Medieval Drama

The Classical tradition of drama was lost in the medieval period apart from some Roman plays, such as those of Terence, six of which were translated by Hrotsvitha of Gandersheim (*c.* 935–*c.* 1002) for her nuns to read or possibly even perform. It was not until *c.* 1250 that Greek drama was rediscovered in the West, with a poor translation of Aristotle's *Poetics* translated into Latin from Arabic sources.

Yet a considerable body of dramatic work survives from the later medieval period, customarily classified into three main types: Mystery plays (biblical stories re-enacted by amateur guild members), Morality plays (moral interludes and allegorical drama), and Miracle plays (mainly continental examples, including saints' plays and edifying stories of miracles). A body of vernacular drama evolved from a range of practices – some popular, such as folk drama and mummers' plays, some ecclesiastical, including the Bible, Church liturgy and sermons. Medieval drama is essentially grounded in religion at a time when literacy was an ecclesiastical preserve. It is a drama of faith, deriving from church rituals and ceremonial which encouraged mimetic re-enactment. Among these liturgical tropes is that enacted by priests at Easter, *Quem Quaeritis?* (Whom do you seek?), which concerns the visit of the three Marys to Christ's sepulchre.* At the heart of Roman

---

* Mary Magdalene, Mary Salome and Mary Cleophas are companions of the Virgin Mary, who were all present at Jesus's Crucifixion, and, in some Gospel accounts, visit his tomb and discover it to be empty.

Catholicism is the central mystery of the Mass, re-enacting the Last Supper in which the Host is ceremoniously consecrated, elevated and consumed as the real body of Christ (the doctrine of transubstantiation). In addition, there were many church processions and playlets which presented dramatic reconstructions of biblical events, so that a rich and multi-faceted tradition of performance was available. The older theory of a lineal development from Latin drama in the church to vernacular works is now largely discredited, the two apparently co-existing and mutually informing one another. The earliest surviving vernacular drama is from the twelfth century, *Le Jeu d'Adam* or *Mystère d'Adam*, which already contains a sizeable cast (of clergy), full stage directions and costume details, testifying to a highly developed form of drama from an early date.

The Feast of Corpus Christi

Most surviving medieval drama comes from the Corpus Christi play cycles. As described above, the body of Christ is at the heart of Roman Catholicism, according to Christ's announcement at the Last Supper, '*hic est corpus meum*' (Lat. 'this is my body'). Receiving the eucharist, one of the seven sacraments, was an article of faith with communion required of all Christians annually following the 1318 Lateran Council. At about the same time, a new annual church feast was introduced based on the injunctions received from a female visionary, St Juliana, a century earlier. Her visions of the eucharist were kept secret for twenty years before they came to the attention of the church. Pope Urban IV first proclaimed the new feast of Corpus Christi in 1264 but died soon afterwards, leaving it to Clement V to promulgate the feast assigned to the Thursday after Trinity Sunday (occurring between 23 May and 24 June). This was the impetus behind the development of a summer

---

* Not all of the surviving cycles adhered to the festival date, however, as the Lincoln Cycle took place on St Anne's day (26 July), while Chester moved its performance to Whitsun and the N-Town Cycle is set for a Sunday performance.

festival, during the time of maximum daylight hours, on which to stage the ambitious cycle of biblical drama known as the Mystery plays.*

The new feast proved immensely popular, giving rise to the foundation of hundreds of dedicated fraternities (organisations which functioned as religious affiliations providing their members with a range of services from helping with funerals, poor relief and legal aid to funding social events). Several university colleges adopted the name, such as those at Cambridge (1352) and Oxford in the sixteenth century. By 1389, forty-four Corpus Christi fraternities are known to have existed in England. These were wealthy and powerful bodies, the York Corpus Christi fraternity (founded 1414) counting Richard III among its members. Cycle drama existed at the intersection of religious belief and civic glory until the Feast of Corpus Christi was abolished in England in 1548, although plays continued to be performed for some time afterwards.*

Non-Naturalistic and Didactic Drama

The cycle plays treat scriptural material and are designed to educate as well as to entertain. They are structured around a system of correspondences known as typology (Gk *tupos*, a mark left by a bow). This type of allegory, as widespread as irony is today, retains a sense of historical reference so that the literal level is important as well as the figurative. This shared system of correspondences explains why different cycles contain a very similar selection of biblical stories. Typology relied on established connections between Old Testament 'types' and New Testament 'antitypes'. For example, Jonah's three days in the whale's belly were seen to prefigure Christ's three days in the tomb; the story of Abraham and Isaac foreshadows that of God the Father sacrificing his son, Jesus; Moses leading the Israelites from slavery across the Red Sea is a figure of Christ releasing the souls from Hell, and so on. Typological

---

* The final performances of the Chester, Wakefield and York cycles were in 1575, 1576 and 1580 respectively.

meanings are explicitly spelled out throughout the Chester cycle by figures such as Doctor, Preco and Nuntius commenting on the action depicted and explaining its significance, as in the play 'Abraham and Isaac', wherein the figure of the Expositor informs the audience:

> By Isaac understand I may
> Ihesu that was obedient aye.[1]

The view of history portrayed by the cycles is a theocentric one, with God as the still, fixed point at the centre of creation. The drama is influenced by a typological conception of time as an unfolding divinely ordained plan, experienced as linear by human beings in its 'earthbound' form, while infinite and contemporaneous from the perspective of God at a point of heavenly timelessness. The treatment of time in the plays balances past, present and future: the Jerusalem setting of the Passion is simultaneously the city space of York, whose citizens are being directly addressed (hence the frequent anachronisms, swearing by Christ, Mary, Mohammed and suchlike). The cycles begin and end 'out of time' with visions of God before Creation and after the end of the world. The Chester Cycle, for example, introduces God poised beyond temporal dimensions:

> It is my will it shoulde be soe,
> Hit is, yt was, it shal be thus. (ll. 3–4)

So we do not come to medieval drama expecting to find fully realised, individual personalities. The dramatis personae of medieval plays are primarily 'types' rather than characters. It would be anachronistic to demand consistency of characterisation, motivation and so on. There were thirty actors playing Jesus in the York Cycle, so any notion of consistency of representation is absurd. Various typical roles developed, so that the Chester Antichrist, York Pharaoh, and N-Town* and Coventry Herod all display similar characteristics constituting a typical

* The designation 'N-Town' serves in the absence of a particular name.

boastful tyrant. One famous stage direction from the Coventry 'Shearmen and Tailors' Play' directs that 'Erode ragis in the pagond and in the street also' (Happé, p. 374) [Herod rages on the pageant wagon and also in the street], delivering this sort of bombastic rant:

> 'I stampe! I stare! I loke all abowtt! ...
> I rent! I rave! And now run I wode!'   [mad]
> (ll. 779, 781)

This is the kind of street performance that Chaucer is referring to in 'The Miller's Tale', where he comically miscasts the effeminate, squeaky-voiced Absolon, 'He pleyeth Herodes upon a scaffold hye' (MilT, l. 3384). Another comedic type is the cheeky boy servant, such as Garcio in the Wakefield 'Killing of Abel', later named as Pikeharness ('amour-stealer', i.e. thief). He opens the play with an instantly assertive presence, bridging the real and play worlds by calling for attention, heralding the arrival of his master, Cain:

> 'All hayll, all hayll, both blithe and glad,
> For here com I, a mery lad!' (ll. 1–2)

This is positively Puck-like! In fact, it is easy to see in medieval drama the prototypes for many aspects of Shakespearean drama: characters such as the frank villain, techniques such as the soliloquy, and mixed modes which juxtapose humour with tragedy. The non-naturalistic drama of the medieval period, which forged Shakespeare's practice, has much more in common with modern drama such as Beckett's sparse existentialism and Brecht's alienation than with the illusion-filled theatrical practice of the nineteenth century. Features which mark many contemporary pieces as boldly experimental are essentially returning to medieval practices: an all-male cast, symbolism rather than realism, bare settings with few props, relying on the audience's active participation in creating imaginative effects. Another core element of medieval drama is music, serving many functions. With no lighting or stage curtain, music is used to mark the beginning and endings of plays but is also thematically charged in some cases. In the Wakefield 'Second Shepherds' Play', the upbeat rather raucous singing of the shepherds, along with the noisy singing of Mak and his wife trying to drown out the sheep's bleating, attests to fallen humanity's raw state before the angel's song inspires the shepherds' inept but sincere efforts to recall and sing it, and their final dignified 'hail' lyrics. The progress from disorder to harmony is underscored. There are usually very few stage directions, although some interesting indications of gesture and movement are found in N-Town suggesting travel between scaffolds and concealing mechanisms which part suddenly to reveal Christ at the Last Supper (p. 445). The Wakefield cycle is especially informative, containing sixty-eight scattered directions in Latin, offering tantalising hints of properties and stage action, such as Abraham sacrificing a ram, the angel seizing the end of his sword, Melchisadech riding and presenting a horse laden with spoils.

Varieties of Cycle Drama

Substantial documentary evidence survives which provides a full picture of the context in which the mystery cycles were produced.[2] The widespread existence of drama is attested. For example, Beverly once had a cycle of thirty-eight plays although none of them have survived. Great losses of material occurred at the Reformation.[3] Luckily, four substantial cycles survive, from York (forty-eight plays performed at twelve stations), Wakefield or 'Towneley'* (thirty-two plays), Chester (twenty-four plays which moved from Corpus Christi to a three-day Whitsun festival, performing nine, eight and seven plays respectively at four stations) and East Anglia or 'N-Town'[4] (forty-two plays) along with many fragments; for example, plays from Newcastle, Norwich and Coventry. Each cycle, grounded in the Bible, spans events from Creation to Doomsday and contains similar episodes, yet it is important

---

* The manuscript containing these plays was in the possession of the Towneley family of Lancashire, and the cycle was named accordingly by some editors. There is some debate about how far the Wakefield attribution given to two plays in the manuscript applies to all of the plays.

not to overgeneralise or to create an impression of sameness where great variety exists. The scale varies, with York requiring thirty actors as Christ, while Wakefield and Chester only feature eleven. Chester alone presents plays of 'Antichrist' and 'Balaam and Balak'. There is evidence for the sharing of material, with Chester and Wakefield both apparently borrowing several plays from the York Cycle (three and five respectively). Some cycles treat individual episodes as fragmented pieces shared among several guilds which others expand, condense or amalgamate. The thriving East Anglian drama seems to represent several towns pooling their resources, as the 'N-Town' Cycle is a mobile performance cycle with no particular city connection (hence the 'N' denoting any name, probably indicating a mobile acting company). This cycle's composite nature has been analysed by Peter Meredith, showing that a once-separate 'Mary Play' (numbers 8–13 of the thirty-eight extant plays) was inserted and divided up into smaller units, and the 'Passion Play' sequence was formed from two independent plays.[5] Marian material rarely survives as it was particularly likely to be expunged by Renaissance Reformers, so the York plays of the Death, Ascension and Coronation of Mary are exceptional. The late Chester banns show erasure of some material deemed sensitive after the Reformation, referring to the Corpus Christi festival and Mary (Happé, pp. 47–8).

There is great stylistic and tonal variety. The Wakefield Pilate is a complex study of evil, while the York Pilate is a figure of some pathos unable to escape the fate foretold in his wife's dream. 'Abraham and Isaac' features an adult Isaac in York but a young child in Brome, to very different effect. York and Wakefield are marked by emotional intensity and occasionally riotous knockabout farce. By contrast, the Chester Cycle is singularly restrained and contemplative, favouring explicit didacticism and with little exuberance or emotive appeal. Chester presents a very stern God, a more divine, less humanised Christ, more miracles than any other cycle, and plenty of direct quotation from the Bible (usually translated quickly into English). It has been described as almost virulently anti-feminist with its many negative depictions of and denunciations of women; for example, in the play of 'Adam and

Eve'. N-Town incorporates a good deal of popular, non-scriptural material into its nativity sequence, such as Joseph's fears of cuckoldry, the cherry tree miracle (p. 232) and the punishment of the irreverent midwives (p. 240). Christ's composure and distance in York contrasts powerfully with the emotional Jesus in N-Town, who displays real fear in the Garden of Gethsemane (p. 457) comparable to the real grief felt by Mary (p. 463).

Mystery Plays

Another term for the cycle drama is 'Mystery plays' (Lat. *mysterium*, 'craft'), coined by nineteenth-century scholars seeking to highlight the guild associations, along with the amateur and folk nature of the cycles (the word 'mystery' in this sense is not attested before 1744). As civic productions, the cycles were occasions for city celebrations. Part of the ceremonial involved the formal proclamation of the forthcoming plays, in banns such as those which survive from Chester:

> By craftsmen and mean men these pagentes are played,
> And to comens and country men accustomably before.
> (ll. 204–5)[6]

Cycles were civic events sponsored by guilds and city councils rather than the Church and performed by amateur craftsmen (although the clergy were probably instrumental as playwrights and producers). As such they were opportunities to advertise wealth and status:

> The said pageants are maintained and supported by the commons and the craftsmen of the same city in honour and reverence of our lord Jesus Christ and for the glory and benefit of the same city. (*York Memorandum Book*, 1399)

This statement reveals an interesting dual purpose, prioritising a religious impulse but according significant weight to civic status and wealth. The distribution of plays among the city guilds could sometimes be clearly suited to their craft; for example, Noah's Ark for the shipwrights, the lavish spectacle of the Last Judgement for the mercers (merchants), the Crucifixion for the pinners (pin makers), the Last Supper for the bakers. Putting on plays was an expensive undertaking, which, as guild fortunes fluctuated, could prove ruinous. In Norwich, the Guild of St Luke petitioned to be relieved of the obligation when they could no longer afford to stage their Pentecost play, claiming to be in great difficulties, 'almost decayed', 'soore charged with reparaciouns, fyndyng, and setting forth of the sayd pageants and disgisinges, which costes and charges causeth many persons being of substaunce and abilities to withdrawe them self and also there goode mynde'.[7]

Although the mystery plays constitute a community enterprise, various elements of society, such as peasants, children, servants and women, were excluded as participants, so that the inclusivity of the 'community' can be exaggerated. As far as we know, women did not act (the female parts, as in Shakespeare's time, were probably played by boys), although there is one tantalising reference to a lost Assumption play by the 'Wives of Chester'.

The York Cycle

The city of York was second only to London in terms of wealth and size, with its Archbishopric to rival Canterbury. The population was small by modern standards (*c.* 20,000) so that roughly one in sixty of the eligible population would be taking part in the cycle, not counting those involved in costumes, set-building and so on. The date of origin for the Corpus Christi play cycle in York is unknown but a cycle was certainly in existence by 1378, and continued for two hundred years before the final performance in 1569. The cycle comprises forty-eight plays, 14,000 lines and three hundred parts, and lasts approximately from dawn to dusk, a total of fourteen hours. Eleven plays present episodes from the Old Testament, thirteen treat the birth and ministry of Christ and twenty-three depict the passion sequence, concluding with the final play of the Day of Judgement. Such a costly event is well beyond modern theatrical budgets. The route followed by the pageant wagons in procession has been reconstructed and scaled-down re-enactments regularly take place, sometimes using original street locations. There was some fixed seating and some prime positions but, generally, the drama was performed as a mobile spectacle. The cycle began at the gates of York's Holy Trinity Church with the 'Creation and Fall of the Angels', performed by the barkers (i.e. tanners, who prepared hides for manufacture into leather goods). As an outdoor festival, the plays provided a vivid and intimate street theatre, with an audience able to wander at will, choosing to experience the plays as individual or continuous performances in any combination.

The detailed composition and circumstances of the cycle are preserved in city records: the *Ordo Paginarum* (1415), also known as 'Burton's List', which itemises the fifty 'pageants' forming the cycle; and *The Register* (1463–77), a copy of the play scripts kept by the town clerk.* Revisions to the texts show the cycle as a fluid piece, evolving and changing organically over time. The size and appearance of the stage area on the pageant wagon, must be inferred from the only surviving description of a pageant wagon in the 1433 inventory of properties and costumes for the Mercers' Guild's production of Doomsday. This account testifies to the elaborate scenic and special effects that could be involved: the wheeled wagon had a hell-mouth with painted clouds, gold stars, two sections of rainbow, red damask curtains enclosing the wagon on three sides, a heavenly space in which God was suspended and, most evocatively of all, nine small angels painted red 'to renne aboute in þe heven' and pulled by a cord. Other details are suggestive of an ornate and symbolic costuming: masks appear to have been worn by certain figures, with a gold mask for God, 'develles faces', wigs, and special costumes appropriate for 'good' and 'evil' souls. The post-Reformation Banns of Chester contain useful details of staging, referring to 'The Devill in his fethers, all ragge[d] and rente' (Walker, l. 123) and 'mynstrills … pipe, tabarte, and flute'

---

* Fifty plays are listed in *The Register*, of which forty-eight survive.

(l. 119). Clearly the cycle drama was a colourful and sensual spectacle, one which offered the audience a lively, interactive event and which was well placed to exploit meta-theatrical potential free from the constraints of naturalistic drama where illusory space must feign 'reality'.

As with all cycles, there are no named dramatists. Cycles were composite productions and periodically revised so the notion of specific authorship is anachronistic. The two crucifixion plays recorded in *The Register* show subsequent versions of a play – one an early fifteenth-century piece attributed to the 'York Realist', an individual playwright with a distinctive style apparently responsible for several plays (see the Extended Commentary in this chapter). Along with the 'Wakefield Master', he is as close as we come to identifying any individual playwright.* These two dramatists' bold style shows that there was potential for very independent, imaginative treatment and invention, even within the confines of the cycle tradition. One of the major objections of the Elizabethan reformers who banned the plays was their wayward, often unscriptural nature:

> I find manie thinges that I muche like because of th' antiquite, so see I manie thinges that I can not allowe, because they be Disagreinge from the senceritie of the Gospell.[8]

The N-Town 'Death of Herod'

The 'Death of Herod' is an unusual cycle play in many respects, but one which demonstrates the inventive and flexible nature of the genre. This play is unique among the cycles in presenting an allegorical figure, Death personified, a feature more typical of Morality plays. This self-proclaimed villain soliloquises as an early example of the role which would later develop into the Elizabethan Vice figure (cf. Shakespeare's Edmund in *King Lear* and Richard III). The staging also seems to be of the 'stage and scaffold' type rather than processional, as there is

---

* Six plays are generally considered to be by the same playwright: the 'Killing of Abel', 'Noah', the First and Second Shepherds' Plays, 'Herod the Great' and the 'Buffeting'.

movement between different fixed locations. A messenger travels from Annas, who is to 'shewyn hym-self in his stage' (Happé, p. 417) to Caiaphas, who 'shewyth him-self in his scaffold' (p. 419), while other actors 'schewyn hem in the place' (p. 421).

The cycle's proclamation describes this play as depicting King Herod, who is 'as wroth as wind', and highlights his wicked despatch of 'cruel knytys and unhende / To sle male chylderyn' [cruel, ignoble knights to kill the male children].[9] The play begins with a steward rushing to report the news that the three kings have escaped, news which prompts a murderous outburst from Herod and provides the catalyst for the main action of the play – the Massacre of the Innocents. Herod, clearly a well-known wicked character, is suitably arrogant and unpleasant, recruiting his 'kene knyghtys [who] kyllyth knave chylderyn' (ll. 28–9). This ironic imagery perverts notions of chivalric honour and forms a recurrent motif; later, Herod addresses the soldiers as 'my jentyll and curteys knyghtys' (l. 142). The play is brief in terms of dialogue but handles the traumatic central spectacle with great pathos. As the staging resources did not allow large-scale treatment, the dramatist, like Shakespeare later, focuses with terrible intensity on a few representative figures. The imminent violence is anticipated early on in the play when Herod looks forward with relish to the violence ahead, a sense of sadism glimpsed in the grimly inappropriate metaphor:

Doth rowncys rennyn with rakynge raftys
Tyl rybbes be to-rent with a reed ray. (ll. 32–3)

[Make your horses run with stabbing spears [ready] until ribs are torn apart in that red dance.]

Herod demonstrates his impiety by disdaining the infant Jesus as 'a beggere' (l. 35) and swearing by Mahound (ll. 36, 209). The three chosen soldiers similarly exult in declaring their evil intentions, 'I xall sle scharlys / and qwenys with therlys / Here knave geryls / I xal steke' (ll. 57–60) [I shall kill churls, women and slaves; their boy children I shall impale]. During the scene of the killing, two brief but emotive speeches by the mothers helps to intensify the horror of the murders, lamenting their tragic misfortune. The phrasing of a mother's anguish for her child prefigures that of Mary, 'Alas, qwhy was my baron [child] borne?' (l. 90). Small details can conjure up grim horror effectively as a mother observes the torn body of her son, 'shanke and sculderyn is al to torn' (l. 93) [his legs and shoulders have been torn to pieces]. The sparse dialogue must have been supplemented by a good deal of stage action involving struggle and gesture. Herod's bombastic speeches dominate the play, verbosity often corresponding to iniquity as he gloats at length following the murders, 'In sete now am I sett as kynge of myghtys most' (l. 129) [I am now established in my throne as the most powerful of kings]. He epitomises worldly pride in his 'bost' (l. 135) so that the entrance of Death, 'Goddys masangere' (l. 177), comes as fitting retribution. The characterisation of Death resembles Herod in some respects, disparaging the king as 'a page' compared with his all-encompassing power:

> All thynge that is on grownd I welde at my wylle ...   [control]
> Wher I smyte ther is no grace   [strike]
> ... aftere my strook man hath no space   [time]
> To make amendys for his trespace. (ll. 182, 190–2)

Death eavesdrops on the tyrant and the soldiers as they celebrate their actions, 'By Sathanas oure syre, it was a goodly sight ... A good game' (ll. 221–2). The climax of the play is achieved by the grimly satisfying spectacle of Death killing them to the accompaniment of trumpets. The hyperbolic terms in which Herod asserts his extravagant consumption are designed to arouse the audience's (perhaps uneasy) antipathy, as he declares himself willing to spend a thousand pounds on a pint of wine, 'for cost take ye no care' (l. 149). A gleeful devil rejoices in his capture of their souls, 'All oure! All oure!' (l. 233), and expresses his relish for the torture to come, perversely described as fun and games, 'pleys ... myrthe ... sportys ... gle' (ll. 235–6, 243). No sooner has the audience been reassured by the humorous moment of complicit comradeship than it is suddenly confronted directly by Death, 'Be-ware of me ... I come sodeynly' (ll. 260, 265). The parting injunction to the audience to learn a moral lesson, 'I xal yow make right lowe to lowth ... Amonges wormes... xul ye dwelle' (ll. 279, 281–2) [I shall make you bow very low, you shall live among worms], employs a lexis and register similar to Herod's earlier. This creates a certain linguistic corollary as speech denotes character and villainy shares a common voice. In many ways, the play shows one monstrous tyrant whose demise we approve being displaced by another, far more disturbing and real. The final word of the play is an emphatically deictic 'me' as Death instructs the audience to contemplate the physical decay he embodies. This unique combination of the biblical story with elements of the Morality tradition achieves an extraordinarily resonant effect.

The Morality Plays

The sixty-odd Morality plays which have survived are far removed from the cosmic scale of the cycles. They present drama on a much more human scale: single plays, often with a small cast and a central human protagonist, deal with the same essential theme – salvation.[10] Some cycle plays show incipient features of morality drama with personified figures, such as vices and virtues (e.g. the Chester Judgement Play), influenced by the Paternoster plays (of which none survive), which depicted sins in conflict. Many literary sources are present, including works by Lydgate and Langland, vernacular poems on sin and redemption, and sermons. The Morality plays dramatise the spiritual trials of an individual representative person with names such as Everyman, Mankind and Life. They are dramatic allegories of temptation and sin, portraying the journey of the soul through life towards salvation and revolving around the conflict between good and evil, as depicted in Marlowe's later *Dr Faustus* with the competing Good and Bad Angels. It is a form of psychological drama, where internal struggles are projected outwards in concrete form and abstractions made real, so that the antagonists are figures such as the World, Flesh, Folly, Greediness and Backbiter. Often virtues and vices engage in battle together for possession of a man's soul. In *The Castle of Perseverance*, a pitched assault on the castle is repulsed by female virtues throwing roses (cf. *Piers Plowman* passus 20). Behind these combat scenes is Prudentius's fourth-century *Psychomachia* ('The War/Battle of the Soul'). *Everyman* is probably the best-known Morality play, presenting the plight of a human being facing death who is suddenly deserted by Fellowship, Kindred, Cousin, Goods, Knowledge, Discretion, Strength, Beauty and Five Wits, with only Good Deeds accompanying him on his final journey. The Moralities feature prototypical figures who later give rise to characters such as Falstaff (tempting Prince Hal into sin in Shakespeare's *Henry IV* Parts One and Two). While in the realm of an imagined allegory, the drama employs many effects to engage the audience through humour and pathos. The applicability of the situation to all is the key feature of such drama, with the audience very much implied participants.

The incomplete *Pride of Life* (mid-fourteenth century) is the earliest surviving Morality play, but the most important in terms of its scale and staging is the *Castle of Perseverance*, found in a manuscript dating from *c.* 1440.[11] It is a huge work with a cast of thirty-six and a total of 3,650 lines crammed full of incident and lots of movement between scaffolds and special effects (including, famously, a devil 'with a firework up his arse'). A diagram accompanying the *Castle of Perseverance* shows a circular acting arena with scaffolds erected at the compass points of the circumference. Here Flesh, World, Belial and God reside, with an extra north-easterly scaffold housing Covetous. Ideally, the perimeter is to be moated as the notes state, 'This is the water about the place. If any ditch may be made, there it shall be played, or else that it be strongly barred all about. And let not over many stytelerys [marshals] be within the place.' In the centre is the Castle of Perseverance, with a bed below for the soul (played by a boy) to lie hidden in until the climactic moment of death. Such visual evidence of performance is unparalleled and clearly suggests an expensive production more suited to professional performance than amateur.

More representative of the norm is *Mankind* (*c.* 1470) with only six or seven actors.[12] The composition of this play can be approximately dated through the type of clothing it describes such as the 'crakows' (pointed shoes) on line 1059, which were fashionable *c.* 1382–1425. It is the most riotous example of a Morality play with extremely colourful vices – Newguise, Nowadays and Nought as well as the devil Titivillus (a folklore figure who also appears in the Wakefield 'Last Judgment'). The ribald language and scatological songs which the audience are duped into joining in with involves outrageously low humour and parody, as in the mock Christmas carol, 'He that shitteth with his hole ... hole-lick, hole-lick' (ll. 338, 343). The collection during the play which precedes the entrance of Titivillus indicates a paying audience, which may have influenced the nature of the comedic treatment and special effects. East Anglia is particularly rich in such modestly staged productions. Although exploiting a crude colloquial idiom, *Mankind* is more than 'popular' fare, as shown by its deft handling of a variety of linguistic registers. Mercy speaks in a lofty, aureate style with complex syntax and ideas, 'Go with me in this deambulatory; [covered walk] / Incline your capacity; my doctrine is convenient' (ll. 842–3). This contrasts strikingly with the speech of the vices, marked by a much simpler syntax and colloquial diction, 'Tish, a fly's wing! Will ye do well?' (l. 789); 'Alas, my jewels! [testicles] I shall be shent of [killed by] my wife!' (l. 381).

Everyman

Everyman[13] is the most famous Morality play. Based on a Dutch original, *Elckerlijc* (*c.* 1490), it treats a widespread eastern folktale of the Faithful Friend. The play survives in two early fragments and two printed editions, the earlier of which (*c.* 1528–29) has a title page announcing 'a treatyse how the hye fader of heven sendeth dethe to summon every creature to come and gyve a counte of theyr lyves in this worlde and is in manner of a morall playe' (p. 61). The accompanying woodcut shows Everyman facing the pointing semi-skeletal figure of Death, surrounded by bones and graves, iconographically aligning itself with the *ars moriendi* tradition (the art of dying well).[14] The sombre theme produces an engaging drama which sensitively depicts the commonplace circumstances of life with which all can identify, 'In prosperity men friends may find / Which in adversity be full unkind' (ll. 309–10). Everyman's plight is extreme, as he realises that his salvation rests on one small expression of charity – the 'Good Deeds' he has performed. The drama gives potent form to the doctrine of the Seven Corporal Acts of Mercy enjoined upon Christians – to feed the hungry, clothe the naked, visit prisoners, nurse the sick, shelter the homeless, give drink to the thirsty and bury the dead.[15]

Unlike other Moralities, this is focused on a very short time period at the end of a man's life and so recalls rather than exhibits youthful indiscretion. The play is celebrated for its economy and compression – its action is restricted to a single day, whereas most Moralities span a whole lifetime. The scene and properties are restricted too, simply specifying a House of Salvation and the *platea* (general acting place). *Everyman* contains no sins, no vices and no psychomachia, eshewing amusing devilry in favour of more worryingly normal, quotidien trials, such as bitter disappointment when trusted friends let you down. The play maintains a dignity and quiet seriousness, devoid of the livelier and more obviously 'entertaining' figures of the Morality genre. The language adopts a neutral register for the most part – a poised 'middle' style, which is less showy than *Mankind* but effective as a medium for its serious message and theme. Sin is still the main topic: the sinful nature of Everyman's past life being threaded into the narrative retrospectively as he has been guilty of each of the Seven Deadly Sins – pride, gluttony, covetousness, lechery, sloth, envy and wrath. For example, Everyman's pride is evident in his ostentatious clothing, 'Whyder arte thou goyng / Thus gaily?' (ll. 85–6).

The dramaturgy is impressive. An opening messenger's speech gives way to a wrathful God who delivers a damning indictment of sinful mankind just as his Mystery play counterparts do in several Old Testament plays, 'I perceive here, in my majesty, / How that all creatures are to me unkind' (ll. 22–3). The intense negativity with which the play begins is counterbalanced by the far more positive Doctor's speech at the end, enacting a progression from Old Testament chastisement to New Testament forgiveness. Structurally, there is a double action with two climactic moments forming a diptych. Halfway through the play, at the very centre, Everyman's soliloquy (ll. 463–78) when he is close to despair acts as a recapitulation, placed at a crucial junction between his meetings with Goods and Good Deeds. These two represent the opposing sides of Everyman's nature, since he has overvalued the one to the detriment of the other, 'All my life I have loved riches' (l. 388). Throughout the course of the play, Everyman is increasingly isolated – first encountered by Death while he is alone, then enduring systematic abandonment by all his erstwhile companions. The gradual nature of the process is heightened by the playwright's addition of a second set of friends. These two groups also operate as part of the prevailing system of contrasts. The first group consists of external attributes, such as Fellowship, whom he addresses with misplaced confidence and affection as 'good friend', 'true friend', eliciting extravagantly hollow promises in return:

> For, in faith, and thou go to hell,   [even if]
> I will not forsake thee by the way. (ll. 232–3)

The second sequence of crushed hopes involves personal qualities, aspects of the self which are lost one by one and which are all the more painful. These figures make no rash promises, but their statements are subtly equivocal:

> Five Wits: And though it were through the world round,
>   We will not depart, for sweet ne sour.
> Beauty: No more will I, unto death's hour. (ll. 686–8)

This is a painful stripping away of illusions, a facing-up to facts, exploring the kind of personal isolation and struggle for self-knowledge later experienced by Lear and Hamlet. Everyman's increasing hopelessness extends by implication to the audience when Good Deeds says to him, 'I am sory of your fall; / And fayn wolde I helpe you, and I were able' (ll. 514–15). There is effective suspense when Good Deeds is too weak to rise, partly a doctrinal necessity, as one could not merit salvation without the gift of grace. The turning point of Everyman's fortunes is signalled by the miraculous reviving of Good Deeds as she recovers her strength. Further surprise follows when Everyman's companion, Knowledge, is unable to go with him on his final journey despite having sworn:

> I wyll go with the and be thy gyde,
> In thy moost need to go by thy syde (ll. 522–3)

Knowledge has been misread as signifying 'intellectual understanding' or 'learning', but is best understood as 'acknowledgement of sin' and 'self-knowledge' (one can compare the figure of Five Wits in *Wisdom*, who bring man to both self-knowledge and knowledge of God). The play contains a good deal of religious material, handled with some delicacy. The 'digression' which eulogises the divine offices of the priest, 'surgyon that cureth synne deedly' (l. 744), is hard-headed enough to include consideration of corruption and simony. The play instructs the audience as well as Everyman by specifying the seven sacraments as the remedy for sin (ll. 722–7) and dramatically presenting the process of repentance, contrition, confession, absolution and satisfaction. While the necessity of communion is underscored as the action which strengthens Good Deeds, Everyman receives it offstage, perhaps as the eucharist was considered inappropriate matter for stage representation.

Everyman's soliloquies are frequent in the first half of the play, enshrining his preoccupations; namely, time – wasted, misspent, and all too short, given the single day he has in which to settle his accounts – his emotional suffering, and abortive prayers for help (e.g. ll. 192, 304, 378). A distinct shift is marked by the complete absence of soliloquy in the second half of the play, and Everyman's prayers are now completed (ll. 581–604). God's mercy and love begin to be appreciated, not just the wrathful side since charity (epitomised by the loving Christ of the New Testament) emerges as the chief virtue. The antidote to Everyman's pride is symbolically demonstrated by his wearing a new garment of contrition.

The effective running metaphor of 'accounting' helps to sustain the central theme. The play exploits the various meanings of the word, in secular and spiritual terms, informed by the new ethos of a proto-capitalistic age which was developing systems of credit and banking. God wants a 'reckoning' (ll. 46, 99); Everyman requests time to prepare his 'counting book' (l. 136), but his 'book of count' (l. 104) is found to be empty or illegible (l. 507); he learns that all his worldly possessions were lent not given (ll. 161, 165), a lesson repeated to him by Goods (l. 440); Death is 'that dreadful reckoning' (l. 521) which all must face. Salvation here is a matter of making one's accounts 'sure' (l. 620), 'clear' (l. 652) and 'crystal clear' (l. 888), so that one may face death in the end ready 'To make my reckoning and my debts pay' (l. 865).

Part of the engaging quality of the play stems from its subtle characterisation. Goods is pert and cheeky, 'Who calleth me? Everyman? What! Hast thou haste?' (l. 393) and declares his nature frankly, 'My condition is man's soul to kill' (l. 442). His callousness grows more obvious in the face of Everyman's anguish and shock at his betrayal:

> 'Marry, thou brought thyself into care,
> Whereof I am glad.
> I must needs laugh ...
> Farewell, and have good day.' (ll. 454–6, 462)

The allegorical figures serve a dual function both as personified emblems of sin and as impersonating individuals (friends, family and so on), so that sin is not an impersonal concept. In the same way, Everyman himself is 'also' the personification of Avarice – which was displacing Pride as the chief sin at this time (cf. Covetousness had his own scaffold in the *Castle of Perseverance*). Everyman's main sin is his excessive love of wealth, which amusingly leads to his futile attempts at bribery, offering Death a thousand pounds to spare him. Everyman is also depicted as a Christ-like figure, with numerous references to Christ throughout supporting the parallels between God's incarnation as man and each individual human life as people follow and imitate the same pattern of fall and ascent. Everyman is first the sinful Son of Adam (l. 145) but later, accepting the scourge of penance, an image of Christ willingly embracing physical suffering (ll. 561–5).

The Moral Interlude of *Mundus et Infans*

Moral interludes ('between games') are short pieces which may have been performed during feasts. The generally sparse staging and small scale seem fitted for indoor performance in modest spaces. A single copy survives of *Mundus et Infans* (*c.* 1522),[16] an adaptation of a poetic dialogue, *The Mirror of the Periods of Man's Life*. The simplicity of the poem is reflected in the play, which can be performed by just two players. Evil is represented by one figure, Folly (a prototypical Vice figure), while Mundus (World) represents the sinful condition of life on earth. Costume functions symbolically, as usual, to mark moral states, first degeneration and then recovery. The inclusion of detailed references to contemporary London helps to ground and vivify the story of a misspent youth (ll. 570–97). The play opens with a speech from Mundus, royally arrayed and most likely seated on a throne as shown in the title page woodcut. Mundus immediately sounds like a cycle-play tyrant, 'Sirs, cease of your saws ... look ye bow bonerly to my bidding!' (ll. 1–2). The alliterative style heightens the impression of pomposity, while the phrasing veers towards sacrilege, echoing Christ's declaration at the gates of hell, 'For I am the World ... Prince of power and plenty' (ll.13–14). Mundus is prone to using a ludicrous style of speech, at times as crass as Bottom's Pyramus:

> Lo, sirs, I am a prince perilous i-proved,
> I-proved full perilous and pithily i-pight.   [firmly established]
> (ll. 216–17)

Mundus assumes a role of lordly benefactor to the human protagonist, renaming him at each stage of his life and offering instructions to respect and serve the seven kings (the Deadly Sins) who are his retainers. The references to numerous other figures who do not feature in the drama helps maintain a sense of a 'wider' world, despite the constraints of the tiny cast. *Mundus et Infans* is far from simple however, particularly in its enormously varied verse. Attenuated speech

149

differentiates character as the infant uses a simple syntax and vocabulary, while young Wanton sounds childlike and selfish, 'Aha! A new game have I found!' (l. 92). The adolescent 'Lust and Liking' (passion and pleasure in love) is assigned a conventional love idiom, 'I am as fresh as flowers in May' (l. 132). Further linguistic registers are used as a shorthand technique to suggest briefly a sense of personality through appealing to generic associations. For example, the adult Manhood is a chivalric hero, 'Now I am dubbed a knight hend' (l. 212), who travels to 'seek adventures' (l. 214). After Mundus leaves the stage to enjoy some female company, Manhood assumes a style of speech which resembles Mundus's and sits on his throne (l. 287), verbally and visually signifying man's complete initiation into worldly values. The egocentricity and hyperbole effectively denote arrogance:

> I am worthy and wight, witty and wise;   [strong]
> I am royal arrayed to reaven under the rice...   [rob under the
>   branches]
>
> I am stiff, strong, stalworth, and stout,
> I am the royallest, redely, that runneth in this rout.   [company]
> (ll. 267–8, 71–2)

Conscience replaces Mundus as the protagonist's mentor, beginning in his first speech to reinstate terms such as 'bonerly', properly applying it to Christ (l. 291). He delivers a sermon addressed to the audience, 'all this comely company' (l. 289). When he states, 'All the world doth Conscience hate' (l. 312), the metatheatrical moment functions to alert the audience who might well prefer the Vice to virtue. Man initially addresses Conscience disrespectfully as 'harlot' and 'bitched brotel' but his tone moderates as their conversation progresses, until he starts to ask questions, 'Spirituality? What the devil may that be?' (l. 335). The 'reformation' of Manhood is not straightforward during the quite comic exchanges as he refutes Conscience's teachings to abjure the sins as 'not worth a stray' and tries to bargain:

Say, Conscience, sith thou wouldest have Pride fro me,
What sayest thou by the king of lechery? (ll. 361–2)

Manhood voices some seductive sentiments as he objects to the pious life:

Fie on thee, false flattering friar! ...
For thou counsellest me from all gladness.
... The devil break thy neck! (ll. 401, 405, 408)

Conscience adapts his strategy according to his subject, circumventing Manhood's resistance by redefining 'covetousness' as constituting devotion to God (l. 441ff.), leading to Manhood's long, reflective speech (ll. 490–520). But Folly, the main vice, now enters in the guise of a melancholic clown like Shakespeare's Feste, 'Heigh-ho! Care away!' (l. 521), immediately interacting with the audience:

Is there any man here that will say nay?
... Ah sir, God give you good eve! (ll. 523, 525)

He is a Londoner who enjoys the taverns and brothels of the city, and speaks in a lively colloquial way, 'I do but claw mine arse, sir, by your leave' (l. 527), 'Yes, by cock's bones' (l. 542). His fencing bout with Manhood expresses in action what is happening verbally, inviting the audience's antagonism, 'This place is not without a shrew!' (l. 564). As with many Tudor Interludes, the topic of education is highlighted through a clash of intellectual faculties. Perseverance succeeds at last in recovering Manhood, using florid alliterative diction:

Christ our comely creator, clearer than crystal clean,
That craftily made every creature by good recreation. (ll. 741–2)

When Manhood reappears as Age, he is in despair as he ruminates upon and catalogues his past experiences:

Alas, alas, that me is woe!
My life, my liking I have forlorn,
My rents, my richesse – it is all i-go;
Alas the day that I was born! (ll. 763–6)

He finally assumes the name, Repentance, comforted and guided by Perseverance through the stages of contrition. He is taught the articles of the Creed in a scene which edifies the audience as much as their dramatic surrogate. The play's simply conceived but persuasive strategies engage by grounding the moral message in the everyday world, while enlivening the theme through effective deployment and varied speech in a manner which echoes in a small way the linguistic feats achieved in *Mankind*.

Medieval English drama demonstrates an extraordinary variety of form and type. For centuries before the Renaissance, there was a widespread tradition of performance which developed a number of key representational techniques. Many of these would be taken up and further refined by the great Elizabethan and Jacobean dramatists.

Extended Commentary: The York Play of the 'Crucifixion'[17]

This is one of the plays which critics ascribe to the writer referred to as the 'York Realist', with a distinctive twelve-line tail-rhyme stanza and robust colloquial diction. It displays the confident and innovative skills for which he is admired, in particular the detailed, tangible realism with which he presents his material. In the 'Crucifixion', Christ is curiously relegated to a minimal presence. He speaks only twice, while most of the action focuses on the workmen contriving to fit him to the badly made cross as he lies flat (out of audience's sightlines). The play incorporates traditions of contemporary devotion (Affective Piety) and iconography (displaying the Arms of Christ, the emblems of his Passion), along with popular material taken from 'The Legend of the

Rood' (the story of a seed from the Tree of Life being placed in Adam's mouth at his death and later growing into the tree from which the Cross was fashioned). It also exploits particular lyric traditions (the Address from the Cross type) and the liturgy of Holy Week. All in all, it is quite a complex and multifarious mix.

The complicated stanza form is ably employed by the playwright, who creates a remarkably flexible verse. A single stanza can accommodate eleven speeches of rapidly moving stichomythia:*

IV Miles	So wille of werke nevere we wore,	[bewildered]
	I hope þis carle some cautellis caste.	[peasant tricks]
II Mil.	My bourdeyne satte me wondir soore;	
	Unto þe hill I myght noght laste.	
I Mil.	Lifte uppe, and sone he schall be þore,	[there]
	Therefore feste on youre fyngeres faste.	
III Mil.	Owe, lifte!	
I Mil.	We, loo!	
IV Mil.	A litill more.	
II Mil.	Holde þanne!	
I Mil.	Howe nowe!	
II Mil.	þe werste is paste.	
III Mil.	He weyes a wikkid weght.	
II Mil.	So may we all foure saie,	
	Or he was heued on heght,	[before]
	And raysed in þis array.	[manner]

(ll. 205–16)

Although there are no stage directions, the dialogue is sharp enough to convey appropriate movement and gesture. Here the jostling voices and busyness, combined with grunts and groans, readily convey discomfort and physical effort. The same stanza can then achieve totally different effects of poise and dignity when dedicated entirely to Jesus:

---

* Stichomythia is a rapid exchange of dialogue, at its most intense, involving single lines of dialogue delivered by alternating speakers.

Jesus: Almyghty God, my Fadir free,
           Late þis materes be made in mynde,
           þou bade þat I schulde buxsome be,   [obedient]
           For Adam plyghte to be pyned,   [tormented]
           Here to dede I obblisshe me,   [force myself]
           Fro þat synne to save mankynde,
           And soveraynely be-seke I the,
           That þai for me may favoure fynde;
           And fro þe fende þame fende,
           So þat þer saules be saffe,
           In welthe withouten ende;
           I kepe nought ellis to crave. (ll. 49–60)

The formal apostrophe is appropriate for intense prayer as Jesus specifies exactly why he is allowing himself to be crucified. Coming after the soldiers' gabble and trivial concerns, this speech strikes a stunning note of simple eloquence and pathos, communicated via a vastly altered register. This one speech has to carry the full weight of Jesus's sacrifice, and it manages to invest the event with great clarity, making tangible the mysterious. The people Jesus is sacrificing himself for are present in the play as unredeemed and undeserving – the crude squabbling soldiers. Their response to this speech juxtaposes their viciousness with Jesus's extraordinary qualities as they mock his 'sawes', swear by 'Mahoundis bloode' (l. 61) and castigate him as 'wikkid' (l. 66).

The audience's attention is then directed towards and remains on these degenerate representatives of humanity until the end of the play. Once more their mundane preoccupations demand the audience's attention in a way that inescapably incriminates. The four figures who speak and labour to achieve their task cause the silent prone figure to become disregarded, so that when Jesus is raised on the cross and addresses the audience again, it creates a sudden, surprising effect. The tone has changed into a direct and emphatic appeal repeatedly using the inclusive personal pronoun ('ye'), and inviting an emotional response to the visual spectacle,

Al men þat walkis by waye or strete,
Takes tente ye schalle no travayle tyne,   [lose]
By-holdes myn heede, myn handis, and my feete,
And fully feele nowe, or ye fine. (ll. 253–6)   [before]

This is masterly manipulation of the audience as the playwright has forced the spectators to admit their culpability after distracting them into disregarding the central act of the Christian faith.

The daring trick is managed by creating such a strong focus of attention on the soldiers. They are amusingly portrayed as ruffians with pretensions, consistently conceiving of themselves as 'Sir knightis' (ll. 61, 97) seeking to 'worshippe wynne' (ll. 14, 199), although the 'dede' they are to perform (ll. 1, 31) involves a grim pun (deed and death). Their activities are performed with thorough attention to detail, creating a sense of life-like realism as they use and mislay specific tools such as hammers and nails. They are fascinatingly engrossed in their work to the point that we forget what they are actually doing. Lost in the minutiae, they are aware of Jesus only as an object. The faulty measurements of the cross mean only a carpentry problem to be solved as they pride themselves on making the best of a bad job, 'Yis, here is a stubbe [peg] will stiffely stande' (l. 102). The casually circumstantial treatment continues as they look for their tools and work at a snail's pace (l. 118) yet unknowingly speak ironic truth, 'this werke will wrie all wrang' (l. 182) [turn out wrong]. The 'realism' extends to the terrible explicitness of Jesus's physical suffering, 'It fallis a foote and more, / The senous are so gone' (ll. 108–09) [The cross is more than a foot too long, his sinews are so destroyed].

Yet, despite the cruelty, the soldiers are presented as engaging comic foils, ironically complaining about their own discomfort, 'My schuldir is in sounder' (l. 190) [I've broken my shoulder], 'Certes, me wantis wynde' (l. 204) [I am totally out of breath]. Most of the time, even as they periodically blame the 'harlot' causing them such problems, they remain deceptively amusing. The audience cannot help but identify with the main speakers' human qualities, amusing comic ineptitude and distracting conversation. The play creates and exploits a powerful discrepancy between the soldiers' manner (chatty, colloquial, supplying a detailed commentary on their work) and the matter (the grim agony and torture they are inflicting). By the end of the play, once Jesus has been raised and is visible, the discord between words and meaning is too powerful to ignore. The soldiers' final comments are increasingly offensive and strike a jarring note of sacrilege and horror as they mock Jesus, 'We! Herke! He jangellis like a jay' (l. 265) [Hey, listen! He's chattering like a magpie].

Overall, this short piece with just five actors and minimal properties creates an unforgettable image of the crucifixion, alerting the audience to its own weaknesses and fallibility even as it provides the central spectacle of the cycle. The peculiar blend of humour and seriousness is still shockingly effective today.

Notes

1   Peter Happé (ed.), *English Mystery Plays* (Harmondsworth: Penguin, 1975), p. 151. All citations are from this edition unless otherwise stated.
2   The University of Toronto undertook the enormous task of publishing all documentary evidence connected with medieval drama, a project known as REED (Records of Early English Drama). See especially, Alexandra F. Johnstone and Margaret Rogerson (eds), *Records of Early English Drama: York*, 2 vols (Toronto: University of Toronto Press, 1979).
3   For evidence of extensive losses, see E. K. Chambers, *The Mediaeval Stage* (Oxford: Oxford University Press, 1903).
4   Earlier editors referred misleadingly to the plays of this cycle as the *Ludus Coventriae* (Coventry Play), but there is no Coventry connection. The confusion stems from a misreading by a library cataloguer. Happé's edition preserves the discredited name. In fact only two plays survive from the genuine Coventry Cycle, one of which is in printed in Happé (play 20).
5   Peter Meredith (ed.), *The Passion Play from the N-Town Manuscript* (London: Longman, 1990). The two versions of the Passion play, like those of the Shepherds in Wakefield, represent alternative texts for performance.
6   The post-Reformation Banns are printed in Greg Walker (ed.), *Medieval Drama: An Anthology* (Oxford: Blackwell, 2000), pp. 201–5. The earlier, pre-Reformation Banns are in Happé (ed.), *Medieval Drama*, pp. 41–8.

7   This account is from the records in the Norfolk and Norwich Record Office, Norwich Assembly Proceedings 1491–1 553, ff. 129ᵛ–130ʳ. Another record of the appeal from the Minute Book was published by Henry Harrod, 'A Few Particulars Concerning Early Norwich Pageants', *Norfolk Archaeology*, iii (1852), 3–18.

8   Matthew Hutton's 'Letter to the Mayor and Council of York' (1567), in Greg Walker (ed.), *Medieval Drama*, p. 206.

9   Norman Davies (ed.), *Non-Cycle Plays and Fragments*, Early English Text Society (EETS) s. s.1 (London: Oxford University Press, 1970), pp. 5–21.

10 G. A. Lester (ed.), *Three Late Medieval Morality Plays: Mankind, Everyman, Mundus et Infans* (London: Dent, 1981). All quotations from these plays shall be from this edition.

11 Mark Eccles (ed.), *The Macro Plays*, EETS, o. s. 262 (London: Oxford University Press, 1969) contains *Mankind*, *The Castle of Perseverance* and *Wisdom*.

12 G. A. Lester (ed.), *Three Late Medieval Morality Plays*, pp. 3–57.

13 G. A. Lester (ed.), *Three Late Medieval Morality Plays*, pp. 63–103.

14 Examples of the popularity of texts treating the *ars moriendi* theme include Chaucer's 'The Parson's Tale', a penitential treatise analysing sin, and William Caxton's bestselling *Book of the Craft of Dying*.

15 Based on Matthew 25:31–46, where the last judgement is detailed as an enquiry into the relief offered to those in need, as the criteria by which souls are sorted into the saved and the damned.

16 G. A. Lester (ed.), *Three Late Medieval Morality Plays*, pp. 111–57.

17 Peter Happé (ed.), *English Mystery Plays* (Harmondsworth: Penguin, 1975), pp. 525–36.

Mystical Love and Devotion

Medieval piety was strikingly dynamic, increasingly vernacular and popular in style. The later part of the period witnessed an explosion of religious texts designed for a wider public beyond the ecclesiastical elite and court circle, addressing an appetite for serious religious devotion concerning core concepts of faith and identity. New audiences, practitioners and occasionally authors were drawn from a far wider social range than previously, extending to women and laypeople. The late fourteenth century produced large numbers of works treating personal perspectives, often shielded behind imagery and motifs in common currency but developing highly innovative and idiosyncratic forms. Certain exploratory voices expressed more confident, emotional and interior perspectives, which led from merely channelling higher intuitions towards a radical enlarging of horizons. The English language became a flexible medium for even the most intellectual and existential of concepts along with an expansion of literacy and access to writing to those previously marginalised or excluded from social discourse. The mystics, many of them female, were appropriating the 'apophatic' voice (inventing a new language for God), discovering and creating strategies of resistance and circumventing prevailing ideologies which restricted learning and tried to impose a univocal, homogeneous discourse. The mystical movement also illustrates processes of intertextuality as key models are appropriated and forged into personal vehicles of expression, exploring new concepts of subjectivity and the 'I' voice. Many significant developments in literature were encouraged or advanced by the dissemination of texts presenting personally oriented enquiry. Mystical writings often originate as private texts intended for private reading, but transfer to the public domain where their inspirational potential broadens.

A new literary genre in English emerges which focuses on individual spirituality in various forms, such as instructive manuals and personal accounts of meditative practice and heightened religious experiences. Such works are regarded here primarily as literary compositions. Much like the Bible, they are products of a specific moment available for scrutiny as texts, whatever their claims to divine inspiration. What is remarkable about these mystical texts is that they share a common Catholic faith, adhering to tropes, conventions and recurrent modes, and yet they display extraordinary diversity and distinctive flair. Although medieval mysticism may appear a remote genre to the general modern reader, these texts undoubtedly offer some intriguing insights into the complexity and richness of late medieval literature and ideas.

Late medieval mystical writing was usually in prose – a medium which proved flexible and adaptive. It presented itself as serious, non-fictional and concerned with elucidating matters of faith and salvation. The imperative to be intelligible and instructive led to a conscious clarity of diction and sensitivity to language, while the construction and deployment of a narrative persona is a crucial feature of mystical writings. Other stylistic preferences were for plainness of style and strategies of authentication. Narrative techniques were focused on vivid description, often acutely visual or tactile, and the persuasive power of personal experience. Storytelling as such was occasional and designed to illustrate a moral point or to render it more tangible. The finest works are sharply evocative and interactive, directly addressing and seeking to affect the reader. Boundaries between author and reader are necessarily dissolved as mystical texts unveil their meaning, seeking to engage and actively involve the reader as participant in ways which non-religious texts emulate and exploit.[1]

English Mysticism in the Fourteenth Century

The concept of mystical union with God as a focus of devotional practice was in vogue from the twelfth century onwards, following the teachings of Bernard of Clairvaux. The image of the *sponsa Christi* (bride of Christ), inspired by the Song of Songs, part of the Hebrew Bible, had been applied particularly to female religious from the third century onwards but really captured the imagination in the later Middle Ages. The Song of Songs was interpreted as an allegorical depiction of Christ's love for and marriage to his Church, and provided devotional treatises with an extensive vocabulary of sensuous, erotic adoration, 'Let him kiss me with the kisses of his mouth' (1:2); 'Thou hast ravished my heart, my sister, my spouse ... how much better is thy love than wine!' (4:9–10); 'My beloved put in his hand by the hole of the door and my heart was moved for him' (5:4).

Among the most famous of medieval mystical writers is Richard Rolle (*c.* 1290–1349). He lived as a hermit, sustained by wealthy patrons, and his writings enjoyed widespread popularity, establishing the standard. In his Latin work, *Incendium Amoris* (The Fire of Love), he took up and propagated an image previously used by Hildegard of Bingen (1098–1179) in her accounts of her visionary experiences. It offers a very personal account of his religious ecstasies, designed to inspire a particular group of women. He wrote many works in Latin and English (e.g. *The Form of Living*), including two English works addressed to Margaret Kirkeby, an anchoress.* Rolle was very influential, describing the 'stirrings' of deep emotional involvement in such events as Jesus's Passion:

> þe prees of þe peple was wonderly strong, þei hurled þe and haryed þe so schamefully, þei spurned þe with here feet, os þou hadde been a dogge. I se in my soule how ruefully þou gost.[2]

---

* An anchoress is a female anchorite, one who withdraws from the world for a life of prayer and contemplative piety.

[The crowd of people was so strong, they pushed and shoved you so shamefully, they spurned you with their feet, as if you were a dog. I see in my soul how pitifully you go.]

Other important mystical writers include Walter Hilton (*The Scale of Perfection*) and Nicholas Love, whose *Myrrour of the Blessed Lyf of Jesu Christ* is discussed below.[3] There are also many anonymous works such as *The Cloud of Unknowing* and *The Book of Privy Counselling*.

Heresy and Lollardy

It is important to remember that this was a time of intense religious persecution and a growing movement of dissent, objecting to Church corruption and demanding reform. John Wyclif was an influential Oxford scholar and popular London preacher whose patron was John of Gaunt.[4] His followers became known as Wycliffites and produced several vernacular translations of the Bible (over 250 examples of which survive in complete or fragment form testifying to an enormous public readership). After the Papal Schism (see Part Two: 'A Cultural Overview'), Wyclif began denouncing papal supremacy.[5]

In this climate, the Archbishop of Canterbury, Thomas Arundel, issued a series of Constitutions (1407; 1409) which sought to extirpate criticism of the Church, outlawing the Bible in English, forbidding possession or production even of brief extracts, and instigating the rigorous persecution of heretics. The first act prescribing burning for heretics had been passed in 1401. This has been related to an unstable political context following the deposition and execution of Richard II in 1399–1400, when the Lancastrians sat uneasily on their usurped throne. Records from East Anglia heresy trials provide useful evidence of Lollard opinion and activity. In 1428, Hawissia Moone was unrepentant in denouncing the official clergy, 'every man and every woman being in good lyf oute of synne is as good prest and hathe as muche poar of God in al thynges as ony prest ordred, be he pope or bisshop'.[6] Such anti-authoritarian attitudes were perceived as extremely threatening by the established Church and represent a radical advance on Wyclif's ideas of opening up the Bible to all, seeing the Church as an entity apart from the formal Catholic structures, envisaging 'a priesthood of all believers'.

The Cloud of Unknowing (c. 1395)

This anonymous text[7] displays many of the central features of the mystical genre. Although it was specifically written to guide a twenty-four-year-old prospective recluse, the work survives in seventeen manuscripts and was later translated into Latin, so clearly held wide appeal. The 'negative way' of withdrawal and seclusion from the world is explored from an authoritative but relaxed position. The text treats complex issues and sets out a detailed analysis of effective meditational practice. Its core conviction is that God remains unknowable and can only be approached from a position of dissolving one's sense of self. The recommended procedures for transcending thought, striving for the necessary inner peace in which to experience the 'nakid beyng' of God (Chapter 4, p. 293), have a long history, stretching back in Christian practices to the sixth-century Pseudo-Dionysius the Areopagite and beyond to Buddhist and yogic traditions. The guidance is delivered through a plain-speaking persona, who develops the central metaphor of the cloud of unknowing which prevents direct access to the divine. This persona refuses claims to omniscience, declaring when considering defining God, 'I wote never' (Chapter 6, p. 293), yet commanding a superior perspective, 'By love may he be getyn and holden, bot bi thought neither' (Chapter 6, p. 294). The usual emotional involvement urged by pious practice is here relegated to a subsidiary, prepatory role, after which the experienced can 'leve hem, and put hem and holde hem far doun under the cloude of foryetyng' (Chapter 7, p. 294).

Even though the devotional subject matter is complex, the style remains resolutely direct and colloquial. A key aspect of this devotional school was a distrust of words as empty signifiers, which may be why there are no references to scripture. The use of mantras is favoured, involving words of one syllable such as 'God' and 'Love' (Chapter 7,

294), which can act as 'thi sheeld and thi spere' in the battle against the obscuring cloud (Chapter 7, p. 295). At times the language intensifies, as when the speaker denounces hypocrites and dissemblers with some vivid metaphor. He deplores excessive histrionics and affectation, such as people who stare intently like witless sheep or loll their heads as if they had a worm in their ear. He ridicules a variety of mannerisms using such homely imagery with an especially memorable image of some who 'rowen with theire armes ... as hem nedid for to swymme over a grete water' (Chapter 53, p. 295). At times the metaphors can become mixed to the point of confusion:

I had lever [rather] be so nowhere bodely, wrastlyng with that blynde nought, than to be so grete a lorde that I might when I wolde be everywhere bodely, merily pleying with al this ought as a lorde with his owne. (Chapter 68, p. 296)

Along the way, the instruction is also enlivened by interaction with an imagined interlocutor, who objects, 'Wher than ... schal I be? Nowhere, by thi tale!' (Chapter 68, p. 296). Rather than being perplexed by the challenge, the speaker uses such comments as cues to provide further explanation, 'nowhere bodely is everywhere goostly' (Chapter 68, p. 296). Subtle understanding is enlisted, as when the speaker distinguishes between inner and outer states of being, inner as 'all', outer as 'nothing' (Chapter 68, p. 296). The emphasis on the uniqueness of each individual whose primary task is self-knowledge, trusting one's inward stirring, clearly has radical potential akin to the exploration in *Piers Plowman* which leads to the discovery that truth resides in one's own heart. The text is resolutely anti-Lollard however, as the earlier insinuation of 'heretikes' among the hypocrites suggests. In another of his works, *The Book of Privy Counselling*, this author pointedly expresses surprise that some regard him as presenting obscure ideas:

Softely, mournyngly and smylingly I merveyle me somtyme whan I here sum men say (I mene not simple lewid men and wommen, bot clerkes and men of grete kunnyng) þat my writyng ... is so harde and so hei3, and so curious and so queinte, þat unneþes it may be conceived of þe sotelist clerk or wittid man or woman in þis liif.

[With both sadness and amusement, I am secretly amazed sometimes when I hear certain people say (I do not mean humble, uneducated men and women, but scholars and men of great learning) that my writing is so hard and so lofty, so complex and so intricate that it can scarcely be understood by the finest scholar or most intelligent man or woman alive].[8]

The need to be alert to charges of heterodoxy is obviously lurking beneath such protestations, necessary even for a thoroughly orthodox writer.

Affective Piety

Medieval lyrics attest to an appetite for heartfelt emotional involvement in the events of Christ's passion with hundreds of poems presenting scenes for the reader to ponder devoutly and meditate upon, as in this very early example:

Quanne hic se on rode	[cross]
Jesu mi lemman...	[beloved]
And his rig iswongen,	[back whipped]
And his side istungen	[pierced]
For þe luve of man	
Wel ow hic to wepen	[ought]
And sinnes forleten	[abandon]
Yif hic of luve kan.	[know]
Yif hic of luve kan.	
Yif hic of luve kan.[9]	

Such poems insist on an imaginative response, urging the reader to participate as it were, to experience the biblical events as immediate and personal. The Passion was primary, religious lyrics having long been exploiting the Classical rhetorical device of *enargia*, elaborating descriptive elements of death and grief. The Passion plays which promoted tears of compassion were castigated by the author of a treatise against Miracle plays but generally such emotive designs were regarded favourably.[10] Other favourite themes in the lyrics were Christ's Reproaches from the Cross and Marian laments, frequently using direct address to heighten the reader's sense of engagement. Parallel artistic fashions for statuary and paintings depicting Jesus in agony, writhing and tortured on the cross, testify to a late medieval fascination with pain and suffering.

The intense focus on the physical suffering of Jesus and the accompanying predilection for empathetic experience of such pain can result in an active participation bordering on the neurotic, from a modern perspective. The Middle English translation of Aelred's twelfth-century work, *De institutione inclusarum*, advises readers to:

> Creep into the wound in that blessed side, from which the blood and water come forth, and hide yourself there … licking the drops of his blood, until your lips become like a red scarlet hood.[11]

The Blessed Angela of Foligno is personally invited by Christ to perform such an act, 'He then called me to place my mouth to the wound in his side. It seemed to me that I saw and drank the blood, which was freshly flowing from his side.'[12] The intimate physicality of this type of devotional practice led to the common trope of mystical marriage with Jesus assuming very physical form. The thirteenth-century Beguine Hadewijch of Brabant was intimately united with Jesus in her visions, 'he came himself to me, took me entirely in his arms, and pressed me to him, and all my members felt in full felicity'.[13] The erotic aspects of this embrace are obviously on one level a sublimation of sexual desire. Such encounters form a staple ingredient in mystical texts, such as Rolle's *Ego Dormio*.[14] The intimacy is not reserved for women, as shown by *Incendium Amoris*:

Truly ... I await my love and kissing, and overflow, as it were, with ineffable desire ... The form of ravishing is the lifting of the mind into God ... available to all who are perfect lovers of God ... appropriately termed ravishing ... for it is done violently and supernaturally.[15]

The description of ecstatic union with God, the aim of mystical practice, is often expressed in sexual terms so that the trope of sexual violence later employed by John Donne is only a variation on medieval piety,

Take me to you, imprison me, for I
Except you enthrall me, never shall be free,
Nor ever chaste, except you ravish me.[16]

Women and Mystical Writings

As the primary audience for texts in the vernacular, women were clearly important in the spread of mystical writings. The extent to which women in particular were informed by and responsive to notions of affective piety is hotly debated. *Ancrene Wisse* is an early thirteenth-century text originally addressed to three sisters who lived together as anchoresses, along with a couple of maids and a kitchen boy.[17]* Its colloquial idiom employs vivid imagery; for instance, Part 4 (ll. 1599–600) describes the devil as a dog to be beaten away rather than told to clear off, 'Ame dogge, ga herut!' [good dog, go away].[18] The women are to imagine themselves in the position of a beloved lady besieged in a tower under assault from sinful sexual desire and with Jesus as their knightly champion. Jesus is presented as the supreme lover, infinitely preferable to any earthly husband:

Ne schaw þu na mon þi wlite, ne ne leote bliðeliche here þi speche, ah turn ham ba to Jesu Crist, to þi deorewurðe spus.

---

* The anchoritic life was not usually one of solitary confinement, as evident in the case of Julian of Norwich, who had at least two servants, called Sara and Alice.

[Show no man your face, nor let him gladly hear your voice, but turn both to Jesus Christ, your precious husband.]¹⁹

Some scholars regard the centrality of women in the mystical context as providing important potential for their enhanced status. It is true that many women were asserting their wishes to engage in religious lifestyles, whether formally, as nuns or anchoresses, or within a secular environment. A wealthy laywoman such as Lady Margaret Beaufort spent regular time in daily prayer and contemplation and commissioned specific translations, while many women's wills show how spiritual works were circulated among women.²⁰ Caroline Bynum is foremost among scholars who see the increased participation of women in areas where they had been largely excluded as significant to female emancipation and access to power. In particular, she traces the evolution of female authority to their inclusion within pious devotion in imitation of Christ (*imitatio Christi*).* This provided women with authorised access to power, validating their experience and self-assertion. Bynum's views on the female body as a site of power can be challenged as overly optimistic.²¹ The focus of Christ's humanity and physical suffering, along with the cult of the Passion, could have fostered new appreciation of and respect for the feminine, traditionally associated with the body as Bynum believes, but David Aers offers an important corrective to generalising ideas about automatic assimilation. He discusses the partiality and restrictedness of such interpretations, which tend to make the contingent and variable appear monolithic and inevitable. Christ's feminine aspect was highlighted by late medieval devotional practice (as opposed to the Germanic representation of Jesus as a stoic warrior or the Byzantine depiction of a Romanesque icon). But, as Aers points out, the image of Christ which was privileged as an emblem of suffering and passivity needs to be set against neglected alternative perspectives of his anti-authoritarianism, egalitarianism and pacifism. Aers maintains that configurations of Christ were 'not inevitable, not uncontested, not politically neutral and not

---

* *Imitatio* Christi is a practice of spiritual devotion, which consciously seeks to emulate Christ's perfection, as a means of intimate connection with God. It often involves meditating upon Christ's Passion and his exemplary humility and obedience.

part of a homogeneous "traditional religion" in a homogeneous world', but deliberately fostered for political ends – one position endorsed and propagated by the powers of the Church and the State.[22] Jesus also offered models of democratic participation and challenge to authority (as in the temple with the moneylenders and opposing institutionalised worship). Wyclif and his followers drew attention to aspects of the established Church which were at odds with Jesus's own example and pronouncements in the gospel, and objected to the veneration of the cross and the cult of the Passion.[23] Nevertheless, officially sanctioned late medieval piety was grounded on images of Jesus's tortured body. The rest of this chapter will consider two women who wrote of their religious experience, contrasting the reclusive devotion of Julian of Norwich with the worldly mysticism of Margery Kempe.

Julian of Norwich (1342–*c.* 1418)

Julian of Norwich was clearly enabled by prevailing conditions to record and disseminate her personal experiences as a visionary. Norwich at the time was a rich and influential city, and Julian seems to have been well respected and sustained in her profession as anchorite attached to the church of St Julian in Conisford. It was common practice to assume the name of the church to which one's anchorite was connected. Very little is known about Julian apart from what her writings reveal. These survive in two versions known as the Short Text (ST) and Long Text (LT), the former being about a third of the length of the latter.[24] It is generally assumed that the expanded version is a later revision; if so, it demonstrates developing confidence and significant changes in strategy, effectively effacing Julian's feminine status.

Julian's Humility as a Woman

Julian's sixteen visions ('shewings') occurred during an illness (as is often the case with mystical experiences) in May 1373 when she was thirty years old. Her account distinguishes between three kinds of 'shewing':

'be the bodely sight', 'be worde formed in mynn understandynge' and 'by gastelye syght' (approaching the ineffable), the last being only partially communicable, 'I maye never fully telle it', so that she is 'stirred to say more' about it ('stirrings' being a Rollean term for mystical inspiration). She is acutely aware of her gender as an impediment:

> Botte god for bede that ȝe schulde saye or take it so that I am a techere, for I meene nouȝt soo, no I mente nevere so; for I am a womann, leued, febille and freylle. (ST, Chapter 6)

It is worth remembering that this may well be a fictive persona, especially since the *Revelations* demonstrate formidable learning. She clearly knew the Bible well, although she noticeably cites no Latin (unlike Langland), biblical references being made entirely in her own English paraphrases and through allusions. She states that her book is addressed not 'to hem that be wise, for thei wote it wele' but 'to yow that be simple' (LT, Chapter 9). Her assertion of her unlettered state refers to illiteracy in Latin but again may be part of the humility topos, a rhetorical strategy to enlist the reader's magnanimity and disarm criticism. The Short Text strenuously denies that she is special, and situates her repeatedly as part of a wider Christian community, her 'evyn cristen'. The Long version dramatically erases her female presence, constructing a very different 'I' persona, one greatly increased in authority. She greatly expands Revelation 14 from one to twenty-three chapters, and treats Jesus's Passion with leisurely, imaginative consideration. Julian develops a searching and subtle analysis of her visions, declaring her own perspectives and insights with bold assertion.

God as Mother

One of the notions which Julian explores is the female aspect of God; indeed, she spends a long time explaining how Jesus is as a mother to us.* There is some modest scriptural basis upon which to ground a

---

* The Christian doctrine of the Trinity conceives of God the Father, Jesus the Son and the Holy Spirit as distinct yet co-existent members of the Trinitarian Godhead.

concept of God as Mother, such as Isaiah 49:15, 'Can a woman forget her suckling child? ... will I not forget ye' and Isaiah 66:13, 'As one whom his mother comforteth, so will I comfort you'. Julian's concept of a maternal presence takes the metaphor much further. This move may be part of what Caroline Bynum identifies as the aforementioned late medieval 'feminisation' of Christ, whereby his body was represented as a source of flowing milk (blood and milk were believed to be the same substance according to medical theory).[25] Female mystical experience often partakes of such imagery – Jesus's bleeding wound symbolising breast feeding, even occasionally vulva-like as a point of entry for the devout.[26] Julian applies the concept of motherhood not just to the acceptable incarnate aspect of the Trinity, Christ as nurturing mother figure, but also extends the metaphor to apply to the Godhead itself – a bold move which is still strikingly radical today. The rather curious result is a masculinised mother figure confounding gender boundaries, 'God Almigty is our kindely [natural/beneficent] fader and ... our kindly moder ... our very trew spouse' (LT, Chapter 58). As a transcendent being who combines all things, God announces his incorporation of both masculine and feminine aspects:

> I it am ... the myght and the goodnes of faderhode ... the wysdom and the kyndnes of moderhode ... the lyght and the grace that is all blessyd love; I it am, the trynyte, I it am, the unyte. I am the sovereyne goodness of all manner of things. (LT, Chapter 59)

Julian expresses a very positive view of motherhood, 'To the properte of moderhede longyth kinde love, wisdam and knowing, and it is good' (LT, Chapter 60). Although Julian regards the transcendent ideal of motherhood as applying only to Jesus and to Mary, her effusive depiction of mothering, along with the presence of her own mother at her bedside, construe childbearing and nurturing in ways which cannot but confer a high status on human motherhood as well:

> The modor may suffre the child to fallen sumtyme and be disesid [upset] in dyvers manners ... but she may never suffre that ony maner of peril cum to the child, for love. (LT, Chapter 61)

Reason and Emotion

Another remarkable feature of Julian's work is its progress from the affective to a much more rational and intellectual mode. As David Aers and Lynn Staley demonstrated, even traditional foci of affective piety receive unusually intense and analytical treatment by Julian.[27] Her first vision is of Jesus bleeding on the cross, 'I saw the reed bloud rynnyng downe from under the garlande, hote and freyshely, plentuously and lively' (LT, Chapter 4) – the intimate physical experience which she had sought. But instead of remaining at the point of emotional outpouring, becoming consumed by grief, the visionary moves quickly on to focus on the goodness of the Trinity.[28] The language is often more abstract and rational than emotive, displaying a propensity to quantify and thus to analyse carefully. This tendency is apparent in Julian's conception of the whole of creation as comparable to a hazelnut, 'a little thing, the quantitie of an hazelnott' (LT, Chapter 5):

> In this little thing I saw iii propreties. The first is þat god made it, the second that god loveth it, the thirde that god kepyth it. But what behyld I ther in? Verely, the maker, the keper, the lover.

The Passion witnessed during the long Ninth Vision (LT, Chapters 16–21) is also similarly depicted, initially as felt suffering with the usual details of Jesus's agonised body, but then moving into a detached tone of scientific enquiry – an 'aesthetic detachment'.[29] Julian's style favours highly individual conceits, producing memorable similes. Christ's bleeding is compared with 'pelottes' [pellets], 'droppes of water that falle of the evesyng [eaves] of an howse after a grete shower of reyne', and 'the scale of heryng' (LT, Chapter 7). The narrator begins to wonder with forensic curiosity how exactly the skin and flesh of Jesus's body was torn open, 'How it was done I saw nott ... Wher thorow it was broken on pecys as a cloth, and sagging downwarde' (LT, Chapter 17). The climactic moment of most Passion sequences, Christ's death, is conspicuously absent here; in fact, he does not die but rather the grim mood suddenly lightens:

The channgyng of hys blessyd chere channgyd myne, and I was so glad and mery as it was possible. Then brought oure lorde meryly to my mynd: Where is now any point of thy payne or of thy anguysse? And I was ful mery. (LT, Chapter 21)

Julian's dialogue with what Aers describes as the 'cheerful Christ' while he is still on the Cross epitomises her extremely radical re-imagining.[30]

Doctrinal Positioning

Julian presents an idiosyncratic view of sin and damnation. Her metaphysical mysticism attends insistently to the spiritual realm of ideas and abstracts. As the main message which emerges from her contemplations is the goodness of God, the firm conviction that God is love, she struggles to accept the 'wrathful' side and finally denies it. Her solution to the dilemma is very much akin to modern yogic philosophy; namely, that our faulty perception creates a sense of sin and evil and we ultimately need to trust and accept, 'Synne is behovely, but alle shalle be wele, and alle shalle be wele, and alle maner of thynge shalle be wele' (LT, Chapter 27). Julian manages to present her radical ideas whilst maintaining orthodox submission to holy church by conceiving of a two-tier system, the official church and personal visionary experience co-existing in harmony, although she undoubtedly privileged individual enlightenment.[31] Her self-presentation as orthodox was successful enough for her to be venerated until the present day as an authentic mystic.

Margery Kempe (*c.* 1373–*c.* 1439)

The same cannot be said for Margery Kempe. She lived in King's Lynn, Norfolk, and enjoyed considerable social status as the daughter of a former Mayor and Justice of the Peace, as well as engaging in several business ventures independently, although with little success. The *Book of Margery Kempe* was discovered only in 1934 in a private library, although selected extracts had been printed in 1501 by Wynkyn de Worde and were later attributed (erroneously, it appears) to 'a devoute ancres'.[32] At some point, Margery's story must have been revered as an account of genuine mystical experience as the manuscript was held in a Yorkshire monastery. Marginal annotations attest to a reader keen to highlight particular affective passages, marking them with heart signs and supplying headings identifying places where the fire of love and Rollean ecstacy occur; for example, Chapters 17, 35. These annotations attest to both the *Book*'s use and processes of selection and control, downplaying certain aspects of the book in favour of others.

Margery's *Book* is much more than a spiritual text; it constitutes the earliest autobiographical account in English. She dictated the work, being unable to read or write herself, which immediately put her at a disadvantage compared with Julian, for instance, leaving her unable to write her own memoirs and dependent upon clerical assistance. Although technically 'lewd' (unlearned), she clearly did not lack 'learning' as she demonstrates an extensive familiarity with the Bible and mystical works, and obviously possessed a hugely retentive memory and notable oral skills as seen when she argues and debates with learned ecclesiasts and ably defends herself as orthodox. The circumstances of the book's composition are discussed in the Proem, or prologues and in Chapter 89. Radical aspects are initially contained and mediated by a number of devices: the careful framing of the two prefaces, introducing the *Book* as a spiritual biography in a conventional genre; the several authorising scribes who both mediate Margery's oral recollection and authenticate it. The Proem is dated 1436 and announces the text as follows:

> Here begynnyth a schort tretys and a comfortabyl for synful wrecchys, wherin thei may have gret solas and comfort to hem and undyrstondyn the hy and unspecabyl mercy of ower sovereyn Savyowr Cryst Jhesu.

The opening sentence refers to 'us unworthy', aligning Margery with the community of sinners. This humble mode is consciously adopted as the narrator presents Margery twice as 'a synful caytyf' before identifying her as female in line 14. The reference to 'hys creatur' (l. 15) marks the first use of a term which will continue to designate Margery as author and subject of the book, consistently employing a distanced third person, referring to her as 'this creatur'. The whole is carefully contrived to present Margery as a worthy spiritual guide and moral exemplum. Her mystical experiences are introduced, from the conventional onset during 'grett bodyly sekenesse' (l. 23) to the miraculous restoration of her wits. Then the Proem enlists penitential and homiletic models, in the style of a sermon, as it relates how she lost her worldly goods, 'Than was pompe and pryde cast down' (l. 27), and was moved to confession, penance and contrition. The particular forms of Margery's piety are briefly outlined; namely, her gifts of tears, the public opprobrium she receives and her experience of ineffable spiritual delights.

Despite the effort at conforming to respected models, already there are hints of the personality and ego which bedevil the work. The detailed personal history advertises her special status, even in the august company of the church elite, 'Then went sche be the byddyng of the Holy Gost to many worshipful clerkys, bothe archebysshopys and bysshopys, doctors of dyvynyte and bachelors also' (ll. 49–51). The casualness with which Margery appropriates God for her own purposes soon reveals itself as a recurrent symptom of her artless lack of self-awareness. As she seeks to situate her self among the revered, 'Sche spak also with many ankrys' (ll. 51–2), the plurality and imprecision express how arbitrarily these figures are invoked. There is a palpable self-regard throughout the *Book* which works against her protestations of simple faith and humility. Many psychoanalytical readings of the *Book* detect an underlying anxiety which is assuaged only by constant striving for validation.[33] Existing as she did on the margins of spiritual authority as a married woman remaining at large in society rather than being cloistered, Margery occupied a distinctly vulnerable position. This may account for her representing herself as divinely favoured, empowered to withstand hostility and with some admirers and acolytes who testify to her as a true font of 'grace' blessed by 'hyr mevynggys and hyr steringgys' (l. 56). The scrupulous account of the writing process suggests a need to substantiate her claim to authority. The death of her first scribe (possibly her son) holds up the work for years while a priest delays and prevaricates, until she heals his poor eyesight by exorcising the devil afflicting him so that he can read the rough drafts. Every detail, even the most banal, is related as if highly significant, while Margery's manipulative and self-aggrandising behaviour is presented as divinely endorsed. The book that Jesus urges Margery to write is very mixed generically, encompassing elements of spiritual autobiography, hagiography, martyrology, chronicle, vision and travelogue. Lynn Staley suggests we 'think of it as a fiction (the first novel?)'.[34] There is a distinction to be borne in mind between the work's subject (Margery) and the self-conscious authorial persona constructing her (Kempe). As it unravels, the *Book* constitutes a complex polyphony filled with many voices.[35]

Margery's Models

Margery's book demonstrates her familiarity with the works of Rolle, Hilton and various mystics (e.g. in Chapters 17, 58) probably as a result of hearing them read aloud. Of the many models of female sanctity available at the time, Margery seems to have been most drawn to several saints whose lives resembled her own in some way. Her favourite saints are Margaret, Katherine and the Virgin Mary, all of whom are present at her mystical marriage. The Mayor of Leicester correctly reads her as consciously imitating St Katherine (l. 2625). Her aspirations to sanctity and veneration are hampered by her status as wife and mother, having married at the age of twenty and had fourteen children. Several female mystics provide her with inspiring models of holiness, attained despite marital and familial constraints. Christina of Markyate (1096–1166) lived chastely with her husband as her 'brother', citing and following the example of St Cecilia by converting him to chastity on their wedding night. Margery resembles Cecilia in several respects, especially in her ability to argue with the learned and defend herself against her accusers. St Bridget of Sweden (1303–73) was an enormously popular figure who successfully combined motherhood with sanctity. Her autobiography proudly names every one of her eight children and describes the admirable religious vocations of several of them, in contrast to Margery who remains conspicuously reticent on the subject apart from mentioning one son. Margery refers to 'St Bride' and at one point enjoys the accolade of being granted a eucharistic vision which God defines as surpassing anything experienced by Bridget (l. 1085).

Margery's Public Piety

Margery's piety is expressed through public weeping, crying out and swooning as she engages in the active life, travelling widely at home and abroad, including pilgrimages to the Holy Land, St James of Compostela, Aachen and Rome. Her first crying fit happens while she is in the Holy Land at Calvalry, 'Sche fel down þat sche mygth not stondyn ne knelyn but walwyd [twisted] & wrestyd [turned] with hir body, spredyng hir armys a-brode, & cryed with a lowed voys' (ll. 1573–4). This form of public lament continues for years as often as fourteen times a day, not unnaturally arousing a good deal of public alarm and hostility:

> Summe seyd it was a wikkyd spirit vexed hir; sum seyd it was a sekenes; sum seyd sche had dronkyn to mech wyn; sum bannyd hir; sum wished sche had ben in þe havyn; sum wolde sche had ben in þe se in a bottumles boyt; and so ich man as hym thowte. (ll. 1599–1602)

This becomes the pattern of her 'ministry': public revilement dominates with very few people accepting her. Even on pilgrimage her behaviour drives her fellow pilgrims to abandon her (ll. 380–1). She relates the experience of one sceptical monk who converts after she correctly identifies his sins (l. 613) and is subsequently (consequently?) promoted to sub-prior (l. 617). The Bishop of Lincoln (l. 763) welcomes her and encourages her to write her book, which she hesitates over for twenty years, conforming to the topos of modesty. He agrees to her receiving the mantle and white clothing, although with reservations as he insists she obtain her husband's consent, advises her first to go to Jerusalem and then sends her to Archbishop Arundel. Arundel approves her wishes, finding her such an engaging speaker that he listens to her all day, 'her dalyawns contynuyd tyl sterres apperyd in the fyrmament' (l. 847). Long-term supporters include her main confessor, a Dominican anchorite in Lynne (Chapter 17), and a White Friar called William Southfield (Chapter 18). Perhaps the most important figure Margery claims is a supporter is Julian of Norwich, whom she visits in Chapter 18. The meeting with Julian forms part of a sequence strengthening Margery's resolve with Julian reassuring her that God is 'al charite', citing St Paul and Jerome to bolster her confidence.

The general hostility towards Margery is seen in the reaction of the Canterbury monk who berates her, 'What kanst thow seyn of God? ... I wold thow wer closyd in an hows of ston that ther schuld no man speke with the' (ll. 627, 629). Challenged about her knowledge of Scripture, she responds by delivering a parable to an assembled company of monks, a thinly veiled allegory about their mistreatment of her which provokes them to pursue her as she leaves, calling out angrily, 'Thow schalt be brent, fals lollare' (ll. 649–50), with a crowd at the gates approving the idea. The threat of execution for heresy is often levelled against her as when a woman in Lambeth tells her, 'I wold thu wer in Smythfeld, and I wold beryn a fagot to bren the wyth' (l. 825). One of her most hostile opponents is the Mayor of Leicester, who condemns her outright, 'þou art a fals strumpet, a fals loller, & a fals deceiver of þe pepyl' (ll: 2625–6).

By failing to conform to the model of enclosed piety, Margery rouses strong antagonisms, her ambivalent status neatly summarised by the steward, 'eyþyr þu art a ryth goodwoman er ellys a ryth wikkid woman' (ll. 2667–8). Margery is imprisoned on occasion and interrogated but always manages to defend herself. In her visions, it is hard not to detect wish-fulfilment, as when Jesus sends St Paul to apologise to her for his disapproval of women preaching (l. 3796); the charge of presuming to preach is one she carefully negotiates, preferring general terms such as 'comownycacyon & good wordys' (l. 2976).

Margery's Visible/Risible Practices

The specific forms which Margery's religious vocation entails were disconcerting to her contemporaries as much as to modern readers. Her priestly scribe is troubled until he reads the life of Mary of Oignies (d. 1213) who also wept, swooned, cried out and wore white clothing (Chapter 62). St Elizabeth of Hungary also expressed her devotion by crying aloud. During her travels, Margery visited many sites associated with holy women, such as Danzig, where the Blessed Dorothea of Montau lived, and Assisi with its flourishing cult of the Blessed Angela of Foligno.

Perhaps the most perplexing of her practices was her insistence on wearing 'synguler' clothing, dressing entirely in white. Clearly this symbolised purity without associations of marriage and virginity, primarily signifying a liminal, transitional identity even in a bridal context. Margery never specifies its meaning and the only interpretation it receives is from the hostile Archbishop of York, who interprets it as an inappropriate sign of maidenhood. Aers speculates that white connoted extreme holiness.[36] Whatever its significance to Margery, she resolutely maintained her decision to distinguish herself by this clothing, visibly setting herself apart and marking her special status.

Margery's choice of devotional practice may appear less strange when set in the context of late medieval piety, where extreme habits were relatively commonplace, such as wearing hairshirts, scourging, fasting, frequent confession and taking of communion. The crisis which led Margery to adopt her distinctive mode of living was a very dangerous delivery (probably not the post-partum psychosis diagnosed by some critics). An incomplete confession, curtailed by an insensitive priest, seems to be the catalyst for Margery's spiritual transformation, depriving her of a vital avenue of psychic release. Confession remained extremely important to Margery as shown by her unusual habit of confessing often, sometimes several times in a day. When temporarily unable to confess, as when she is travelling abroad, Margery finds miraculous substitute confessors such as St John the Evangelist and a German priest who, astoundingly, is able to understand her English. The *Book* itself may function as a way of confessing, although she never specifies the nature of the terrible secret sin which haunts her conscience. In view of her avowed enjoyment of sexual intercourse in her youth and an adulterous affair, the sin may be sexually oriented.

Virtual Virginity

This is the main area of Margery's life which detracts from her saintly aspirations, her constant awareness of her imperfect physical condition. She provides an intimate account of her sexual experience, describing her revulsion from sex in Chapter 3:

> The dette of matrimony was so abhominabyl to hir that sche had levar, hir thowt, etyn or drynkyn the wose, the mukke in the chanel, than to consentyn to any fleschly comownyng saf only for obedyens. (ll. 256–9)

After twenty years of marriage, she finally obtained her husband's consent to chastity by offsetting the marital debt with a settling of his financial debts, effectively buying back control of her own body. This bargain is made in Chapter 11, one Friday in Midsummer, near Bridlington, 'Grawntyth me that ye scal not komyn in my bed, and I grawnt yow to qwyte yowr dettys er I go to Jerusalem' (ll. 567–8).

She lived in a culture where the highest status was accorded to virginity but which had few nunneries, reserved for the wealthy (unlike on the continent). The fetishisation of virginity is a marked feature of the Middle Ages, with virgin martyrs such as St Ursula and her 11,000 virgins exemplifying the exalted and wondrous heavenly future in store for the virginal. Since Margery was necessarily debarred from this, chastity and sexual abstinence were the highest state to which she could aspire. Saints' lives detailed and popularised tales of virgin martyrs such as St Katherine, St Juliana, St Margaret, St Agnes, St Lucy and St Cecilia suffering imprisonment and torture before death. Marriage was often represented as a terrible fate best avoided by voluntary enclosure and dedication to Christ, as in *Hali Meiðhad* where intending anchoresses are regaled with pictures of a husband who 'beateð þe and busteð þe as his ibohte þrel ant his eðele þeowe' (l. 138) [beats you as his bought slave and his born serf].[37] Time and again, Margery expresses anxiety about her sexuality. She asks Christ, 'Maydonys dawnsyn now meryly in hevyn. Schal not I don so? For becawse I am no mayden, lak of maydenhede is to me now gret sorwe' (ll. 1150–1) and is reassured by Christ, 'I lofe þe as wel as any mayden in þe world' (ll. 1118–19); 'þu art a mayden in þi sowle' (l. 1198). A kind of honorary virginity is bestowed upon her, regarding her as worthy of the same grace which is accorded to the virgin saints, Katherine, Margaret and Paul (l. 1188).

Margery's Mystical Marriage

Margery undertakes a typical mystical union with Christ, becoming *sponsa Christi*, but takes things a step further by marrying the Godhead too (ll. 2004–6). She does so awkwardly, for once unable to speak, so that Christ says her vows for her (l. 2025). Margery envisions her marriage to Christ as a standard wedding with guests in attendance as witnesses and formal vows (ll. 2030–4). The transcendent union follows her pilgrimage to Jerusalem. Margery fulfils the strategy recommended by *The Cloud of Unknowing* by ascending from mystical engagement with the incarnate deity to the higher realm of the abstract (from the bodily to the sublime). However, although she attains union with the whole Trinity, she returns insistently to her love for Christ which she conveys in terms that are sometimes far from sublime; for example, Chapter 36 which describes her physical intimacy with Christ with what Windeatt characterises as her 'endearingly earthbound awkwardness'.[38]

Margery's account of her spiritual development is one highly idiosyncratic version of late medieval mysticism. Margery and Julian of Norwich present two very different experiences of female authorship and reception. Both testify to the energy and enthusiasm of the late medieval mystical movement, as well as to some of its restrictions and dangers.

Extended Commentary: Love, *The Mirror of the Blessed Life of Jesus Christ*

Nicholas Love was prior of a Carthusian monastery* at Mount Grace in North Yorkshire. *The Mirror of the Blessed Life of Jesus Christ*[39] (1410) is a translation of a mid-fourteenth century Latin work, *Meditationes vitae Christi*. It is a solidly orthodox piece, strenuously opposing Lollard sentiments by asserting the efficacy and centrality of the Eucharist in Christian worship. It survives in fifty-six manuscripts and was printed nine times before the Reformation (after which its conspicuous Catholicism and eucharistic focus rendered it unpalatable). As a document designed to counter heresy, it probably represents a more mainstream current of late medieval religion than either Julian of Norwich's or Margery Kempe's work. Archbishop Arundel officially sanctioned it, as Love declares at the beginning.

Yet, producing works of spiritual guidance in the vernacular was itself an acknowledgement of the need to address a lay audience keen for such material. Love uses an appealingly plain style, favouring a simple vocabulary with an array of intensifying adverbs. Many of the features of his prose relate to an oral style appropriate for the dual audience he has in mind – of readers and listeners. The *Mirror* demonstrates much of the style and technique of contemplative mystical tracts, using words such as 'stirrings' and 'felynges'. It addresses a presumed male audience of lay pious (although the male pronoun may be of the non-gendered, inclusive type), 'Who-so desireth ... he moste with bisy meditacion abide'; Jesus's sacrifice must be 'inwardly consideret with alle the inwarde mynde and beholding of mannes soule', and the reader is urged to 'serche the passioun of oure Lorde with alle his herte and alle his inwarde affeccion'. The *Mirror* proposes a mixture of feeling and intellect, with the devout practitioner 'makynge himself as [as if] present in alle that befelle' (p. 313).

---

* The Carthusian order is one of the monastic orders, named after the Chartreuse mountains in the French Alps, where its founder first established a hermitage.

Passionate emotional engagement is advocated, in accord with the affective practice of the time, including the main aim of cultivating the Rollean fire of love (with a pun on his name?). Love (*caritas*) is prized as the greatest virtue, as the *Mirror* describes '[Christ's] charite, the which reasonably shold alle holely enflaume and brenne oure hertes in his love' (p. 314). The overall tone is easy and straightforward and the diction is idiomatic and direct, avoiding any complexity of expression, even as he envisages the same kind of intense ardour envisaged by the *Cloud of Unknowing*. The *Mirror* repeatedly emphasises the joy and bliss which result from earnestly contemplating Christ's suffering, stressing the 'new' (renewed, unprecedented, novel) emotional response which awaits, 'newe compassion and a newe love and newe gostly confortes'. The reiterative style matches the subject matter, which is the regular repetition of devotional practices.

The central event of Christ's Passion is treated at some length, covering many of the stages in the sequence traditionally represented in the cycle drama, such as the scourging of Christ (Chapter 41).* This chapter epitomises in its structure and narrative strategies those of the whole work as it proceeds meticulously in stages and focuses in turn on small details of the story, suspending the narrative at intervals to elaborate and encourage certain responses and to highlight particular images. The apparently artless language combines with calculated effects of tempo and variety of rhythm to achieve a carefully orchestrated impact on the reader.

Subsequent sections begin with clear temporal connectives which control the flow of the text and enact an oscillation between past and present: 'And than, Sothely, Take now here, Than was, Bot sothely, After, Now beholde, O wrecches, And yit, Se now' (p. 314). The systematic procedure starts by relating biblical events in a factual, chronological manner from the moment when Pilate orders Christ to be scourged. The neutral register then shifts to evoke a vivid picture

---

* Christ's Passion (Lat. *passum*) refers to Jesus's suffering (physical, spiritual, and mental) at the crucifixion, while scourging (cf. flagellation) refers to the whipping of Jesus during the events leading up to the crucifixion.

precisely guiding the reader's imaginative participation, using studied superlatives and intensifiers:

> And so stant he naked before hem alle, that fairest yonge manne of alle childrene that ever were born, taking paciently of thoo foulest wrecches the hardest and moste bitter strokes of scourges … moste innocent, faireste and clennest flesh. (p. 314)

The imagery drawing upon human experience invites empathy while the free-flowing sentence expands to accommodate an elaboration of detail. The cumulative effect of the multiplied sub-clauses creates a crescendo of words, enacting linguistically a kind of mimetic resonance in heavy plosive couplets:

> [A]lle to-rent and full of woundes, rennyng out of alle sides that preciouse kynges blode, and so longe beten and scourget, with wounde upon wounde and brisoure upon brisour, til bothe the lokeres and the smyters were werye. (p. 314)

This powerful image of Jesus shifts suddenly from a human to a regal context, yet maintains the focus on the bodily torment. The long sentence concludes at the moment of general exhaustion, quietly returning to the initial 'biddyng' of Pilate that Jesus be bound and beaten, 'and then was he biden to be unbounden'. The neatly contrived 'envelope' creates a satisfying sense of closure and respite, ending the beautifully deployed unravelling of the scene. Pilate is not named again until later after an interjection from the narrator.

The next stage of the guided meditation involves the narrator rapidly moving via a brief reference to contemporary actuality, the 'stories' which tell of the pillar still bearing the bloodstains, to a direct address. He begins with the prophesies of Isaiah, cited in English (rather oddly for an anti-Wycliffite), to demonstrate the fulfilment of scripture. But his own prayer to Jesus soon displaces the biblical citation, using a very colloquial address and rhetorical questions, 'O Lorde Jesu, who was he so fole-hardy that dorste despoile the?' (p. 314). The speaker proceeds

Medieval Literature

to consider who among those present behaved worst of all, 'althere-
werste and moost foole-hardye'. Again, there is a smooth triple
gradation. The narrator now assumes a strident sermonising tone as a
representative figure, addressing Jesus and setting out the contrast
between 'thi love and oure malice'. He demonstrates an easy intimacy
with Jesus marked by the plethora of personal pronouns, 'thou ... thi ...
thine ... thou ... thi ... thou', appropriate for the adopted persona of
priestly authority.

The heightened tone and declamatory style of this section then
modulates with the return to the biblical narrative, recovering a neutral
register and homely idiom, linking statements with the simple
conjunction 'and'. Factual narration and emotive commentary now
alternate more quickly as the narrator tells of the despoiling of Jesus's
clothes with a touch of actuality in the reference to the cold weather
noted by St John 18:18. He instructs his audience to 'have compassion
of him in so grete colde quaking and tremelyng, for as the Gospelle
witnesseth it was thanne harde colde'. Then the scene is presented with
the vivid detail of a miniature drama, supplying details of clothing,
gesture and speech as some of the most wicked approach Pilate with a
request that they be allowed to dress Jesus up in mockery as a king.
They take 'an olde silken mantelle of redde', the garland of thorns and
sceptre reed, kneel and salute him. We are invited to ponder this
tableau, 'beholde him with sorowe of herte' (p. 314). The narrator
rather anxiously leaves nothing to chance, specifying the requisite
responses and directing our gaze to the precise point of most shocking
impact as Jesus is beaten about the head, 'ful of sharp thornes, the
which persede grievously into the brayne-panne and made it alle full of
blode'. At each moment, Jesus's lack of response is highlighted – after
the mock 'hailing', 'he heeled his pees and spake not'. The crown of
thorns abuse is followed by the terse observation, 'alle he suffreth as hir
servante or knafe' (p. 314). The exemplary humility of Jesus, occupying
the roles of the low-born and servile, insinuates an ideal to be admired
and emulated.

The chapter is brought to an end by the once-more impassioned
narrator whose exclamation of antipathy towards Jesus's tormentors

functions to express the audience's presumed feeling, 'O wrecches, how dreful sal that hede apere at the laste to yow' (p. 314). The immediacy of the scene is brought once more to the fore, 'how he stant ... hanging the face doun towarde the erthe' (p. 315). The final image is of Jesus, abject amidst the baying crowd, suspended in time at the end of the chapter.

The crucifixion is described in Chapter 43 in characteristically emotive terms, 'that stinking hille of Calvarie', 'make the there present in thi mynde' (p. 315). Again, the narrator leads us step by step through the process, sharing the perspectives of those preparing the cross and those hammering the nails. Mary serves as a surrogate for the reader in her emotional response to the situation, characterised in human terms as a grieving mother, poignantly covering Jesus's nakedness (explicitly total) with her headscarf. The narrator enters the scene imaginatively, although with some awkwardness, 'Sothely, I trowe that she miht not speke one worde to him for sorowe. Bot she miht do no more to him, nor help him; for if she miht, without doute she wolde'. The reader is given explicit instructions, 'Take hede now ... Now take hede diligently ... Now take gude hede' (p. 315). The guided meditation upon the details of Christ's passion is said to provide access to what is paradoxically 'a piteuous siht and a joyful siht'. The whole recreated experience is designed to enable worship, as:

> By devout ymaginacioun of the soule ... sume creatours ... after longe exercise of sorouful compassioun thei felen sumtyme so grete likyng, not onely in soule bot also in the body, that thei kunne not telle'.

The mode of praxis over theory is preferred, 'no man may knowe, bot onely he that by experience feleth it' (p. 318).

This work exemplifies a painstaking, attentive approach to guiding popular devotional habits. The controlling presence of the narrator is marked and frequently foregrounded, although the authoritarian tones are generally modulated to an informal and colloquial register. The involvement of the reader at all times is one of the most innovative features of such didactic texts, forging an entirely new type of literary experience.

Notes

1   Gail McMurray Gibson, *The Theatre of Devotion* (Chicago: University of Chicago Press, 1989) discusses meditation as a kind of spectacle, with the devout projecting themselves into the drama of the Passion.

2   *The English Writings of Richard Rolle, Hermit of Hampole*, ed. Hope Emily Allen (Oxford: Clarendon, 1931; repr. 1963), p. 21.

3   Nicholas Love, *The Myrrour of the Blessed Lyf of Jesu Christ*, eds James Hogg and Lawrence F. Powell, 2 vols (Salzburg: Institut für Anglistik und Americanistik, 1989).

4   David Aers and Lynn Staley, *Powers of the Holy*, (Philadelphia: University of Pennsylvania Press, 1996), pp. 165–6.

5   See Anne Hudson, *The Premature Reformation* (Oxford: Clarendon, 1988), esp. chapter 9, 'The Context of Vernacular Wyclifism'.

6   Cited in Aers, *The Powers of the Holy*, p. 48.

7   Selections can be found in Derek Pearsall (ed.), *Chaucer to Spenser: An Anthology* (Oxford: Blackwell, 1999), pp. 292–6.

8   Cited and translated by Thorlac Turville-Petre, *Reading Middle English Literature* (Oxford: Blackwell, 2007), p. 137.

9   Carleton Brown (ed.), *Religious Lyrics of the Thirteenth Century* (Oxford: Clarendon, 1932), item 35b.

10   Cited in Thorlac Turville-Petre, *Reading Middle English Literature*, p. 145.

11   *Aelred of Rievaulx's De institutione inclusarum: Two English Versions*, eds. John Ayto and Alexandra Barratt, Early English Text Society (EETS), o.s. 287 (Oxford: Oxford University Press, 1984), p. 22.

12   *Angela of Foligno: Complete Works*, trans. P. Lachance (New York: Paulist, 1993), p. 128.

13   *Hadewijch: The Complete Works*, trans. Mother Columba Hart (New York: Paulist Press, 1980), p. 281.

14   Richard Rolle, *Ego Dormio et cor meum vigilat*, in *The English Writings of Richard Rolle, Hermit of Hampole*, ed. Hope Emily Allen, p. 66.

15   Richard Misyn (trans.), *The Fire of Love and the Mending of Life or The Rule of Living* (1435), ed. Ralph Harvey, EETS, o.s. 106 (London: Kegan Paul, 1896), pp. 56–7.

16   John Donne, 'Holy Sonnet 10' (12–14) in John Carey (ed.), *John Donne: The Oxford Authors* (Oxford: Oxford University Press, 1990).

17   A modern English translation of *Ancrene Wisse* and other works designed for female recluses, such as the Katherine Group saints' lives, can be found in *Anchoritic Spirituality: Ancrene Wisse and Associated Works*, trans. Anne Savage and Nicholas Watson (New York: Paulist Press, 1991).

18   Thorlac Turville-Petre, *Reading Middle English Literature* (Oxford: Blackwell, 2007), p. 129.

19   Ibid., p. 134.

20   See Carol M. Meale (ed.), *Women and Literature in Britain 1150–1500* (Cambridge: Cambridge University Press, 1993) especially Chapter 6 by Felicity Riddy, '"Women Talking about the things of God": a late medieval sub-culture', pp. 104–27.

21   Aers, *Powers of the Holy*, p. 33.

22   Aers, *Powers of the Holy*, p. 44.

23   Aers, *Powers of the Holy*, pp. 51–8.

24   For both the Long and Short Texts, see Eric Colledge and James Walsh (eds), *A Book of Showings to the Anchoress Julian of Norwich*, 2 vols (Toronto: Toronto Pontifical Institute of Medieval Studies, (1978). For a modernised edition, see Elizabeth Spearing (trans.), *Revelations of Divine Love: Short Text and Long Text* (London: Penguin, 1998).

25   Caroline Bynum, *Holy Feast and Holy Fast: The Significance of Food To Medieval Women* (Berkeley: University of California Press, 1987) and *Fragmentation and Redemption: Essays on Gender and the Human Body in Western Christianity, 200–1336* (New York: Columbia University Press, 1991). Other important studies include: Sarah Beckwith, *Christ's Body: Identity, Culture and Society in Late Medieval Writings* (New York: Routledge, 1993); Miri Rubin, *Corpus Christi: The Eucharist in Late Medieval Culture* (Cambridge: Cambridge University Press, 1991); J. Cadden, *Meanings of Sex Differences in the Middle Ages: Medicine, Science and Culture* (Cambridge: Cambridge University Press, 1993); Elizabeth Robertson, 'Medieval Medical Views of Women and Female Spirituality in the *Ancrene Wisse* and Julian of Norwich's *Showings*', in *Feminist Approaches to the Body in Late Medieval Literature*, eds Linda Lomperis and Sarah Stanbury (Philadelphia: University of Philadelphia Press, 1993), pp. 142–67; and Sarah Salih, *Versions of Virginity in Late Medieval England* (Cambridge: Brewer, 2001).

26   Aers, *Powers of the Holy*, pp. 91–2.

27   Aers, *Powers of the Holy*, Chapters 3 and 4.

28   Aers, *Powers of the Holy*, p. 82.

29   Aers, *Powers of the Holy*, p. 91.

30   Aers, *Powers of the Holy* p. 91.

31   Aers, *Powers of the Holy*, pp. 145–6.

32   Lynne Staley (ed.), *The Book of Margery Kempe* (Consortium for the
       Teaching of the Middle Ages, Middle English Texts Series, Kalamazoo, MI:
       Western Michigan University, 1996). For a good modern English
       translation see B. A. Windeatt (trans.), *The Book of Margery Kempe*
       (Harmondsworth: Penguin, 1985).
33   See Julia Long, 'Mysticism and Hysteria: The Histories of Margery Kempe
       and Anna O', in Ruth Evans and Lesley Johnson (eds), *Feminist Readings
       in Middle English Literature* (London: Routledge, 1994), pp. 88–111.
34   Lynne Staley (ed.), *The Book of Margery Kempe*, p. 8.
35   Sarah Beckwith, 'A Very Material Mysticism: The Medieval Mysticism of
       Margery Kempe', in David Aers (ed.), *Medieval Literature: Criticism,
       Ideology and History* (Brighton: Harvester, 1986), pp. 34–57.
36   Aers, *Powers of the Holy*, pp. 217–21.
37   Selections can be found with facing-page translation in Elaine Treharne
       (ed.), *Old and Middle English c. 890-c. 1400: An Anthology* (Oxford:
       Blackwell, 2004), pp. 293–305.
38   Windeatt (trans.), *The Book of Margery Kempe*, p. 23.
39   Selections can be found in Derek Pearsall (ed.), *Chaucer to Spenser: An
       Anthology* (Oxford: Blackwell, 1999), pp. 313–18.

Part Four
Critical Theories and Debates

The Emergent Individual

A marked feature of many medieval texts is their representation of conflict between an individual and society (e.g. Sir Gawain, Piers Plowman, Margery Kempe). New forms of subjectivity and individuality develop during this period as narrative strategies. The mystical movement helped to foster new attitudes towards discourses of authority as new kinds of writing, framed as personal experience, asserted individual perspectives which were challenging or modifying established modes of thought. Also, as vernacular literature diversified, several genres such as the lyric, hagiography (i.e. writing on the subject of revered figures, especially biographies of saints) and fictional narrative experimented with tone and personae: all contributing to an environment in which writing came to be less the preserve of an educated, religious elite and greater access to texts fostered a more confident approach to self-expression. It has been estimated that about half the population was literate by 1500, so that a broader audience for literature was emerging. Cultural changes were informing a major shift in self-awareness with late medieval concepts of personal religion, conscience and individual accountability prefiguring the Reformation. Accompanying developments in living conditions and leisure activities involved a shift from communal to private space and a new habit of solitary reading. Social changes included the disintegration of longstanding structures of community, hospitality and charity as a proto-capitalist mentality of the market and consumerism grew, with concomitant anxiety and unrest.[1]

Applying Reader-Response Theory to Medieval Texts

This chapter will take as its theoretical model a branch of modern literary theory which is well suited to exploring the phenomenon of late medieval individuality. Reader-response theory privileges the reader of a text as the primary site of its meaning. It is the most recent of a series of critical practices over the last hundred years or so which progressively shifted attention from the author to the text to the reader. Its focus on how meaning is produced has appealed to various critics including feminists, Marxists and deconstructionists. Reader-response theory developed from the late 1960s as a challenge to patriarchal models of the determining author, the objective text and the unified subject. In place of an author in complete control of the text, determining its meaning, or a self-sufficient text, it proposed a new approach, privileging the reader as co-creator if not the sole creator of meaning. The reader recognises and responds to sets of codes and conventions, such as the fairytale conventions by which beauty denotes goodness, while ugliness denotes evil. Consciousness of such conventions and codes helps to reveal the constructed nature of the text and the artificiality of hierarchical concepts (e.g. between high and low culture) and oppositions (good/bad).

In terms of its analytical bent, reader-response theory is close to semiotics, the science of signs (e.g. Saussure). Roland Barthes in France and Stanley Fish in America formulated key concepts of reader-response theory such as the 'horizon of expectations' which operates as a text is read.[2] As this involves the assumptions and expectations brought to the text as well as questions raised and answered, the context is important since the expectations of a twentieth-century reader are very different to those of a fifteenth-century one.[3] It is important to take account of the fact that different readers experience a text in different ways, filling the gaps and silences of a text as much as constructing meaning from the words. This variability prevents the experience from being controlled since any text provides space for codes and conventions to be resisted, reconfigured and violated. The reader creates meaning alongside hesitation, conjecture and self-correction, so that reading becomes a subjective and organic process of continually refining and revising impressions cued by the text. The process of establishing meaning involves continuous negotiations and interpretative activities, constituting the hermeneutical circle. The achieved result entails concretising meaning; that is, making it firm, finalising the sense.

The possibility of infinitely varying readings is countered in practice by the reader's situation as part of an 'interpretative community', which prevents absolute relativism. The dynamics of reading and creating a text range widely but are constrained by shared community values and experiences, constituting a 'group' response. This is what Jauss called a 'situation of understanding' – namely, how understanding is shaped by certain tropes and so on. Norman N. Holland coined the term 'transactive' to describe the relation between reader and text as a two-way process.[4]

One of the main achievements of reader-response theory has been to sensitise critics to their own interpretative strategies. For instance, analysing the strategies by which a text makes the male perspective the norm highlights the constructed nature of the subject, with consequent implications for a female reader who must learn to 'read like a man'. Further feminist criticism has worked on the construction of woman as the object of a male gaze. The socio-political dimensions of reading have been explored, investigating how literature functions in society, shaping identity and informing the 'self' through vicarious experiences of texts into which the reader projects her/himself. Reading serves to inculcate ideological values and to promote, endorse and condemn certain behaviour, even if by teaching implicitly; for instance, that adultery is wrong and leads to disaster. Exploring how the reader experiences a text has led to new questioning of the extent to which texts represent or reflect reality, how discourse functions and how the audience receives, contributing to the ongoing debate about the influence of the media on everyday life.

The texts to be considered here demonstrate a range of initiatives and impulses to explore inner worlds, individual differentiation, self-consciousness and self-esteem. The Chaucerian narrator will be discussed as a key aspect of *Troilus and Criseyde*, *The Legend of Good Women* and 'The Clerk's Tale', with brief reference to the 'Wife of Bath's Prologue'. Two non-fictive works will also be examined, *The Testimony of William Thorpe* and Thomas Hoccleve's autobiographical work, *The Series*. Interpretative strategies will involve consideration of the community of readers implied or inferred, the means by which each text facilitates an unfolding horizon of expectations, and some of the conventions exploited or violated. Comments are necessarily suggestive and in no way attempt to provide a single model or prescriptive readerly response.

A key author in looking at the development of the narrator is Chaucer, who favours prominent mediating personae who shape and colour the material they present, drawing attention to the processes of writing and communicating. He engages the reader in a variety of ways. One of his most characteristic interests is in voice. He experiments from the earliest period of his writing with a range of voices and, in particular, develops the self-revelatory monologue, often presenting female subjects. This section will examine these features of several works, in chronological order.

Troilus and Criseyde

In form and subject matter this poem announces itself as a serious work with epic aspirations. Very little needs to be read before a series of associations is set in motion. The story is set during the Trojan War, framed by an elaborate series of structuring devices such as the formal prologues, apostrophes to the gods, appeals to the muses, and division into five parts, familiar from Classical works such as Virgil's *Aeneid* and Homer's *Iliad* (although the latter was unknown in the West except by report). The rime-royal stanza connotes serious material which the generally high register and heightened style support. The centrality of

Criseyde means that she is a primary subject, and the representation of her subjectivity comprises a large part of the poem. The figure of Criseyde derives from earlier literary treatments, her name being patronymic (Gk Chryseis, 'daughter of Chryses', Chryseida being the accusative form). This figure, mentioned in Homer, became conflated with a separate figure, Briseis, when the twelfth-century poet Benoit invented a love story concerning Troilus.

Chaucer's interest in female subjectivity is evident in the version of Criseyde he presents – a complex, multi-layered persona, given subtle shades of personality and interiority. As soon as she is named at line 99, the narrator's emotional involvement is apparent as he praises her, 'As to my doom' [in my opinion] for being exceptionally lovely, employing hyperbolic terms, 'forpassynge every wight ... aungelik ... like a thing immortal ... an hevenyssh perfit creature' (I. 101–4). Readers familiar with Criseyde as the archetypical unfaithful woman, a byword for prostitution and infidelity, would be perplexed by this positive perspective. The narrator almost acts pre-emptively to defend her against negative responses. The failure to adhere to the norm forces the reader to reappraise Criseyde while at the same time questioning the reliability of the narrator, who remains a challenging presence until the end.

The narrator is an extremely ambivalent figure throughout and is deployed in sophisticated ways. He explicitly seeks to counter the hostility of 'som envious' (II. 666). At the height of the lovers' ecstatic union, the narrator seems seduced as well (III. 1317–23). His reluctance to relate events presenting Criseyde unfavourably is insinuated at intervals, putting him fundamentally at odds with his own story. At one point he explicitly distances himself from popular opinion, 'Men seyn, I noot, that she yaf hym hire herte' (V. 1050). The narrator becomes embroiled in issues of textual authority by resisting his sources, resenting his dependence upon them, omitting and altering wherever possible the tone and impact of his story. Finally, as he sends out his work, it is with conspicuous anxiety about miscopying and reception (V. 1795–6). The concluding dismissal of the 'corsed' pagans represents a puzzling volte-face which critics struggle to explain.[5]

By rewriting the emblem of infidelity as a complex and sympathetic figure, Chaucer frustrates an easy moral response. The narrator repeatedly refuses to condemn or to denigrate her, thereby making transparent the process by which impressions of character and personality are constructed. Instead of a one-dimensional, conventional figure, the narrator presents Criseyde in ways which invite the reader not necessarily to agree but to be aware of a range of responses. The archetypical 'bad' woman is encountered as a virtuous, quiet, reserved figure, very slow to yield to romantic advances, so that Chaucer's longest and most complex study of a female character constitutes Criseyde as someone who 'eludes category', according to Priscilla Martin.[6]

Much of this complex representation stems from the manner of the presentation. The self-conscious narrator matches his self-conscience narratee. Whereas other Chaucerian heroines such as Emily, May, Griselda and Constance are silent or say very little, Criseyde is voluble. She is given a large amount of space in the poem in which to express her thoughts and desires, achieving a distinct and definite presence. Chaucer greatly expands the amount she has to say from his sources; in Boccacio's *Il Filostrato* she has 747 lines of speech, compared to 1154 lines in *Troilus and Criseyde*, while the reduction of Troilus's speech enhances her heightened impact. Direct first-person narration, the primary means by which Criseyde emerges as a tangible and realised figure, is one of Chaucer's great contributions to English literature. He enjoys in its potential for self-revelation through speech, especially later in the *Canterbury Tales*. There he creates the voluble Wife of Bath, whose assertive discourse voices the perspectives of a marginalised community of women readers. Chaucer's exploration of subjectivity through speech is not simply an issue of gender, but part of a wider interest in the power of discourse, authorised and normative writing, and the use and abuse of language. Linguistic play, the indeterminacy of meaning, and acute awareness of language as contingent and unstable form recurrent themes in much of his work (e.g. 'The Nun's Priest's Tale', 'The Pardoner's Tale', 'The Wife of Bath's Prologue', especially lines 687–96).

Criseyde in Public

In Book I, Criseyde is spoken about and remains 'offstage'. When she appears in Book II, various devices prepare and colour her reception. The Book opens with a May setting filled with associations of love, prompting her uncle Pandarus to visit her to prosecute Troilus's suit. Pandarus tries to inscribe the topic of love, wrongly anticipating it as the subject of the book she is listening to being read aloud, the 'romaunce' of Thebes.* When Pandarus suggests merrymaking appropriate to the season, Criseyde expresses outrage, 'I! God forbede! ... Be ye mad?' (l. 113). In place of the identity he assigns her (young widow, ready for pleasure), she consistently asserts her sense of herself as sober-minded, preferring to read saints' lives to love stories. As she grapples to understand the meaning of his cryptic speeches, it becomes clear that she is also resisting reading the message he insinuates (Troilus's love for her). The extreme delay in her grasping his meaning is coded as the result of a number of factors, not the least of which is her marginal status and vulnerability as the daughter of a traitor. Her first thought is of danger, 'I am of Grekes so fered that I deye' (l. 124). Pandarus works hard to entice her interest through extended delay, obliqueness, using hints and insinuations, which rouse her to a pitch of curiosity. When he finally reveals the secret, the power of words continues to be made manifest in his performance as he chooses loaded terms, 'adventure', 'honour', which are calculated to excite and intimidate her; he tells her that she is free to yield to Troilus or not, but threatens to kill himself if she does not. While he continues for ten stanzas, she listens thoughtfully, pondering what he really means (l. 387), which shows how little definite or trustworthy meaning is conveyed by his bluster. Criseyde is constantly aware of elision and nuance, conducting herself accordingly with self-conscious alertness.

During her long speech with Pandarus, she remains clearly on the defensive, lines 140–4 revealing the gap between what she says and what underlies her words – the caution with which she has to present herself,

---

* The medieval connotation of the word 'romance' was 'written in vernacular French', originally to distinguish it from Latin. No associations of love are implied.

catering for her audience. Tone is often hard to determine; for instance, as she responds to Pandarus's encouragement to yield to Troilus (ll. 409–27). Her speech registers a shifting array of emotion, encompassing shock, playfulness, haughtiness and sadness. The words depend on delivery to clarify their import, which veers wildly between possibilities, 'This false world—allas!—who may it leve?' (l. 420). Her carefully balanced rhetorical questions might be contrived, histrionic, calculated, indicative of intense emotional strain or, equally, of supreme artifice. She reads Pandarus as a performer, denouncing his speech as 'this paynted proces' (l. 424). The multiple levels of her characterisation are part of the reason why the poem is held in high regard, considered as the first novel. Criseyde's self-dramatising tendencies have been read by some, such as David Aers, as her immasculated self, compelled to play societally prescribed roles.[7] Pandarus shows himself to be an adept reader, able to manipulate her fears and underlying tensions. He incites her compliance by playing upon her fearfulness, using emotional blackmail and predicting terrible consequences should she refuse. This causes her to restrain him from leaving, to reconsider and to agree to meet Troilus, concerned with public opinion:

> What men wolde of hit deme I kan nat seye;
> It nedeth me ful sleighly for to pleie. [act]
> (ll. 461–2)

This is extremely ironic in the mouth of the avatar of female duplicity. The key word here is 'sleighly', with a scale of meaning ranging from deceitful through cunning and cleverness to carefulness. Chaucer reconfigures Criseyde so powerfully as misread and misjudged that such terms acquire imprecision. This heroine's resolve to remain above suspicion, her delicate scruples and unwillingness to yield, justify the narrator's position as partisan apologist.

Criseyde in Private

The strain of maintaining a brave face for Pandarus shows when she is left alone, 'as stylle as any ston' (l. 600). She happens to see Troilus riding by and is struck suddenly by love as if intoxicated, 'Who yaf me drynke?' (l. 651). Her mood now changes and her lengthy internal debate is delivered by the narrator who deliberately positions this account alongside previous versions. As ever, the narrator emphasises how far he is constrained by his source material:

> And what she thoughte somwhat shal I write,
> As to myn auctour listeth for t'endite. (ll. 699–700)   [to write]

In private, Criseyde is marked by her introspection and self-analysis (Troilus is also accorded an interior life but to different effect). Lines 694–812 reveal her internal thoughts as comprising shifting inclinations, half-admitted doubts and fears alongside apparent clear-mindedness, 'Al were it nat ... yet ... Ek ... And sith ... if I wolde ... Peraunter he myghte ... I myghte ... I woot ... I woot ... I knowe ... seith men ...'. She is aware of men's bad behaviour in love, 'I knowe also, and alday heere and se' (l. 633). Tellingly, her chief concern is how others will interpret her:

> Men myghten demen that he loveth me.
> What dishonour were it unto me, this? (ll. 730–1)

Her doubts weaken once she begins to envisage herself as exercising power, 'his lif al lith now in my cure' (l. 741). The special status she enjoys seems to seduce her as she ponders the exciting event, 'myn aventure' (l. 742). There are moments of self-regard and independence, 'I am myn owene womman' (l. 750), alongside uncertainty, 'What shal I doon?' (l. 756). Grim irony is again in play as she resolves to keep 'myn honour and my name' (l. 762), just as an ominous metaphor refers to the sun being clouded over, with a sudden fear of love as misery, 'we wrecched wommen' (l. 782). She is tormented by thoughts of 'wikked tonges' (l. 785) and by the weight of past stories of tragic love, 'How ofte tyme hath it yknowen be / The tresoun that to wommen hath ben do!' (ll. 792–93). Other people's perception is constantly in the forefront of her mind (l. 799ff). Her decision is finalised, significantly, by hearing a song celebrating love which is composed by a woman and performed by a woman:

But every word which that she of hire herde,
She gan to prenten in hire herte faste. (ll. 899–900)

By following the example of the woman in Antigone's song, Criseyde is very much fashioning herself in accord with a recommended code of conduct. The tragic irony is that, despite her best efforts to 'read' the song's lyrics and to adapt so as to conform to the model of a 'good' lover, she ultimately fails to adhere to the ideal and provides a lasting negative exemplum.

The Legend of Good Women

As in *Troilus and Criseyde*, Chaucer focuses on female subjectivity in the *Legend of Good Women*, but here women feature as victims not perpetrators of infidelity. Written soon after *Troilus and Criseyde*, the *Legend* presents itself as a form of atonement, its inscribed purpose being to tell stories of good women through the ages. The God of Love casts the poet in the role of women's champion as a remedy against the kind of prevalent misogyny which preoccupied writers such as Christine de Pisan, who wrote her own anthology of virtuous and intelligent women, *The Book of the City of Ladies*. The Classical and mythological material was quite new at the time, many of the tales also featuring in Gower's work as novelties. The repudiation of 'corsed' pagans which concludes *Troilus and Criseyde* typifies one strand of opinion which was strenuously opposed to the use of pagan material. So Chaucer is treating potentially inflammatory material just by writing about Classical and mythological women.

The *Legend* was popular and influential in the fifteenth century but then fell into disfavour. The 'Prologue' is generally more highly regarded than the tales. It is set as a framing dream vision in which the God of Love and his consort Alceste commission the work. The 'Prologue' establishes the poem's theme as love through multiple generic cues. The May-time setting, the seasonal flowers, natural description and courtly diction connote love; the dream vision mode suggests an enlightening, instructive journey in the imagination; the legend or saint's life model evoked by the title conjures up associations of women of exceptional virtue, strength and loyalty to be held up as admirable models of female conduct. The *Legend* is among Chaucer's longest works, occupying him for several years, and is his earliest foray into iambic pentameter couplets (heroic couplets), the form which dominates the *Canterbury Tales*.

Of the apparently intended twenty tales of abused women, only nine were completed. The unfinished nature of the work suggests to some an unwillingness or loss of interest on Chaucer's part, while others interpret it as intentionally unresolved.[8] The God of Love's precise instructions mean that each story is reduced to a brief account, fulfilling a rigid set of conventions with little room for manoeuvre. A single narrator relates a series of tales with the same essential plot. The resulting monotony is open to variety of interpretations, which makes it an ideal text to explore from the point of view of reader-response theory.

Reading the *Good Women*

For a start, it is possible to challenge the accusation of monotony, depending on one's horizon of expectations. Many of the heroines are famous figures with lively past stories behind them, such as Cleopatra, Medea, Ariadne and Dido. Those unfamiliar with Chaucer's sources – Ovid's *Heroides*, Virgil's *Aeneid* and Boccaccio's *De Claris Mulieribus* – will not be judging it against them. Those who are able to compare the differing portrayals will find plenty to amuse and intrigue them. A number of alterations to the original source material suggest deliberate design. The 'Legend of Dido', for instance, consistently portrays the men as cruel despots, greatly reducing the role of the gods, thereby making Aeneas more personally culpable and unsympathetic. Elsewhere, incidental female roles are manipulated to enhance their impact, so that in the 'Legend of Ariadne' the passing mention of the story of Nysus's daughter, Scylla (ll. 1908–21), presents her simply as an innocent abused. Only the most oblique reference is made to her colluding with Mynos to enable him to conquer her father. Similarly partial is the omission and subtle insinuation when Anna advises her sister, Dido, on the subject of marriage to Aeneas. Her speech is pointedly left unreported, just deemed to be well-intentioned. The *Aeneid* gives her a long rhetorical speech helping Dido to decide in favour but Chaucer's version obliquely suggests that she is opposed to the idea (ll. 1182–3).

Among its stories of Classical women, the *Legend* provides the first extended treatment of the Cleopatra legend in English. The story leaves out everything negative about her – incest, murder, adultery and treachery – although this probably was not apparent to many readers. Chaucer was obviously inspired sufficiently by her story to invent an imaginative death for her, in a snake pit, a fate not found in any other version except in Gower's derivative account. The death in a pit filled with venomous reptiles makes a vivid and appropriate end for a martyr (reminiscent of Daniel in the lion's den, and saints' lives where heroines face exposure to wild animals). The pit carries allegorical connotations of a descent into hell as well as being a motif found in medieval romances. Thus it works as a multiple signifier, evoking a range of associations.

The main point debated by critics is the extent to which the work is a parody or ironic. In terms of representing women's experience, its attention to the plight of the victimised women varies, crudely measured in terms of assigned speech: Cleopatra enjoys a fifteen-line final speech; Thisbe's story is related at some length, her thoughts conveyed in lines 855–61, while her dying lament takes up twenty-six lines, including an assertive advocacy of gender equality:

> But God forbede but a woman can
> Ben trewe in lovynge as a man!' (ll. 910–11)

Dido's story is even longer, but ends abruptly with the curious reader being advised to consult Ovid. The 'Legend of Medea' also terminates with the same advice (thereby neatly sidestepping the issue of infanticide). The narrator passes over the contents of Ariadne's letter, telling readers to go to 'Naso' (l. 2220). This dismissive gesture, coupled with the repeated rhetorical devices of *abbreviatio** and *occupatio*,[†] seems to convey blatant lack of interest and boredom. Alternatively, it may be read as a narrative strategy of condensing the material or of heightening tension. The point is, such techniques occur in other contexts without irony. The women of the *Legend* are accorded a voice but it is largely the same voice and all end up silenced for good by death if not by the termination of the narrative. The unfinished work need not indicate failure of interest (cf. *Canterbury Tales, House of Fame*); indeed, Elaine Tuttle Hansen regards it as purposeful when the narrative stops at this point, 'This tale is seyd for this conclusioun –'.[9] The editorial punctuation (a long dash) plays its own part, as alternative punctuation (a period) could signal finality rather than hiatus. Ultimately, the *Legend* remains an enigma and is open as much to a satirical reading as to a sympathetic one – its monotony potentially pointed rather than pointless (exposing the inanity of the material), reductive moralising habits, the folly of the patron's rigid prescription, or the badness of the men as much as the goodness of the women. Perhaps it demonstrates the inadequacy of plot alone, or condemns writing which reduces everything to a common matrix in favour of a deeper exploration of individual subjectivity.

The Canterbury Tales: Alison and Griselda

Alison, the Wife of Bath, and Griselda in 'The Clerk's Tale', are two of the most famous 'sites' of Chaucer's exploration of female subjectivity. They contrast absolutely, as bourgeois and peasant, respectively – one excessively voluble by any standards, the other extremely terse – but both experience repressive control, patriarchal definition and social inferiority. While Alison is often read as a complex portrait, a rebel who counters misogynistic assumptions even as she embodies many of them,

---

* This condenses (abbreviates) material, foreshortening the narrative.
† This claims a lack of time (the narrator being fully occupied) in which to fully recount or describe events.

Griselda is equally a puzzle, as a reductive exemplar of obedience, an allegorical construct apparently disempowering women. The extraordinary vitality of Alison's extensive self-revelatory speech (her 800-line Prologue dwarfs those of the other pilgrims) may be compared with the extreme passivity and virtually silent subordination of Griselda. Yet some contend that the Wife's autonomy is illusory while Griselda exerts a paradoxical power.

The Wife of Bath seems to present an essay in subjectivity from the very first words, 'Experience, though noon auctoritee / Were in this world, is right ynogh for me'. The trouble is, she can be analysed as a composite construct formed from texts – a ventriloquist's dummy, part of an elaborate hoax. The impression of a subversive character is dazzling, as the Wife seems to counter textual authority at the same time as embodying its premises. Her monologue is engaging, lively and deceptively naturalistic in places as when she loses her thread. She seems to pose a radical challenge to patriarchal control with her bold manipulation of the Bible and refutation of male discourses condemning women (epitomised in the 'Book of Wicked Wives'), particularly when she objects to the bias of 'clerks' (scholars/author/clergy):

> For trusteth wel, it is an impossible
> That any clerk wol speke good of wyves,
> But if it be of hooly seintes lyves. (ll. 688–90)

Lack of Subjectivity: The Clerk's Tale of Griselda

One clerk does 'speke good of wyves' in accord with her expectation. 'The Clerk's Tale' provides a case of female virtue *in extremis*, a secular saint's life. Griselda is raised from poverty by marriage with the marquis, who then proceeds to test her obedience by depriving her of her children, apparently ordering their deaths, then divorcing her to marry a younger woman. Throughout, she remains steadfastly loyal and uncomplaining. Walter is finally satisfied of her wifely submissiveness and reveals all his actions to have been a trial of her enduring loyalty. But far from achieving secure status as a model of exemplary behaviour,

Griselda's story disturbs many readers by its depiction of extreme callousness and degradation. From the outset, the tale aspires to an elevated style. The rime-royal form contributes to the serious tone, signalling material of weight and gravity supported by the formal division into parts and the apparatus of closure, consisting of a formal moral gloss and concluding envoy. The setting, 'whilom' in Italy, is modestly distant geographically and temporally. All seems designed for an unproblematic reception. The story is introduced as a tale derived from Petrarch, establishing its solid, unimpeachable origins. Chaucer's source may be the Latin prose version by Petrarch but the story enjoyed wide circulation, not least as the climactic final tale of the final day of Boccaccio's *Decameron*.

What complicates the Tale is its transposition of a secular saint's life (cf. *Emaré*) into a realistic milieu with heightened pathos and complex narrative strategies which complicate the basic folktale. The Clerk himself, the inscribed reader, displays increasing antipathy to his story from a point early on when he disapproves of Walter as a thoughtless ruler, 'I blame him thus' (l. 78). Walter is presented as a tyrant, requiring absolute obedience from his subjects and from his lowly born wife. Griselda's humble origins are markedly evocative of Christ's, with references to the ox's stall. Her submissive response to Walter's proposal is likewise reminiscent of the Virgin at the Annunciation, 'Lord ... as ye wole yourself, right so wol I' (ll. 359, 361).

The Clerk cannot refrain from comment, as Walter subjects her to terrible trials, 'hir sadnesse [constancy] for to knowe' (l. 452):

> But as for me, I seye that yvele it sit   [it is wrong]
> To assaye a wyf whan that it is no nede,
> And putten hire in angwyssh and in drede. (ll. 460–2)

Many modern readers feel likewise, as Walter ostensibly has her children killed, divorces her to marry a younger woman, insisting on her ungrudging approval and participation, before sending her back to her father, a pitiable figure whose old clothes no longer fit. The narrator's charged emotional response guides our own:

O nedeless was she tempted in assay!
But wedded men ne knowe no mesure,   [restraint]
Whan that they fynde a pacient creature. (ll. 621–3)

Within the tale, the people grow to hate Walter as a murderous tyrant
and many readers concur. A hint as to the unreliability of the people's
opinion comes as they welcome the replacement wife, much to the
Clerk's dismay, 'O stormy peple! Unsad and evere untrewe!' (l. 995).
The Clerk venerates Griselda's saint-like fortitude and loyalty in
adversity:

Men speke of Job ...
Ther kan no man in humblesse hym acquite   [match]
As womman kan, ne kan been half so trewe
As womman kan, but it be falle of newe.   [unless there is a
(ll. 932, 936–8)   recent case]

The empathy may strike a chord, or it may arouse suspicion as
hyperbolic exaggeration or as a recommendation of the least appetising
ideal of womanhood. The final quiet modifier might undercut the lofty
assertion. As the Clerk vociferously objects to Walter and the fickle
people, he disrupts precisely the straightforward allegorical reading he
advances at the end.

The scholarly technique of *dispositio*, the artful arrangement and
purposeful shaping of received material, becomes ever more apparent as
Chaucer manipulates the reader's response. By keeping the moral until
after the tale, unlike his source, Chaucer is frustrating the
straightforward generic meaning necessary to receive the story without
unease. The final sequence of irreconcilable 'interpretations' draws
attention to the reading processes. The Clerk first supplies the inherited
moral reading, claiming a universal application, but then reverts to a
more literal and gendered reading, addressing the 'lordynges',
commenting on how hard it would be to find such a woman 'now-a-
dayes', and casually referring to the Wife of Bath 'and al hire sect' as
deserving their dominant position. When he dismisses Griselda in his

song, 'Grisilde is deed, and eek her pacience' (l. 1177), the shift of tone is strange indeed. He urges wives to ignore Griselda's example; in fact, to act with completely contrary behaviour, with increasingly ironic implications. Even as allegory, the Tale is ambivalent since Griselda may be interpreted as a figure of the obedient soul, or even as God. The reader remains unclear as to whether spiritual allegory is being ironised or parodied. The Clerk's implied rebuttal of both allegorical and realistic readings leaves the tale hanging in perpetual suspense. A reading of the Tale as a direct example of ideal womanly behaviour is rejected as insupportable but that is exactly how it is read by the Host and the Merchant. Much depends upon the 'situation of understanding'. Scholars divide sharply between those such as Robertson and Winny who consign it to an allegorical plane and remain thereby untouched by its cruelties, and those such Hansen and Martin who respond to the silences and 'deficiencies', the over determination and the manipulation of conflicting discourses.[10] The fictive audience of pilgrims provides an inscribed community of readers but not a common reception since the Host and the Wife represent utterly incompatible responses. The discord may be the point, revealing questionable reading habits, or it may be an indictment of the Clerk or his tale. In terms of enabling a reader to concretise meaning, it is a perplexingly open text.

The Testimony of William Thorpe (1407)

If Griselda is an enigmatic fictional character who resists easy interpretation, William Thorpe provides a comparable historical figure. His *Testimony*[11] occupies the midway space between fiction and historical record as a document purporting to be an accurately reported account of an examination for heresy. Nothing certain is known of Thorpe, who appears to be a priest but his account is self-consciously 'staged' and shaped with clear purpose: to present Thorpe as a heroic spirit resisting authority, which designates him 'a roten membre, kitt aweie from holi chirche' (l. 1219). It purports to be a personal account of his examination by the Archbishop of Canterbury, Thomas Arundel, apparently following reports of Thorpe preaching heresy in Shrewsbury, although no external records corroborate this nor is there any record of a subsequent trial. He had already been held in prison for five months before the examination. The *Testimony* coincides exactly with the Archbishop's issuing of the *Constitutions*, intensifying and prosecuting the suppression of dissent. In some respects, Thorpe displays a similar attitude to Margery Kempe in that he seems to thrive on persecution, entrenched in a position of self-righteousness. If Thorpe's statement that he had been preaching his beliefs for thirty years is correct, then this supports his unyielding stance. With the example of Jesus's suffering in mind, such figures felt empowered to defy the church authorities, interpreting hostility and persecution as signs of their favoured status in God's eyes.[12] The text establishes a glorious pedigree for Thorpe's beliefs, identifying as his teachers all the central figures associated with Lollardy, John Wyclif, Philip Repingdon, John Aston, Nicholas Hereford and John Purvey – all of whom were either dead or had recanted by then. As a text it proves that the general Lollard disapproval of fable need not preclude edifying accounts of Lollard doctrine. It presents itself rigorously as authentic with a Prologue outlining its historical situation, specifying the date of the event as 7 August 1407, identifying the subject and author as William 'of Thorp', and stating its aims of recording and publicising his experience for the benefit of others.

Dramatised Debate

The core of the *Testimony* is a series of questions and answers as Thorpe cleverly fends off charges of unorthodoxy, as much by making petty objections and prevaricating as by direct refutation. Much like a courtroom drama, the language comprises double-edged statements, pitting two antagonistic sets of ideas against one another. The perspective is partial and the debate unequal as the whole event is staged by the underdog, presenting himself as outwitting and evading Arundel's efforts to incriminate him. Thorpe's contributions dominate and dwarf those of Arundel, reducing the Archbishop to the role of bystander for most of the debate.

Some of the techniques of the presentation are evocative of the saint's life genre. There too the clash of beliefs between Christian and pagan is frequently represented as a duel of words. This reading would daringly cast Thorpe as martyr and the Archbishop as equivalent to a pagan tyrant. The learned disputation involves both parties competing as priests and scholars, each seeking to display a superior knowledge of scripture. Generally Thorpe wins by manipulating language ambivalently when asked to specify his doctrinal position. He counters the charge of intended disruption of holy church by 'youre cursid sect' (l. 1994) with a polite rejoinder, 'Ser, I knowe no men that traveilen so bisily as this sect ... to make reste and pees in holy chirche' (ll. 1997–8). When pressed on key matters of Lollard disapproval, he declares pilgrimage *sometimes* lawful, the swearing of oaths *sometimes* permissible, regularly enlisting key modifiers which exploit the crudeness and vagueness of his accuser's phrasing. Essentially it is a demonstration of evasiveness, which was a tactic of Lollard dissenters at the time, with church prosecution of heresy intensifying. One fifteenth-century handbook for Lollard defendants is called 'Sixteen Points on which the Bishops accuse Lollards'.[13] This text shows how Lollards such as Thorpe felt the need to prepare themselves for possible interrogation. Such a text might help to explain Thorpe's performance as well rehearsed, especially given the moment when his unpreparedness leaves him temporarily at a loss. He has to think on his feet when Arundel asks him his view of John Chrysostom's statement about swearing, stating frankly that he had never thought about it (l. 1705), which seems to imply that most of his arguments are prepared in advance, 'Certis I was sum deele agast to answere herto, for I hadde not bisyed me to stodie aboute the witt thereof' (ll. 1706–7). This momentary lapse reveals his discourse as carefully controlled and premeditated.

Semantic Struggle

The text highlights the malleability of language – the shifting senses of words which function variously to infer, to threaten, to insinuate, to authenticate and to undermine.

Thorpe uses many specific terms associated with Lollard-coded expressions, such as calling themselves 'followers of truth', their opponents 'enemies of truth' and the pope 'antichrist'. Neutral terms are invested with hidden negative inference, such as 'prelate' used as a derogative term for the higher clergy while 'poor men' signifies Lollard communities, and 'poor priests', Lollard preachers. Sensitivity to language informs the Lollard project of rendering the word of God accessible to all in the form of vernacular bibles. Lollard sermons focused on elucidating biblical texts, glossing meaning in scrupulous detail without distracting stories and anecdotes, rejecting the layers of textual annotation and patristic commentary which had accumulated and become attached to the Bible with no scriptural authority. Their particular interest in demystifying the language of the Bible, making meaning plain and accessible, included reformulating Latin terms for the sacrament of the eucharist ('transubstantiation') distinguishing between 'accydent' (attribute) and 'sugette' (essence) where the official Church held to a belief in 'accident without subject' (i.e. the literal and bodily presence of Christ in the eucharist). In this climate, words were loaded with potentially dangerous meanings.

Thorpe acquits himself well fencing off verbal traps. When he is urged by Arundel's associate, Malvern, 'leve alle thi fantasies' (l. 2011), he offers a prayer for Arundel, 'that he wole leeve his indyngnacioun that he hath ayens me' (ll. 2014–15). Thorpe poses a series of questions himself (ll. 2025–40), all of which elicit surprisingly meek accord from Arundel, 'Ye', while on one occasion Arundel is reduced to wordless fury, striking a cupboard with his fist (ll. 2070–1). Malvern and a clerk attempt to intimidate him, 'I schulde, thei seiden, be degratid [defrocked], cursid and brent and so thanne dampned' (ll. 2081–2), urging him to follow the example of those who have recanted, the very same named individuals he cited earlier as formative influences. Instead of accepting the view of them as enjoying 'savoure and ... delite' (l. 2096), Thorpe describes them as 'schamefulli and schlaundrousli' corrupt (l. 2111), commiting 'opin blasfemye and sclaundre' (l. 2125) by 'revokinge and forsakinge of truthe' (l. 2126). He usurps the role of advisor with firm, monosyllabic command, 'Wherefore, seres, I preie you that ye bisien you not for to move me to sue these men' (ll. 2128–9). Thorpe's text does not allow much space for the reader to ponder interpretation as he controls the discourse, so that those who recant are redefined as victims of the 'enemyes of treuthe' (l. 2134), serving not as a positive example to follow but as a warning as he denounces 'the worldly covetyse, the lusty lyvynge and the slydinge fro treuthe of these renegatis' who are appeasing 'tyrantis' (ll. 2136–8). He constructs an alternative source of inspiration, reiterating his confidence in the Lollard community, 'manye other men and wymmen' (l. 2138), 'right many men and wymmen' (l. 2140), 'manye men and wymmen' (l. 2149).

Thorpe as Hero

Thorpe presents himself as a victim of abuse, characterising Arundel as abusive, vindictive and prone to outbursts of temper and swearing, repeatedly calling him 'losel' [wretch], and threatening him, 'Bi seint Tomas [presumably Becket, former Archbishop of Canterbury] I schal turne thi joie into sorwe!' (ll. 2171–2). Arundel seems to regard Thorpe as the embodiment of his 'fals sect' (l. 2182), 'I schal pursue you ... I schal not leve oo stap [a single trace] of you in this londe!' (ll. 2182–4). The model of *imitatio Christi* is evident as Thorpe describes himself beset by persecutors, 'And thanne I was rebukid and scorned and manassid on ech side ... But I stood stille and spak no word' (ll. 2224–6).* He remains polite and calm, ever ready to comply with Arundel's demands but always conditionally. By maintaining an air of dignity and reasonableness in the face of increasingly frustrated and angry figures, he conforms to the model of Jesus's lone composure. In an extended debate, he and Arundel disagree about the meaning of words such as 'false', 'true', 'wise' and 'foolish' (p. 39). Early on in the questioning, as Arundel threatens burning, Thorpe reflects interestingly:

---

* Compare Thorpe's composure with that of Jesus in the York 'Harrowing of Hell' play.

And anoon herfore I was moved in alle my wittis for to holde the
Archbischop neither prelat ne prest of God; and, forthi that myn
inner man was altogidre thus departid from the Archbischop, me
thow3te I schulde not have ony drede of him. (ll. 419–23)

This asserts an unassailable inner freedom of conscience. At the end of
his examination, the only time he is shown alone he appears to enjoy the
solitude and peace. He relishes the opportunity to commune with God,
turning to prayer. This inner strength and reliance on personal access to
the divine proved a formidable element in the reformers' armoury,
although Thorpe's individual fate remains unknown. The existence of
two Latin versions of his *Testimony* in Hussite Bohemia suggests that he
may have escaped punishment.

Thomas Hoccleve, *The Series*

Another 'autobiographical' text of the period is written in poetic form
by Thomas Hoccleve (*c.* 1368–*c.* 1426).[14] Sometimes regarded as a
'Chaucerian', along with writers such as Lydgate and Henryson,
Hoccleve's work shows little signs of imitation, apart from the presence
of a chatty, self-referential narrator. Hoccleve was a professional writer as
a clerk in the office of the Privy Seal, part of the government
administration based in Westminster. He enjoyed some favour under the
Lancastrian regime, presenting the future Henry V with his *Regement of
Princes* (1411–12) where he develops a narrative persona characterised
by self-pity:

> Many men ... weenen that wrytyng
> No travaile ys, they hold hyt but a game:
> Art hath no foo but swyche folk unkunnyng. (ll. 988–90)

[Many men believe that writing is not hard work at all, they
consider it to be simply a game; craft has no enemy except such
ignorant people.]

210

Elsewhere his comments on the arduousness of his job lay emphasis on the demanding nature of the concentration required to combine 'Mynde, ye and hande' (l. 997), a comment which assumes added piquancy in view of his later mental breakdown. This illness struck in 1416 and forms the subject of his most famous collection of pieces known as *The Series*, which he may have hoped to present to Humphrey, Duke of Gloucester as part of his rehabilitation efforts. Written *c.* 1421, *The Series* comprises five poems of which the first, the 'Complaint', describes his experience of madness. Madness features in many genres as an illness afflicting the sinful (archetypically, the biblical figure of Nebuchadnezzar), a malady brought on by excess passion (Lancelot and Tristan), and a trope for disparagement (e.g. Langland's 'lunatyk lollares').[15] This kind of personal, firsthand account of madness is very rare.

Written in rime-royal, the *Complaint* forms the first part of a sequence of poems dealing with the processes of their own composition. The poem is both fictive as a poetic shaping of experience and autobiographical, functioning on many levels as a means of self-expression, release, consolation and as an antidote to loneliness and despair. This kind of anxious self-scrutiny prefigures later forms of religious autobiography such as John Bunyan's *Grace Abounding to the Chief of Sinners*.

The opening invokes associations of melancholy, following the harvest time after Michaelmas (29 September), 'the broun sesoun' setting the mood which dominates of decay, hopelessness, misery and death. The genre of moral lament typically concerns loss of love, life's transience, or the mutability of fortune; this complaint begins with suicidal depression which 'sanke into myn herte roote' (l. 7). Every detail evokes bleakness as the situation is specified, a late November night, and the narrator introduced as sleepless and in bed, sighing, 'So vexid me the þouȝtful maladie' (l. 21).* Some of the cues prompt expectations of love-sickness, while generally a moral allegory appears to

---

* Since each stanza comprises seven lines, any line number divisible by seven represents a climactic stanza-sealer.

be likely given the hints of universality with reference to the season (cyclic, continuous), observations on the habitual state of 'this worlde' with strong negatives denying any departure from the inevitable norm of decay and death, 'noon ... no þing ... endure it shal not ... no mannes myȝt'. The 'personal' at this point is being expressed through traditional means, the speaker's suffering functioning apparently as a trope for moral philosophy. More immediate and precise experience is related towards the end of the Prologue, with a shift from the general and commonplace to the particularised and personal as the macrocosm is figured in microcosmic form:

> I sy wel sithin I with siknesse last
> Was scourgid, cloudy hath bene þe favour
> That shoon on me ful briȝt in times past. (ll. 22–4)

The experience rings psychologically true as, close to the anniversary of his trauma, 1 November (All Saint's Day), he experiences grief, which prompts a melancholy mood and the poem itself. The complaint genre is explicitly flagged at the end of the prologue, 'Here endith my prolog and folwith my compleinte'. The poem seems designed as both a means to attain and an expression of acceptance of his illness as God's will. By the end, the narrator-poet fulfils a penitential purpose while achieving personal consolation and recovery of his confidence by means of a spiritual text which leads to his final prayer and composure. But this complaint becomes more of an indictment of other people, whose suspicious attitudes disturb his sanity.

As the poem develops, it documents the process of constructing a self-image with extraordinary self-analysis and self-consciousness.[16] There is almost a painful honesty about the account, as the poet-narrator describes his habit of examining his face in the mirror to assess the impression he is conveying. He attempts to fix his features in as 'normal' an expression as possible, trying to read himself as others read him. This might be dismissed as paranoia, but he plausibly describes the ways in which people try to avoid him. The friend who visits appears doubtful of the poet's mental stability too, as he tries to dissuade him from publishing the poem; indeed, dissuading him from writing at all, blaming his original breakdown on overwork. He is trapped in a 'Catch 22' situation whereby his efforts to resume a normal life are met by mistrust, fear and hostility, while isolation and confinement seem to corroborate his dysfunction. The text works as a therapy, allowing him to assess past and present (objectively and subjectively) and reintegrate himself into society. One might compare the early nineteenth-century poet John Clare, who also explored his madness through his poetry.

The first stage of the process for Hoccleve involves an excessive grief, which swells up within:

> That nedis oute I muste therwithal
> ... I braste oute on þe morrow. (ll. 31, 36)   [burst out]

He accepts his illness as divine chastisement, aligning himself with the everyday reality, as God 'Vesiteþ folke al day as men may se' (l. 37). This invites the reader in before he delivers the full details of the terrible affliction he received, a 'wilde infirmite' which 'me oute of my silfe caste and threwe' (l. 42); the inversions and doublets are part of Hoccleve's usual style, but work well here to effect aggressive disruption. As he itemises the reactions of those around him, there may be a degree of exaggeration, or egotism, but the intense anguish is clear as he feels rejected by 'þe peple', 'every mannes mouþe', 'my frendis' (ll. 43–6). He has a cool perspective on his mental breakdown as a temporary loss of self:

> But al þou3 the substaunce of my memorie
> Wente to pleie as for a certein space. (ll. 50–1)

For five years he has been restored to health, which he characterises as a reunion of separated selves:

> My wit and I have bene of suche acord
> As we were or the alteracioun. (ll. 59–60)   [before]

Elsewhere he describes recovery as 'my wit weer hoom come aзein' (l. 64). This detached view of oneself, observing the presence of component elements as if they are discrete entities, is reminiscent of Thorpe with his 'inner man'. But whereas Thorpe maintains his composure and draws strength from perceiving his interior nature, Hoccleve's inner harmony is fragile and conspicuously opposed by other people who remain hostile and shun his company. This ostracisation causes him pain, expressed with fervent imagery, 'sette on fire ... greet turment and martire' (ll. 63–4), as his 'herte sore gan to tourment' (l. 71).

One of the most engaging aspects of the poem is its representation of this crowd of friends and colleagues through their speeches, which he overhears predicting his imminent relapse into madness. He is a keen observer of other people, noting their gestures, facial expressions, behaviour and especially their words. He tries to define himself against their misperception through a series of strategic actions. His first response is distress, causing him to fulfil their expectations:

> Men seiden I loked as a wilde steer,
> And so my looke aboute I gan to throwe. (ll. 120–1)

The critical voices judging him multiply, 'anothir seide ... seide the thridde ... somme seiden eke ... Another spake ...'. He anticipates the effect of this, 'To harme wole it me turne and to folie' (l. 140).

His next strategy is withdrawal. He compares his enforced silence to losing the key to his tongue (l. 144). He suffers from uncontrollable shaking, fear, shame, panic attacks, alternating between hot and cold, sweaty hands but struggles to appear normal, 'to peinte countenaunce, chere, and look' (l. 149). He examines himself in the mirror when safely at home ('mysilfe aloone') in order to create a pleasing image, clearly possessing self-belief and resources:

> For fain wolde I, if it not had bene riзt   [I wanted]
> Amendid it to my kunnynge and myзt.   [to the best of my
> (ll. 160–1)   knowledge]

The intense self-scrutiny is poignant as he strives to present 'noon errour / Of suspecte look' (ll. 164–5):

> This countinaunce, I am sure, and þis chere
> If I it forthe use is no thing reprevable
> To hem þat han conceitis resonable. (ll. 165–7)

This clearly posits the reader in the role of reasonable observer, invited to concur: yes, he is well, obviously. The narrative continues, describing the ongoing conflict within him about how best to act, resolving to bear with the hostility rather than object. His inner conflict is conveyed as a kind of debate, recalling Criseyde's technique of inner dialogue. Both sides of the argument are given in a balanced, sensible way, which strikes a chord with any 'resonable' reader. Judging by appearances is clearly not sensible, knowing the truth about anyone is clearly impossible – actions should count for more than appearance. The statements employ a forceful lexis, insisting on definite facts, 'Therby ... he may not determine ... Shal ... as it is writen in bokes ... Othir preef is ther noon' (ll. 204–5). A proverbial colouring helps the arguments convince, 'Communynge is the beste assay' (l. 217), 'Preve may the dede' (l. 224). Towards the end, he can confidently assert his recovery from the 'grevous venim / That had enfectid and wildid my brain' (ll. 234–5). But he still feels despair and self-pity, despite the concern of sympathetic friends. It marks a new stage when he stops blaming them and assumes personal responsibility:

> But nowe mysilfe to misilfe have ensurid
> For no suche wondrynge aftir this to mourne. (ll. 304–5)

Three stanzas recount the fictive complainant's woes followed by five stanzas from Reason, after which he reads 'a lamentacioun ... of a wooful man ... wordis of consolacioun' (ll. 309–11) which eases his heart.[17] The 'communynge' he needs comes via writing, both the book he reads and the poem he writes.

The force of the philosophical lesson is abruptly terminated. Casually, the poet proceeds to explain how he could not finish the book as it was only on loan from someone else, who reclaimed it. This serves to interrupt the lesson (for him and for us). 'Sum of the doctrine' only can be grasped (l. 376), but enough to content him,

> For evere sithen sett have I the lesse
> By the peples ymaginacioun. (ll. 379–80)

The improvement is internal, the external problem remains. The final image of himself is as a model of stoical fortitude, 'Not grucching but ... in souffrance' (l. 384), able to leave behind his suffering, 'Farewel my sorwe!' (l. 386). The poem closes with trust in God made evident in prayer in a deliberate, elevated style:

> Laude and honour and thanke unto thee be ...
> Thanke of my welthe and myn adversitee,
> Thanke of myn elde and of my seeknesse,
> And thanke be to thin infinit goodnesse. (ll. 407, 409–11)

The poet-narrator subsumes his identity in that of the Creator, immersed in reassuring phrases of equanimity. However, as a conclusion it is a false ending, for the trials continue across the next four poems with intervening scenes with his sceptical friend.

Hoccleve's poem serves as a firm corrective to any view of the medieval period as one lacking a sense of individual subjectivity. He deploys texts and textuality deliberately to evade being forced into any position as a fixed signifier, resisting forces which seek to elide him in textual traditions. Instead, he posits himself as a distinct entity, using poetry, not being identified by it.[18]

Each of the texts examined in this chapter attests to a subtle and complex interplay between text and reader. Many works treat issues of self-representation and individual identity in ways which foreground the constructed and arbitrary nature of these concepts. Medieval writers show an increasing awareness of and interest in the means by which internal and external perceptions are shaped. In particular, there is a widespread consciousness of discrepancy between self-image and socially defined identity. Reader-response theory provides tools with which to analyse and articulate the emerging self-consciousness of the period.

Notes

1   For an extensive analysis of these social and economic developments, see R. H. Tawney, *Religion and the Rise of Capitalism* (Harmondsworth: Penguin, 1964; repr. 1973).
2   Key works are: Roland Barthes, 'The Death of the Author', in *Image-Music-Text*, essays selected and translated by Stephen Heath (London: Fontana/Collins, 1974); Stanley Fish, *Is There a Text in This Class? The Authority of Interpretive Communities* (Cambridge, MA: Harvard University Press, 1980).
3   An earlier 'reception' theory focused on original reception as having the same importance as modern responses, whereas reader-response theory tends to demote original responses as subsidiary or irrelevant.
4   Hans Robert Jauss, 'Literary History as a Challenge to Literary Theory', trans. Elizabeth Benzinger, in Ralph Cohen (ed.), *New Directions in Literary Theory* (London: Routledge and Kegan Paul, 1974). Norman Holland, *Dynamics of Literary Response* (New York: Oxford University Press, 1968).
5   The main strands of interpretation are summarised succinctly in *Riverside Chaucer*, ed. Larry D. Benson (Oxford: Oxford University Press, 1989), p. 1056, n.1772–1869.
6   Priscilla Martin, *Chaucer's Women: Nuns, Wives and Amazons* (Basingstoke: Macmillan, 1996), p. 163.
7   David Aers, 'Chaucer's Criseyde: Woman in Society, Woman in Love' in his *Chaucer, Langland, and the Creative Imagination* (London: Routledge, 1980), pp. 117–42.
8   See Elaine Tuttle-Hansen, 'Irony and the Anti-Feminist Narrator in Chaucer's *Legend of Good Women*', *Journal of English and Germanic Philology* 82 (1983), pp. 11–31.
9   Elaine Tuttle-Hansen, 'Irony and the Anti-Feminist Narrator'.
10 Priscilla Martin, *Chaucer's Women* (1996), Elaine Tuttle-Hansen, *Chaucer and the Fictions of Gender* (1992), D. W. Robertson, *A Preface to Chaucer: Studies in Medieval Perspectives* (Princeton, NJ: Princeton University Press,

1962), James Winny (ed.), *The Clerk's Tale* (Cambridge: Cambridge University Press, 1966).

11 Selections can be found in Derek Pearsall (ed.), *Chaucer to Spenser: An Anthology* (Oxford: Blackwell, 1999), pp. 308–12. The Middle English version is available in an edition by Anne Hudson in *Two Wycliffite Texts*, Early English Text Society (EETS) o.s. 301 (Oxford: Oxford University Press, 1993). See also her *Selected English Wycliffite Writings* (Cambridge: Cambridge University Press, 1978) and *The Premature Reformation* (Oxford: Clarendon, 1988).

12 For a discussion of the strategies of passive-aggressive resistance, see Rita Copeland, 'William Thorpe and his Lollard Community: Intellectual Labor and the Representation of Dissent', in *Bodies and Disciplines: Intersections of Literature and History in Fifteenth-Century England*, eds David Wallace and Barbara Hanawalt (Minneapolis: University of Minnesota Press, 1996), pp. 199–221.

13 See Hudson (ed.), *Selected English Wycliffite Writings*, pp. 19–29, 145–55.

14 Selections from several of Hoccleve's works can be found in Derek Pearsall (ed.), *Chaucer to Spenser: An Anthology* (Oxford: Blackwell, 1999), pp. 319–42. Supplementary material is taken from J. A. Burrow (ed.), *Thomas Hoccleve's Complaint and Dialogue*, EETS o.s. 313 (Oxford: Oxford University Press, 1999).

15 For a discussion of madness which analyses the moral application and function of the trope, see Penelope B. R. Doob, *Nebuchadnezzar's Children: Conventions of Madness in Middle English Literature* (London: Yale University Press, 1974).

16 See James Simpson, 'Madness and Texts: Hoccleve's *Series*' in Julia Boffey and Janet Cowen (eds), *Chaucer and Fifteenth-Century Poetry*, King's College London Medieval Studies 5 (London: King's College, 1991), pp. 15–29 for an excellent reading of the poem as self-fashioning.

17 The book has been identified as Isodore of Seville's *De Lamentatione animae doloris*.

18 For a full discussion of this self-situating, see James Simpson, 'Madness and Texts: Hoccleve's *Series*'.

Gender and Power

A number of feminist approaches can be usefully applied to medieval literature, particularly to genres such as romance which compulsively reiterate norms and depict homosocial bonding, and texts which relentlessly polarise male/female, Eve/Mary, goddess and whore.[1] Women are routinely classified as 'Other', systematically defined in catalogues of 'good' and 'bad' women (e.g. Dorigen's lament, Gawain's rant, *The Legend of Good Women*, the Wife of Bath's 'Book of Wicked Wives'). Lurking behind medieval discourses of praise and blame there is a persistent strand of misogyny, yet a large proportion of the existing textual record of the period preserves the views of a tiny minority, comprising less than 0.5 per cent of the population (the clerical elite). This distorts the impression of predominant anti-feminism. Even within the most rigid of systems (e.g. patriarchal religion) women were finding a voice. This chapter will explore the configurations of gender and power within a range of late medieval works.

From the 1960s, the women's liberation movement developed a new awareness of the constructed nature of gender and its self-fashioning partly through literature. These ways of reading do not form a unified school but rather comprise a variety of critical practices constituting 'feminisms'. Elaine Showalter distinguished various stages of feminist criticism, involving analysing the representation of women in literature ('images of women'), rediscovering and privileging female authors (practising 'gynocritics' as a counter to traditional 'androcentic' criticism), then extending to broader issues of gender.[2] Varieties evolved which focused on reading against the text as Judith Fetterley's 'Resisting Reader',[3] or developing a theory grounded in the body and language (*écriture féminine*) – the French school associated with Hélène Cisoux.

The concept of woman as 'Other' in a social system designed and controlled by men was explored in the 1940s by Simone de Beauvoir.[4] A good example of the way in which a patriarchal culture stigmatises women as abnormal is Freud's theory of penis envy, which constitutes women as fundamentally 'lacking'. Many feminists employ psycho-analytical models which build upon Freud and Jung in ways which open up less prescriptive interpretations – considering the function of archetypes and analysing relationships between women, such as mothers and daughters and female friendships. In this light, feminist critics reassess the role of Noah's wife's female gossips and the important validating function of Julian of Norwich for Margery Kempe. Feminisms examine how gender functions surreptitiously, informing a culture with writing as a male preserve – the pen acquiring phallic connotations and generative force as it acts upon the blank (virginal) page of the text. Carolyn Dinshaw's study of Chaucer's *Canterbury Tales* explores this topic in depth.[5] Desire is constructed as masculine – an urge to know, to master, to possess.[6] In such a context, female creativity becomes a site of anxiety (for both male and female). In order to enter patriarchal discourse, a woman needs to act deceptively by internalising social norms.[7] Christine de Pisan, the first professional female writer in medieval Europe, describes the despair she fell into by internalising the misogynistic views of her contemporaries. In *The Book of the City of Ladies*, she consciously sets out to provide a corrective to the prevailing hostility towards women.[8]

The dangers of 'essentialising' or 'totalising' (e.g. identifying the 'feminine' as an essential essence, objectifiable and eternal) loom large in discussions of gender and sexuality. For example, the roles played by women in romance can be seen as rigidly prescribed, inculcating nurturing and catalysing behaviour against which male identity is defined. Similarly, the notion of 'what women want' ('The Wife of Bath's

Tale') presumes a single, unchanging identity for women as a class, denying individual agency and variation. These 'totalising' effects are precisely what feminist criticism seeks to identify and to expose as fallacious. Gender and sexuality themselves have been reconceived as acts not identities, shaped by what Judith Butler terms 'reiterative and citational practice'.[9] Judith Butler has opened up new concepts of identity and subjectivity, asserting that 'The reconceptualisation of identity as an *effect*, that is as *produced* or *generated*, opens up possibilities of "agency" that are insidiously foreclosed by positions that take identity categories as foundational and fixed.' The norms asserted by literary texts do not necessarily impose conformity or acquiescence as there are always strategies of resistance, subversion and displacement. Eve Kosofsky Sedgewick's notion of the 'homosocial' develops the psycho-analytical 'mirror stage' of development* to explore the representation of heterosexual relationships as covert male-bonding: a man sees and seeks to emulate another with whom he competes to possess a woman.[10]

Women in Medieval Literature

In this chapter, a range of texts from different genres will be discussed: the saint's life which appears to glorify and celebrate abused female bodies, in the form of Chaucer's 'The Second Nun's Tale' of St Cecilia; the drama, particularly the 'Noah' plays, where popular antifeminist satire of women finds expression in the figure of Noah's Wife; allegorical modes representing women will be explored with reference to Langland's *Piers Plowman*, in particular the polar opposites of Holy Church and Lady Mede. It will be seen that even genres which apparently reproduce female inferiority and sinfulness can work in surprising ways; for example, in the romance, where women function as much more than stereotypical accessories and catalysts for male heroism. The roles and disposition of female figures in Malory's *Morte Darthur*

---

* Jacques Lacan identified this as a stage in the development of the ego, as the human infant between the ages of six and eighteen months begins to differentiate itself from the world.

will be appraised to determine how far strategies of resistance and agency disrupt gender boundaries in romance.

Chaucer, 'The Second Nun's Tale'

Although usually printed as one of the final fragments of the *Canterbury Tales* (fundamentally dismembered!), this tale seems to have been written early on in Chaucer's career as it is referred to in the 'Prologue' to the *Legend of Good Women* (l. 246) as the 'lyf of Seynt Cecile', therefore it is usually dated before 1386–7. Other stylistic elements also suggest an early composition, such as the use of the rime-royal stanza and the evident influence of Dante during Chaucer's 'Italian' period. This is Chaucer's only saint's life and one of the very few tales assigned to women on the pilgrimage (the others being, 'The Prioress's Tale' and 'The Wife of Bath's Tale').* It is regarded as the finest saint's life in Middle English verse.[11] Saint Cecilia (variously assigned to periods *c.* AD 177 and *c.* AD 362) was very popular in the medieval period, especially among women. She was an early Christian martyr who converted her husband to Christianity and chastity on her wedding night, and was put to death by the Roman Prefect for refusing to conform to the (pagan) state religion. Accounts of female martyrdom, while featuring the bodily abuse common to the genre, can contain lurid details of physical abuse, although seldom eroticised.[12] The experience of sadistic torture is usually conveyed from an oddly detached and pain-free perspective (e.g. boiling lead is felt to be like a warm bath). Death by beheading is common, with associations of masculinity and nobility.[13] Although the saint's life is a highly stylised and formulaic genre, it should not be treated as if it occupies a rarified zone of sanctity assuring its sublime indifference to politics and cultural norms. Hagiography (Gk 'sacred writing') concerns power and the nature of authority, often involving a clash of forces. It habitually stages

---

* 'The Physician's Tale' also celebrates a virgin martyr with clear allegorical potential, embodying virtue opposing sin.

contests between pagan and Christian and, in the case of female virgin martyrs, their struggles to resist familial control. The female saint sustained by God as she opposes authorities, such as rulers and parents, presents aspects of self-assertion which run counter to the prevailing models of the medieval period. Also, the genre may provide opportunities for subtle political overtones to exist. Chaucer's Tale of St Cecilia is set during the time of the endowment of the Church, a topic of intense topical dispute, and shows the early Church as a modest but unified community, in sharp distinction to its fragmented state at his time of writing during the Papal Schism which fractured Christendom.[14]

Female Agency

Like Emaré, Cecilia is an instrument of conversion. Whereas Emaré travelled to Rome, Cecilia is a native, situated at the heart of Christendom. She convinces a series of people of the truth of Christianity, beginning with her husband Valerius, which leads to a chain of events converting her brother-in-law Tiburtius and many Roman soldiers, starting with Maximus. Valerius and Tiburtius are executed for refusing to worship pagan idols, and Cecilia is brought before the Prefect Almachius for interrogation. She defends herself ably in a debate with Almachius before being executed, bequeathing her property to the fledgling Church. This land becomes the site of a church in Rome commemorating her. The centrality of her role and the myth of foundation which it fosters would seem to offer possibilities of enhanced status for Cecilia as a woman, yet the genre of the saint's life which is predicated upon martyrdom necessarily requires extinction, while also asserting the extraordinary quality of its subject as *rara avis* (exceptional among women). This tends to reduce the radical implications of the text.

Significantly, the Tale is narrated by a nun (not described in the 'General Prologue'). She calls herself 'unworthy sone of Eve' (l. 62), possibly an authorial slip, a sign of the text's revised nature, or a revealing moment where the female must assume a male guise in order to speak or write. The Tale begins with a long invocation to Mary, 'flour

223

of virgines' (1. 29), 'virgine wemmelees' (1. 41), filling fifty-five lines (ll. 29–84). The elaborate prayer, fashioned as a Classical appeal to the Muses, demonstrates literary knowledge as well as rhetorical force. It incorporates material from Dante's *Paradiso* (ll. 36–56) and cites the collection of saints' lives, the *Legenda Aurea* (Golden Legend) by Jean de Vignay (1280s–1348), as its source for the etymology of Cecilia's name. The identity of the saint–heroine is symbolically affirmed by her name, meaning, variously, 'heaven's lily' – marking her virginal purity – 'the wey to blynde' (Latin *caecus*), 'Wantynge of blyndnesse', 'hevene' and 'leos'. The multiple etymological significance almost dissolves the notion of identity. At the very least, the elaborate over-determined definition draws attention to itself as a construct, an extendable sequence, and quite loses the point, which was announced as authoritative clarification, 'I wolde yow ... Expowne' (ll. 85–6).

The Status of Virginity

Jocelyn Wogan-Browne assesses the central image of the female saint's life, 'In this vast genre, extending throughout the middle ages and beyond, the *passio* of the dismembered virgin is the dominant representation of female sanctity'.[15] In both 'The Second Nun's Prologue' and the Tale, female chastity is active and personally asserted. Cecilia's virtue is constituted by her virginal status, which enables her to transcend her gender and become an honorary man, a 'vir-ago' [mannish woman]. For Priscilla Martin, Cecilia's 'active and celibate virtue is empowered by the marginality of the Church and the liminality of her time'.[16] Her agency is initially impressive as she persuades her husband to maintain chastity, using the leverage of a guardian angel who will kill him if he touches her. She despatches her slightly sceptical spouse to Urban* where he is convinced to convert to Christianity. Upon his return, the couple receive crowns of roses and lilies from two angels. Cecilia's initiating action leads to a chain reaction as Valerian

---

* Pope Urban I reigned AD 222–30 but was mistakenly associated with Cecilia by being wrongly assigned in the *Liber pontificalis* to the reign of Diocletian (*c*. 245–316).

seeks his brother's conversion and assumes an explicatory role, 'That shal I thee devyse' (l. 266). The narrator explicitly accords the agency to Cecilia, 'The mayde hath broght thise men to blisse above' (l. 281). It is she who demonstrates to Tiburtius the vanity of idols (l. 284) and forcefully charges him to give them up (l. 287). She guides him towards baptism but Tiburtius consults his brother for advice, although his fears about being burnt are allayed by Cecilia who 'answerede boldely' (l. 319), explaining to him the divine purpose and the heavenly afterlife. Here, in a kind of catechism, she elucidates the nature of the Trinity, comparing it to the three 'sapiences' of man, memory and imagination ('engyn') and intellect:

> Tho gan she hym ful bisily to preche
> Of Cristes come, and of his peynes teche.   [coming, passion]
> (ll. 342–3)

The potentially unsettling nature of this female preaching (contrary to St Paul's prohibition)* is modified by it being couched primarily as reported rather than direct speech. The deliberate vagueness also helps to lessen the radical implications, 'And manye pointes ... Al this thyng she ... tolde'. The narrator states that the wonders which followed are 'ful hard by ordre to seyn' (l. 358), insinuating a double sense to the words: her words are both difficult to report accurately and also awkward to relate as they do not conform to the 'order' of St Paul. It is noticeable that at this point the pronouns work to erase Cecilia, referring only to the men, and the actions detailed are theirs alone.

When the two brothers are arrested for failing to worship as prescribed, they have already been established as saints, 'the seintes lore' (l. 370), and form a plural entity, which achieves the conversion of Maximus 'with hir prechyng'. The mass christening only takes place with the help of Cecilia, who brings the priests (l. 380). She addresses them 'with a ful stedefast cheere' [very resolute bearing/manner/

---

* For example, St Paul's influential injunction, 'I suffer not a woman to teach', 1 Timothy 2:12.

expression] as they go to face interrogation, inspiring them with her words by using metaphors of knights in battle and armour. They are quickly beheaded (ascending to heaven with angels, inspiring Maximus to recount it and convert 'many a wight') whereas she is arrested later while burying them and is subjected to prolonged enquiry and torture.

The Power of a Woman's Word

Cecilia is accorded prominence as the central voice of the divine will, even though some parts of the story relegate her to a subsidiary position. During her interrogation (ll. 421–511) her powers of intellect and strength of will are fully realised. Here she is empowered to engage in debate, to explicate theology (l. 319ff.) and to preach, even as she dies, continuing 'the feith to teche ... to preche' (ll. 538–9). The biblical models for such resistance to tyrants include Moses with Pharoah and Christ with Pilate (John 18:33–8; 19:9–11). When challenged as to what kind of woman she is, Cecilia replies with details of her social status (her only use of 'I') and responds to his insistence on her defining her identity in terms of religion and belief by rebuking his poor grammar, 'Ye han bigonne youre questioun folily' (l. 429). She demonstrates perfect confidence as she mocks him for ignorance, 'ye axed lewedly' (l. 430), and belittles his claims of power and intimidation as like 'a bladdre ful of wynd' (l. 439) easily pierced by the point of a needle. All this insouciance provokes him to parody her own method, 'Ful wrongfully bigonne thow' (l. 402). Secular power and prestige do not impress her, 'Yowre princes erren, as youre nobleye dooth' (l. 449). She speaks as a representative of Christians as a body, referring to 'us', 'our', 'we' and 'my syde' (l. 475). She proves herself a formidable logician and rhetorician, balancing criticism with defence, using antithetical terms and clauses, 'ye, that knowen ... we that knowen' (ll. 452, 456). Her laughter as he offers her two choices, to comply or die (l. 462), casts her in the exultant mode of heroic literature. Far from being intimidated by Almachius posing as her 'juge', she remains as blasé as Shaw's St Joan and uses a similarly familiar tone:

O juge, confus in thy nycetee,	[foolishness]
Woltow that I reneye innocence,	[renounce]
To make me a wikkid wight? (ll. 463–5)	[person]

The text stages her absence of personal arrogance by having Almachius accuse her of pride so that she can calmly deny the charge. Words are shown to be unstable signs as she redefines the terms he uses, such as might and power, demonstrating them to be hollow lies against which she proposes truth. Wogan-Browne argues that this linguistic expertise is a marked feature of female saints in the Katherine Group, whose 'speeches exhibit deft syntactic control, and a capacity for lucid, fervent and rational eloquence, and bluntly effective rebuke'.[17] Cecilia boldly denounces Almachius as 'lewed officer and a veyn justise' (l. 497), employing prophetic tones to warn him of his iniquity, 'I rede thee' (l. 502), and condemning his idols as worthless, 'nat worth a myte' (l. 511). This final redefinition is the last direct speech from her, although it is reported that she continued at some length before the enraged Almachius orders her execution.

The Staging of Cecilia's Death

Cecilia is condemned to be burned in a bath of fire in her house, and survives for a day and a night utterly untouched by the flames, feeling cold and without a drop of sweat – a precise detail which highlights the abnormality. In fact, this represents a relatively decorous and privately contained torture in a genre where extraordinary public humiliation is the norm. There may be a voyeuristic element to the retelling of stories of violated and dismembered female bodies by male clerics, whose writing in some senses re-enacts the deed. But Cecilia's execution markedly excludes sexual suggestiveness, compared with other female saints, such as Katherine, Margaret and Agnes, who suffer being publicly stripped, beaten and dismembered. No such threat is countenanced in this tale, although, as an example of a potentially revealing silence, the very exclusion may imply a latent voyeuristic impulse repressed.

Her death is achieved by an inept beheading which leaves her able to preach for three days with a half-severed head. As she dies, she continues to preach the faith which she had 'fostered' in life, the metaphor used being significantly charged with connotations of motherhood supplying an alternative nurturing model to the conventional one. The displacement or sublimation of a woman's procreative potential figures throughout the story, as Cecilia displays a strong sense of family and community and generates a stream of Christian converts from the moment of inception in her marriage bed. Her final act is to make her will, bequeathing her considerable wealth to Urban, which effects a myth of endowment with pointed resonance at a time when the Church's status as wealthy beneficiary of estates and bequests was a highly contentious issue. The end seeks to account for every detail, so that Cecilia's last words affirm the miraculousness of her three days' grace as a specific response to her prayer. She also acts as an intermediary with God by commending the souls of her faithful supporters and commissions a church to be built on the site of her house. This bequest indicates an awareness of posterity and endorses a practice which many were troubled by; namely, a woman bestowing her own property upon the Church. When the narrator swiftly concludes that Urban did as she bade, 'as he wel myghte' (l. 551), it is double-edged, implying both 'as he indeed ought to have done!' as well as 'to the best of his ability'. Clearly such tales offer plenty of support for feminist readings of the female body as a site for resisting male control and for displaying heroic endurance, courage and rationality. Above all, the saint's life privileges and demonstrates female discourse as authorised, albeit mediated through a male author. This is a matter of no small import in the context of the prevailing prohibition and disapproval of women daring to preach or teach.

The Allegorical Representation of Women: Holy Church and Lady Meed

The semi-mythologised figure of St Cecilia may be compared with more purely fictional representations of female agency. In Langland's *Piers Plowman*, various female figures personify a range of qualities. The feminine gender of Latin nouns such as Constance and Prudence encouraged versions of personified virtue embodied in female form. In the drama, allegories of female virtue (and vice) developed from abstract expressions into concrete representation (e.g. *Everyman, Castle of Perseverance*). It is a point at issue whether such figures demonstrate or realise any potential for empowering women or modifying negative perceptions. As with the phenomenon of Courtly Love, liberating aspects of 'positive' incarnations can be exaggerated, yet some readers are always likely to respond in ways which resist the norm, so that the authoritative presence of Langland's Lady Holy Church or even the lively exoticism of Lady Mede might inspire radical ideas of female potential.

Passus 1–4 of *Piers Plowman* present a sequence foregrounding these two female figures. After Will's vision of the field of folk, an unnamed female figure descends from the castle, 'a lovely lady of leere in lynnen yclothed' (l. 3), and addresses him, 'Sone, slepestow?' (l. 5).[18] Initially, her allegorical connotations are primary as she is invested with vague beauty, her pure linen garment marking her as an emblem of simplicity and humility. The motherly tone of her words is resonant of abstracted entities associated with instructive discourse (e.g. Boethius's Lady Philosophy) as well as the Virgin Mary as she is characterised in medieval lyrics and mystical texts. Exegetical training and inculcated reading habits may well seek to construct coherent systems around signs as fixed entities, but in practice, the shifting literal and figural layers are not always perfectly controlled. This figure, later revealed to be Lady Holy Church, serves to voice the concept of a heavenly life beyond most people's understanding, elucidating the meaning of the preceding vision. Will's first reaction is fear, and he addresses her in terms appropriate at once to a mother and to Mary, 'Mercy, madame, what [may] this [be] to mene?' (l. 11). The discussion proceeds in the form of a catechism, as she explains the meaning of the allegorical landscape, specifically focusing on the location of 'Truthe' in the tower at the top of the hill. The explanation expands upon the notion of an initially shadowy 'he' who wants obedience as a father who created all people and a courteous lord who requires three things, which she proposes to elucidate in a scholarly way:

Are none nedfulle but tho, and nempne hem   [name them]
I thynke,   [intend]
And rekene hem by reson – reherce thow hem after. [enumevate,
(ll. 21–2)   repeat]

Her tone is strikingly authoritative, absolutely prescriptive, as she asserts a superiority of intellect alongside an automatic assumption of compliance. Here she is being constructed as a teacher, motherly in the sense of instructing a young child, although in some tension with the traditional reticence of Mary, who spoke seldom and only in submissive tones. Schmidt glosses 'resoun' as 'in order' but that evades the primary import, which is determinedly rational: that is, not womanly but masculine, intellectual as opposed to physical.[19] The female figure names herself at line 75 and demands respect, 'Holi Chirche I am ... thow oughtest me to knowe'.

The Female Preacher

Holy Church goes on to deliver a kind of sermon, which, like the 'teaching' of St Cecilia, confounds the assumptions which excluded women from preaching. Whereas Cecilia is permitted to speak as a divinely inspired miracle, here a woman who preaches is resolutely contained within a dream and fictive personification allegory. Her sermon selects biblical quotations in Latin, then translates and expounds the meaning, pointing out the explicit moral lessons for Will to heed. Will's pleasure is phrased in the same terms as his initial awe, 'A, madame, mercy ... me liketh wel youre wordes' (l. 43). But he does raise objections in the manner of a prompter, developing the discussion, for example, to consider the role of money in society (l. 44) as a treasure on earth. She directs him to the Bible, 'Go to the Gospel ... that God seide hymselven' (l. 46), the first explicit naming of God. The episode to which she refers is that of Jesus in the temple with the moneylenders. 'Go to' is not the same as saying 'listen to me telling you about it'. She is in the guise not just of a preacher but of one who encourages a personal experience of the Bible akin to that of the Lollards (see Part

Three: 'Mystical Love and Devotion', for more on the Lollards). The inscribed response is one of awe as the dreamer falls to his knees in supplication (connoting humility) asking for 'grace', begging her to pray for his sins, 'And also kenne [teach] me kyndely on Crist to bileve'. His particular desire is for guidance, 'How I may save my soule' (l. 84), a question which drives the whole poem with Will journeying far and wide in search of the answer. At this stage it seems to be a simple matter, ask humbly and the church will provide, although the rest of the poem explores far more radical possibilities.

The main theme of Holy Church's sermon is 'Whan alle tresors arn tried ... Treuthe is the beste' (l. 85), which she repeats at intervals in the manner of a contemporary sermon (ll. 135, 207). But the meaning of truth proves hard to pin down as she is driven to more and more explication while the concept resists definition. 'Truth' held a wide range of meanings, encompassing speaking truthfully, behaving honourably, maintaining loyalty and physical chastity as well as justice and religious faith, so it is not surprising that her explanation is complicated. This attention to the evasiveness of meaning and to the slippery nature of words recurs throughout the poem. Holy Church's sermon is controlled by an underlying structure, comprising six questions and answers. She deals not just with biblical history but also with social models of conservatism, expressing the platitude that kings and knights ought to rule well (l. 94) from a position of complacency and ecclesiastical partiality, 'Lereth it thus lewed men, for lettred it knoweth' [teach it to uneducated people for educated men know it'] (l. 136). The didactic format and arid material threaten to undermine the impact, although Langland occasionally injects some engagingly 'life-like' qualities, such as her impatience:

'Thow doted daffe!' quod she, 'dulle are thi wittes. [stupid idiot]
To litel Latyn thow lernedest leode, in thi youthe.' [man]
(ll. 140–1)

Her authority is not entirely aligned with the dominant orders as there are gestures towards restoring traditional charity, with the rich being advised to succour the needy poor (l. 175). An interesting juxtaposition of styles and registers occurs as she enjoins the wealthy to be charitable:

> But ye loven leelly and lene the povre,   [faithfully]
> ... Ye ne have na moore merite in Masse ne in houres   [divine
>   office]
> Than Malkyn of hire maydenhede, that no man desireth.
> (ll. 181, 183–4)

This comparison with a suddenly introduced woman, called Molly, strikes a discordant note. Schmidt equates the name with a type of ugly, sluttish woman, so that the image insinuates a whole repertoire of long-lived misogynist opinion that only an ugly woman whose virginity no one wants can remain chaste.[20] The effective shock tactic may well alarm the rich but primarily aligns itself with assumptions which seriously undermine her position as a figure constructed as female. Here the artificiality of the gender construct is highlighted by misogynistic discourse in the mouth of a woman, rendering her as problematic as the Wife of Bath.

Lady Meed

Lady Meed* appears at the beginning of passus 2, following Will's request for knowledge of 'the false'. In every way she contrasts with Holy Church. She appears as 'a womman wonderliche yclothed' (l. 8), wearing luxurious clothing, fur-trimmed, bejewelled, crowned and in a red scarlet robe. Eight lines elaborate upon her attire, seducing Will to wonder, 'What is this womman ... so worthili atired?' (l. 19). An extended allegory now develops in which Meed is Holy Church's antagonist as Holy Church presents her, 'Mede the mayde ... hath noyed me ful ofte' (l. 20). Holy Church objects to Mede's inferior lineage (her father being False whereas Holy Church is the daughter of God), declaring, 'I oughte ben hyere than heo [her] – I kam of a bettre'

---

* Meed means payment or reward.

(l. 28). Such issues of status and social relationships define Meed as the allegory develops, with Holy Church betrothed to Mercy while Meed is set to marry 'Fals Fikel-tonge, a fendes biyete' (l. 41) [a devil's offspring]. The impending marriage is described fully by Holy Church before she leaves Will to learn from what he sees. Meed's story then unfolds as a dramatic action witnessed by Will, taking up the next three passus.

Meed Accused

At the centre of the Meed episode which forms the basis of the first dream of the poem is a scathing satire. Serious matters of corruption and unstable loyalties, represented as the intoxicating effects of Meed, are handled with a comic touch however. This type of satire, known as venality satire, traditionally criticises the pernicious effects of money. Langland employs the metaphors of maintenance* and marriage to demonstrate the vicious effects of a monetary economy on social and political structures. The sacrament of marriage is presented, closely emulating contemporary procedures with a formal gathering of witnesses, legal charters and a parodic service. The underlying cynicism and greed which typified many marriages at the time are baldly stated, 'Falsnesse is fayn of hire for he woot her riche' (l. 78). As Simpson discusses, the institution of marriage serves to enact a semantic alliance or overlap associating Meed with falsehood, then with conscience.[21] As with all good weddings there is an objector, in this case Theology, who opposes the proposed match with Falsnesse since God intends her to marry Truth (l. 120). This necessitates the journey to London to consult the king, which Langland uses as an opportunity to satirise maintenance. Meed's enormous retinue purchased with gold mocks the system of personal maintenance, combined with ecclesiastical satire, as the mounts on which they ride include deans, sub-deans and archdeacons.

In passus 3, the action passes to the king's court where Meed is welcomed and rewards her coterie of new supporters, her 'meynee' (l. 24). It appears as if Meed is powerful enough to corrupt the centre of

---

* Maintenance is maintaining a personal, liveried retinue (a contentious matter at the time); cf. bastard feudalism, Part Two: 'A Cultural Overview'.

government. Particularly disturbing and pointedly satirical is the means by which Meed poses as a Church benefactress (ll. 47–63), prompting a disembodied narrative voice, which seems unlikely to be Will, to decry such practices in stern moral fashion. The fictive frame is shattered by a long direct address which suspends the story until line 87. At court, Conscience, the royal advisor, rejects the king's idea that he should marry Meed, 'Crist it me forbede!' (l. 120). Conscience denounces her as an unsuitable wife by invoking customary disparagement of women as fickle, weak and evil, '[she] maketh men mysdoe many score tymes' (l. 123). He accuses her of infecting wives and widows, teaching them wantoness, and lechery. Here the personification allegory tips over into regarding an abstract concept as a representative of womankind, thoroughly confusing the separate strands of the allegory. As is so often the case, hostility to women infects the discussion of issues in which gender has no relevance. Earlier (ll. 1–19), Mede's physical splendour displayed her as a seductive female comparable to the Great Whore of Babylon (cf. Revelations 17–18). Now Conscience launches his attack on her as a whorish woman in explicitly human terms, 'tikel of her tail [sexually promiscuous] ... as commune as the cartwey' (ll. 131–2). Sexual politics is clearly colouring what should be an analysis of the political system, so that a woman is being used to epitomise corruption. Meed's insidious threat to justice, kingship and the social order is detailed in Conscience's damning catalogue of her baleful influence.

Meed Speaks Back

If that were the final word, Meed would be a dismal example of misogyny, deployed reductively as a type of female vice. However, Langland's art is more subtle than that for he moves on to invest this figure with a startling degree of autonomy and eloquence. In the face of Conscience's accusations, Meed defends herself persuasively (ll. 175–227). Her speech accords her a central position in the narrative for a tour de force of reasoned argument. She insinuates a sense of restraint through an appropriately maidenly, hesitant syntax, 'Yet I may, as I myghte, menske [honour] thee with yiftes' (l. 184). She specialises in caesura addresses, 'And that thow knowest, Conscience, I kam noght to chide' (l. 178), 'Wel thow woost, wernard, but if thow wilt gabbe' (l. 180). With casual cunning, she invokes contemporary events at Normandy and Calais, so as to impute pacifist disloyalty to Conscience, 'Cowardly, thow, Conscience' (l. 206). As Meed proposes herself as a superior military strategist, declaring that had she been in charge victory would have been assured, the satire grows ever more complex. Given the context of royal policy prosecuting war against France in the face of parliamentary disapproval, Meed is treating matters of huge topical delicacy. Meed proves adept at exploiting a range of grievances and social tensions, appealing to prevailing *mores* of aristocratic largesse as well as the humbler orders' desire for adequate pay, 'Alle kyn crafty men [craftsmen] craven mede for hir prentices' (l. 225). She associates herself especially with the mercantile classes, 'Marchaundise and meed mote nede go togideres' (l. 226). Langland conveys through her speech the dangerously smooth plausibility and widespread appeal she exerts. As a vice made concrete in woman's form, she is worryingly alluring. As so often in Langland's art, subtle touches undermine the ostensible impact of words as when she asks the mayor to be more permissive towards trading:

'For my love', quod that lady, 'love hem echone,
And suffre hem to selle somdel ayeins reson'.   [at unreasonable
(ll. 90–1)   prices]

Every word strikes a note of sound sense until the last two words reveal the extortion being veiled as fair trade. Meed's speech of self-defence ranges across a myriad of colliding discourses (submissively feminine appeals for mercy and leniency, aristocratic arrogance, laissez-faire callousness). Her manipulative linguistic facility and artful misrepresentation are exactly what Conscience seeks to counter by defining two types of Meed. At this point the multiple meanings of Meed's name deserve clarification. In Middle English the word exists on a continuum, variously connoting gift, reward, wages, fee, bribe, spiritual reward and grace. By eliding these meanings, Meed is able to deceive until

Conscience restores the accurate definitions, so that her power to misrepresent herself is curtailed. His exposure provokes a shattering of the false image she has constructed, provoked by his aspersions upon her linguistic expertise:

> Also wrath as the wynd weex Mede in a while.
> 'I kan no Latyn?' quod she, 'Clerkes wite the soothe!'   [know the
> (ll. 331–2)   truth]

While on one level this indicts Meed and the implicated clerks, it also mocks female aspirations to learning. Conscience smugly belittles her as having only half-read the text in question, a biblical injunction to try everything, omitting the important conclusion, 'hold fast to that which is good'. Once again the allegory is infused with disruptive, realistic import, when Conscience dismissively characterises her, 'thow art lik a lady that radde a lesson ones' who lacked 'a konnyng clerk' to explain fully (l. 338). The war of words between them continues in the style of a learned disputation, their arguments supported by snippets of the Bible in Latin.

The episode is brought to a close by the king summoning Reason to reconcile them, leading into a new narrative focus on the trial of Wrong. What appears to be a diversion turns out to be resolution as Meed's attempt to bribe the plaintiff, Peace, during the trail held at Westminster (formally conducted in a realistic way) finally convinces the king of the need to punish her. The demonstration of her pernicious influence, as she tries to circumvent the legal process, educates the king where spoken assertion failed. The allegory concludes with the king totally aligned with Reason and Conscience against wrong, and Meed is publicly denounced as a whore and left in a dejected state (l. 166).

The temporary empowerment granted to female figures in personification allegory clearly offers some scope for reappraisal of gender assumptions as they are accorded unusual presence and personality. Dramatic treatment dependent on speech tends to render such characters ambiguously however, so that the impact may be to promote responses contrary to the moral requirements. We may respond more warmly to Meed's daring assertiveness than to Holy Church's mild conformity. The difficulties of sustaining a personification allegory are evident in the periodic discrepancies which destabilise the meanings. The representation of vice and virtue in female guise may be easier to control when handled briefly as a small-scale device. As the allegory expands, the moral message proves harder to contain. The cohesiveness of such a personified female character is harder to sustain as the narrative develops, so that notions of fixity and gender identity become looser. This renders the text more open to a range of responses, including feminist ones, which in many ways run counter to the dominant mode of satire, so that Meed may be seen to embody an attractive self-assertiveness rather then a morally dubious corrupting influence.

The Dramatic Treatment of Mrs Noah

Many of the issues which problematise the depiction of female figures in personification allegory also affect the representation of women in the drama. As medieval drama operates in a strongly allegorical (typological) mode, the same tensions result between naturalistic and symbolic attributes. In the biblical account of the Flood, Noah's Wife is mentioned just twice (Genesis 6:18, 7:7) as a casually inserted presence accompanying Noah and her sons onto the Ark to escape the destruction. She, like the sons' wives, presumably supplies a procreative potential, mirroring that of the animals in their pairs of male and female. In the Mystery cycles, Noah's Wife provides a key case-study as she is a composite figure derived not from the Bible, where she barely features except as a momentarily glimpsed appendage, but from exegetical traditions and popular anti-matrimonial satire.

The combination of this disparate material leads to a generally negative characterisation of Noah's Wife. She is accommodated within the cycle drama framework as a site of 'low' humour who threatens to disrupt the moralising scheme by being vividly embodied as a type of human disobedience who is more entertaining than admonitory.

Energetic wickedness is inherently an easier topic for drama to treat engagingly than accomplished virtue. According to the typological logic informing the selection of Old Testament incidents for inclusion in the cycle, Mrs Noah is usually allegorised as the disobedient soul whose salvation demonstrates the extreme bounty of God's grace. In this reading, the Ark is the Church, Noah is a type of Christ as well as an obedient soul and Mrs Noah is the repentant sinner who is initially unwilling but then amends her ways. With the originary wickedness of Eve shadowing her, woman provides a challenging locus of reformation, especially suggestive of salvation as a miraculous possibility: in the case of Mrs Noah, if she can be saved, anyone can. Two different versions of the Noah story – namely, the Chester and Wakefield 'Noah' plays – exhibit differing emphases and different ways of constraining the disruptive potential of his recalcitrant wife. [22]

The Chester Wife

Noah's Wife is introduced as the last in a sequence, following the willing efforts of Noah and his three sons as they set about constructing the Ark in accordance with God's command. Each deploys their tools eagerly (axe, hatchet, hammer and pegs) until the Wife strikes a note of disharmony. Instead of compliance she voices complaint, specifically as a representative of her sex's frailty, 'Women be weake to underfoe [undertake] / Any great travayle [hard work]' (ll. 67–8). The immediate juxtaposition of the sons' wives all participating without demur serves to underline her isolation as the lone rebel. The man playing her role is likely to be burly, given the tradition of unruly wives as forceful and contentious, so her words claiming physical delicacy will be visually belied to comic effect. A good deal of the comedy will stem from gestures and verbal nuance, opposing the rather cowed Noah who addresses her respectfully as 'Good wife' with his crabbed spouse who curtly calls him by his first name. Behind her back he appeals to the audience for sympathy, 'Lord, that women be crabbed aye ... In witnes of you each one' (ll. 105, 108). Presumably, as with all jokes denigrating women, the audience's easy collusion depends on their gendered perspectives. The women watching may laugh, trained and responsive to the dynamics of the crowd, but no entirely unanimous 'masculine' community can be expected. The Wife's statements of wilful disobedience, 'I will not doe after thy red [advice]' (l. 101), are bound to reflect or even inspire the aspirations of some. The proximity of the audience in every respect means that much of the play's method relies on interaction, so that there are frequent addresses to the audience as when Noah admits his Wife's dominance, 'All they wene that thou arte master, / And so thou arte, by St. John' (ll. 111–2).

The central moment of her disobedience is her refusal to board the Ark. In this version her reluctance to leave is given a motive which complicates the otherwise consistent reading of her as obstreperous. She refuses to leave behind her 'gossips' [female friends], perhaps indicating some of the women in the audience. Certainly her gesture of attachment to 'this towne' helps to concretise the situation. Her determination to save the lives of her friends as she swears by Saint John is hardly an unobjectionable stance, 'They loved me full well, by Christ' (l. 205). This aspect of her as benign, compassionate, and heroic is at odds with the prevailing portrayal of her as an archetypically shrewish woman. The momentary dignity is quickly undercut by her return to the language of matrimonial dispute, 'rowe forth ... and get thee a new wife' (ll. 207–8). Emblematically, she embodies the sin of wrath as noted by Noah as well as a nightmare incarnation of the world's worst wife, 'For sooth, such another I do not know' (l. 210). The Good Gossips enter, frightened, huddled together against the storm, but any potential for pathos is denied as they display their inordinate capacity for alcohol, 'at a draught thou drinkes a quarte' (l. 231), 'a pottell full of malmesy good and stronge' (l. 233). Given the drunken revelry, Shem's intervention, forcibly removing his mother and carrying her on board the Ark, is as much a rescue from sin as from physical danger. As agency is taken from her, she reasserts herself by striking Noah, a matter of neat comic timing as well as a juxtaposition of male reason and female unreason:

Noah: Welcome, wife, into this boate.
Noah's Wife: And have thou that for thy note! [to take notice of]
(ll. 245–6)

Some sort of cartharsis seems to occur as there is no further word or action from her, simply Noah's relieved comment that 'It is good to be still' (l. 248) suggesting a reconciliation. In all God's speeches about the damned condition of humanity as well as its future redemption, man and woman are spoken of as a unit, sharing God's benign promise (ll. 305, 313). The marital union witnessed seems to subjugate the Wife entirely to the point of silencing and stilling her completely.

The Wakefield Wife

This play contrasts strongly with the Chester version of the story. The antagonism between husband and wife is more extreme, more extensive and more violent. The transformation of the Wife is more astonishing as, after three refusals, she boards the ark voluntarily and assumes the role of helpful advisor. The play begins not with omnipotent God but with Noah characterised as a decrepit old man (600 years old), 'Seke, sory, and cold, / As muk apon mold / I widder away' (ll. 61–3). God appears when called, confidently asserting the special merit of Noah and his wife, 'For thay wold never stryfe / with me then me offend' (ll. 107–8). These preliminary moves unsettle expectations, making the eruption of domestic violence much more shocking. There are hints of discord as Noah rushes home, fearing trouble, 'For she is full tethee, [bad tempered] / For litill oft angre' (ll. 186–7). His affectionate greeting is rebuffed brutally:

Noah: God spede, dere wife! How fayre ye?
Uxor: Now, as ever myght I thryfe, the wars I the see. (ll. 190–1)

The Wakefield Master captures accurate speech rhythms and idiom, which lends huge naturalism to her performance as the epitome of wifely nagging while fulfilling age-old stereotypes as she berates him for being late (what time do you call this?) and accuses him of neglect (we could starve for all you care). The use of proverbial phrases contributes to the authentic tone of her mockery of him as 'Wat Wynk' (l. 382), 'Nicholl Nedy' (l. 405), 'thou were worthi be cled in Stafford blew'* (l. 200), 'there is garn on the reyll'† (l. 298), 'Go cloute thi shone!'§ (l. 353). She is the one who complains to the audience, 'God knowes I am led ... full ill' [treated so badly] (ll. 203–4). Much like the Wife of Bath, she appears to be self-consciously performing, demonstrating the techniques of female resistance to patriarchal control, 'We women may wary all ill husbandis' (l. 208). As an accomplished performer, she adapts her behaviour to his, meeting his anger with feigned sorrow, complete with gestures and expressions (contrite face, hands wringing), and seeking her chance to repay him, 'with gam and with gyle' (l. 214), 'I shall smyte and smyle / And qwite hym his mede' (l. 215–6). It is Noah who resorts to violence first, 'Hold thi tong, ramskyt, or I shall the still' (l. 217), instigating an extended physical struggle reminiscent of Punch and Judy. The fighting is clearly prolonged, forceful and noisy as the Wife vents an animalistic fury (we are told that she can bite, whine, roar and shriek). Eventually they are reduced by exhaustion to a bickering exchange of verbal abuse.

The impending destruction shocks her senseless, 'I dase and I dedir' (l. 313). The reason for her delay is to finish her spinning, threatening violence to anyone who hinders her. The change of heart is due to panic as her feet start to get wet. The frustrated Noah chastises her, 'Ye shal lyk on the whyp ... betyn shall thou be with this staf to [until] thou stynk. Are strokis good? Say me' (ll. 378–82). In this context, her wish to be widowed would surely enlist some sympathy:

So wold mo, no frees, that I se on this sole   [doubt]
Of wifis that ar here,
For the life that they leyd,
Wold thare husbandis were dede. (ll. 389, 391–4)

---

* 'You deserve to be clothed in Stafford blue' means covered in bruises, black and blue from being beaten.
† 'There is still yarn on the reel' means there is something more to be done.
§ 'Go and mend your shoes' means clear off, get lost.

Both enter the Ark battered and bruised, rebuked by their children and, in a scene of double reform, suddenly agree, 'we will no more be wroth' (l. 418). The moral allegory suffers from the imbalance between farcical humour and didactic effect with a clash of modes. As with Meed, the energetic and engaging personality of Noah's Wife tends to overbalance the allegory, so that her spirited resistance could well inspire certain sections of the audience to support and emulate her. The intensely comedic mode encourages a wayward festive attitude which might endorse rather than condemn the feminine recalcitrance she represents.

Women and Power in Malory's Morte Darthur

Whereas satirical and allegorical modes treat women as symbolic figures, romance, however fantastic its guise, essentially presents a more realistic realm. Medieval romance is a genre in which women feature prominently. They are visible in the records as prolific consumers and patrons, from the first appearance of romance in the twelfth century courts of France until the era of Caxton's printed editions in the fifteenth and sixteenth centuries.[23] Over such an expanse of time, the form and nature of romance changed considerably, as did the composition of the audience. But the involvement of women as patrons and as consumers remained substantial. In the light of this, it is intriguing to consider how far medieval romance testifies to the pervasive female influence. Romance seems to have originated as a complement, or even counter to the masculinist ideologies of the martial exploits of the *chansons de geste*.* Just like romance fiction today, medieval romance seems to have provided escapist or compensatory entertainment for a primarily leisured female audience.[24]

Yet, at first glance, romance appears to be a relatively hostile environment for women, one denying them much effective subjectivity or agency. Helaine Newstead's definition of romance as, 'A narrative

---

* Lit. 'songs of deeds', a style of Old French poetry from the late eleventh and twelfth centuries treating of the heroic exploits of figures such as Roland. These poems privileged male realms of conquest and martial prowess.

about knightly prowess and adventure' remains typical of the general perception.[25] The male is at the centre of romance plots: his journeys, maturation and active self-development are the prime concerns of the text. Again and again narratives configure the female as subsidiary, marginal, conspicuous by her anonymity, absence or victimhood. Plots tend to revolve around male heroics, for which the female provides only the catalyst. This of course makes her something of a necessary evil – important for the plot and the male-centred adventures but largely disdained or denied whenever her role threatens to become too significant or challenging.[26] The primary roles of the female would seem to be those of victim (damsel-in-distress) and trophy (inspiring or even demanding male heroics).

It is indeed possible to gather plentiful examples of female roles which fit the reductive model. As an object moved by and between men, the vulnerable female seems to offer little radical possibility for interpretation. For example, one of the main plot devices in romance is the abduction topos. The male in romance achieves his reputation and his masculine identity largely as a direct consequence of his effecting rescue of vulnerable women. The paths of romance are littered with such helpless, hapless females. Nymue sets the pattern very early on in Malory's narrative,[27] arriving at Arthur's newly fledged court in Book III in search of a champion. Her attempted autonomy is swiftly foreshortened when she is casually abducted by a passing villain, 'He toke the lady away with forse with hym, and ever she cryed and made grete dole' (I, p. 63, ll. 39–40). Her abduction leads to the establishment of the Round Table as a brotherhood of knights dedicated to the protection of women:

Than the kynge stablysshed all the knyghts ... and charged them ... allwayes to do ladyes, damesels, and jantilwomen and wydowes sucour [help]: strengthe hem in hir ryghtes, and never to enforce them, uppon payne of dethe. (I, p. 75, ll. 36–44)*

---

* This famous 'Oath of Knighthood' seems to have been formulated by Malory.

Malory's Gwenever is probably the most prominent example of the vulnerable female at the centre of romance. Her serial abductions form the framework on which the increasing moral casuistry of Lancelot is predicated. By the time he rescues the queen from the flames (VIII, p. 684, ll. 31–5), he is blatantly contravening justice and compromising his own chivalric principles.[28] He is failing to adhere to the chivalric code, as formulated in the Oath of Knighthood, which enjoins knights to 'take no batayles in a wrongefull quarrell for no love'. Just as knightly reputations are made via women, so are they lost.

However, recent feminist perspectives have opened up romance to new areas of understanding to reveal some of the limitations of earlier interpretations. Critics have explored the gender dynamics and potentially radical nature of many romance texts. A new critical aesthetic has developed which no longer seeks to measure texts against presumed ideals of coherence and unity associated with the liberal-humanist consensus which dominated the twentieth century. Over the past few decades, scholars investigating the nature of gender and power have found romance to be a site where, despite appearances to the contrary, gender boundaries are explored and frequently challenged. In fact, female figures often function in ways which destabilise any notion of fixed gender-identity. They can embody radical ideas, which run counter to the prevailing orthodoxy which sought to constrain men and women to sharply differentiated roles. Traditional dichotomies are less stable when the literary material is re-interrogated according to new perspectives.

Reader-response theory, for example, invites multiplicity of interpretation, what Bakhtin described as 'heteroglossic readership'.[29] Even the most conservative texts can allow unintended and resistant responses.[30] A genre as self-reflexive and self-referential as medieval romance can afford to flirt with notions of female autonomy and monstrous images of female agency. Many traditional romance motifs are reconfigured by different texts to achieve, for example, inversions which challenge gender assumptions. Thus, the archetypically active hero can be represented as 'feminised' (consider Chaucer's swooning Troilus in *Troilus and Criseyde*), emasculated (Lancelot wounded in the thigh by the huntress of Windsor forest) and, more generally, embody passive submission to chance as he 'takes the adventure'.[31] Another useful approach to what is famously a rather intractable genre is to contextualise a given text within the broader tradition. It is fruitful to investigate the fluidity of certain roles to determine how far gender intersects with function. A diachronic reading of texts reveals how unstable representation of gender and power can be.

This variation across time is illustrated in the changing depiction of those employing magic. Power here resides in access to arcane, restricted areas of knowledge. Historically, such spheres of influence as healing and medicine are usually associated with women – an area of life where they are 'ritually potent' according to the historian Julia Bolton Holloway.[32] In literature, magic and healing tend to denote danger when employed by women. The arts of enchantment and healing are by and large reserved for females clearly demarcated as 'Other', either as fairy mistresses or as exotic foreigners. The female empowered in this way is habitually demonised, marginalised and ultimately divested of her force for evil. Subsumed as docile wives or displaced by male figures who appropriate her powers, the evil sorceress clearly serves to express and to assuage patriarchal anxiety.[33]

The most famous male practitioner of magic in romance is undoubtedly Merlin. Dominating the early Books, Merlin's powers of prophesy and enchantment combine effectively to enable Arthur's accession. He is readily revered, received by King Mark as 'a merveylous man' (I, p. 45, l. 19). He clearly represents an unproblematic expertise. When invested in a female figure, however, such magical ability has very different connotations. Morgan le Fay is almost his exact counterpart – the archetypal sorceress. Yet she is positioned as an opponent of civilisation, as a disruptive, malevolent force requiring strenuous control. From her very first appearance as a child, Morgan is an unquestionably dark figure associated immediately with the black arts. She is sent to school in a nunnery where 'she lerned so moche that she was a grete clerke of nygromancye' (I, p. 5, l. 29). Her own son, Sir Uriens, calls her an 'erthely fende' (I, p. 90, ll. 40–1). This distinctly negative aspect reflects male anxiety, whereby power in the hands of a female is a fearful concept needing to be assuaged. As the narrative proceeds, Morgan is constantly thwarted in her efforts to harm Arthur and to undermine Camelot. None of her many plots succeed. Yet, at the final collapse of Arthurian society, Morgan is mysteriously reconfigured as a white witch, accompanying Arthur to Avalon. Behind this version of Morgan lie earlier incarnations in which her original identity as Celtic Mother Goddess invests her with admirable power worthy of veneration, albeit mixed with awe.[34] This benign role is accorded to her in Geoffrey of Monmouth's *Vita Merlini*. Later romances such as Malory's retain this aspect of Morgan le Fay only as contingent and constrained.

Minor magical females reappear throughout the narrative. Arthur is served by several Ladies of the Lake and there are numerous solicitous damsels who periodically fulfil maternal, nurturing functions, such as equipping, guiding and protecting the hero. While Morgan is resolutely depicted as hostile and murderous until her final volte-face, other figures embodying the female capacity to offer miraculous healing are plentiful and venerable. A whole bevy of minor female characters provide expert medicinal care and are accorded the respect due to their authority, as evident in one such damsel who overseas the recovery of Tristram:

> Than the kynge lette sende for all maner of lechis and surgeons, bothe unto men and women … Than cam ther a lady that was a wytty [wise] lady and she seyde playnly unto the king Marke … that he sholde never be hole but yf that sir Trystrames wente into the same contrey that the venym cam fro, and in that contrey sholde he be holpyn, other ellys never; thus seyde the lady unto the kynge. (V, p. 238, ll. 10–17)

Other prominent female healers include the three Isoldes (Tristram's lover, her mother and his wife) and Brengain. It is notable that these 'positive' representations of females engaging in magical arts are all in the section of Malory's narrative which is of Irish origin, retaining something of that earlier, validated power of Morgan. The power of the goddess has fragmented and dispersed; she herself has descended into villainy. Morgan is displaced to an extent by the figure of Nymue, one of the ladies of the lake. Nymue's role is considerably enlarged and developed by Malory. She repeatedly acts to counter Morgan's evil, rescuing Arthur from murderous plots.* She and other 'white' witches even assume the masculine role of rescuer for abducted knights taken prisoner by Morgan and her cronies (e.g. III, p.151; V, p. 392). Not only does Nymue assume the role of chief enchantress but she also takes on Morgan's original roles of seductress and conqueror of Merlin. In earlier versions of the Arthurian story, it is Morgan who is at first Merlin's willing pupil and who then betrays him. This splitting of roles, or doubling in the Jungian sense, is typical of romance.† In magical narrative, as Anne Wilson asserts, all the figures are one, projections of the central psyche, in this case presenting the two sides of Arthur – his good and evil propensities.[35] The various Isoldes also display this tendency to fragment and to duplicate as narratives encircle and revisit anxieties. The more versions of 'good' Morgan there are, the less her threatening aspect unsettles the narrative. By the end, as we have seen, both sides of the goddess are reconciled uniquely in Malory. The fractured pieces of the self are reconciled. But, from a gender-conscious perspective, the transgressive power of the female has been recuperated.

Nevertheless, although romance texts such as Malory's may seek to displace or to discredit female agency in order to assert male superiority, they need not succeed, either in laying to rest unwelcome notions of female power or in rendering female agency impotent. Resistant readers abound, now as then. Overall, there is no simple dichotomy between male and female roles or identities. Rather there is continual scope for reading disruptively, for countering the norm, for multiplying textual meaning(s) and for reading against the grain. Categories of 'good' and 'bad', contained/safe and errant/dangerous become unstable. Despite the formulaic elements, type situations and repeated motifs, romance is a world in which gender and power are shifting, multivalent concepts. In this it is both endlessly provocative and equivocal.

* Examples occur in I, pp. 85–7 and pp. 93–4.
† Compare the young and aged females in *Sir Gawain and the Green Knight* who function as a diptych, representing the dual nature of womanhood as seductress and sorceress/crone.

Attending to the representation of women across different genres reveals the deployment of many recurrent types and pervasive misogyny but, from feminist perspectives, also ensures plenty of room for dissent, for alternative sympathies and for a variety of resistant readings. Whether as the embodiment of cultural stereotypes, allegorical figures, or symbolic values, women are accorded shifting and polyvocal presence.

Notes

1   Alcuin Blamires, Karen Pratt and C. W. Marx (eds), *Woman Defamed and Woman Defended: An Anthology of Medieval Texts* (Oxford: Clarendon, 1992).
2   For an excellent overview of the early decades of feminist theory, see Elaine Showalter (ed.), *The New Feminist Criticism: Essays on Women, Literature and Theory* (London: Virago, 1985), Introduction. Showalter defines the evolution of feminist approaches to women's difference as following several stages: i) biological (focusing on biological difference, favouring analogies using the female body); ii) linguistic (attending to the male-constructed *parole*, as well as blanks, gaps, silences); iii) psychoanalytic (concepts of the phallic lack, entering the symbolic realm of language and its laws); iv) cultural (interested in elucidating context, enlisting anthropological models, e.g. 'dominant' and 'muted' cultures).
3   Judith Fetterley, *The Resisting Reader: A Feminist Approach to American Fiction* (Bloomington, IN: Indiana University Press, 1978).
4   Simone de Beauvoir, *The Second Sex* trans. H. M. Parshley (London: Vintage, 1999), explores the construction of femininity, encapsulated in her famous dictum, 'One is not born a woman, one becomes one'.
5   Carolyn Dinshaw, *Chaucer's Sexual Poetics* (Madison: University of Wisconsin Press, 1989).
6   The literary treatment of desire is discussed by Toril Moi, *Sexual/Textual Politics* (London: Routledge, 2000).
7   Judith Butler's work has been particularly influential, see especially, *Gender Trouble: Feminism and the Subversion of Identity* (New York: Routledge, 1990), *Bodies That Matter: On the Discursive Limits of 'Sex'* (New York: Routledge, 1993), *Excitable Speech: A Politics of the Speech Act* (New York: Routledge, 1997).

8   Christine de Pisan, *The Book of the City of Ladies*, trans. E. J. Richards (London: Pan, 1983).

9   See Judith Butler, *Bodies That Matter*.

10 Eve Kosofsky Sedgewick, *Between Men: English Literature and Male Homosocial Desire* (New York: Columbia University Press, 1985).

11 V. A. Kolve, 'Chaucer's Second Nun's Tale and the Iconography of St Cecilia', in *New Perspectives on Chaucer Criticism* ed. D. M. Rose (Norman, OK: Pilgrim, 1981), p. 139.

12 Kathryn Gravdal argues for latent sexual violence underpinning representations of the abused female body in saints' lives, in *Ravishing Maidens: Writing Rape in Medieval French Literature and Law* (Philadelphia: University of Pennsylvania Press, 1991), p. 24. Jocelyn Wogan-Browne counters such a totalising view, in 'The Virgin's Tale' in Ruth Evans and Leslie Johnson (eds), *Feminist Readings in Middle English Literature: The Wife of Bath and All Her Sect* (London: Routledge, 1994), pp. 165–94.

13 Sarah Salih, *Versions of Virginity in Late Medieval England* (Cambridge: Brewer, 2001), p. 67.

14 David Aers and Lynn Staley, *The Powers of the Holy: Religion, Politics and Gender in Late Medieval English Culture* (Pennsylvania: Pennsylvania State University Press, 1996), p. 210.

15 Wogan-Browne, 'The Virgin's Tale', p. 165. Wogan-Browne discusses the particular function of the female body in the saint's life as part of the fashioning of cultural and gender boundaries and explores the female body as a trope for male possession, operating as a site in which to posit notions of male territory and conquest. This notion clearly informs later expressions, such as that of John Donne, *Elegy 2*, 'To His Mistress Going to Bed', 'O my America, my new-found land!' (l. 27) in *John Donne: The Oxford Authors*, ed. John Carey (Oxford: Oxford University Press, 1990).

16 Priscilla Martin, *Chaucer's Women: Nuns, Wives and Amazons* (Basingstoke: Macmillan, 1996), p. xvi.

17 Wogan-Browne, 'The Virgin's Tale', p. 179.

18 William Langland, *The Vision of Piers Plowman: A Complete Edition of the B-Text*, ed. A. V. C. Schmidt (London: Dent, 1984).

19 Schmidt (ed.), *Piers Plowman*, p. 10.

20 Schmidt (ed.), *Piers Plowman*, p. 16.

21 James Simpson, *Piers Plowman: An Introduction to the B-Text* (Harlow: Longman, 1990), p. 56.

22 Both Noah plays discussed here can be found in Peter Happé (ed.), *English Mystery Plays* (Harmondsworth: Penguin, 1975).

23   See for example, Felicity Riddy, 'Middle English Romance: Family, Marriage, Intimacy' in Roberta L. Kreuger (ed.), *The Cambridge Companion to Medieval Romance* (Cambridge: Cambridge University Press, 2000), pp. 235–52; Jennifer R. Goodman, '"That women holde in ful greet reverence": Mothers and Daughters Reading Chivalric Romances', in Lesley Smith and Jane H. M. Taylor (eds), *Women, the Book and the Worldly: Selected Proceedings of the St. Hilda's Conference, 1993* (Cambridge: Brewer, 1995), pp. 25–30; another relevant chapter in this volume is that by Jennifer Summit, 'William Caxton, Margaret Beaufort and the Romance of Female Patronage', pp. 151–65.

24   A study of modern romance fiction and its compensatory function with interesting ramifications for medieval romance is Janice Radway's *Reading the Romance: Women, Patriarchy, and Popular Literature* (Chapel Hill: University of North Carolina Press, 1984).

25   Helaine Newstead, *A Manual of Writings in Middle English 1050–1500*, gen. ed. J. Burke Severs (New Haven, CN: Connecticut Academy of Arts and Sciences, 1967), p. 11.

26   For a discussion of the role of women as items exchanged by men and their function as the premise upon which the romance construction of masculinity depends, see Marion Wynne-Davies, *Women and Arthurian Literature: Seizing the Sword* (London: Macmillan, 1996), p. 64. See also Angela Jane Weisl, *Conquering the Reign of Femeny: Gender and Genre in Chaucer's Romance* (Cambridge: Brewer, 1995), p. 84.

27   Eugène Vinaver (ed.), *Malory: Works* (Oxford: Oxford University Press, 1977).

28   For discussion of this point, see Terence McCarthy, *Le Morte Darthur and Romance*, Arthurian Studies (Woodbridge: Brewer, 1991), pp. 160–75.

29   Pam Morris (ed.), *The Bakhtin Reader: Selected Writings of Bakhtin, Medvedev, Voloshinov* (London: Arnold, 1994).

30   Anne Clark Bartlett, *Male Authors, Female Readers: Representation and Subjectivity in Middle English Devotional Literature* (Ithaca: Cornell University Press, 1995), p. 27.

31   Jill Mann, 'Malory: Knightly Combat in *Le Morte D'Arthur*', in Boris Ford (ed.), *Medieval Literature Part One: Chaucer and the Alliterative Tradition*, New Pelican Guide to English Literature, vol. 1 (Harmondsworth: Penguin, 1991), pp. 331–9.

32   Julia Bolton Holloway, Joan Bechtold and Constance S. Wright (eds), *Equally in God's Image: Women in the Middle Ages* (London: Lang, 1990), p. 168.

33   Margaret Hallissey, *Venomous Woman: Fear of the Female in Literature* (New York: Greenwood, 1987) p. 62.

34   For a broad discussion of this subject, see Juliette Wood, 'Celtic Goddesses: Myths and Mythology' in Carolyne Larrington (ed.), *The Feminist Companion to Mythology* (London: Pandora, 1992), pp. 118–36.

35   A psychological reading of romance is given by Anne Wilson, *The Magical Quest: the Use of Magic in Arthurian Romance* (Manchester: Manchester University Press, 1988).

Fun and Games

Aristotle (*c.* 350 BC) had observed the distinctively human quality of laughter, 'Of all living creatures, only man is endowed with laughter' (*De Anima*, III.10). Early Christianity had condemned laughter (e.g. Tertullian, Cyprian, John Chrysostom), particularly suspicious of festivities associated with pagan practices and debauchery. Yet the medieval period contains continuing forms of ancient rituals such as folk drama commemorating death, rebirth and renewal, apart from the culturally condoned form of Jesus as reviled, executed 'king' who is miraculously restored to life. The impulse to comic relief was acknowledged by various church festivals such as the feast of fools, the boy bishop, parodic services, Paschal laughter* and Christmas games. Some of these were occasions of extreme high spirits, involving the clergy hurling excrement from carts. Within the most sacred part of the church where divine offices were sung, the underside of the choir seats often preserve medieval carvings known as misericords ('places of merciful rest'). These frequently depict scenes of robust domestic comedy with wives beating husbands, grotesque imagery such as monsters and devils, and highly explicit deviant sexuality. Manuscript marginalia similarly attests to an embracing of the vulgar and obscene even in sacred contexts.

* Paschal laughter was officially condoned laughter at Easter, when the sermon would be jocular, even obscene, as part of the celebration of rebirth and resurrection.

Humorous literature of the period has been largely neglected apart from critical attention on Chaucer's fabliaux. In fact, comedy is a common mode in the medieval period with many fantastic tales from as early as the thirteenth century, such as the *Land of Cockayne* and *Aucassin and Nicolette*, which imagine topsy-turvy worlds in which geese fly while roasting on spits and men become pregnant.[1] The motifs of fantasy and inversion are the primary characteristics of medieval humour as norms are violated and values ironised. A moral purpose was generally attached as Henryson explains using a traditional metaphor of the nut and its shell:

> The nuttes schell, thocht it be hard and teuch,   [tough]
> Heildis the kirnill, and is delectabill.[2]   [holds]

The justification for humour was usually as release; another commonly invoked metaphor being that of an overstrung bow needing to be relaxed. Henryson asserts the necessity of mixing 'merie sport' with 'ernist', 'To light the spreit, and gar [make] the tyme be schort' (l. 21). Pure entertainment was not a point at issue as the prevailing moralising imperative insisted on the didactic value of all created works:

> For seint Paul seith that al that writen is,
> To oure doctrine it is ywrite, ywis;
> Taketh the fruyt, and lat the chaf be stille.[3] (ll. 3441–3)

The aesthetic that judged a 'mixed' mode most effective produced the richly varied texture of medieval drama, Chaucer's *Canterbury Tales* and Langland's exhuberant medley of theological cruxes, *Piers Plowman*. Polarising habits of thought cohering around oppositional repre- sentation produced depictions of the 'bad' and 'low' in order to counterbalance and to enhance the 'good' and the 'sublime'. Therefore, in the serious didactic mode of the cycle drama, there is plenty of farce and frivolity with squabbling in the York 'Harrowing of Hell'. The elastic boundaries of acceptability could extend to include a parodic nativity with a stolen sheep alongside the genuine nativity of Jesus in the

'Second Shepherds' Play'. Deadly sin could be luxuriated in as an occasion for scandalous behaviour to be manifest, to gross comedic effect, as in *Piers Plowman*. The most famous comedy of all is Chaucer's experimentation with the genre of fabliau. His works portray the baser elements of human nature affording his courtly audience a taste of lowlife shenanigans. An illuminating approach to this material can be made from the perspectives of the 'carnivalesque'.

Bakhtin and the Notion of the Carnivalesque

Mikhail Bakhtin (1895–1975) developed a thorough analysis of social release mechanisms and communal festivities which popularised the notion of the carnivalesque. He developed his ideas in his book, *Rabelais and His World*, first published in the West in 1968 to immediate critical acclaim.[4] This work focused particularly on Francois Rabelais' *Gargantua and Pantagruel* (published as five books between 1532 and 1553) with some attention on the late-medieval context from which it sprang.[5]

Carnival as an occasion for public revelry continues today in exotic form in Rio de Janeiro as well as smaller-scale community events such as the Notting Hill Carnival in London. The end of winter is associated with celebratory feasting in many cultures, while customs of suspending regulations and inverting hierarchies stem from the pagan Saturnalia of the Roman period when slaves were freed and there was a general licence for ridicule in honour of Saturn's temporary reinstatement. Cross-cultural analogies include the Jewish Purim and Indian Holi, suggesting a deeply embedded human impulse. The medieval festival of carnival evolved as a religious occasion marking the eve of Lent with the giving up of meat, *carnem levare*, or farewell to meat, *carne vale*. All fat had to be consumed before Lent, hence the name 'mardi gras' (fat Tuesday). Bakhtin identifies various occasions of medieval carnival, including public fairs, which were large scale and frequent, as at Lyon where the fair was held four times a year for two weeks at a time. Holidays on saints' days and street processions were numerous. The

French custom of the charivari mocked marriages involving notable disparity of age or rank, expressing social unease, although hardly asserting decorum as the drunken youths tended to become violent. The anarchic aspects of mass revelry are analysed approvingly by Bakhtin as 'a suspension of all hierarchical rank, privileges, norms, and prohibitions' (p. 10). His view of the 'folk' as an enduring popular entity, one representing a force for energetic resistance to official culture and serious ideology, clearly has its foundations in Stalinist Russia.

He distinguishes three forms of carnivalesque expression: ritual spectacle (performance), written works (such as parodic texts) and vulgar language (including curses, obscenities and swearing, often involving the verbal dismembering and isolation of bodily parts). He regards it as an unbounded, participative, free-playing realm where generative energy is celebrated sometimes with chastisement and mockery, although 'bare negation is completely alien to folk culture' (p. 11). Unlike official culture which maintains rigid distinctions (p. 168), carnival is always 'ambivalent and festive' (p. 13), mingling positive with negative, praise with abuse. Carnivalesque expression can involve violence and harsh treatment, although Bakhtin carefully asserts that it is 'in no way hostile to women' (p. 240). It serves as an outlet, a temporary channel for pent-up and latent antagonisms. In particular, an underlying repudiation of mortality is identified by Bakhtin as the essence of carnival, 'Laughter, food and drink defeat death' (p. 299).

The Carnivalesque Body

This indulgence in excess is the key to the carnivalesque mode, which presents distorted images of grotesquely distended and hideously emaciated bodies (p. 292). Physical squeamishness was not a feature of a period routinely venerating dismembered saints' bodies as part of the cult of relics, and where public execution, branding and amputations were de rigueur. Carnival relishes 'grotesque realism' (p. 18) particularly involving 'degradation', an inclination downwards, physically and metaphorically, hence transposing the lofty, spiritual and abstract onto a material plane (p. 19). The body is typically fluid, partial, dismembered, incomplete, in the process of becoming (pp. 24ff., ll. 316–17). Above all, the focus tends to be on rendering the body as openness and swelling, a site of orifices and protuberances. The medieval concept of the body as social and universal is far removed from modern notions of the particular, individual and private. The carnivalesque representation of the body places the emphasis on expulsion (bodily fluids, excrement) and sexual organs. An image of hell as a gaping mouth is quintessentially carnivalesque, portraying death as a swallowing, a descent into the nether regions.

Bakhtin's analysis has been subjected to a good deal of modification, especially questioning his assumptions about the liberating force of carnival. It may function as a permissive event but need not be essentially radical. Temporary licence can be seen as functioning paradoxically to sustain and shore up structures of repression and restraint. Two additional Bakhtinian concepts have become part of general critical vocabulary: heteroglossia and multiplicity of styles, which explore the multivalence of language and the disruptive effects of mixed modes.

The Ludicrous and the Ludique

A related theory is concerned with analysing the nature and function of play. Game theory investigates texts from the perspectives of the playfulness of language (especially as transgressive and volatile), form (e.g. pastiche) and genre (violating boundaries, reconfiguring and inverting conventions). This attends to features such as gross exaggeration, farcical excess, extreme scurrility, sordidness, indecency and irreligiousness. Clearly fabliau provides plenty of material for such an analysis as it exhibits precisely the cocktail of excess and distortion that constitutes the ludique. The fabliau world of Chaucer's 'The Miller's Tale' and 'The Reeve's Tale' exploits folk traditions and is imbued with the spirit of mockery and release associated with carnival in which riot displaces restraint and chaos is celebrated over order. Stories revolve around fast-paced sexual riot and intensely competitive energies. Ludicrous texts may provide fantasy escapism, enacting a collective reassurance, helping to assuage anxieties and loosen tensions. Game theory is alert to the operation of restraining mechanisms and the promotion of controlling rather than liberating impulses.[6] Games require rules, with penalties for nonconformity. Games are predicated upon distinction, point scoring and rivalry. There are losers and winners. So too with texts such as fabliaux which appear to scorn authority; recent studies have revealed that their licence is authorised, their discourse officially approved.[7] Mockery and satire are forms of humour which create an illusion of play space and free rein.

Humour and comedy are notoriously difficult to assess. An enigmatic group of pilgrim badges discovered in the Netherlands, dated *c.* 1375–1425, represent phalluses and vaginas in extraordinary forms.[8] Badges shaped like winged genitalia may possibly record the kind of scenes enacted in carnival as occasions when such badges might be worn. The imagery is reminiscent of French fabliau stories of talking vaginas.[9] One badge is in the form of three phalluses bearing a crowned vagina, apparently a mock-religious image possibly referring to a procession of the Virgin. Other badges are in the form of a vagina on stilts and a vagina on pilgrimage, complete with staff, hat and rosary beads. These mysterious artefacts have no known provenance or function, but testify to the bizarre and elusive nature of medieval humour.

Robert Henryson's *Moral Fables*

Little is known about Robert Henryson (*c.* 1420/35–*c.* 1508), a Scottish Chaucerian who wrote a continuation of *Troilus and Criseyde*, *The Testament of Cresseid*. He is primarily remembered for his collection of beast fables, many from the Aesopic tradition.[10] His *Moral Fables* contains a variety of tales affronting and confronting norms, demonstrating a keen sense of linguistic play. The lexis of play and pretence appears at intervals, particularly in 'The Wolf and the Wether' with a sheep disguised as a dog, a foolish 'counterfait' (l. 2497) who protests his intention 'bot to have playit' (ll. 2558, 2578), but is treated as 'bourding in ernest' (l. 2560), offending against 'fair play' (l. 2564) and is killed despite his 'prettie play' (l. 2583).

Several aspects of the *Fables* appeal to a folk sensibility. They are filled with proverbial lore and often display values of plain speaking and practical wisdom over book-learning, along with an ethic of practical common sense. Henryson was a schoolmaster, but combines his learning and didacticism with exactly the prescribed dose of humour which his Prologue recommends. The morality of each fable is often playfully concealed or withheld and tends to be unpredictable. The humour is one of dour irony and understatement rather than sheer fun, but Henryson's adaptation of the beast fable form is as innovative as Chaucer's use of fabliau. The stories are shaped into a complex structure and the genre acquires unprecedented levels of psychological realism. The narrator is subtly deployed along with skilful manipulation of style and register. The whole work encompasses penetrating satire, alongside plenty of wily roguery of a sufficiently bold kind as to evince many of the techniques of carnivalesque humour.

Parodic language is plentiful as Henryson juxtaposes different styles of speech and different registers for comic effect, as with the hens in 'The Cock and the Jasper', his version of the story told by Chaucer as 'The Nun Priest's Tale'. The three hens are assigned strikingly contrasting speech modes in a rhetorical set-piece juxtaposing formal complaint, proverbial sententiousness, vulgarity and religious funda-mentalism to ludicrous effect. In 'The Wolf and the Wether', the shepherd mourns his dead sheepdog in the elevated tones of a courtly lover, 'Now is my Darling deid, allace' (l. 2355). Elevated and Latinate language is frequently deployed by the rogues although they are just as adept at feigning simplicity at times as part of their repertoire of guile.

There are also set pieces which formally parody religious practices and texts, such as the parody of the formal lament for the dead in the tale of 'The Cock and the Jasper':

'Quha sall our lemman be? Quha sall us leid?
Quhen we are sad, quha sall unto us sing?' (ll. 502–3)

The 'Confession of the Fox' treats false confession by the sinful in a manner which is reminiscent of Passus 5 of *Piers Plowman*, where reform is inimical to the character's identity. The Fox partakes of each stage of the formal sacrament of confession, while exhibiting an unrepentant appetite for 'Lambes flesche that new ar lettin blude' [newly bled] (l. 701). The reference to a lamb evokes associations with Jesus, the 'Lamb of God', while later a mock-baptism turns a kid goat into a salmon for the resourceful fox, 'Ga doun Schir Kid, cum up Schir Salmond agane!' (l. 751). This transformation of forbidden flesh into permissible fish involves exactly the sort of sacrilegious play of carnival. The same religious prohibition is evaded in the 'Fox, the Wolf and the Cadger' [travelling food seller] which is set during Lent. In an inversion of official moral codes, cunning and fraud are approved in beast fables representing the proverbial trickery of the fox. This fable celebrates the Fox's ruse to cheat the Cadger, 'bleir yon Carllis Ee' [fool that peasant] (l. 2041), repeating the trick on the Wolf, according to the established comic principle of repetition. No sympathies attach to the duped; rather, rough justice prevails as the foolish Wolf is beaten with a club (l. 2196), 'neir weill dungin to the deid' [nearly beaten to death], while 'blude wes rynnand over his heillis' (l. 2202). The 'Wolf and the Lamb' depicts a parodic Passion, with 'The selie Lamb ... meik and Innocent' (l. 2625), advocating New Testament mercy as opposed to Old Testament vengeance, but being killed without 'grace' and consumed in a mock-eucharistic scene, 'Syne drank his blude and off his flesche can eit' (l. 2702). Grim bodily dismemberment forms the climactic conclusion to the *Fables*, as the hapless mouse and the predatory paddock [toad/frog] both fall prey to the kite, who 'belliflaucht ful fettilie thame fleid' [flayed them very skilfully, in one movement removing their skin] (l. 2904).

Carnivalesque Language

Bakhtin's carnivalesque language plays a major part in the creation of humour. Oaths and curses are common, but no consistent consequences occur; sometimes oaths are fulfilled and curses effective, but at other times even apparently heartfelt and justified appeals for divine intervention are futile. In 'The Fox, the Wolf and the Farmer', the angry farmer curses his sluggish oxen, consigning them to the Wolf. But when the literally minded Wolf claims them, he protests that he did not mean it:

'Schir ... ane man may say in greif,
And syne ganesay, fra he advise and se'   [retract]
(ll. 2273–4)

The tale explores notions of intention and distinctions between the spirit and the letter of an utterance, so that when the Wolf swears to fulfil the man's oath (l. 2250), insisting that a gift freely given cannot be rescinded, the dangerous entrapment of word-play is scathingly satirised. The Farmer's protest, 'God forbid, Schir, all hechtis [oaths] suld haldin [kept] be!' (l. 2276) is double-edged, asserting an innocence which, strictly speaking, his loose tongue does not endorse. Chaucer's 'The Friar's Tale' deals with the same issues.

Many of the 'crimes' and ruses of the villainous animals revolve around bodily appetite and greed with no firm distinction between the two. Physical appetites tend to lead to danger as when the Wolf is tricked into believing that the moon's reflection in a well is a great cheese, a 'Somer Cheis, baith fresche and ffair' (l. 2276). Scatology is a rare but occasionally prominent ingredient in the comedy. The 'Tale of the Wolf and the Wether' provides the comic spectacle of the terrified Wolf fouling himself three times as he flees for his life from what he believes to be a vicious sheepdog, described in an odd mix of linguistic registers:

Thryis (Be my Saull) ye gart me schute behind,   [made]
Upon my hoichis the senyeis may be sene.   [haunches]
(ll. 2567–8)

The moral orientation of the *Fables* is as topsy-turvy and unpredictable as the plots. A sheep may be innocent in one tale and deserve to die in another; a fox may escape justice as the perpetrator of one crime only to become the victim of another. The explicit moral import is revealed retrospectively after each tale and frequently proves surprising, like a murder-mystery with misleading clues. As the tales progress, the instability of meaning and symbol intensifies. The final tale shows a mouse attempting to interpret the nature of the paddock, considering the learned view of physiognomy, whereby an ugly exterior betokens evil, but being swayed by the humanistic reasoning of the paddock to reject such a crude philosophy of character. The rational approach proves disastrous and the paddock's evil intent perversely substantiates the cruder opinion. By confusing the reader in such ways, Henryson insists on an alert and fluid mode of reading, as the misleading manipulation of our sympathies tends to implicate us as morally suspect. We are tricked into condoning and condemning wrongfully, every bit as prone to folly as the beasts in the stories.

Deadly Sin Without Deadly Seriousness

Comedy is similarly enlisted for serious purposes in Passus 5 of Langland's *Piers Plowman*, which presents the inherently absurd spectacle of the Seven Deadly Sins trying to amend their ways.[11] From this ludicrous scenario, Langland develops a series of comic vignettes. Moved by Reason's powerful sermon, the Deadly Sins resolve to reform, a proposition which would effectively cause their non-existence. Langland employs a range of colourful idiom and a colloquial register filled with realistic detail to present the ensuing farce of sin sinning. He selects choice details of physical repulsiveness, so that Envy resembles a shrivelled leek and Wrath has white eyes and a running nose. Primarily, it is through a semi-dramatic self-presentation rather than description that each sin is presented. Envy admits his habitual resentment of others in the dialectal timbre of everyday chatter:

> I wolde be gladder, by God! that Gybbe hadde meschaunce
> Than though I hadde this wouke ywonne a weye of   [week]
> Essex chese. (ll. 91–2)

Langland is exceptionally skilled in capturing authentic tones of speech, be it gossipy insinuation, 'She hadd child in chirie-time' (l. 159), or blunt slander, 'Dame Johane was a bastard' (l. 156). Avarice is sketched with savage observation of his physical attributes (ll. 188, 191), 'bitelbrowed and baberlipped, with two blered eighen ... his berd was bidraveled' [with beetling brows, thick lips and inflamed eyes ... his beard was covered in grease]. Langland can orchestrate a conversation to subtle comic effect, so that Reason's approving comment that Envy's sorrow is a fine step towards salvation is undercut by Envy's artless reply, 'I am evere sory ... I am but selde oother'. The deadpan delivery points up incongruous meanings of sorrow as contrition and envious misery. The semantic range of words is constantly in sight, as with Wrath's distinction between general 'spiritualite' and his own particular brand (ll. 147–8). Fine lines are constantly being made apparent, attuning the reader to the elastic and misleading nature of words as the conman speaks of the 'grace of gile' (l. 203) and Wrath concocts food from 'wikkede wordes' (l. 160).

The humour resides in the absurdity of the situation too, exacerbated by the realistic elements of the presentation. The pervasive attention to tactile and visual aspects, coupled with colloquial verisimilitude, forges a tangible concreteness to the fantastic nonsense (cf. *Alice in Wonderland*). The allegory takes on a life of its own, developing into mini-narratives featuring special cameo appearances by speaking subjects (whose 'I' voice works powerfully to self-incriminate). Avarice is characterised as a conman married to Rose the Regrater (retailer), an ale-brewing cheat like her husband. Asked if he ever makes amends, he fails to understand the term, 'restitucioun', misconstruing it absolutely:

> I wende riflynge were restitucioun ... for I lerned nevere rede on boke,   [stealing]
> And I kan no Frenssh, in feith, but of the fertheste ende of Northfolk. (ll. 234–5)

This is akin to Chaucer's mockery of the Prioress with her 'Frenssh ... After the scole of Stratford atte Bowe' (GP, ll. 124–5). Such multi-targeted satire greatly enlivens what could be a rather arid topic. Much of the humour comes from staging double acts between the straight man (Reason) and the fall guys (the Sins) as in the exchange with Avarice: Do you pity the poor? 'I have as much pite of povere as pedlere hath of cattes' (l. 254); Are you hospitable? 'As hende as hounde is in kitchene' (l. 256). When the exasperated Reason gives up the effort of trying to save Avarice, relinquishing him as an impossible job, Avarice falls into despair and wants to hang himself. This is indeed a world of carnival filled with incongruous elements in antagonistic disharmony.

The grotesque and parodic aspects are perfectly realised in the sorry tale of Glutton's abortive efforts to reform. He sets out for confession, 'kirkwarde his coupe to shewe' (l. 298) – with a pun on *culpa*, 'sin' – but is tempted into an alehouse on the way to employ a different cup. The aromatic appeal of her wares is seductively conveyed by the alewife,

> I have pepir and pione ... and a pound of garleek,
> A ferthyngworth of fenel seed for fastynge dayes. (ll. 305–6)

The tavern scene is painted with finesse, describing the gathering of motley regulars, including 'Cesse the Souteress' (shoemaker), Watte the Warner (warrenkeeper), Tim the Tinker, Clarice of Cocks' Lane (prostitute), Dawe the Dykere' and Griffyn the Walshe. As in 'The Pardoner's Tale', drink leads to gambling and oath-swearing, so that sins multiply. The low comedy proceeds, with extremes of behaviour such as 'laughynge and lourynge' (l. 337) co-existing as if natural bedfellows. Religious activities are casually incorporated in perverse ways, as the Lord's prayer signifies no more than the time Glutton takes to relieve himself and the Horn of Hope (l. 507) is farcically anticipated in a reductive manner:

> His guttes bigonne to gothelen as two gredy sowes;   [rumble]
> He pissed a potel in a Paternoster-while,   [half a gallon]
> And blew his rounde ruwet at his ruggebones ende,   [trumpet]
> That alle that herde that horn helde hir nose after. (ll. 341–4)

The scabrous language becomes ever more outrageous. Glutton's unsteady gait as he leaves is compared to the darting of a 'glemannes bicche' (l. 347), and his vomit is too stinking even for a starving dog to lap up. Boundaries of taste are clearly being crossed as the poem has veered wildly from the solemn sermon with which the passus began. Yet, curiously, Langland manages to contain the scandalous elements and achieve an enlightening effect. The representation of sin through personified individuals enables him to shock as well as to engage the reader, employing excess in many forms, linguistic and behavioural, to present sin as truly repugnant in a way which the sermon alone could not.

Devils in the Drama

A similar incorporation of extreme low comedy into serious religious material occurs in drama. The York play of the 'Harrowing of Hell' includes a group of devils who are given mock-heroic treatment while squabbling childishly.[12] This diminishing of fiendishness into frivolity is even more apparent in the unruly devils of the closely related Wakefield play. Yet, in a culture with widespread and officially endorsed belief in devils, there must be some edge to such comedy. The laughter may be partly nervous, or even work to associate laughter with devilry. As part of the Passion sequence, in a cycle of plays re-enacting the Christian faith, the depiction of hell cannot be entirely free of serious import. The dramatic representation is set within a holiday context as part of a communal festivity, but the serious relevance of damnation and salvation is always reinstated no matter what diverting potential for laughter is exploited. The mixed mode is part of the design, attesting to the easy confidence of medieval religion which can incorporate fun and games into the place of eternal pain.

The York 'Harrowing' assigns to the devils a range of specific linguistic registers associated with official culture (knightly comportment, law, aristocratic French lexis) creating satirical implications. There is also a frank admission about the representation of the fiends as energetic, gleeful and cheerfully expressing the lower aspects of human nature. Recurrent comedic types appear, such as the big-mouthed boaster, disguising his cowardice, the over-delegating boss, the willing-but-inept fool and the inveterate moaner. Realised in drama, such personalities provide boisterous entertainment:

> 1st Devil: Helpe, Belsabub, to bynde thes boyes! ...
> 2nd Devil: Why rooris thou soo, Rebalde? Thou royis.
> (ll. 97, 99)   [you're raving]

This exploits an antagonism between the first devil, who is consistently nervous unless following orders, and the second devil, whose mockery asserts his sense of superiority. The multiplication of devilish figures creates a cacophony, multiplying the interactive potential while fragmenting the fiends into smaller comic units. Belsabub claims to be in charge and commands other devils to be summoned, 'Calle up Astrotte and Anaball ... Bele-Berit and Belial' (ll. 113–5). The pre-fallen angel Lucifer, 'lovely of lyre', exists as a separate character from Satan, their 'sire'. In his bluster and bombast, Satan is characterised as akin to an arrogant tyrant in the mould of Pharaoh and Herod. Preparing to repulse Jesus's assault on hell, Satan reassures his forces:

> I bidde you be noght abasshed
> But boldely make youe boune,   [prepare yourselves]
> With toles that ye on traste   [weapons]
> And dynge that dastard doune. (ll. 177–80)

He virtually repeats himself a bit later on (ll. 201–4), suggesting a restricted command of rhetoric. Generally the devils are assigned a lively colloquial diction which degenerates under pressure into hollow expletives ('We!', 'Harke!', 'Owe!'), contrasting strongly with Jesus's composure and forceful commands. As Jesus breaks through the gates of hell, the devils fall into disarray and are rebuked by Satan, drawing scornful mockery from Belsabub in classic tones of deflating superiors:

'Ya, sette hym sore, that is sone saide,   [attack]
But come thi selffe and serve hym soo.' (ll. 205–6)

Disappointed in his minions, Satan rises to the challenge and calls for his 'gere' [armour] to repulse the besieger. He specialises in disparaging terms, scorning his underlings as 'faitours' and Jesus as a 'gedlyng' [insignificant fellow]. Whereas Jesus employs portentous Latin phrases, Satan affects French, addressing Jesus ironically as 'belamy' (l. 213) [My dear friend]. The war of words with Jesus forms the core of the 'Harrowing' episode, with typical touches of flyting matches.* Satan casts aspersions upon Jesus's parentage and repudiates his claim as unjust, but is out-argued at every turn. Desperately trying to negotiate some small scraps of consolation in defeat, he ends up shackled and reduced to incoherent madness:

Owt! Ay! Herrowe! Helpe, Mahounde!
Nowe wex I woode oute of my witte. (ll. 343–4)

The final spectacle of the devils sinking down into the pit of hell provides a very satisfying visual climax, probably staged as them being swallowed by a hell-mouth. The grotesque image is quintessentially carnivalesque.

Sacred and Profane

It is not just the more obvious material involving devils and Deadly Sins which can receive comic treatment. Similarly bold, comedic treatment marks the 'Second Shepherds' Play' of the Wakefield cycle which treats the most sacred material of the birth of Christ with extraordinary light-heartedness.[13] It parodies the Nativity by rendering the biblical metaphor of the Lamb of God in literal form as a stolen sheep. The

---

* Flyting is a formalised, ritual contest of words, a popular poetic genre; for example, *The Owl and the Nightingale, Winner and Waster*.

farcical plot has the sheep swaddled and set in the cradle, where the three shepherds come and present gifts to the newborn in a ludic foreshadowing of the play's conclusion. The mock saviour has a mock holy family, Mak and Gill, who function as a quarrelsome double-act. A good deal of the play is spent on the villainous pair, presenting the familiar anti-matrimonial perspectives of the 'Noah' plays. Gill as a nagging wife is evenly matched with her husband, so that the two share a raucous song. Their attempt to conceal the evidence of their sheep rustling resembles in some respects the inverted morality of the beast fable, where the wily are covertly admired. It also serves, along with the representation of the shepherds as downtrodden labourers, to assert the dire condition of fallen humanity which the Christ child has come to redeem. Like the shepherds' lengthy complaints about the abuses they endure, Mak and Gill's resort to theft to feed their expanding family brings the play very much into the contemporary world of the cycle. The lower orders are privileged, albeit temporarily. Of the 754 lines of the play, only the final 125 are concerned with the birth of Jesus. When the play turns to its supposed primary matter, the genuine nativity is quieter and more affecting after the mayhem and confusion. The return to 'order' enacts a kind of exemplary restoration, wherein Jesus is aligned with the reimposition of decorum and propriety. In this way, the temporary carnivalesque release is contained.

The Wakefield Master's keen ear is attuned to nuances of speech. Mak pretends to imitate a proud yeoman, adopting the lofty tone of a lord's messenger, 'Fy on you! Goyth hence! ... Why, who be ich?' (ll. 204, 207). His affected style of speech perplexes them, 'Why make ye it so qwaynt?' (l. 206). His adoption of a southern accent meets with the first shepherd's blunt mockery, 'Take outt that southren tothe, / And sett in a torde!' (ll. 215–6). Their speech is peppered with oaths and insults, 'the dewill in thi maw' [mouth] (l. 110), 'Crystys crosse me spede [favour] and Sant Nycholas!' (l. 118), 'Chrystys curs, my knave' (l. 147), 'the dewill in youre ee!' (l. 217). Mak also swears easily, combining an anachronistic oath with some pig Latin as he steals the sheep:

'*Manus tuas commendo,*   [Into thy hands I commend]
Poncio Pilato,   [O Pontius Pilate]
Cryst crosse me spede!' (ll. 265–7)

The incomplete Latin citation is a parody of the Office of the Dead,*
tellingly omitting mention of his soul.

Mak and his wife provide the most boisterous comedy. Mak indulges
in a spot of black magic by casting a spell over the shepherds to keep
them asleep. Back home with his booty, the battle between the sexes
common in folk material occupies a considerable space. Before she even
appears, Gill has been spoken of by the others, always in abusive tones.
Mak wishes her dead (ll. 251–2) along with his many children (l. 392),
which breaches some taboos in a jocular fashion. Each time he arrives at
his house, his agitated knocking causes her to complain about being
disturbed, the recurrence helping to create a sense of habitual
behaviour. When accused of laziness and nagging, she retorts with a
rhetorical catalogue of complaints:

'Why, who wanders, who wakys? Who commys, who gose?
Who brewys, who bakys? What makys me thus hose?'   [hoarse]
(ll. 415–6)

Despite the bickering they cooperate well in villainy, sharing a stanza
and completing each other's statements with palpable unity, a device put
to very different effect in Shakespeare's *Romeo and Juliet*.[14]

Mak: Go spar   [fasten]
       The gaytt-doore.   [outer door]
Gill: Yis, Mak,
       For and thay com at thy bak-
Mak: Then myght I by, for all the pak.   [fare badly]
(ll. 327–30)

---

* The Office of the Dead is the prayer cycle of the Roman Catholic liturgy prescribed for funerals
which begins, 'Into thy hands I commend my spirit', recalling the last words of Jesus on the cross
(Psalms 31:6; Luke 23:46).

The idea of disguising the sheep as a newborn baby in her cradle is Gill's but Mak approves with an ironic aside, 'Yit a woman avyse [advice] helpys at the last' (l. 342). The shepherds' visit prompts a noisy, melodramatic farce with Gill feigning post-partum distress as they search the house for their lost sheep:

> Gill: I swelt!   [am dying]
>   Outt, thefys, fro my wonys!   [house]
>   (ll. 525–6)

The bold parody continues with the shepherds offering gifts in direct parallel to the later scene of homage to Jesus, addressing the sheep with the same affectionate phrase, 'lytyll day-starne' (ll. 50 cf. 727). The comic denouement is gradual, delaying the inevitable recognition so as to heighten the comedy:

> 3rd Shepherd: Gyf me lefe hym to kys, and lyft up the clowtt.
>   [swaddling cloth]
>   What the dewill is this? He has a long snowte.
>   (ll. 584–5)

During the couple's strenuous defence of their ugly 'baby', a variety of folk beliefs are invoked, 'He is merkyd amys' [carries a disfiguring birthmark] (l. 586), is 'a hornyd lad' (l. 601), has been bewitched (l. 613) and was 'takyn with an elfe' (l. 616) at midnight. Another folk tradition seems to underlie the punishment meted out to them – of being tossed in a blanket, perhaps a festive ritual symbolising death. The play's themes of transformation and metamorphosis are resonant with pagan practices. All these features combine to endow the play with a distinctive 'folk' quality perfectly in accord with Bakhtin's theories.

Chaucer's Fabliaux

Chaucer's *Canterbury Tales* contains five fabliaux, namely the tales told by the Miller, the Reeve, the Cook, the Summoner and the Shipman, as well as others which strongly resemble fabliau told by the Merchant and the Friar. Previously regarded as a genre enshrining popular material, the fabliau has been analysed as a courtly genre – an appropriation of the obscene and irreverent by the nobility for whom fabliau provided an occasion to enjoy scandalous diversion.

Most surviving examples of the genre are from France – stories of sometimes extreme vulgarity featuring sexual adventures among the lower classes and young scholars. They display a marked propensity for the carnivalesque, focusing frequently on bodily orifices and monstrosities such as multiple and talking vaginas. They fulfil all of the criteria formulated by Bakhtin as typical of the carnivalesque, including a frank interest in lower bodily functions and emissions (excrement, urine, vomit, discharges of all sorts), grotesquely exaggerated behaviour and offensive language. Chaucer's are the only English examples of medieval fabliaux and they are quite unlike their continental counterparts. Chaucer's bawdy tales exhibit a far greater complexity of plotting and thematic layering, as sophisticated products of his art.

Narrators

Chaucer's projected pilgrim persona shows awareness of the 'scandalous' nature of the material as he apologises in advance for any offence that might be caused, advising the squeamish reader to turn to another page. This strategy is comparable to that of a medieval diptych where a conspiratorial figure bears a banner telling the onlooker not to open the painting. The provoked disobedience leads the viewer to an image of a backside excreting thistles, emblazoned with the triumphant message, 'I told you so!'[15] The revelation of a shocking scene which was secretly anticipated provides the comic frisson which Chaucer is also inviting. 'The Miller's Tale' is preceded by a disingenuous injunction to avoid the upcoming offensive material which whets the appetite even as it unsettles:

> And therefore, whoso list it nat yheere,   [to hear]
> Turne over the leef and chese another tale. (ll. 3176–7)

The confusion between a listening audience and a reader draws attention to the artfulness of the device which engages the reader's expectations while protesting innocence a little too much. Chaucer prefaces his 'cherles tale' with a disclaimer, whereas other writers of scurrilous tales, such as Boccaccio, acknowledge the potentially offensive material as an afterthought. A warning in advance paradoxically enhances the appeal as much as it discourages or disarms criticism:

> Avyseth yow, and put me out of blame,
> And eek men shal nat maken ernest of game. (ll. 3185–6)

Only the Reeve seems to be offended, as it happens, and his response is to what he perceives as a personal insult rather than to the 'low' material, which his own tale emulates and surpasses. His tale is motivated by the desire to 'quite' the Miller (l. 3916), employing a similarly base language, 'Right in his cherles termes wol I speke' (l. 3917).

As the First Fragment continues, Chaucer seems to have unleashed a series of increasingly gross tales, culminating in 'The Cook's Tale' of complicit marital prostitution. It is not long before a subsequent fragment returns to the indecorous mode of fabliau with 'The Merchant's Tale' of January and May. This pilgrim is a more ambivalent narrator, possibly venting hostility towards women as an unhappily married man despite his Prologue's mock-paean to marriage. He frames his story as a complex, multi-generic piece, mixing styles bewilderingly. But essentially it is a fabliau, with its central motif of *senex amans* (the aged lover) whose sexy young wife commits adultery amid recourse to crude language and base physicality. The Merchant affects an aversion to vulgarity, referring euphemistically to her sexual activity as her being 'dressed' [treated]:

> In swich manere it may nat been expressed
> But if I wolde speke uncurteisly. (ll. 2362–3)

This is artfully misleading as the Merchant, while claiming to be plain speaking, 'I kan nat glose, I am a rude [simple] man' (l. 2351), and apologising to the ladies present (l. 2351), goes on to speak what he claims to be unspeakable.

Twisted Plots

The fabliau plot invariably revolves around sex or intrigue. The pleasure lies less in discovering what happens than in how the stratagems are contrived and how far anyone will emerge unscathed. 'The Miller's Tale' and 'The Merchant's Tale' share a typical triangular scenario between a jealous old husband, his young wife and a young student or squire. Chaucer constructs elaborate plots as he delays and orchestrates the sexual encounters. Nicholas and Alison spend time groping and playing but have to concoct a complicated scenario involving a prophesied second Flood in order to entice the husband to seclude himself in a barrel hanging from the roof and to ensure that the house is emptied of servants. In 'The Merchant's Tale', May and Damien manage to exchange love notes and she passes on a wax imprint of the key to the garden, yet they have to wait a long time before finding a way to exploit January's blindness and circumvent his jealousy. The plot-delays work to promote desire and frustration in the reader.

Fabliau treats sex not love. Perhaps most repulsively presented is January's laborious efforts on his wedding night with May as still as a stone, enduring his attentions:

> With thikke brustles of his berd unsofte,
> Lyk to the skyn of houndfissh, sharp as breer. (ll. 1824–5)

The narrator expresses unease at the grotesque, animalistic coupling but his reservations merely require the reader to supply the missing details:

But lest that precious folk be with me wrothe	[fastidious/ prudish]
How that he wroughte, I dar nat to yow telle. (ll. 1962–3)	[acted]

The bestial nature of the sex depicted is enhanced by prevailing imagery of farmyard animals and wild creatures, so that May is compared to a weasel, while January is 'al coltissh' (l. 1847) and chatters with excitement like a magpie (l. 1848). Casually adding human beings to a list of creatures who rest after sex, 'fyssh, or bryd, or beest, or man' (l. 1865), the narrator slyly reduces people to the level of animals. 'The Reeve's Tale' depicts John as a crazed stud, 'He priketh harde and depe, as he were mad' (l. 4231).

Base Physicality

The body also features in a number of ways which conform to Bakhtin's models, frequently involving orifices and violence. 'The Miller's Tale' famously presents not just one but two arses projecting from windows – one of which is a site of a misdirected kiss, the other the receptacle for a vengeful branding. 'The Reeve's Tale' also predicates its physical violence upon retaliation. The two students claim compensation for their lost corn by sowing their seed among the miller's womenfolk. The antagonism escalates to the final violent mêlée with clearly erotic undertones to the broken nose and bald head cracked by a staff. The woman's body is an open receptacle, 'Yon wenche wil I swyve' (l. 4178). Lower bodily functions occur as casual events, freely admitting snoring, farting and urinating; slight plot-function may accompany the acts, so that the miller's wife getting out of bed to 'pisse' (l. 4215) enables the cradle-switching trick, while May pretends a similar urge as a means of reading her lover's letter (ll. 1950–1). The vulgarity serves a serious satirical purpose in 'The Summoner's Tale' as explicitly announced by the Prologue. The Summoner's vision of hell parodies a legend of friars in heaven being sheltered beneath Mary's skirts. In the inverted version, a legion of friars is discovered up the devil's arse. This prefigures the Tale's scatological focus, concerning a friar who rummages around a sick man's buttocks and 'tuwel' [anus] (l. 2148) in search of his bequest. The bestowed fart becomes a scholarly conundrum with a lengthy debate about how to divide it equally which reaches an ingenious solution. The courtly audience of the *Canterbury Tales* clearly relished breaches of decorum in ways far removed from the folk festivities treated by Bakhtin. Yet perhaps the difference is more apparent than real as the vulgar language and crude exposure of the body's lower functions tends to exercise a levelling function. Chaucer's relatively restrained fabliaux are sophisticated pieces involving more than a game of dirty jokes. As we shall see, they exploit the genre to insinuate all sorts of critiques.

The Literary and Linguistic Style of Chaucer's Fabliaux

The plots are typically structured around a protracted delay in gratification which is followed by a rapid resolution. This is stylistically marked by an energetic syntax effecting a frantic finale with a brief narrative summary to mark closure. 'The Miller's Tale' concludes by highlighting selected terms which encapsulate the nature of the tale in a gleefully amoral resumé, 'Thus swyved [screwed] was this carpenteris wyf ... Absolon hath kist hir nether ye [lower eye] / And Nicholas is scalded in the towte' (ll. 3850, 3852–3). 'The Reeve's Tale' competes by doubling the amount of sexual activity, concluding merrily, 'His wyf is swyved and his doghter als' (l. 4317).

The low register of terms such as 'swyve' [copulate with] sets an appropriate tone for the tales, which habitually expose and debase language. The lamentable 'churles termes' include oaths and curses which moralists such as the Parson routinely deplore. In 'The Reeve's Tale', Alan wishes a 'wylde fyr' to fall upon the bodies of the miller's family (l. 4172), which the heated couplings and violent grapplings metaphorically accomplish. 'The Friar's Tale' hinges on the intended meaning of a curse, 'The carl spak oo thing, but he thoghte another' (l. 1568). Casual swearing is disregarded, while the widow's considered and repeated curse 'in ernest' damns the summoner to hell. Latent meaning often informs the language of Chaucer's fabliaux with plentiful punning. 'The Miller's Tale' employs a number of terms in ways which reveal their multiple meanings. 'Hende' is applied to the scheming Nicholas eleven times, becoming almost a heroic fixed epithet. Its sense is far from fixed however, ranging from the elevated (rather archaic) sense, 'noble, courteous', through the neutral, 'close to hand, nearby', to more dubious suggestiveness, 'handy, available, good with his hands'. In a tale specialising in parody, inverting the elements of courtly romance in the preceding 'The Knight's Tale', a number of terms usually associated with refined love are comically invoked. 'Deerne' love is transposed from its usual courtly milieu to a coy euphemism severely at odds with its context (ll. 3200, 3278, 3297). The most outstanding example of wordplay is the use of 'queynte'. Its primary meanings are 'elegant, pleasing, cunningly wrought, clever' and, by extension, it can be applied to female genitals as a pleasing thing (cf. the Wife of Bath's 'bele chose', l. 447) with a vulgar pun on 'cunt'. Contrasting import is beautifully aligned as Nicholas gropes Alison:

As clerkes ben ful subtile and ful queynte;
And prively he caughte hire by the queynte (ll. 3275–6)

Sexual *double entendre* fills 'The Merchant's Tale', with the warm *wax* in which May imprints the shape of the *key* to the garden *gate*. The garden metaphor of courtly love familiar from the *Roman de la Rose* onward is made concrete, so that as Damien gains access it prefigures his sexual conquest, 'And in he stirte' (l. 2153), directly parallel to 'and in he throng' (l. 2353). This tale specifically accords the woman a persuasive tongue, so that May can successfully designate her exploit a 'strugle' designed to restore January's sight, although he demurs, 'Strugle?' quod he, 'Ye, algate in it wente!' (l. 2376).

Those who gloss meaning professionally are exposed with particular satiric force. 'The Summoner's Tale' satirises the friar's smooth tongue, love of glossing and exploitation of double meanings by both word and gesture. His Prologue played with the homophones 'tale' and 'tail', focusing repeatedly on the devil's tail (three times) and 'ers' (four times), using a carnival coalescence of mouth and anus (both emitting hot air). In the Tale, the fart which has to be equally divided among the friars presents a case of 'ars-metrike' (l. 2222), punning with almost deconstructionist skill on the art of measurement – arithmetic. The friar is mocked for his affectation as he peppers his speech with French and

Latin and despises 'burel folk' [laypeople] (ll. 1872, 1874). He cynically manipulates words, even sacred text, describing a glutton breaking wind (l. 1934), 'Lo, "buf!" they seye, "*cor meum eructavit!*"' [my body has spoken]. The quotation from Psalm 45 is refashioned in the context so as to draw attention to the secondary meaning of *eructare*, to belch. This kind of pun clearly relies on an educated and literate audience to appreciate its subtleties.

What emerges from all the wordplay is the essential mutability of language as words resist stable definition and conceal disparate meanings. Bloch has analysed French fabliau as a genre intrinsically concerned with the poetic craft as a self-conscious literary medium.[16] Chaucer's fabliaux seem to be equally concerned with exploring the ambivalence and arbitrary signification of words.

Generic Subversion and Parody

In typical carnivalesque fashion, inversion and parody are central aspects of the comedy. A solemn deathbed bequest becomes a site of scathing anti-fraternal mockery in 'The Summoner's Tale', while 'The Friar's Tale' elevates the devil to the role of an anti-hero. The primary source of parodic inversion is the courtly love ethos. 'The Miller's Tale' exists as a distorted mirror image of 'The Knight's Tale', transferring the pathos of Arcite's death 'alone withouten any companye' (KtT, l. 2779 cf. MilT, l. 3204) into a sordid bedroom farce. The distant figure of Emily is reconfigured as the teasing young wife Alison, and the associated similes are not otherworldy or angelic but of the sensuous weasel and the softness of a wether's wool. An extended *descriptio** revels in her physicality, comparing her with a swallow, a kid goat, a calf and a colt, as well as thirst-quenching sloe, bragot and mead. The rhetorical catalogue of her attributes ends fittingly with the diminutive terms 'popelote' [doll] and wench [lower class woman]. Unlike 'The Knight's Tale', where the two knights debate whether Emily is a real woman or an angel, the only philosophy applied to deciphering Alison's essential

* A head-to-toe physical description as recommended in medieval manuals of rhetorical style.

nature is a cynical comment on her equal suitability as a bedmate fit for a lord or as a yeoman's wife (ll. 3269–70). The male lovers in fabliau often serve to parody courtly behaviour. Absalon's inflated style of speech, 'Lemman, thy grace, and sweete bryd, thyn ore' (l. 3726), elicits 'healing' of an unexpectedly crude form as she presents him with her 'hole' and 'naked ers' (l. 3734). This might almost serve to epitomise the recurrent motif of deflated pretensions. The hymn sung by Nicholas, *Angelus ad virginem* [the angel to the virgin], sacrilegiously evokes the Annunciation in a context of a not-so-immaculate desire. Similarly, the animalistic coupling in 'The Reeve's Tale' is incongruously accorded a courtly *aubade*, the lovers' dawn-song which laments the need to part with the rising sun. The formal parody adopts a refined diction and chiasmic patterning, 'Fare weel ... sweete wight' (l. 4236), 'deere lemman ... far weel' (l. 4240). One small but telling detail breaks the spell, as Maline *almost* weeps. This deflationary touch is similarly applied in the designation of May as 'gentil', filled with 'pitee', bestowing her 'grace' upon the squire (l. 1995), while unceremoniously tearing up his love letter in the privy. 'The Merchant's Tale' also parodies the Song of Songs (l. 2138ff.), conjuring up sublime associations which are suddenly degraded by the narrator's derision of the 'olde lewed wordes' (l. 2149). The elaborate exegetical mystification of the erotic material of the Song is conspicuously lacking; there is nothing metaphysical about January's garden, which serves as an outdoor sexual arena.

Amorality and Inverted Morality

Instead of adhering to the medieval norm which asserted the moralising potential of fiction, this kind of storytelling is predicated upon rivalry and hostility. Several antagonistic pairings provide a dynamic of mutual vindictiveness as between the Friar and the Summoner, and the Miller and the Reeve, whose final word is to exult, 'Thus have I quyt the Millere in my tale' (l. 4324). A robust amorality rules where the miller, whose wife and daughter have been sexually assaulted, is treated dismissively as a rogue well repaid. The judgement that the students 'bette hym weel' is true in both a literal and a metaphorical sense. Above all, fabliau occupies a space in which prevailing morals may be temporarily suspended or challenged. Like the beast fable, fabliau celebrates an ethos of basic self-preservation and instinctive cunning. The plots approve of a variety of rebellious, anti-authoritarian behaviour, where the non-conformist can acquire the status of anti-hero. The audience is invited to share the perspectives of freewheeling sexuality exhibited by 'hende' Nicholas, John and Alan, to collude with May's adultery and join in with Alison's laughter, 'Te-hee!' (l. 3740).

Much of the force of the comedy is driven by its exploitation of tensions between different classes of society. Social and professional tensions are evident from the moment the Miller first disrupts the orderly arrangements by insisting on following the Knight. Longstanding conflict underlies the recurring motif of young scholars pitting their wits against representatives of the peasantry and the bourgeoisie; other recurrent axes of hostility are age and youth, male and female. 'The Miller's Tale' sets up a double rivalry – between a wealthy bourgeois and a poor student from Oxford, as well as between the student and the parish priest competing for Alison's attentions. Strangely, the one who emerges as the winner is, for once, the woman. Those who are duped tend to be characterised as dim-wits who deserve it. John the carpenter is not only older than his wife and jealous (fulfilling the charivari criteria nicely), but also ignorant enough to believe in a second Flood. The 'mixed mode' characteristically confuses the question of sympathy as John's suspicions are well-founded (as are January's) since Absalon's night-time serenades are clear evidence of other men seeking his wife. He displays a touching concern for her safety when convinced of the imminent destruction. However, the comic resolution requires public humiliation, as 'neighebores, both smale and grete' (l. 3826) mock him, 'The folk gan laughen at his fantasye' (l. 3840). In such a situation, the audience seldom pauses to sympathise with the designated butt; instead, the holiday mode encourages identification with the crowd, who 'turned al his harm into a jape' (l. 3855).

'The Reeve's Tale' relies upon presumed hostility towards the stereotypical thieving miller, 'deynous Symkyn', and his haughty wife, the illegitimate daughter of the town priest. The comedy of their degradation is combined with a clash of dialects as the two students are given a distinctive Northern accent, the first time dialect is consciously employed in English literature. Their speeches contain characteristically Northern vowels, pronouns, harsh consonantal clusters and forms of the verb 'to be' which had not yet migrated south and become Standard English, 'Whilk way is he geen?' [which, gone] (l. 4078); 'I is ful wight, God waat, as is a raa' [strong as a roe] (l. 4086).

Prejudices may be invoked by small details, such as the setting of 'The Merchant's Tale' in Lombardy – a byword for lechery and greed. This fosters a predisposition against the 'worthy knyght' who rules there and who turns out, satisfyingly, to be a randy sixty-year-old idiot. The symbolic names and fixed epithets, January and 'fresshe' May, alert the audience to an archetypal mismatch, suggestive of unnatural union. Other figures appear to support an allegorical reading – the flattering Placebo ['I shall please'] and Justinus, the voice of reason. Although sympathy is being manipulated, they can occasionally switch momentarily as when January repudiates the amassed learning and advice of his counsellors, 'Straw for thy Senek, and for thy proverbes!' (l. 1567). His sweeping aside of the weight of textual tradition appeals to a certain strand of anti-intellectualism, 'I counte nat a panyer ful of herbes / Of scole-termes' (ll. 1568–9).

'The Miller's Tale' also invites concurrence with John's sentiment, 'Blessed be alwey a lewed man' [unlearned] (l. 3455). The carpenter's touching concern for the 'sick' student as a brother in arms, 'we ... men that swynke', meets the riposte, 'Fecche me drynke' (ll. 3491–2). The rhyme brutally rejects any connection between them, and asserts the dominance of bodily needs over romanticised hard work. The role of dupe can be versatile, so that the students in 'The Reeve's Tale' begin as the 'sely' [naive, hapless] ones (ll. 4108, 4100, 4090), suffering a string of humiliations and discomfort. Then the situation is reversed as they retaliate. For one moment the triumphant miller shares his inner thoughts with the audience in a soliloquy, which reveals his cleverness at spotting their plan and wry resolve to 'blere hir ye' (l. 4049). His disdain for the 'sleighte in hir philosophye' (l. 4050) and 'quenynte crekes' [clever tricks] (l. 4051) appeals to an anti-intellectual inclination as well as to prejudices against students, and marks the miller's success in the first round.

Many medieval texts are imbued with the carnivalesque spirit, sometimes in unexpected contexts. An awareness of the jocular and comedic aspects of medieval literature helps to enable a fuller understanding of the period. The experimental and innovative treatment of 'low' humour and edgy satire can be unnerving even today in a much more generally permissive culture. Bakhtin's analysis of popular subculture provides a useful model for examining a relatively neglected aspect of the medieval period. A theory of the comic as a site for revealing tensions and expressing antagonism assures that the material is not dismissed as grotesque or quirky, but is accorded more respectful attention. This leads to exciting discoveries about the transgressive potential of humour and the ways in which 'offensive' material may be subtly nuanced.

Notes

1   *The Land of Cockayne* in J. A. W. Bennett and G. V. Smithers (eds), *Early Middle English Verse and Prose* (London: Oxford University Press, 1966; repr. 1974). *Aucassin and Nicolette and Other Tales*, trans. Pauline Matarasso (Harmondsworth: Penguin, 1971).

2   *Robert Henryson: Moral Fables*, ed. George D. Gopen (Notre Dame, IN: University of Notre Dame Press, 1987), Prologue, 15–16. All quotations shall be taken from this edition.

3   Chaucer, 'The Nun's Priest's Tale', *The Riverside Chaucer*, Larry D. Benson (Oxford: Oxford University Press, 1989).

4   Mikhail Bakhtin, *Rabelais and His World*, trans. Hélène Iswolsky (Bloomington, IN: Indiana University Press, 1984). All quotations shall be taken from this edition.

5   Bakhtin regards later forms of caricature, involving grotesque distortion and vulgar physicality (e.g. Swift, Hogarth) as fundamentally different to the medieval and early Renaissance phenomenon of the carnivalesque, as a shift

from public and popular practices to a more elitist milieu as folk festivals were increasingly contained, even prohibited, as during the period of Puritan government when Christmas and Easter were banned as pagan events.

6 Play as a fundamental element in culture is discussed by Johan Huizinga, *Homo Ludens: A Study of the Play Element in Culture* (London: Routledge and Kegan Paul, 1944; repr. 1947).

7 See R. Howard Bloch, *The Scandal of the Fabliaux* (Chicago: University of Chicago Press, 1986).

8 The catalogue of an exhibition of art related to the carnivalesque presents these and many other remarkable images: *Carnivalesque*, eds. Timothy Hyman and Roger Malbert (London: Hayward Gallery, 2000).

9 The obscene nature of many French fabliaux is discussed by R. Howard Bloch, *The Scandal of the Fabliaux.*

10 For a full discussion of the use of fables in the medieval period, see Marianne Powell, *Fabula Docet: Studies in the Background and Interpretation of Henryson's Morall Fabillis* (Odense: Odense University Press, 1983).

11 A. V. C. Schmidt (ed.), *Piers Plowman: A Complete Edition of the B-Text* (London: Dent, 1984).

12 Peter Happé (ed.), *English Mystery Plays* (Harmondsworth: Penguin, 1975, Play 32). Passus 18 of Langland's *Piers Plowman* contains a very similar depiction of the Harrowing as a matter of squabbling devils, and seems to have been influenced by dramatic performances.

13 Happé, (ed.), *English Mystery Plays*, Play 14.

14 In *Romeo and Juliet* I.iv. 206–19 the lovers' speeches form a sonnet.

15 This painting provides the cover images of the exhibition catalogue, *Carnivalesque*, eds Timothy Hyman and Roger Malbert.

16 Bloch, *Scandal of the Fabliaux.*

Society and Class

The later Middle Ages was a tumultuous period of crumbling traditions and shifting perspectives. Any picture of the period as one of untroubled harmony, predicated upon a stable foundation of religious equanimity, can be firmly laid to rest. There is a widespread unease evident among all ranks and classes of society. One area where such unease is especially evident is in the genre of Estates Satire.* This provided a theoretical model of sorts for a well-ordered society based on traditional distinctions of class (in the loose sense of the term). At the most basic level, this enshrined a view of society as comprising fixed groups or estates, each essential to the others. During the later medieval period, texts detailing such a view begin to demonstrate greater anxiety about the model's reliability. From being an assertion of the immemorial constitution of society, estates theory developed into an increasingly discontent and searching critique. Writers such as Langland and Chaucer invoke the theory mainly to draw attention to the gaps and fissures which are becoming apparent. The Prologue to *Piers Plowman* and the 'General Prologue' to the *Canterbury Tales* are based upon the Estates Satire genre but greatly extend its scope and import. The conventional division of society into fixed, hierarchical orders was always at odds with reality to some degree but it became increasingly

* Estates Satire is a genre that satirises the corruption within the three medieval social estates (clergy, nobility and peasantry).

untenable. The movement from a late feudal to an early capitalistic system of government entailed huge social disruption. There had long been important gaps and blurred boundaries which the simplistic tri-partite system did not accommodate, such as the status of wealthy peasants, impoverished knights and, above all, women, who were subsumed within the categories without overt acknowledgement. The anachronisms were becoming harder to sustain.

Voices of Dissent

The literature of the period attests to this widespread sense of discontent, along with growing unease at social mobility, which was confounding traditional distinctions and challenging notions of order. In particular, more critical and more vocal opposition to fundamental inequities mark the fourteenth and fifteenth centuries. Prevailing practices in the Church which were at odds with scriptural conduct (the gap between precept and practice) proved especially incendiary. At the same time, centres of secular power such as the royal court were also being scrutinised more intensely. As social, religious and political tensions intensified, there was increasing fragmentation and plurality of allegiance. The many voices deploring the state of affairs usually share a claim to be preserving and/or restoring order, often making nostalgic appeals for re-establishing control and coherence. However, it is interesting to note that writers from widely divergent ends of the spectrum assert similar purposes as they denounce the status quo. At one extreme end of the scale is the reactionary Gower whose *Vox Clamantis* (Lat. 'voice of one crying out') castigates the radical underclass. Those classes of people whom he condemns as insubor-dinate rarely have their opinions preserved, except in records of their persecution. Suggestive hints of popular dissent can be gleaned from documents such as the letters attributed to the rebel John Ball. The economic and social upheaval was intensifying age-old conflicts and creating new antagonisms. The early stages of a market-driven economy coinciding with natural disasters such as the plague exacerbated a wide range of tensions. Henryson's *Moral Fables* present a world of poor sheep and ravenous wolves, exposing callousness and cruelty along with juridicial corruption. Piers Plowman became a figurehead, appropriated as a symbol for the aspirations of various discontented elements of society. Anonymous texts such as the fifteenth-century *Piers the Plowman's Creed* openly satirise the established Church, developing a vociferous and lively polemic, denouncing corruption. It provides an example of the flourishing anti-fraternal satire.

New Theories Contextualising Literary Texts

One branch of modern critical theory which attends closely to such socio-economic phenomena is Cultural Materialism. Approaching medieval literature using some of its analytical tools and premises will allow an exploration of how issues of society and class were shaping and being shaped by texts.[1] Cultural Materialism grew out of Marxist and post-structuralist theory, cohering around two closely related but distinct critical practices largely in reaction to the 1980s phenomenon of right-wing politics in Great Britain and America. The primary conviction underlying the theory is that a literary text is not ahistorical, divorced from its specific historical and personal context, nor is it simply to be read against a cultural 'background'. Literature is one discourse among many, a product and producer of meaning in a wider social and cultural context. Latent tensions, as well as gaps and silences, are attended to as valuable indicators of interpretative potential. Reacting against an 'aesthetic' approach, which attended purely to matters of style and form, cultural materialists seek to restore the social and collective nature of the text. Whereas the dominant critical mode after the Second World War was Formalism, paying close attention to the text in isolation, Cultural Materialism explores the complex dialogue between literature and history; for example, engaging with the 'General Prologue' to the *Canterbury Tales* as a product very much of the social and political forces at work at the time.

New Historicism

Rather confusingly, two distinct forms of the new theoretical approach exist. New Historicism is associated principally with American critics, while Cultural Materialism is associated with British and European ones. John Brannigan's excellent introduction to the theories of both spells out a clear general distinction between the two.[2] Both critical practices trace connections between texts, discourses, power and 'subjectivity': that is, 'the individual as an effect of sociohistorical and linguistic forces, and therefore "subject" to those forces'.[3] The theory adopted techniques from emerging disciplines such as anthropology and sociology, favouring 'thick description' – the close reading of texts attending to specific details in the manner of a case study. Cultural systems are conceived of as involving 'dominant', 'transitional', 'emergent' and 'residual' stages. This means that a text can reveal a variety of assumptions, some entrenched (embedded core values and practices), some incipient, some divergent and fluid; for instance, attitudes towards the shift from feudalism to capitalism, or from exchange-and-barter to a cash economy. The main point of interest concerns whether writings which challenge prevailing cultural norms constitute effective mechanisms of subversion or dissidence.

'New' Historicism defines itself as unlike 'Historicism', which classified the past as a series of notable epochs composed of strictly defined periods (e.g., the Enlightenment, the Renaissance). It takes account of divergent sub-cultures, the marginalised and neglected, and operates with a broader perspective on culture. Louis Montrose's famous dictum, 'The historicality of texts and the textuality of history', neatly sums up the approach, which treats all texts equally (bus ticket and sonnet are of equal relevance) and often juxtaposes disparate items to explore what emerges as their interconnection. Even apparently subversive artefacts are interpreted as functioning in the interests of the ruling ideology by justifying repression or reasserting the need for order. Useful as New Historical approaches are, they tend to produce too totalising a notion of power, influenced by Foucault's perspectives on the power system as ultimately controlling and benefiting from all cultural expression.[4] New Historicist readings can result in all forms and formats of art, society and literature being reduced to a common model. By insisting on the equal value of texts, distinctions are erased; for example, between fact and fiction, fantasy and actuality, propaganda and personal opinion. The view that everything is subject to political control (text, image, institution) has led to what some feel to be rather a bleak outlook, inculcating 'the politics of apathy'.[5]

Cultural Materialism

Cultural Materialism, associated with Raymond Williams from the 1980s, is also concerned with new perspectives on the past and its artefacts, considering 'material' aspects of culture: that is, specific, concrete activities and experiences. Brannigan characterises its remit as 'studying the construction and function of culture within the materialist fabric of society' (p. 96). In this practice, history serves the present, usually through relating the past to the present and foregrounding the relevance of the past within a contemporary context. Like New Historicism, it has been particularly applied to the Renaissance, Victorian and modern periods, although selecting very different kinds of texts to New Historicists and preferring to target the 'canonical'. A prime focus is on investigating how texts police and contain ideas; for example, how Tennyson deals with the colonisation and domestication of the exotic and foreign (*Idylls*) and threatens to subvert sexual decorum but ends safely with heterosexual marriage (*In Memoriam*). The existence of multiple and conflicting readings is an important element as part of a destabilising strategy, making apparent and possible divergent views, exposing identity and subjectivity as con-tingent constructs. Drawing attention to the partial and variable nature of opinion and response dismantles an outmoded liberal-humanist criticism, which was based on coherence (e.g. unified character) and the chimera of eternal verities (e.g. concepts such as honour). Again, the practice is open to some criticism in that it tends to neglect the text, engaging as it does with selected extracts considered in isolation and from very partial perspectives. Another objection to the practice is that it too readily maps contemporary concerns and attitudes onto the past.

Both Cultural Materialism and New Historicism have been criticised for being 'essentialising': that is, portraying human nature and cultural values as given and unchanging (e.g. madness in the past is appraised in the same way as madness today). Brannigan regards both as slow to adapt to the notion of reading as a destabilising act (i.e. reader-response theory, with its plurality of interpretive positions, positing a far from singular, univocal experience of a text). Incorporating certain approaches from reader-response theory enables Cultural Materialism to relate texts to 'the conditions in which they *were* and *may be* read' [emphasis mine] which Sinfield asserts as a primary aim.[6] Derrida's notion of 'translation' is helpful, too, as Brannigan notes, 'each reading is an event of transgressing the unknowability of text (because of the inexhaustibility and extinction of meaning) and because of this transgression, a pretence at knowledge and communication'.[7] In other words, the reader participates, filling in spaces and competing with latent interpretations akin to background noise. This relates to Bakhtin's notions of dialogism, which concerns a multiplicity of competing voices within a text and of heteroglossia, the range of variant readings a text can receive.

Applying Cultural Materialist Theory to Medieval Literature: The Beast Fable

This chapter will examine the social aspects of some key works of the later medieval period to consider how they interact with, challenge, reconfigure and seek to destabilise power. The concept of a harmoniously ordained society is clearly under strain as a unifying notion with many texts expressing critical awareness of and opposition to forces of restraint and repression. Robert Henryson uses his *Moral Fables* to speak out for the poor and oppressed by castigating injustice and the wrongful exercise of power. His collection of beast fables exploits the genre's potential for satire, aligning his work with the practice of Langland (cf. the Belling of the Cat episode) and Chaucer ('The Nun's Priest's Tale'). Several of the *Moral Fables* are predicated upon instances of tyranny and intimidation, particularly in scenes of unjust trials (perhaps related to Henryson's own legal training). 'The Trial of the Fox' presents justice as triumphant, embodied in the person of the lion as king presiding over scrupulous court procedures; the murderous fox is duly found guilty and hanged. However, the very next tale, 'The Sheep and the Dog', presents a sharply contrasting scene – a court in which the presiding arbitrator of justice is a wolf. Satirical analogies are immediately apparent in the identities of the court officials: the clerk of the court is a fox, the advocates are a kite and a vulture. The whole process of the court is contrary to the law, convening at an illegally late hour and refusing the plaintiff a defence lawyer. When the accused sheep challenges the court's authority, a farcical justification follows with the bear and badger being appointed to mediate and diligently consulting their law books, only to declare the sheep's objections invalid. The fable is a pointed indictment of contemporary abusive practices. The narrator ostentatiously reserves his opinion, 'On Clerkis I do it, gif this sentence wes leill' [I leave it to scholars whether this decree was just] (l. 1229). The hapless sheep is judged guilty and fined, forced to sell the wool off his back to pay – a very literal representation of the usual metaphor. He is a pitiable representative of the 'fleeced' peasant as 'Naikit and bair syne to the feild couth pas' [naked and shorn he returned to the field] (l. 1257). In the subsequent Morality (the formal moral reading that follows each tale), the narrator denounces the proceedings more overtly, railing against 'This Cursit Court, corruptit all ffor meid [profit]' (l. 1241). The specifics of the moral allegory are spelled out at some length, identifying the sheep as the 'pure commounis [poor common people], that daylie ar opprest' (l. 1259). The wolf is identified as a sheriff, having purchased his position in order to extort money from the poor. The narrator pointedly declines to identify the fox and kite, 'Of thair nature, as now I speik no moir' (l. 1281), suggesting scandalous material too dangerous to reveal. Such a gesture opens up possibilities, encouraging the reader to supply missing material and to reflect upon their own experience and propose their own candidates.

The strategy of exposing social ills, not by listing standard abuses but in the form of dramatised, pathos-filled stories, evokes emotional and intellectual responses. The narrator claims to be a witness to the events, having personally heard the sheep's 'sair lamentatioun', asking why God sleeps, and takes up the same lament, 'Seis thow not (Lord) this warld overturnit is' (l. 1307). There is frank sympathy for the oppressed poor, 'the pure is peillit, the Lord may do na mis' [the poor man is stripped bare, the great man can do no wrong] (l. 1309). Finally, the narrator identifies with the lower orders who are suffering oppression, 'We pure pepill'. Although he takes refuge in the argument that our sinful state entails suffering, the narrator spends little time on this commonplace compared with his impassioned exposure of injustice and expression of concern. This is a severe indictment, possible only because it is safely couched in the form of a beast fable. But the timeless and generalised mode of moral allegory is given greater immediacy by the involved narrator, who engages directly with the material, intervening and expressing a strong awareness of 'nowadays'.

The Three Estates Model of Society

The notion of 'estates', separate classes of society, was at the centre of the dominant social theory of the period. The most usual model was of the Three Estates – comprising knighthood, priesthood and commons – which enshrined a trinitarian ideal, albeit one highly inaccurate as a description of the actual composition of society. The theory retained a symbolic rather than literal value, yet was widely propagated. A public sermon preached by Thomas Wimbledon at St Paul's cross in London, 1388, makes deliberate and pointed use of it.[8] Wimbledon carefully expounds the ideal division of society using a number of biblical texts and associated imagery. His primary metaphor employs a parable of a vine needing to be trimmed and tended in order to thrive:

Some kutten awey the void branches, some maken forkis and railis
to beren up the vine, and some diggen away the old earth fro the
rote ... right so in the church beth nedefull these three offices,
priesthood, knythode, and laborers. (p. 550)

The easy equivalence makes it indeed seem natural, one of the main
ploys of persuasive rhetoric. The resulting picture is of mutual service
and organic design benefiting everybody, 'Every state should love other;
and men of o craft shuld not despise ne hate men of none other craft,
sith they be so nedefull everich to other' (p. 551). He describes how
'travailing [working] in this world' is everyone's proper lot and will be
rewarded, while those who live 'after none state ne order' will go 'in
that place that no order is in but everlasting horror and sorrow, that is,
in hell'. Everyone is advised to adhere to their allotted role, 'everich
man see to what state God hath cleped him, and dwell he therein by
travile according to his degree' (p. 551).

Words such as 'state', 'order', 'travail' and 'degree' are loaded with
connotations, which paradoxically betrays an underlying flux and
multiplicity even as the sermon seeks to promote fixed stability in
harmony with the divine will. Several key referrents resist a single
meaning. 'State' can refer to estate as a social class, specific and general
rank, an office, particular status, or condition. 'Order' (Latin *ordo*)
potentially denotes sequence, group, religious, social and vocational
grouping, controlled design and established hierarchy. 'Travail' refers
primarily to physical work but covers a range of connotations, including:
religious   calling,   contemplative   solitude   and   prayer;   knightly
governance, fighting and the display of force; as well as humble,
domestic work and manual labour. 'Degree' designates a position in the
hierarchical society and is closely associated with notions of rank and
order. The audience listening to the sermon would clearly have a variety
of concepts in play as they sought to understand the meaning of the
words. The ostensible purpose of Wimbledon's sermon is clearly to
counter pernicious effects undermining the social strata, coming as it
does within a few years of the Peasants' Revolt. Wimbledon grounds his
arguments categorically upon biblical authority. In particular, he

endorses and is endorsed by the sentiments of St Paul – that every man should know his own order (I Corinthians 15:23) and abide in the same calling wherein he was called (I Corinthians 7:20). In such a context, the Three Estates model served to authorise a rigid view of society as permanently fixed and to repudiate change as sacrilegious.

It is interesting to compare this sermon with the one which concludes Chaucer's *Canterbury Tales*, 'The Parson's Tale'. This is cast as a sermon, albeit a fictive one, and discusses the same issues as Wimbledon. 'The Parson's Tale' in many ways aligns itself with serious moral discourse, explicitly rejecting poetry and fable. This sermon also outlines a systematised moral programme while denouncing abuses of power and position. It supports the traditional ideal of divinely approved stability:

> I woot wel ther is degree above degree, as reson is ... for as
> much as the estaat of hooly chirche ne myghte nat han be, ne
> the commune profit myghte nat han be kept, ne pees and rest
> in erthe, but if God hadde ordeyned that som men hadde
> hyer degree and som men lower, therfore was sovereyntee
> ordeyned.[9]

However, the Parson carefully elaborates the responsibilities which need to be met on both sides in order to uphold the system as legal, decent, honest and truthful. He plainly denounces wicked lords and rulers who treat their underlings harshly as the originators of base behaviour, asserting the levelling effect of wickedness, 'Every synful man is a cherl to synne' (l. 763). This definition of status according to behaviour promotes a relativist position with the potential to undermine presumptions about status, which is exactly what the hag does in 'The Wife of Bath's Tale', 'He nys nat gentil, be he duc or erl, / For vileyns synful dedes make a cherl' (ll. 1157–8).[10]

Estates Satire: Chaucer and Langland's Prologues

Traditionally, the genre of Estates Satire was an occasion to lament the sinful state of society, appraising and reprimanding various social classes. Jill Mann's groundbreaking work in 1973 situated Chaucer's 'General Prologue' firmly in the literary genre of Estates Satire, which she defined as 'any literary treatments of social classes which allow or encourage a general approach'.[11] The 'general approach' need not mean simply endorsing stereotypical social stratification however, as illustrated by 'The General Prologue' and Langland's 'Prologue' to *Piers Plowman* which employ the genre to devastatingly novel effect.

Piers Plowman begins from a very conservative position, seeking reform from a position of some anxiety in the face of threats from a new commercialism and cultural shifts. It is generally agreed that the poem moves towards a more radical stance with much more open perspectives on individual responsibility (partly what gained the poem some prestige during the Reformation as a proto-Protestant tract).

The 'Prologue' presents an allegorical landscape with a 'tour on a toft' [tower on a hill] and 'depe dale binethe, a dongeon therinne', connoting heaven and hell. The world is set between them as 'a faire felde ful of folke':

> Of alle manere of men, the meene and the riche,   [humble]
> Werchynge and wandrynge as the world asketh. (ll. 18–19)[12]

The dreamer appraises, apparently at random, the various activities and behaviour of those in the field, observing first ploughmen, then wasters, the proudly dressed, the devout (anchorites and hermits), merchants, greedy beggars, lying pilgrims, oddly sociable and lecherous hermits, and friars. As a survey, it quickly becomes a conspectus of social ills, fraudulent practices and impropriety. The reference to hermits 'on an heep' (l. 53), with 'hire wenches' (l. 54) destabilises identity as it nullifies the meaning of the name/vocation, just like the fat beggars, 'Roberdes knaves' (l. 44). Basically, Langland is acutely aware of social tensions and corruption, attributing the decay of morals to the changes in the constitution of society. His satirical representations reveal the dislocation occurring to a culture of exchange-and-barter, with duties of almsgiving and hospitality based on principles of service. The friars have abandoned their principle function, honouring apostolic ideals of poverty, in a society corrupted by a cash economy with new goals of profit-seeking, bargaining and negotiating. These are intrinsically wrong according to the moral perspectives of the reactionary 'Prologue'. Commerce as a profession and as a metaphor is consistently regarded with suspicion and hostility:

> Sith charite hath ben chapman and chief to shryve lordes
>   [confess]
> Many ferlies han fallen in a fewe yeres ...   [strange events]
> The mooste meschief on molde is mountynge up faste.   [earth]
> (ll. 64–5, 67)

This attributes the demise of traditional social interaction (based on Christian charity) to rising commercial forces ('chapman'), foreseeing dire consequences if the appetitive financial outlook is not checked. The problem Langland explores is: where does the authority and will to check such appetites reside? *Piers Plowman* essentially poses a problem and then exhaustively explores potential solutions, developing more radical proposals as it proceeds (privileging individual conscience above a corrupt institutionalised practice, such as pilgrimage, for instance).

The 'Prologue' includes Estates Satire but in a much less systematic way than is usual in the genre. Some of the targets of Langland's ecclesiastical satire are traditional ones, also attacked (if much more obliquely) by Chaucer, such as the fat monk driven by bodily appetites rather than spiritual and the pardoner selling absolution and thus profiting from sin and fraudulent relics. But much of the 'Prologue' deals with less familiar territory, exploring innovative and bold techniques. The 'Prologue' quickly progresses beyond the normal range by considering the failings of bishops and the pope. Langland the satirist adopts a subterfuge, protecting himself to some degree by the dream vision form but also phrasing his critique in ambiguous ways. For instance, when he moves from condemning the exploitative pardoner to assessing the support structures and collusion which enable his exploitation:

Were the bisshop yblessed and worthe bothe his eris,   [ears]
His seel sholde noght be sent to deceyve the peple.
Ac it is noght by the bisshop that the boy precheth. (ll. 78–81)

The bishop is arraigned obliquely with the idea of his guilt being couched in a hypothetical conditional, alongside an indignant imperative, before turning on 'Ac' into a statement of exoneration. This masterfully says one thing then twists it to say the opposite! As he appraises the church hierarchy, Langland makes transparent the shifting semiology of words. Lines 100 onwards discuss 'power' in a variety of guises, legitimate and illegitimate ('power presumed'), as 'vertues' (denoting both power and virtue) and as cardinals (applying to virtues, gates and high church officials). The narrator takes pains to moderate any disconcerting edge of criticism, claiming no such intent, 'impugnen I nelle' [I do not wish to cast aspersions upon them] (l. 109). This is a daring ploy, highlighting the urgency of Langland's critique as he takes risks by presenting very frank cynicism which is hardly veiled by gestures of 'denial'. The theoretical basis of the Church's power is laid open to consideration from a searching viewpoint, querying whether names and actions accord and whether terms fit the deed. When he refrains from comment, it is framed in a double-edged way, 'I kan and kan naught of court speke more' (l. 111). This evokes the traditional modesty topos, combined with unspeakablity and not being permitted. The multiple signification of the verb 'kan' ranges among 'know how to' to 'be able to' and even shades into 'be allowed to', conjuring up a whole complex of potential meaning. Such obfuscating gestures reveal rather than veil radical implications of his 'further' knowledge, which the reader is left to speculate upon.

The 'Prologue' then moves from ecclesiastical satire to the secular sphere – the king and his systems of justice. The originary foundation of state power and control is imagined as a coronation scene with the ruler being led by knighthood and approved by the 'Might of the communes' (l. 113). The social structure which is established forms the typical tripartite hierarchy of the estates system. Langland presents the scene in a chaotic, disorderly way, layering the text sometimes to the point of obscurity and regularly retreating into Latin, excluding the 'lewed men' (ll. 132–8). He sets various discordant voices against one another in the form of a lunatic, an angel and a goliard (loud-mouthed jangler) in rapid succession with little time for pausing to consider how they connect or follow on from one another. The result is to create confusion, amidst which the narrator abdicates responsibility, 'construe whoso wolde' (l. 144), inviting anyone who wishes to do so to try to make sense of it. What we are challenged to interpret is the people's cry (in Latin), 'the king's commands have the force of law for us'. Whether it signals obedience or grievance, it triggers the mock-parliament that follows.

Langland's Beast Fable

The Belling of the Cat episode (ll. 146–210) exemplifies Langland's diffuse technique. It fills up a considerable portion of the Prologue, constituting 65 lines out of 231, more than a quarter of the text (28 per cent), so is clearly far more than an incidental diversion. The illusion of (chaotic) verisimilitude is suddenly broken by the appearance of talking rats and mice, 'Comen to a counseil for the commune profit' (l. 148). Their problem is an unruly cat, assaulting them at will; they aim to resist and become 'lordes olofte and lyven at oure ese' (l. 157). Clearly this concerns status aspirations and antagonisms, but between which particular social groups? The fable is given some topical suggestiveness by references to the City of London, the wearing of chains of office and mention of France and England (within three lines). This kind of satire anticipates later deflationary representations of parliament such as Milton's mock-parliament of the fallen angels in Book II of *Paradise Lost* and Swift's Lilliputians in *Gulliver's Travels*. Langland's mock-parliament of rats and mice agrees that belling the cat to give them advance warning of his presence is a good idea, but the plan falls down when no one is bold enough to hang the bell on the cat. The precise purpose of the restraint remains unclear; the phrase 'commune profit' is repeated (ll. 148, 169), but the shift from the definite pronoun, 'the', to the possessive pronoun 'our' betrays the self-interest masquerading as general well-being. A mouse objects to the proposal, 'Though we hadde ykilled the cat, yet sholde ther come another' (l. 185). His misgivings voice an extreme solution, albeit negatively phrased as a wild hypothesis. His counsel is of compliance, collusion, for 'while he cacceth conynges he coveiteth noght oure caroyne' [while he is catching rabbits, he is not after our carcasses]. His appeasement strategy is supported by proverbial lore from past generations as he relates his father's saying, 'Ther the cat is a kitoun, the court is ful elenge' [wretched] (l. 195). Again, the casualness conceals an artful implication coupled with a reference to 'Holy Writ, whoso wole it rede', referring the reader to Ecclesiastes 10:16, 'Woe to the land where the king is a child'. Gradually, dangerous insinuations emerge to cast doubt upon the minority of Richard II, who acceded to the throne aged ten in July 1377. The narrative typically retreats, via a human perspective on the situation, arguing that rats and mice afflict mankind adversely, so need to be kept in check by a cat. The situation shifts from a problem to a solution in just a few glib statements. While some cryptic political import lurks behind the vignette, Langland inserts a deliberate attention-grabbing disclaimer with emphatic parentheses functioning like a loud whisper in the ear:

(What this metels bymeneth, ye men that ben murye,   [dream]
Devyne ye—for I ne dar, by deere God in hevene!) (ll. 109–210)

The conspiratorial disavowal seems to invite consideration of the significance of the beast fable as an image of tyrannical authority – a power based on fear. But the narrative moves swiftly on, returning to the everyday sights and sounds of contemporary London. A human assembly convenes, comprising hordes of lawyers, 'Barons and burgeises and bondemen al' [aristocracy, middle-class townsfolk and unfree peasants], an oddly mixed gathering despite the normalising tone of the statement. The 'Prologue' ends by dissolving into sheer noise with the cries of the street sellers advertising their wares. As a conspectus of society, the 'Prologue' frustrates the usual satirical model, combining safe targets with extremely dangerous ones. It cunningly exploits the dream vision to enable a potentially radical critique. We could argue that the resolute social and political focus of the 'Prologue' in confronting topical abuses and conflict requires a cultural materialist perspective to be brought to bear in order to explicate its meaning and appreciate the boldness of its treatment.

Estates Satire in the 'General Prologue'

The same is true of Chaucer's 'General Prologue', although its techniques differ in many respects from Langland's.[13] James Simpson sees Langland's 'Prologue' as loosely within the Estates Satire tradition while covering groups who are not usually part of the 'occupational' range, although more general in its methods and with a more critical narrator than the 'General Prologue'.[14] Also, whereas Langland exploits fully the opportunities presented by his dream vision to castigate and indict a wide range of social and political practices, Chaucer minimises the moralising potential (using a hesitant, naïve narrator and the infamously ironic tone). Langland's setting is the world of work as opposed to Chaucer's tavern/pilgrimage – a space set apart from the everyday. There is also an absolutely inverse proportion of normative detail (what should be) over descriptive (what is) when comparing Langland's 'Prologue' with Chaucer's: Chaucer describes the pilgrims' appearance and behaviour with much more circumstantial detail and at greater length than Langland without drawing explicit moral conclusions. Much of the distinctive quality of Chaucer's satirical Prologue proceeds from his characterisation of the narrator of the 'General Prologue'. This narrator declares his intention with an excessive attention to propriety, characterising the speaker as fastidious in the extreme:

Me thynketh it acordaunt to resoun
To telle yow al the *condicioun*   [circumstances]
Of ech of hem, so as it semed me,
And *which* they weren, and of what *degree*,   [social rank]
And eek in what *array* that they were inne.   [clothing]
(ll. 37–41, emphasis mine)

The 'General Prologue' conforms in general terms to the Estates Satire genre as it contains representatives from a variety of different social ranks, includes an idealised portrait of each of the Three Estates (Knight, Parson, Plowman), and covers a good deal of stereotypical material. Many of the details of the individual pilgrim portraits are more general than they may initially seem, as shown by Jill Mann's study. Although the pilgrimage framework removes the figures from their usual occupations, there is a good deal of material describing their 'everyday' lives, and the predominant categorisation is according to the type of work each performs (or fails to perform). The one character who may appear excluded as a worker is the Wife of Bath, but in many respects marriage is her profession. The satire depends upon invoking associations and traditional prejudices (e.g. the standard fare of thieving millers, greedy friars and smooth-talking lawyers). Each figure is praised as a superb representative of their profession with an abundance of superlatives and intensifiers ('ful wel', 'ful faire'). Some details reveal discrepancies between what is required and what is delivered, especially among the clergy: the Monk wears expensive fur contrary to the rule of his order; similarly, the Prioress keeps pet dogs and feeds them expensive high-quality bread and roast meat; the Wife's cloth-making expertise rests on the West Country's reputation for poor quality material.

Clothing and physical appearance play an important part in defining character and often serves as a kind of shorthand, so that the Monk's white neck denotes lechery, the Wife's gat-toothed smile is associated with negative connotations including lechery, and the Miller's red hair, wart and bald head add up to a physiognomist's dream. No detail is innocent and animal imagery insinuates a good deal of information, as when the Pardoner is described with reference to a hare, a gelding and a mare, the Miller in terms of a sow and a fox, whereas the Parson is fittingly associated with sheep, suiting his role as pastoral good shepherd. Quite a lot of the personality with which the pilgrims are invested stems from traditional medical classification, such as the theory of four bodily humours, rendering the Reeve typically choleric and the Franklin quintessentially sanguine.

Yet, Chaucer is not constrained by the generic model. He develops the blueprint to deal with figures who do not form part of the tripartite model or who are not usually included in the satirical conspectus, such as the Manciple, Summoner and Shipman. Only three specific names are supplied – Harry Bailey, Madame Eglantine and Friar Huberd – while specific places are plentiful, including the Tabard Inn, Rouncivale Hospital and the Reeve's hometown of Bawdeswell in Norfolk. The presentation through the diffident narrator creates subtlety by means of which opinion is left relatively open, so that critics can debate how far a portrait is negative or positive, regarding the Knight, for instance, as exemplary or as a travesty.[15] The Prioress receives relatively gentle satirical treatment, as teasingly ambivalent as the inscription on her brooch, *Amor vincit omnia* [love conquers all], while the Pardoner is accompanied in his love song by the Summoner's 'stif burdoun' (a strong bass, with a pun on 'heavy weight'), conveying an altogether more vulgar insinuation.

There are many variant views of Chaucer as an apolitical poet, a staunch conservative, even a covert Lollard sympathiser. The fact is that there are very few overt references to contemporary events and people, apart from one notable exception. The farmyard mêlée of 'The Nun's Priest's Tale' is described with a passing mention of the Peasants' Revolt, comparing the uproar to that of the rioting rebels:

So hydous was the noyse – a, benedicitee!– [Lord bless us!]
Certes, he Jakke Straw and his meynee   [band]
Ne made nevere shoutes half so shrille
Whan that they wolden any Flemyng kille. (ll. 3393–6)

Chaucer's openness to a variety of readings stems largely from his deployment of inscrutable narrative disguises. The naïve reporter of the pilgrims' activities and words shifts at times to appear more knowing, more ironic, some times alert and omniscient, and at other times dim-witted and baffled. Primarily the narrator is a flexible vehicle for exposing directly and adducing indirect self-exposure. The presence of the mediating narrator supplies a transparently boundaried perspective – one which maintains polite approval irrespective of the attitudes and behaviour he encounters. This effectively de-authorises the discourse, for, if all is excellent, then finer distinction and discernment must rest with the reader. The 'General Prologue' uses material associated with dream vision and Estates Satire but consistently denies criticism in favour of ostensible magnanimity, resulting in the dominant mode of irony.[16] Dream vision's investigative and interrogative modes are markedly absent, as is Estates Satire's overt criticism. Instead, the narrator serves to insinuate critical perspectives, constructed ambiguously as an enthusiastic simpleton or as a clever dissimulator, honing in on the telling detail which modifies or undercuts the ostensible approval; for example, suddenly revealing the Prioress's largeness, 'For, hardily, she was nat undergrowe' (l. 156), and the Cook's running sore, 'But greet harm was it, as it thoughte me, / That on his shyne a mormal hadde he' (ll. 385–6).

The impression of artlessness is fostered by a series of manoeuvres, such as the apparently random ordering, a developing sense of the speaker's filtering consciousness, through a variety of different acts, authenticating personal avowals ('I trowe', 'as I was war'), studied casualness of omission ('But, sooth to seyn, I noot how men him call'), inside knowledge ('Ther wiste no wight that he was in dette'), intriguing insight hinting at more acute observation ('And yet he semed bisier than he was'), and occasionally harsh appraisal ('I trowe he were a geldyng or a mare'). Not entirely naive, not entirely ironic, this is the teasing persona who shifts ground and refuses to be defined.

The subtle critique of society in the 'General Prologue' responds well to a Cultural Materialist reading, particularly one in alignment with reader-response theory. A key technique of Chaucer's is to demonstrate the partiality of perspectives and the power of the unspoken. One aspect of the text which enriches the experience and enlists active participation on the part of the reader is a gradual loosening of semantic value, so that key value judgements rest upon inadequate linguistic grounds. For instance, the designations 'gentil' and 'noble' assume a less and less stable import, applied as they are to the Knight, the Parson, the Manciple, the Summoner ('gentil harlot'!), the Pardoner and, finally, to the Tabard Inn. 'Worthy' is another term whose semantic weight shifts so as to become indeterminate, being applied twice to the Knight, the Friar and the Merchant, and once to the Franklin and the Wife. Similarly, clear linguistic markers of high status, such as 'Madame', 'curteisie', 'lord' are accorded only and conspicuously to those among the religious pilgrims who profess or aspire to an aristocratic status, such as the Prioress, Monk and Friar. Outright labelling of social status is rare, restricted to definitions of the Knight, 'a verray parfit gentil knight' (l. 72), and the Miller, a 'stout carl' (l. 545).

The two unambiguous portraits – of the Parson and his brother the Plowman – contain the only instances of the term 'good' as a personal epithet. Elsewhere the term is slippery, more often to be distrusted as a smokescreen (comparable to 'interesting' today), so that the Monk despising his religious duties is condoned, 'And I seyde his opinion was good' (l. 183), and the murderous piratical Shipman, wearing a dagger around his neck (not the usual place for such an accessory!), is deemed 'a good felawe' [a fine rogue] (l. 395). Moral judgements, like social status, emerge as severely compromised. They rest on infirm markers which are liable to alter their meaning or become perversely inverted. The judicious anatomy of language in which Chaucer specialises alerts the reader to the power of ironic juxtaposition and inconsistent application, unsettling any notion of fixity. Through their choice of language and acute social commentary, Chaucer and Langland show themselves to be keenly aware of the tensions lurking within society, unsurprising in view of their proximity to the violent uprising in 1381 known as the Peasants' Revolt.

John Ball and the Peasants' Revolt

John Ball was one of the leaders of the protest movement labelled the Peasants' Revolt. He is reported by Froissart as delivering a rousing sermon to the assembled rebels, advocating communism and revolution, 'Good people, things cannot go right in England and never will, until goods are held in common, and there are no more villeins and gentlefolk, but we are all one and the same' ('tout un').[17] Citing Adam and Eve as the common ancestors of mankind, he reputedly expounded upon the notion:

> When Adam delved and Eve span
> Who was then the gentleman?

As a priest, Ball seems to have been a prominent dissenting figure, possibly a Lollard. He was released from the Archbishop of Canterbury's prison by the rebels during the revolt in 1381 and accompanied them to London, where he was later executed. Six letters exist attributed to him, contained in chronicles of the time, by Henry Knighton and Thomas Walsingham, which are essentially hostile to the rebellion.[18] The letters may or may not be genuine, but they attest at least to a perception of what rebellion entailed. They appear to be cryptic, coded messages gathering forces to prepare for rebellion. They are presented as seditious documents contained within 'authorised' accounts of events, so clearly are open to charges of misrepresentation or, at the very least, mediated expression. Yet, as rare samples purporting to be the discourse of the disenfranchised, they offer tantalising glimpses of the fourteenth-century underclass. Their primary function within the context of the chronicles which preserve their sentiments is as incriminating evidence justifying repression and harsh reprisals, speaking mainly perhaps of the fears of a compromised regime. Walsingham's letter is said to have been found on the person of a hanged felon, and John Ball is reported to have admitted writing it.

The 'letters' are in various forms, most often as short rhyming pieces introduced by a prose statement (Walsingham's chronicle, two items in

Knighton's chronicle). They are generally delivered in the personae of honest-sounding labourers with miscellaneous occupational surnames, John Sheep, John the Miller, Jack Miller, Jack Carter and Jack Trueman; two are explicitly phrased as statements by John Ball. As vernacular compositions from the lower orders, who are usually denied access to literacy, they suggest a community cooperating in their production and dissemination. Even shrouded as they are in oblique coding, they represent a challenge to authority simply by existing and addressing a public, both damnable offences among those seeking to silence and subjugate dissent. The letters adopt the authoritative form of official letters with elaborate formulae of address. The epistolary formula is so emphatic as to be almost parodic. The central premise conceives of a community of workers, a fraternity open to those excluded from elite crafts guilds and religious confraternities. The very idea of an open association, of collective action among peasants, was itself outrageous to the ruling orders, whose legislation had for many decades been aimed at confining peasants to their lords' manors, restricting their movement and independence, and imposing wage restraints and punitive measures for even minor instances of resistance, such as reduced tax payments.

In their straightforward diction and immediacy, favouring present-tense verbs, such as 'greet', 'bid', 'ask', 'pray', 'doth yow to understande' [wishes you to know], the letters assert a direct appeal to the community. Simple statements are phrased as direct imperatives, as instructions, or as messages of support and encouragement. The detached mode slips only once into a plural pronoun, 'oure mylne' [our mill], denoting a collective enterprise.

In themselves, the sentiments expressed hardly seem objectionable, 'seketh pees', 'fleth sin'; it is by association and retrospectively that the pieces become incendiary. The documents situate themselves in opposition to falseness and guile, sins of pride, greed and so on which have been allowed to proliferate for too long. A figure who embodies the reviled sins is characterised repeatedly as 'Hob the Robber', who will receive chastisement. The writing style has the classic feature of polemic in that it employs an oppositional style, using loaded terms which are balanced antithetically:

Lat myght helpe ryght,
And skyl go before wille,
And ryght befor myght. (I, ll. 7–9)

The verse deploys sets of oppositions, such as war/woe, friend/foe, right/might, in an elaborately alternating pattern, oscillating in different combinations which enact the tendency of value-laden terms to operate differently depending on context. Although the verse is far from sophisticated, its techniques can be subtle as when the relationship between skill (ability) and will (intention) is pointed by their rhyming proximity. The dominant tone is of strident confident moralising with certain actions deemed unambiguously 'gode'. Key terms such as 'true' are reiterated, underpinning a pose of reliability and truthfulness.

The recurrent message of the letters is to be resolved and to take action against sinners, but without any explicit detail. People are apparently urged to follow a single leader, or cause, 'loke schappe you to on heved'. Cryptic remarks such as 'bee war of gyle in borugh' and 'nowe is tyme to be ware' suggest a climate of suspicion, perhaps of infiltrators or, more generally, of threats to liberty and livelihood. The unspecified nature of the threats creates a sense of ubiquitous persecution. There are vague mentions of projects under way, 'make a gode ende of that ye have begunnen', 'stondith togidre'. John Ball reassures people that 'he hath rungen youre belle', suggesting some sort of alarm, a call to action, in a context where the ringing of the church bells was the prime method of alerting the parish in time of need. The mode of distrust and vague threat was clearly equally unsettling to those in power, who felt threatened by the rebels, probably capable of fuelling anxiety on both sides.

Imagery and Allusions

The language of the letters is colloquial and idiomatic, yet full of biblical cadences. The coded call to arms is couched in terms resonant of parables and proverbs. In regard to religious language and imagery, the letters refer to the 'kynges sone of hevene' who shall 'pay' for everything, to God, Mary and the Trinity, usually in opening and closing prayers (two end with 'amen') or oaths (e.g. 'in the name of the Trinite'). One Latin allusion occurs, '*si dedero*' [if I shall give] from Psalm 131:4. John Ball's preaching credentials are relatively invisible, apart from two references to his priestly status – one set in the past, 'somtyme', the other, in the present, 'seynte Marye prist'.

The biblical image of a mill, symbolising divine justice, is appropriated as a metaphor for impending uprising, through the recurrent persona of a miller who grinds 'smal, smal, smal'. The image conveys a neat impression of patient, dedicated effort, while also suggestive of a mill's wheel turning, connoting transformation as well as the shifting wheel of fortune. In letter I, there is a progressive shift in the ownership of the mill (in some respects a symbol of the means of production, the sustaining labour of the peasantry), moving from 'Jakke Mylner ... his mylne' (l. 1), to 'thi mylne' (l. 4) and a double reference to 'oure mylne' (ll. 10, 13). A certain menace underlies the image of slow inevitability suggestive of an approaching climactic event. Elsewhere there are anticipated future achievements, 'at the even men heryth [praise] the day', and hints of taking justified action, 'For if the ende be wele, than is alle wele'. These remarks contain religious undertones, alluding to a day of reckoning. Among the more prominent and recurrent images is the figure of Piers Plowman, twice invoked by name, as well as two mentions of other figures in Langland's poem – Dowel and Dobet. The fundamental style and method of the letters owes a lot to *Piers Plowman*, with their colloquial diction steeped in biblical language and focus on labouring figures who represent virtue in a vicious world.

The Influence of *Piers Plowman*

The popular appeal of *Piers* is evident not just in these letters but in other texts which take up and continue its moral indignation. *Piers* was in the process of being written and rewritten before and after the Peasants' Revolt with uncertain distribution and audience, but it definitely proved influential during the following century of discord.

Throughout the period of civil and international war, with the throne bitterly contested and factions multiplying, many poetic satires appeared and claimed an affinity with *Piers*, including *Winner and Waster*, *Piers the Plowman's Creed* and *Mum and the Soothsegger*. These texts form part of a climate of opposition as challenging voices advocating urgent reform. In hindsight, they can be associated with the stirrings of discontent which would fuel the Protestant revolution and the disestablishment of the Catholic Church in England. Langland's text provided a model for many dissident voices and was appropriated for various polemical ends.

Winner and Waster

This poem[19] survives in a unique copy in Robert Thornton's book *c.* 1440, alongside the *Parliament of the Three Ages* (one other copy of which exists elsewhere). In the monumental *Manual of the Writings in Middle English*, it is classified under the category 'Poems Dealing with Contemporary Conditions', prioritising its subject matter above all.[20] The poem clearly is highly topical, apparently commenting on conditions following the plague, during the period of repressive labour legislation. Chief Justice William Shareshull (d. 1370) is referred to (l. 317) and the motto of the Order of the Garter, founded in 1349, is included (l. 68). These references allow for only the sketchiest of dating. It is impossible to prove whether or not *Winner and Waster* preceded *Piers* or followed it. The poem presents a dream vision in which two opponents debate in front of the king, largely consisting of four formal exchanges.

In a Prologue, a critical, unidentified speaker laments the contrast between 'Whilom' and 'nowe'. He makes cryptic comments about a 'child' who is favoured undeservingly more than the poet, but takes comfort from future recognition:

> But, never-the-lattere, at the laste when ledys bene knawen,
> [men are known]
> Werke wittnesse will bere who wirche kane beste.   [can best act]
> (ll. 29–30)

This bears some resemblance to the ominous anticipation of a day of judgement looming which characterises the letters of John Ball. Such political prophesy was specifically outlawed in 1402. Elements of parody are soon visible as the dream vision landscape is described at a ludicrously excessive length. The birds who sing, include less-than-mellifluous barnacle geese, woodpeckers and jays, while it is no gentle brook which lulls this narrator to sleep:

> So ruyde were the roughe stremys and raughten so heghe
>
>   [reached high]
>
> That it was neghande nyghte or I nappe myghte.   [sleep]
>
> (ll. 42–3)

The narrator then witnesses a tournament, identifying the various groups with their banners and heraldic devices as the king, aristocracy and ecclesiasts. Then, through the persona of the king's messenger, an appraisal of the gathered forces takes note of various classes, including friars, merchants, squires and archers. At times the observer-messenger is evidently straining to maintain impartiality as when he asserts the likelihood of the friars winning, 'If I sholde say the sothe, it semys no nothire' (l. 178). The narrative perspective shifts without warning, so that the narrator describing knights riding to the king is suddenly foregrounded as an inebriated participant, 'Me thoghte I sowpped so sadly it sowrede bothe myn eghne' [It seemed I drank so deeply it bleared both my eyes] (l. 215). This may be a defensive ploy to prepare for 'loose' speech to come.

    The grievances of Winner are declared, employing the metaphor of agricultural labour beset by a cash economy, aligned with sin:

> Alle that I wynn thurgh witt he wastes thurgh pryde;
>
> I gedir, I glene, ...   [gather]
>
> ... and he the purse opynes' (ll. 230–2).

Waster's counter-argument inveighs against accumulating riches while poor people suffer, sinning against charity. Winner replies by accusing

Waster of reckless consumption, causing famine, with another prophetic warning, 'The more colde es to come, als me a clerke tolde' (l. 293). In turn, Waster depicts Winner as mean and acquisitive, 'Mangery ne myndale ne never myrthe lovediste' [You never enjoyed feasting, memorial drinks nor merrymaking] (l. 304), portraying himself as the embodiment of hearty generosity as opposed to thrifty niggardliness. The debate continues in an evenly balanced form with each side deploying effective arguments. The question of who is in the right is increasingly difficult to ascertain as, at one point, Winner is accused of profiting from scarcity – a negative exemplum of market forces in action. Similarly, Waster asserts the need for social distinctions, not just as a matter of rank but, interestingly, for reasons which blur traditional social distinctions and appeal to broader, less partisan interests:

> Woldeste thou hafe lordis to lyfe as laddes on fote?
> Prelates als prestes that the parischen yemes?   [look after]
> Prowde marchandes of pris as pedders in towne?   [wealth/worth]
> (ll. 3750–2)

The confusion of degree confounds a sense of order and propriety, not least by applying an aristocratic concept of excellence ('of pris') to a merchant elite. Prelates (an derogatory term favoured by Lollards) are placed parallel to 'proud', aligning the two suggestively. The shocking proposition that the higher clergy (bishops) should act to take care of their assigned diocese, when most were absentee landlords, is a point lightly skipped over. As the poem unfolds, the complications accumulate. Waster makes a beautiful point about winning depending on spendthrift clientele, 'Whoso wele schal wyn, a wastour moste he fynde' (l. 390). Winner changes his attack to a more general disapproval of extravagant lifestyles, exalting the humble examples of Mary and Joseph. In response, Waster invokes freedom of choice, disparaging Winner's mean spiritedness, 'For gode day ne glade getys thou never' (l. 440). The poem concludes with the king sending Waster into temporary exile and turning his affections upon Winner, whom he encourages to profit from wasters in order to finance his imminent wars.

This achieves a sophisticated, multi-layered satirical critique. The poem as a whole works to expose subterfuge with particular attention placed upon the malleability of words and values. What emerges is the pernicious yet irresistible profit ethic. The preliminary assumption that winning is good and wasting is bad is modified by the evolving debate and the somewhat cynical solution. The state (in the person of the king) protects and privileges money-generating entrepreneurs over the old aristocratic elite. In the context of the proto-capitalistic society of the period, this poem could hardly expose more clearly the relations between power and profit.

Piers the Plowman's Creed

Piers the Plowman's Creed declares its literary associations in its title. It is essentially an anti-fraternal satire, extolling a Lollard critique of the corruption of apostolic ideals. As the TEAMS* editor says, 'the poem has both literary and cultural value–indeed, it is difficult to separate the literary from the cultural'.[21] Written *c.* 1398–1401 and surviving in two manuscripts from the sixteenth century, the poem clearly appealed to some readers during the Reformation.

Without recourse to the distancing frame of a dream vision, the narrator travels in search of spiritual instruction, encountering friars of every order, none of whom can help; it is the figure of Piers who teaches the seeker the Apostolic Creed (ll. 795–821). Each speaker he meets denounces the others while praising themselves, so strong criticism is voiced by mediating personae whose lies and artful misrepresentation highlight the scurrilous unreliability of words. As verbal testimony is scrutinised, the narrator reflects, 'Here semeth litel trewthe' (l. 138). The poem is unusually bold in its assertion of Lollard opinion, favouring apostolic poverty, citing the Bible in English and being suspicious of fables. There are some colourful and striking images; for example, the Dominicans, 'digne as dich water that dogges in bayteth' [proud as

---

* TEAMS is the acronym for the Consortium for the Teaching of the Middle Ages. Details of the TEAMS website can be found in Part Five: 'Further Reading'.

ditchwater in which dogs feed] (l. 375). Piers the plowman, named at line 473, is 'a sely man' (l. 421), who is the central figure of wisdom and authority. He denounces the four orders of friars, while approving of Wyclif, 'Wytnesse on Wycliff, that warned hem with trewthe' (l. 528). He respects Wyclif as a good man who was persecuted, 'lollede him with heretykes werkes' (l. 532) and also mentions the Lollard Walter Brut (l. 657), who was tried and executed for heresy in 1393. But the creed stops short of following Wyclif in denying transubstantiation (l. 823) and refers respectfully to 'generall Holy Chirche' (l. 816) as an overarching body separate from the corrupt elements in need of reform.

Each of the works examined in this chapter reveals a critical awareness of the tensions fuelling unrest. A cultural materialist focus can explore attitudes of dissent and subversion which run counter to much of the dominant ideology of the medieval period. The rapid social and economic changes were producing a broader diversity of occupation and greater social and geographical mobility which traditional models could only accommodate by modification. Some texts observe the processes at work in society from a position of sympathy, others seek to oppose the cataclysmic forces at work. Always, gaps and inconsistencies work to expose deeper issues of uncertain meaning. The circulation of texts helped to inculcate a wide spectrum of views, which gradually eroded entrenched dogma in many areas of life.

Notes

1   Jonathan Culler, *Literary Theory: A Very Short Introduction* (Oxford: Oxford University Press, 2000) presents succinct overviews of major critical theories in an Appendix. Two excellent anthologies providing substantial primary sources are: David Lodge and Nigel Wood (eds), *Modern Criticism and Theory: A Reader*, 2nd edn. (Harlow: Pearson, 2000) and K. M. Kenton (ed.), *Twentieth- Century Literary Theory: A Reader*, 2nd edn. (London: Macmillan, 1997).

2   John Brannigan, *New Historicism and Cultural Materialism* (Hampshire: Palgrave Macmillan, 1998), p. 108.

3   Brannigan, *New Historicism and Cultural Materialism*, p. 118.

4   For an excellent introduction to the works of Michel Foucault, see Gary Cutting, *Foucault: A Very Short Introduction* (Oxford: Oxford University Press, 2005).

5   Brannigan, *New Historicism and Cultural Materialism*, p. 78.

6   Jonathan Dollimore and Alan Sinfield, 'Culture and Textuality: Debating Cultural Materialism', *Textual Practice* 4:1, 1990, pp. 91–100 (p. 99).

7   Brannigan, *New Historicism and Cultural Materialism*, p. 181.

8   See G. R. Owst, *Literature and the Pulpit in Medieval England*, rev. edn (Oxford: Blackwell, 1933; repr. 1961), pp. 550–1.

9   *The Riverside Chaucer*, ed. Larry D. Benson (Oxford: Oxford University Press, 1989), pp. 314, ll. 763, 772–3.

10   'The Wife of Bath's Tale', pp. 105–22 in *Riverside Chaucer*.

11   Jill Mann, *Chaucer and Medieval Estates Satire: The Literature of Social Classes and the General Prologue to the Canterbury Tales* (Cambridge: Cambridge University Press, 1973). At the time Mann was offering a novel response to and corrective of the prevailing modes of 'autobiographical' and psychological character-based criticism.

12   William Langland, *The Vision of Piers Plowman: A Complete Edition of the B-text*, ed. A. V. C. Schmidt (London: Dent, 1984).

13   For a detailed comparison, see Helen Cooper, 'Langland's and Chaucer's Prologues', *The Yearbook of Langland Studies* 1, (1987), pp. 71–81. For 'General Prologue' see pp. 23–36.

14   James Simpson, *Piers Plowman: An Introduction to the B-Text* (London: Longman, 1990), p. 21.

15   For a closely argued negative reading of the Knight, see Terry Jones, *A Knyght ther Was: A Portrait of a Medieval Mercenary* (London: Weidenfeld and Nicholson, 1980).

16   On the role of the narrator, see Mann, *Estates Satire* (1973), pp. 190–202.

17   Froissart, *Chronicles*, trans. Geoffrey Brereton (Harmondsworth: Penguin, 1978), p. 212.

18   Derek Pearsall (ed.), *Chaucer to Spenser: An Anthology* (Oxford: Blackwell, 1999), pp. 227–9.

19   Warren Ginsburg (ed.), *Wynnere and Wastour and The Parlement of the Thre Ages*, Consortium for the Teaching of the Middle Ages (TEAMS) (Kalamazoo, MI: Western Michigan University, 1992).

20   Rossell Hope Robbins in *A Manual of the Writings in Middle English 1050–1500* (New Haven, CT: Connecticut Academy of Arts and Sciences, 1975), vol. 5, p. 1358.

21   James Dean (ed.), *Six Ecclesiastical Satires*, TEAMS (Kalamazoo, MI: Western Michigan University, 1991), p. 1.

Part Five
References and Resources

Timeline

	Historical Events	Literary Events
1066	Battle of Hastings, Duke William of Normandy becomes king of England	
1096–9	First Crusade	
1100	Accession of Henry I	
c. **1100**		Earliest Welsh Arthurian story, *Culhwch and Olwen*
1106	Henry I defeats Robert of Normandy at Tinchebrai	
1114	Henry's daughter Mathilda marries the German Emperor	
1120	Death of Henry I's heir	
1127	Mathilda recognised as Henry's successor and marries Geoffrey Plantagenet of Anjou	
1133	Henry of Anjou born	
1135	Death of Henry I; accession of Stephen of Blois	
1135–54	Civil war between Stephen and Mathilda	
c. **1136**		Geoffrey of Monmouth's *Historia Regum Britanniae*

Timeline

	Historical Events	Literary Events
1137	Eleanor of Aquitaine marries Louis VII of France	
1144	Geoffrey of Anjou becomes Duke of Normandy	
1152	Eleanor of Aquitaine divorces Louis and marries Henry of Anjou and Normandy	
1154	Death of Stephen; accession of Henry of Anjou as Henry II of England	
c. **1155**		Wace's *Roman de Brut*
c. **1160–90**		Chrétien de Troyes' French Arthurian verse romances
c. **1160–90**		Marie de France's *Lais*
1161	Thomas à Becket becomes Archbishop of Canterbury	
1167–8	Second Crusade	
1170	Becket killed	
1173	Armed revolt by Eleanor and her sons against Henry; Eleanor imprisoned	
c. **1180**		Andreas Capellanus's *De Amore*
1183	Henry's heir dies	
1188–92	Third Crusade	
1189	Death of Henry II; Eleanor released; accession of Richard I	
c. **1190s**		*The Owl and The Nightingale*
1191	King Arthur's grave 'discovered' at Glastonbury	
1199	Death of Richard I; accession of John	
c. **1200**		*Hali Meiðhad*
c. **1200–10**		Laȝamon's *Brut*

Historical Events		Literary Events
1202–4	Fourth Crusade	
1203	Death of Arthur of Brittany	
1204	John loses control of Normandy; death of Eleanor	
1208–14	England under papal edict	
1208	Pope Innocent III proclaims a crusade against the Cathars in Albi, southern France ('the 'Albigensian' Crusade)	
1215	Magna Carta; universities of Paris and Oxford founded	
1216	Death of John; accession of minor Henry III, William Marshal is regent	
1217–21	Fifth Crusade	
c. 1225		*Ancrene Wisse*
1227	Henry assumes his majority	
1236	Henry III marries Eleanor of Provence	
c. 1237		Guillaume de Lorris's *Roman de la Rose*
c. 1270		Jean de Meun completes Guillaume de Lorris's *Roman de la Rose*
1272	Death of Henry III, accession of Edward I	
1290	Edward I expels Jews from England	
c. 1300		*Cursor Mundi*
c. 1300–50		*Sir Landevale, Sir Orfeo*
1307	Death of Edward I; accession of Edward II	
1327	Death of Edward II; accession of Edward III	
c. 1330–40		Auchinleck manuscript written

Timeline

	Historical Events	Literary Events
1337	Beginning of the Hundred Years' War	
c. **1340**		Geoffrey Chaucer born
1348–51		Boccaccio's *Decameron*
1349	Arrival of the Black Death in England	Richard Rolle dies
1362	English displaces French as language of law and government	
c. **1352–70**		*Winner and Waster*
1360s–1390s		William Langland's *Piers Plowman* (B-Text *c.* 1377)
c. **1369–72**		Geoffrey Chaucer's *Book of the Duchess*
c. **1375–1400**		*Sir Launfal*
1376	Wyclif contests papal authority and clerical privileges	Earliest reference to the York Cycle
1377	Death of Edward III; accession of minor Richard II	
1378–1417	Great Papal Schism	
1379	Wyclif challenges the doctrines of the eucharist	
c. **1380**		Geoffrey Chaucer's *Parliament of Fowls*
c. **1380–1400**		*Sir Gawain and the Green Knight, Patience, Pearl* and *Cleanness*
1381	Peasants' Revolt	
1382	Official condemnation of Wyclif's opinions	
c. **1382–85**		Geoffrey Chaucer's *Troilus and Criseyde*
1385		John Trevisa's translation of Ralph Higden's *Polychronicon*
c. **1385–86**		Geoffrey Chaucer's *Legend of Good Women*

	Historical Events	Literary Events
1386	Council of Regency	John Gower's *Confessio Amantis*
c. **1387–1400**		Geoffrey Chaucer's *Canterbury Tales*
1389	Richard II resumes full royal power	
c. **1390**		Alliterative *Morte Arthure*
c. **1395**	Second Wycliffite Bible in English	*Cloud of Unknowing*
c. **1398**		*Piers the Plowman's Creed*
1399	Deposition of Richard II; accession of Henry IV	
c. **1400**		Chaucer dies, Stanzaic *Morte Arthur, Emaré*
1401	Statute prescribing the burning of heretics	
c. **1408**		Gower dies
1410		Nicholas Love's *Mirror of The Blessed Life of Jesus Christ*
c. **1411–12**		Thomas Hoccleve's *Regement of Princes*
c. **1412–20**		John Lydgate's *Troy Book*
1413	Death of Henry IV; accession of Henry V	First copying of Julian of Norwich's Long Version of her *Revelations*
1415	Battle of Agincourt; Council of Constance ends Papal Schism (1417)	York *Ordo Paginarum*
1420	Treaty of Troyes: dual kingdom of England and France	
c. **1421–2**		Hoccleve's *Series*, Lydgate's *Siege of Thebes*

Timeline

Historical Events		Literary Events
1422	Death of Henry V, accession of the infant Henry VI	Earliest reference to Chester Cycle
c. **1425**		*Castle of Perseverance*
1426		Hoccleve dies
1431	Burning of Joan of Arc in Rouen	
1431–8		Lydgate's *Fall of Princes*
1443	Henry VI's first episode of madness	
1436-8		*Book of Margery Kempe*
c. **1440**		Robert Thornton's manuscript written
1449		Lydgate dies
1450		First English Arthurian prose romances (*Merlin*)
1453	End of the Hundred Years' War, beginning of the Wars of the Roses; Turks gain Constantinople; exodus of scholars to the West	
1456	Johann Gutenberg prints the Bible	
c. **1460**		Findern manuscript compiled
c. **1460s–80s**		*Wisdom, Mankind*
c. **1460–80**		Paston Letters
c. **1460s–1505**		Robert Henryson's *Moral Fables, Testament of Cresseid*
1461	Deposition of Henry VI; Edward IV proclaimed king	
1470	Henry VI restored to the throne	
1471	Deposition and murder of Henry VI; Edward IV restored	Sir Thomas Malory dies
1476	William Caxton sets up the first printing press in England	
1483	Death of Edward IV; accession of Richard III	

	Historical	Literary Events
1485	Richard III killed at Bosworth. Accession of Henry VII	Caxton's printed edition of Malory's *Morte Darthur*
***c.* 1490**		Dutch precursor to *Everyman*, *Elkerlijc*, produced in Antwerp
***c.* 1490–1510**		The Towneley Cycle manuscript
1492	Christopher Columbus lands in the West Indies	
1497	John Cabot lands in North America	
***c.* 1500–22**		*Mundus et Infans* (extant in a printed copy, 1522)
1502	Death of Prince Arthur, Henry VII's heir	
1509	Death of Henry VII; accession of Henry VIII	
***c.* 1510**		*Everyman* printed
1513	James I of Scotland killed at the Battle of Flodden	
1517	Martin Luther publishes his 'Theses' in Wittenburg	
1564		William Shakespeare and Christopher Marlowe born
1567		Moves to suppress the York Cycle
1575		Last performance of the Chester Cycle
1576		Suppression of the Wakefied Cycle
1580		Final attempt to stage the York Cycle fails
1591		Earliest extant text of the Chester Cycle

Further Reading

Introductions and Historical Background

Introductions, Anthologies and General Resources

Lewis, C. S., *The Discarded Image: An Introduction to Medieval and Renaissance Literature* (Cambridge: Cambridge University Press, 1964, rept 1971)
> A classic work offering a detailed account of medieval literature

Pearsall, Derek (ed.), *Chaucer to Spenser: An Anthology* (Oxford: Blackwell, 1999)
> Superb collection of poetry and prose from the period

Treharne, Elaine (ed.), *Old and Middle English c. 890–c. 1400: An Anthology* (Oxford: Blackwell, 2004)
> A very accessible edition with facing-page translations

Websites

www.lib.rochester.edu/camelot/teams/tmsmenu.htm
> The TEAMS (Consortium for the Teaching of the Middle Ages) website contains an extensive collection of medieval texts and is an invaluable resource

www.courses.fas.harvard.edu/~chaucer/
> Harvard University's Chaucer pages with many links to valuable resources.

http://quod.lib.umich.edu/m/med/
> The Middle English Dictionary online

Social and Historical Background

Brewer, Derek, *Chaucer in His Time* (London: Longman, 1973)
> An excellent general overview of the social and historical background to Chaucer

Coleman, Janet, *English Literature in History 1350–1400* (London: Hutchinson, 1981)
Contains valuable material on literacy and education, and on social unrest reflected in literature

Dobson, R. B. (ed.), *The Peasants' Revolt of 1381* (London: Macmillan, 1970)
A full and very readable account of the Revolt

Hicks, Michael, *Bastard Feudalism* (London: Longman, 1995)
Discusses the breakdown of feudal relationships between lords and their followers, and the contentious issues of private retinues

Justice, Steven, *Writing and Rebellion: England in 1381* (Berkeley: University of California Press, 1994)
Thorough account of the Peasants' Revolt, including consideration of the influence of *Piers Plowman*

Keen, M. H., *England in the Late Middle Ages* (London: Methuen, 1971)
Classic historical account of the period, particularly focused on political history

Leyser, Henrietta (ed.), *Medieval Women: A Social History of Women in England 1150–1350* (London: Weidenfeld and Nicolson, 1995)
Includes an extensive body of primary sources relating to the lives of medieval women

Rigby, S. H., *English Society in the Later Middle Ages: Class, Status and Gender* (Manchester: Manchester University Press, 1995)
Thorough overview of the topic

Tawney, R. H., *Religion and the Rise of Capitalism* (Harmondsworth: Penguin, 1964; repr. 1964)
Extensive study of the economic and cultural transformations occurring during the period

Tuchman, Barbara, W., *A Distant Mirror: The Calamitous Fourteenth Century* (London: Macmillan, 1979)
Immense work of scholarship that covers the big events of history in a very readable narrative

Texts and Genres

Chaucer: *The Canterbury Tales*

Boitani, Piero and Jill Mann (eds), *The Cambridge Chaucer Companion* (Cambridge: Cambridge University Press, 1986)
> A collection of essays covering all aspects of Chaucer's work

Cooper, Helen, *The Structure of the Canterbury Tales* (London: Duckworth, 1983)
> Considers the encyclopaedic nature of the *Canterbury Tales*, assessing its generic variety

— *Oxford Guides to Chaucer: The Canterbury Tales* (Oxford: Clarendon, 1989)
> Excellent introduction to Chaucer

— 'The Girl with Two Lovers: Four Canterbury Tales', in P. L. Heyworth (ed.), *Medieval Studies for J. A. W. Bennett* (Oxford: Clarendon 1981), pp. 65–79.
> Comparison of love triangles in various *Canterbury Tales*

Correale, Robert M. (ed.), *Sources and Analogues of the Canterbury Tales*, 2 vols (Cambridge: Brewer, 2002–5)
> Provides an updated edition of Bryan and Dempster's 1941 anthology of source materials and analogous versions of Chaucer's *Canterbury Tales*

Finlayson, John, 'The Satiric Mode and the Parson's Tale', *Chaucer Review* VI (1971–2), pp. 94–116.
> Analyses the narrative strategies of 'The Parson's Tale'

Hines, John, *The Fabliau in English* (London: Longman, 1993)
> Good introduction to Chaucer's fabliaux

Pearsall, Derek, *The Life of Geoffrey Chaucer: A Critical Biography* (Oxford: Blackwell, 1992)
> Wonderful introduction to the life and works of Chaucer

Schweitzer, E. C., 'The Misdirected Kiss and the Lover's Malady in Chaucer's Miller's Tale', in Julian N. Wasserman and Robert N. Blanch (eds), *Chaucer and the Eighties* (Syracuse, NY: Syracuse University Press, 1986), pp. 223–33
Discusses the central motifs of 'The Miller's Tale'

Chaucer: *Troilus and Criseyde*

Windeatt, B. A., 'Troilus and the Disenchantment of Romance', in Derek Brewer (ed.), *Studies in Middle English Romances* (Cambridge: Brewer, 1988), pp. 129–47
Discusses the element of anti-romance present in *Troilus and Criseyde*

— *Oxford Guides to Chaucer: Troilus and Criseyde* (Oxford: Clarendon, 1992)
An excellent introduction covering the main themes and features of the poem

Dream Visions, Lays and Lyrics

Andrew, Malcolm and Ronald A. Waldron (eds.), *Poems of the Pearl Manuscript* (Exeter: University of Exeter Press, 1977)
Superb edition with excellent introduction and notes

Dronke, Peter, *Poetic Individuality in the Middle Ages: New Departures in Poetry 1000–1150* (Oxford: Clarendon, 1970)
A thorough study of early medieval lyrics in Europe

— *The Medieval Lyric* (Woodbridge: Brewer, 1996)
A survey of medieval lyrics, including the European and Latin traditions

Duncan, Thomas, G. (ed.), *A Companion to the Middle English Lyric* (Cambridge: Brewer, 2005)
Excellent collection of essays covering all aspects of the genre

Field, Rosalind, 'Apocalyptic Consolation in the Middle English *Pearl*', in N. Morgan (ed.), *Prophecy, Apocalypse and the Day of Doom:*

Proceedings of the 2000 Harlaxton Symposium (Donington, Lincolnshire: Shaun Tyas, 2004), pp. 86–96
Considers the apocalyptic tradition which informs the poem

Griffin, Miranda, 'Gender and Authority in the Medieval French Lai', *Forum for Modern Language Studies* 35 (1999), pp. 42–56
Deals with the vexed question of determining female authorship, considering whether gender is evident in style.

Krueger, Roberta, 'Marie de France', in Carolyn Dinshaw and David Wallace (eds), *Cambridge Companion to Medieval Women's Writings* (Cambridge: Cambridge University Press, 2003), pp. 172–83

Pearsall, Derek (ed.), *Piers Plowman: An Edition of the C-Text* (Exeter: Exeter University Press, 1994)
Excellent edition which it is very useful to compare with the earlier B-text

Phillips, Helen, 'Structure and Consolation in *The Book of the Duchess*', *Chaucer Review* 16 (1981), pp. 107–18
Discusses the confusing nature of the structure of the poem which problematises it as a consolation

Phillips, Helen and Nick Havely (eds), *Chaucer's Dream Poetry* (Harlow: Longman, 1997)
An edition of all four of Chaucer's dream-vision poems

Ransom, Daniel J., *Poets at Play: Irony and Parody in the Harley Lyrics* (Norman, OK: Pilgrim, 1985)
Detailed consideration of linguistic and thematic subtleties in the lyrics of the Harley manuscript

Salter, Elizabeth, *Piers Plowman: An Introduction* (Oxford: Blackwell, 1962)
Excellent starting point for a study of the poem

Spearing, A. C., *Medieval Dream Poetry* (Cambridge: Cambridge University Press, 1976)
Definitive guide to the genre

— 'Marie de France and her Middle English Adapters', *Studies in the Age of Chaucer* 12 (1990), pp. 117–56

Traces the development of the Breton lay in Middle English

— *Textual Subjectivity: The Encoding of Subjectivity in Medieval Narratives and Lyrics* (Oxford: Oxford University Press, 2005)

Analyses the narrative personae in lyrics alongside a range of other medieval works

Stevens, John, 'Medieval Lyrics and Music', in Boris Ford (ed.), *The New Pelican Guide to English Literature*, vol. 1, *Medieval Literature Part One: Chaucer and the Alliterative Tradition* (Harmondsworth: Penguin, 1982), pp. 248–76

Discusses a range of lyrics which survive with music

Stokes, Myra, *Justice and Mercy in Piers Plowman* (London: Croom Helm, 1984)

Considers the wider significance of the allegory of the four daughters of God as a key thematic thread in the poem

Waldron, Ronald A., 'Langland's Originality: The Christ-Knight and the Harrowing of Hell', in Gregory Kratzmann and James Simpson (eds), *Medieval English Religious and Ethical Literature* (Cambridge: Brewer, 1986), pp. 66–81

Examines the literary traditions behind Langland's depiction of the Harrowing of Hell

Wilhelm, James J., *The Cruelest Month: Spring, Nature and Love in Classical and Medieval Lyrics* (London: Yale University Press, 1965)

Considers the central motifs of love poetry

Windeatt, B. A. (trans.), *Chaucer's Dream Poetry: Sources and Analogues* (Cambridge: Brewer, 1982)

Provides full source material for Chaucer's dream visions, including the poetry of Machaut and Froissart

Drama and Theatrical Culture

Axton, Richard, 'The Miracle Plays of Noah', in Boris Ford (ed.), *The New Pelican Guide to English Literature*, vol. 1, *Medieval Literature Part One: Chaucer and the Alliterative Tradition* (Harmondsworth: Penguin, 1982), pp. 277–89
A good general account of the Noah plays

Beadle, Richard (ed.), *Cambridge Companion to Medieval English Theatre* (Cambridge: Cambridge University Press, 1994)
A collection of indispensable essays

Clopper, Lawrence M., *Drama, Play, and Game: English Festive Culture in the Medieval and Early Modern Period* (Chicago: University of Chicago Press, 2001)
Full survey of folk festivals and drama

Davenport, W. A., *Fifteenth-Century English Drama* (Cambridge: Brewer 1982)
A classic study of the genre

Davidson, Clifford, *Festivals and Plays in Late Medieval Britain* (Aldershot: Ashgate, 2007)
Examines a wide range of drama including the Corpus Christi Cycles

Gibson, Gail MacMurray, *The Theater of Devotion: East Anglian Drama and Society in the Late Middle Ages* (Chicago: University of Chicago Press, 1989)
Examines medieval drama as a site where performance and subjectivity are explored

Happé, Peter (ed.), *Medieval Drama: A Casebook* (London: Macmillan, 1984)
A collection of useful critical essays on medieval theatre

Harty, Kevin J. (ed.), *The Chester Mystery Cycle: A Casebook* (London: Garland 1993)
A collection of useful critical essays on the cycle

Kolve, V. A., *The Play Called Corpus Christi* (London: Arnold, 1966)
A thorough discussion of the cycle drama

King, Pamela M., 'Morality Plays', in Richard Beadle (ed.), *Cambridge Companion to Medieval English Theatre* (Cambridge: Cambridge University Press, 1994), pp. 240–64
Excellent overview of and introduction to the genre

Owens, Margaret E., *Stages of Dismemberment: The Fragmented Body in Late Medieval and Early Modern Drama* (Newark: University of Delaware Press, 2005)
Explores the representation of dismemberment and beheading in a range of plays

Robinson, J. W., 'The Art of theYork Realist', *ModPhil* 60 (1963), pp. 241–51
Considers the characteristic features of the York Realist's work

Stevens, Martin, 'Language as Theme in the Wakefield Plays', *Speculum* 52 (1977), pp. 100–17
Thorough consideration of the linguistic range and registers in the plays

Van Emden, Wolfgang (trans.), *Le Jeu d'Adam* (Edinburgh: Société Rencevals, 1999)
Facing-page edition of the earliest extant medieval drama

Walker, Greg (ed.), *Medieval Drama: An Anthology* (Oxford: Blackwell, 2000)
An invaluable resource, covering the whole range of medieval and early Tudor drama

Websites

www.luminarium.org/medlit/playlink.htm
Various useful links and resources

http://vos.ucsb.edu
Voice of the Shuttle

http://www.reed.utoronto.ca/index.html
REED project online

http://chass.utoronto.ca/~plspls/
The website of *poculi ludique societas* (the cup and game society), a company of medieval players

Mystical Writings

Beckwith, Sarah, 'A Very Material Mysticism: The Medieval Mysticism of Margery Kempe', in David Aers (ed.), *Medieval Literature: Criticism, Ideology and History* (Brighton: Harvester, 1986), pp. 34–57
Superb piece which challenges assumptions about the liberating potential of female mysticism

Glasscoe, Marion, *English Medieval Mystics: Games of Faith* (London: Longman, 1993)
A fine introduction to mystical writings

— *The Medieval Mystical Tradition in England* (Cambridge: Brewer, 1992)
Full appraisal of the phenomenon of medieval mysticism

Phillips, Helen (ed.), *Langland, the Mystics, and the Medieval English Religious Tradition: Essays in Honour of S. S. Hussey* (Cambridge: Brewer, 1990)
A collection of essays which relate Langland's work to the mystical movement as a whole

Rubin, Miri, *Corpus Christi: The Eucharist in Late Medieval Culture* (Cambridge: Cambridge University Press, 1991)
Examines the importance of the eucharist as a symbol

Staley, Lynne, *Margery Kempe's Dissenting Fictions* (University Park: Pennsylvania State University Press, 1994)
Thorough analysis of Margery Kempe as a non-conformist mystic, with particular attention placed on her 'authorial' presence

Tanner, N. P. (ed.), *Heresy Trials in the Diocese of Norwich, 1428–31*, Camden Fourth Series vol. 20 (London: Royal Historical Society, 1977)

Watson, Nicholas, 'The Medieval English Mystics', in Carolyn Dinshaw and David Wallace (eds), *Cambridge Companion to Medieval Women's Writings* (Cambridge: Cambridge University Press, 2003), pp. 539–65
> Excellent starting point for a study of medieval English mysticism

— 'Julian of Norwich', in David Wallace (ed.), *The Cambridge History of Medieval English Literature* (Cambridge: Cambridge University Press, 1999), pp. 210–221
> Examines Julian's writings as innovative and challenging works by a female visionary claiming access to the power of writing

Websites

www.holycross.edu/departments/visarts/projects/kempe
> A teaching resource devoted to Margery Kempe

Romance

Andreas Capellanus De Amore, trans. P. D. Walsh (London: Duckworth, 1982)
> The founding treatise on courtly love

Archibald, E. and A. S. G. Edwards (eds), *A Companion to Malory* (Cambridge: Brewer, 1996)
> A wide-ranging collection of critical essays

Benson, Larry D., 'Courtly Love in the Later Middle Ages', in Robert Yeager (ed.), *Fifteenth-Century Studies: Recent Essays* (Hamden, CT: Archon, 1984), pp. 237–57
> Good introduction to the phenomenon of courtly love

Bloch, R. H., *Misogyny and the Invention of Western Romantic Love* (Chicago: University of Chicago Press, 1991)
> A fine corrective to an overly 'romantic' view of courtly love, with particular attention to twelfth-century French literary manifestations

Further Reading

Brewer, Elisabeth, *Sir Gawain and the Gr een Knight: Sources and Analogues* (Woodbridge: Brewer, 1992)
Provides the Celtic and folkloric source materials which are reworked in the poem

Bruckner, Matilda Tomaryn, *Shaping Romance: Interpretation, Truth, and Closure in Twelfth-Century French Fictions* (Philadelphia: University of Pennsylvania Press, 1993)
Detailed study of Chrétien de Troyes and early courtly romance

Cowen, Janet (ed.), *Malory: Le Morte D'Arthur*, 2 vols (Harmondsworth: Penguin, 1969)
Caxton's edition of 1495

Davenport, W. A., *The Art of the Gawain-Poet* (London: Athlone, 1978)
Considers all four poems as the product of a single author

Field, P. J. C., *Romance and Chronicle: A Study of Malory's Prose Style* (London: Barrie and Jenkins, 1971)
Full stylistic analysis of Malory's prose style, particularly relating it to chronicle

Hahn, Thomas, 'Gawain and Popular Chivalric Romance in Britain', in Roberta L. Krueger (ed.), *The Cambridge Companion to Medieval Romance* (Cambridge: Cambridge University Press, 2000), pp. 218–34
Focuses on the figure of Gawain in Middle English romances

Hudson, Harriet E., 'Toward a Theory of Popular Literature: The Case of the Middle English Romances', *Journal of Popular Culture* 23 (1989), pp. 31–50
Good overview of the later Middle English romances in relation to their non-aristocratic audiences

Kay, Sarah, 'Courts, Clerks, and Courtly Love', in Roberta L. Krueger (ed.), *The Cambridge Companion to Medieval Romance*, (Cambridge: Cambridge University Press, 2000), pp. 81–96
Examines the literary contexts of courtly love

Lacy, Norris, *The Craft of Chrétien de Troyes: An Essay in Narrative Art* (Leiden: Brill, 1980)
Good introduction to the structure and style of Chrétien's romances

329

Mehl, Dieter, *The Middle English Romances of the Fourteenth and Fifteenth Centuries* (London: Routledge and Kegan Paul, 1968)

A vast study, covering the whole corpus of verse romance, including discussion of *Emaré* and other tail-rhyme romances

Rider, Jeff, 'The Other Worlds of Romance', in Roberta L. Krueger (ed.), *The Cambridge Companion to Medieval Romance* (Cambridge: Cambridge University Press, 2000), pp. 115–31

A discussion of various 'otherworlds' in Medieval literature, including that of *Sir Orfeo*

Robson, Margaret, 'Cloaking Desire: Re-reading *Emaré*', in Jennifer Fellows et al. (eds), *Romance Reading on the Book: Essays on Medieval Narrative Presented to Maldwyn Mills* (Cardiff: University of Wales Press, 1996), pp. 64–76

Pays particular attention to the mysterious agency of Emaré's robe

Wittig, Susan, *Stylistic and Narrative Structures in the Middle English Romances* (Austin, TX: University of Texas Press, 1978)

A full and detailed analysis of the characteristic stylistic features of verse romances

Websites

Three superb websites devoted to all things Arthurian:

www.lib.rochester.edu/camelot/

Arthuriana/Camelot project

www.georgetown.edu/labyrinth

Labyrinth

www.netserf.org/Arthuriana

NetSerf

www.lib.rochester.edu/camelot/teams/tmsmenu.htm

For editions of the two main analogues to 'The Wife of Bath's Tale', *The Marriage of Sir Gawain* and *The Wedding of Sir Gawain and Dame Ragnelle*

Critical Perspectives

Feminisms and Gender Studies

Aers, David and Lynn Staley, *The Powers of the Holy: Religion, Politics and Gender in Late Medieval English Culture* (Philadelphia: University of Pennsylvania Press, 1996)

Brooke, Christopher N. L., *The Medieval Idea of Marriage* (Oxford: Oxford University Press, 1989)
> An account of the essentially business-like nature of marriage in the Middle Ages, and the development of marriage during the period

Dinshaw, Carolyn, *Chaucer's Sexual Poetics* (Wisconsin: University of Wisconsin Press, 1989)
> Groundbreaking reading of Chaucer in the light of theories about the anxiety of authorship and the gendered nature of writing

Evans, Ruth, 'Feminist Re-enactments: Gender and the Townley *Uxor Noe*', in Juliette Dor (ed.), *A Wyf Ther Was* (Liège: University of Liège Press, 1992), pp. 141–54
> Discusses the play's interaction with its audience

Fenster, Thelma S. (ed.), *Arthurian Women: A Casebook* (New York: Garland, 1996)
> A survey of Arthurian characters and themes, with particular attention on women such as Morgan le Fay in Malory and *Sir Gawain and the Green Knight*

Fisher, Sheila, 'Women and Men in Late Medieval English Romance', in Roberta L. Krueger (ed.), *The Cambridge Companion to Medieval Romance*, (Cambridge: Cambridge University Press, 2000), pp. 150–64
> Discusses the marginalisation of women in romances by Chaucer, the *Gawain*-poet and Malory

Fries, Maureen, '"Slydynge of corage": Chaucer's Criseyde as Feminist and Victim', in Arlyn Diamond and Lee R. Edwards (eds), *The Authority of Experience: Essays in Feminist Criticism* (Amherst: University of Massachusetts Press, 1977), pp. 45–59

Considers Criseyde as constrained by her situation as a widow, lacking a male protector, in the light of contemporary marriage laws

Gerould, G. H., 'The Second Nun's Prologue and Tale', in W. F. Bryan and Germaine Dempster (eds), *Sources and Analogues of Chaucer's Canterbury Tales* (Chicago: University of Chicago Press, 1941, rept. 1958), pp. 664–84

Good survey of scholarship relating to this text

Kinoshita, Sharon, 'Cherchez la Femme: Feminist Criticism and Marie de France's *Lanval*', *Romance Notes* 34 (1994), pp. 263–73

Considers *Lanval* as a 'feminist' critique of courtly society

Knight, Stephen, *Geoffrey Chaucer* (Oxford: Blackwell, 1986), pp. 32–65

Analyses Criseyde as an individual, new self-consciousness, site of exploration of privacy

McQueen, John, *Complete and Full with Numbers: The Narrative Poetry of Robert Henryson* (New York: Rodolpi, 2006)

Considers fiendish equivocation and tragedy in the *Moral Fables*

Minnis, A. J., *Medieval Theory of Authorship: Scholastic Literary Attitudes in the Later Middle Ages* (Philadelphia: University of Philadelphia Press, 1988)

Classic survey of attitudes towards authorship, especially the barriers restricting female authorship

Moi, Toril, 'Desire in Language: Andreas Capellanus and the Controversy of Courtly Love', in David Aers (ed.), *Medieval Literature: Criticism, History, Ideology*, (Brighton: Harvester, 1986), pp. 11–33

Fascinating, complex analysis considering whether courtly love served the interests of aristocratic women and women in general, essentially from a post-structuralist position

Murphy, Colette, 'Lady Holy Church and Meed the Maid: Re-envisaging Female personifications in *Piers Plowman*', in Ruth Evans and Leslie Johnson (eds), *Feminist Readings in Middle English Literature: The Wife of Bath and All Her Sect* (London: Routledge, 1994), pp. 140–64

Examines the radical potential of female personification allegory

Strauss, B. R., 'The Subversive Discourse of the Wife of Bath: Phallocentric Discourse and the Imprisonment of Criticism', *English Literary History* 55, no. 3 (Autumn, 1988), pp. 527–54

A feminist reading of the Wife of Bath

Tuttle-Hansen, Elaine, 'Irony and the Anti-Feminist Narrator in Chaucer's *Legend of Good Women*', *Journal of English and Germanic Philology* 82 (1983), pp. 11–31

A reading of the narrator as the primary object of the satire

Websites

www.haverford.edu/library/reference/mschaus/mfi/mfi.html

Feminae, formerly the Medieval Feminist Index, a bibliographical resource covering articles, reviews and essay on medieval literature from feminist perspectives

Cultural and Historical Readings

Benson, Larry D., and Theodore M. Andersson, *The Literary Context of Chaucer's Fabliaux* (Indianapolis: Bobbs-Merrill, 1971)

Invaluable for situating Chaucer's fabliaux within the wider literary tradition

Blackham, H. J., *The Fable as Literature* (London: Athlone, 1985)

A broad study of the fabliau genre

Copeland, Rita, 'William Thorpe and his Lollard Community: Intellectual Labor and the Representation of Dissent', in Barbara Hanawalt and David Wallace (eds), *Bodies and Disciplines: Intersections of Literature and History in Fifteenth-Century England* (Minneapolis: University of Minnesota Press, 1996), pp.199–221

Explores the construction of a dissenting identity in late medieval culture

Gradon, Pamela, 'Langland and The Ideology of Dissent', *Publications of the British Academy* 66, (1980), pp. 179–205

Places Langland within the context of late fourteenth-century radical dissent

Green, R. F., 'John Ball's Letters: Literary History and Historical Literature', in B. A. Hanawalt (ed.), *Chaucer's England: Literature in Historical Context* (Minneapolis: University of Minnesota Press, 1980), pp. 176–200

Considers the letters as social documents

Hanawalt, Barbara and David Wallace (eds), *Bodies and Disciplines: Intersections of Literature and History in Fifteenth-Century England* (Minneapolis: University of Minnesota Press, 1996)

A collection of essays from different disciplines, centred on images of the body in law, literature and other documents

Lawton, David, 'Lollardy and the *Piers Plowman* Tradition', *MLR* 76 (1981), pp. 780–93.

Explores *Piers Plowman* in the context of Lollard radicalism

Leicester, H. Marshall Jr., *The Disenchanted Self: Representing the Subject in the Canterbury Tales* (Berkeley: University of California Press, 1990)

A thorough analysis of the construction of identity and individual subjectivity

McQueen, John, *Complete and Full with Numbers: The Narrative Poetry of Robert Henryson* (New York: Rodolpi, 2006)

Considers fiendish equivocation and tragedy in the *Moral Fables*

Patterson, Lee, *Negotiating the Past: The Historical Understanding of Medieval Literature* (Madison: University of Wisconsin Press, 1987)

A challenging work exploring the intersections between literature and history

Simpson, James, 'The Constraints of Satire in *Piers Plowman* and *Mum and the Soothsegger*', in Helen Phillips (ed.), *Langland, the Mystics and the Medieval English Religious Tradition* (Cambridge: Brewer, 1990)
  Traces the development of satirical strategies across several late fourteenth-century works

Storey, John, *An Introductory Guide to Cultural Theory and Popular Culture* (New York: Harvester Wheatsheaf, 1993)
  An excellent introduction to the topic

Strohm, Paul, *Hochon's Arrow: The Social Imagination of Fourteenth-Century Texts* (Princeton: Princeton University Press, 1992)
  A fine series of essays considering various aspects of the medieval historical context alongside literary representations

—*Social Chaucer* (Cambridge, MA: Harvard University Press, 1989)
  Focuses particularly on Chaucer as part of a social circle and the influence of his situation on his work

Waldron, Ronald A., 'Langland's Originality: The Christ-Knight and the Harrowing of Hell', in Gregory Kratzmann and James Simpson (eds), *Medieval English Religious and Ethical Literature* (Cambridge: Brewer, 1986), pp. 66–81
  Examines the literary traditions behind Langland's depiction of the Harrowing of Hell

Index

Index

Index

Index

Matter of England 79
Matter of France 79
Matter of Rome 79
Matthew, gospel of 116
media, influence of 191
Meditationes vitae Christi 181
meed, defined 235–6
memento mori 68
mendicant orders 17, 62
Mercers' Guild 138
merchants 20–1
Meredith, Peter 135
Merlin 86
middle classes 20–1
Middle English 38–40
Milton, John, *Paradise Lost* 295
Miracle plays 129, 165
The Mirror of the Periods of Man's Life 149
mirror stage of development 221
misericords 252
misogyny 198, 220, 232, 234, 248
mock-parliaments 295–7
mockery 252, 257
monks, monastic orders, monasteries 9, 16, 62, 181
Montrose, Louis, 'The historicality of texts and the textuality of history' 285
Monty Python and the Holy Grail 80
Moone, Hawissia 18, 161
moral interludes 149–52
morality, inverted 277–8
Morality (following a beast fable) 288
Morality plays 129, 139, 142–8
More, Thomas 14–15
Mort Artu 92
mortality
    and the carnivalesque 255
    lyrics on 68–9, 70
motherhood 228
    of God 170
    and sanctity 175–6
multiplicity of styles 256
Mum and the Soothsegger 306
Mundus et Infans 149–52
music 133–4

Muslims 15–16
My Woeful Heart 71–2
Mystery plays 14*n*, 129, 131, 134–9, 145
    authorship 139
    as civic events 136–7
    comedy in 253–4
    Noah's wife in 237–42
mystical union with God 160
mystical writings 159–86, 189
mysticism 19, 104

N-Town Cycle 130*n*, 132, 134, 135, 136, 139–42
narrative
    circular 54
    delay in 52
    double 49
    fictional 189
    linear 106
narrative techniques 37, 40, 189
    Chaucer's 43, 193–4, 297
    in lyrics 65–6, 73
    Malory's 92, 93, 97
    in mystical writing 159
    in sermons 62
    shifting perspective 307
narrator(s)
    authoritarian 185–6
    Chaucerian 192–4, 297–8, 299, 300
    disembodied 234
    dreamers as 110–12, 116, 117
    emotional involvement of 193–4
    of fabliaux 270
    Hoccleve as 210, 212, 216
    in lyrics 67, 75
    Marie de Frances's 35, 36
    mediating 67, 192, 300
    neutrality of 295
    reliability of 193
    in *Sir Orfeo* 47–8, 50
Nennius 81
New Historicism 285–7
Newcastle 134
Newstead, Helaine 242–3
Nicholas of Lyra 109

345

Index

YORK NOTES COMPANIONS

Texts, Contexts and Connections from York Notes to help you through your literature degree ...

- ✔ **Medieval Literature**, Carole Maddern
  ISBN: 9781408204757 | £10.99

- ✔ **Renaissance Poetry and Prose**, June Waudby
  ISBN: 9781408204788 | £10.99

- ✔ **Shakespeare and Renaissance Drama**, Hugh Mackay
  ISBN: 9781408204801 | £10.99

- ✔ **The Long Eighteenth Century: Literature from 1660 to 1790**
  Penny Pritchard
  ISBN: 9781408204733 | £10.99

- ✔ **Romantic Literature**, John Gilroy
  ISBN: 9781408204795 | £10.99

- ✔ **Victorian Literature**, Beth Palmer
  ISBN: 9781408204818 | £10.99

- ✔ **Modernist Literature: 1890 to 1950**, Gary Day
  ISBN: 9781408204764 | £10.99

- ✔ **Postwar Literature: 1950 to 1990**, William May
  ISBN: 9781408204740 | £10.99

- ✔ **New Directions: Writing Post 1990**, Fiona Tolan
  ISBN: 9781408204771 | £10.99

Available from all good bookshops

For a 20% discount on any title in the series visit
www.yorknotes.com/companions and
enter discount code JB001A at the checkout!